CHARLES RENNIE MACKINTOSH

CHARLES RENNIE MACKINTOSH
AND THE MODERN MOVEMENT

THOMAS HOWARTH

ROUTLEDGE & KEGAN PAUL
LONDON, HENLEY AND BOSTON

First published in 1952
Second edition 1977
by Routledge & Kegan Paul Ltd
39 Store Street,
London WC1E 7DD,
Reading Road,
Henley-on-Thames,
Oxon RG9 1EN and
9 Park Street,
Boston, Mass. 02108, USA
Printed in Great Britain by
Redwood Burn Limited, Trowbridge & Esher
© Thomas Howarth 1952, 1977

British Library Cataloguing in Publication Data

Howarth, Thomas
    Charles Rennie Mackintosh and the modern
    movement.—2nd ed
    1. Mackintosh, Charles Rennie
    720'.92'4   NA997.M3   77–72348
    ISBN 0–7100–8538–9

CONTENTS

ILLUSTRATIONS

58. (A) 1898. Interior at Munich. Cupboards by Mackintosh, furniture by K. Bertsch.
    1900. Secessionist Exhibition, Vienna.
    (B) Secretaire by C. R. Ashbee.
    (C) Cabinet by Josef Hoffmann.

59. 1900. Secessionist Exhibition, Vienna.
    (A) Scottish section by Mackintosh.
    (B) Furniture exhibited by Josef Hoffmann.
    (C) Furniture exhibited by Mackintosh.

60. *circa* 1902. Wärndorfer Music Salon, Vienna.
    (A) General view, showing fireplace.
    (B) The Grand Piano, with window seat in background.

61. 1901. *Haus eines Kunstfreundes* Competition Drawings.
    (A) View from the North-West.
    (B) View from the South-East.

62. 1901. *Haus eines Kunstfreundes* Competition Drawings.
    (A) and (B) North and South elevations by Mackintosh.
    (C) and (D) North and South elevations by Baillie Scott—the winning design.

63. 1901. *Haus eines Kunstfreundes* Competition.
    (A) Dining-Room by Baillie Scott.
    (B) Dining-Room by Mackintosh.
    (C) Music-Room by Baillie Scott.
    (D) Music-Room by Mackintosh.

64. 1902. International Exhibition of Decorative Art of Turin.
    (A) Pavilion by Signor D'Aronco of Constantinople, Architect to the Exhibition.
    (B) *The Rose Boudoir* by Mackintosh.
    (C) Display cabinet by Mackintosh.

65. 1902. International Exhibition of Decorative Art at Turin. Typical Stands.
    (A) Salon by Bugatti, Italy.
    (B) Interior with balcony by Sneyers & Crespin, Belgium.
    (C) The Scottish Section. Herbert & Frances MacNair.
    (D) Display cabinet by Henry van de Velde, Belgium.

66. (A) 1888. James Sellars. Industrial Hall, first International Exhibition, Glasgow.
    (B) 1901. James Miller. Industrial Hall, International Exhibition, Glasgow.

67. (A) 1898. Mackintosh. Perspective drawing of project for the International
    Exhibition, Glasgow, 1901, with Kelvingrove Art Gallery in the background.
    (B) 1898. Mackintosh. Side elevation of Industrial Hall (not executed). Glasgow
    University Collection.

68. 1898. Mackintosh. Project for Concert Hall, International Exhibition, Glasgow,
    1901 (not executed). Glasgow University Collection.

69. 1901. *Daily Record* Office, Glasgow. Perspective drawing of the building as executed. Glasgow University Collection.

70. 1897. Queen's Cross Church of Scotland, Glasgow. Perspective drawing by Mackintosh of building as executed, and a sketch (1895) of Merriott Church, Somerset. Glasgow University Collection

71. 1897. Queen's Cross Church, Glasgow.
    (A) The Chancel.
    (B) The Aisle, with gallery above.
    (C) 1898. Gravestone, Kilmacolm.

72. 1903. Liverpool Cathedral Competition. The design submitted by Mackintosh. Perspective view from the South-West; plan of the Cathedral, cloister and chapter house. Glasgow University Collection.

73. 1903. Liverpool Cathedral Competition.
    (A) South elevation. Glasgow University Collection.
    (B) West front. Glasgow University Collection.

74. 1906. Holy Trinity Church, Bridge of Allan.

75. 1904. Scotland Street School, Glasgow.
    (A) Perspective drawing, view from the North-East. Glasgow University Collection.
    (B) Plans of Scotland Street School.
    (C) 1914. Walter Gropius. Exhibition Building at Cologne.

76. (A) 1904. Scotland Street School. View from North-East.
    (B) 1916. No. 78. Derngate, Northampton, for Mr. Basset-Lowke.
    (C) 1925. *New Ways*, Northampton, designed by Peter Behrens.

77. 1916. No. 78, Derngate, Northampton. Remodelled interior.
    (A and B) Lounge Hall and Guests' bedroom.

78. 1920. Proposed Artists' Studios, Chelsea.
    (A and B) Elevations to Glebe Place and to Cheyne House garden. Mr. H. Jefferson Barnes' Collection.

79. (A) 1920. Proposed Studios for the Arts League of Service, Chelsea. Mr. H. Jefferson Barnes' Collection.
    (B) 1920. Proposed Theatre in Chelsea for Margaret Morris. Glasgow University Collection.

80. Flower studies by Charles and Margaret Mackintosh, $10\frac{1}{2}'' \times 8\frac{1}{2}''$.
    (A) Japonica, Chiddingstone, Dorset, 1910. Glasgow University Collection.
    (B) Larkspur, Walberswick, 1914. Glasgow University Collection.
    (C) Stagthorn, Walberswick, 1914. The Author's Collection.
    (D) Mimosa Amelie, Les Bains, 1924. Glasgow University Collection.

81. (A) *circa* 1919. *The Little Hills*. Painted on canvas: two panels 40″ × 40″. Mrs. Dunderdale's Collection. Now in Glasgow University Collection.
    (B) *circa* 1920. Flower study. 9″ × 9″.   Fabric design. Glasgow School of Art Collection.
    (C) *circa* 1918. Adhesive labels. 2¼″ × 1⅝″. The Author's Collection.

82. 1927. C. R. Mackintosh. *The Rocks*. Water-colour. Hamish R. Davidson Collection.

83. 1927. C. R. Mackintosh. *Le Fort Maillert*. Water-colour. Glasgow School of Art Collection.

84. 1927. C. R. Mackintosh. *La Rue du Soleil*. Water-colour. Glasgow University Collection.

85. 1927. C. R. Mackintosh. *The Little Bay*. Water-colour. Glasgow University Collection.

86.   Honeyman & Keppie's Staff, *circa* 1890.
    Margaret Macdonald Mackintosh, *circa* 1903.
    Miss Catherine Cranston.
    Francis H. Newbery. Portrait by Maurice Greiffenhagen. Original in Glasgow Art Gallery.

87. The English Revival.
    (A) 1881–6. Philip Webb. *Clouds*.
    (B) 1881–6. The Hall at *Clouds*.
    (C) 1891. W. R. Lethaby. *Avon Tyrrell*, Hampshire.
    (D) 1876. R. N. Shaw. *Swan House*, Chelsea.
    (E) 1899. A. H. Mackmurdo. 25, Cadogan Gardens.

88. (A) 1876. Philip Webb. Rounton School, Yorks.
    (B) 1901. George Walton. *The Leys*, Elstree.
    (C) 1900. C. F. A. Voysey. *The Orchard*, Chorley Wood.
    (D) 1906. George Walton. *The White House*, Shiplake.

89. Edgar Wood.
    (A) 1910. *Upmeads*, Stafford.
    (B) 1891. Drawing-Room in the Architect's own house, Oldham, Lancashire.
    (C) 1901. Clock Tower, Lindley, Yorks.

90. (A) 1898. English Art Nouveau. Sydney Greenslade. A Town Church.
    (B) 1895. Smith and Brewer. Mary Ward Settlement, London.
    (C) 1899. Leonard Stokes. Convent, St. Albans.
    (D) 1897–9. C. H. Townsend. Whitechapel Art Gallery.
    (E) 1910. Sir John Burnet and Partners. Kodak House, Kingsway, London.

91. (A) 1893. Victor Horta. No. 12 Rue de Turin, Brussels, Façade.
    (B and C) 1895. Henry van de Velde. House at Uccle, Brussels. Exterior and Dining-Room.
    (D) 1906. Antonio Gaudí. Casa Batlló, Barcelona.
    (E) 1914. Henry van de Velde. Exhibition Theatre, Cologne.

92. Josef Hoffmann, Vienna. 1904. Pürkersdorf Sanatorium, Vienna.
    (A) Perspective drawing of the main façade by the Architect.
    (B) Subsidiary doorway.
    (C) The Dining-Room, painted white.
    (D) *circa* 1904. A Villa at Vienna.

93. J. M. Olbrich, Vienna.
    (A) 1898. The Secession House, Vienna.
    (B) 1901. Ernst Ludwig House, Künstlerkolonie, Darmstadt.
    (C) 1901. Sketch of house for Ludwig Habich at Darmstadt.
    (D) 1901. Pavilion of the plastic arts, the Künstlerkolonie, Darmstadt.

94. (A) 1901. Peter Behrens' house at the Künstlerkolonie, Darmstadt.
    (B) *circa* 1900. Lloyd Wright. Fricke House, Chicago.
    (C) 1909. Peter Behrens. A.E.G. Factory, Berlin.
    (D) 1910. Adolf Loos. House, Vienna.

95. Otto Wagner, Vienna. 1905. Postsparkasse, Vienna.
    (A) Elevation faced in granite slabs.
    (B) Main Hall in steel and glass.

96. 1907–9. Mackintosh. Glasgow School of Art. Detail of the Library Wing.

List of Figures in Text

Jacket illustrations: Reproduction of a design for inside of white cabinet doors (See also Plate 13.) and a panel of lettering. (Glasgow University Collection)

Endpapers: Fabric design, *c*. 1916, Foxton & Sefton (Glasgow University Collection)

PREFACE TO THE FIRST EDITION

Cʜᴀʀʟᴇs Rᴇɴɴɪᴇ Mᴀᴄᴋɪɴᴛᴏsʜ, architect, designer and water-colourist, has been one of the most enigmatic of the personalities contributing to the rise of modern architecture. Some have acclaimed him the father of the modern movement and the greatest Scottish architect since Robert Adam. Others have found in his work nothing but vain caprice, and have dismissed him out of hand as little more than an eccentric *art nouveau* decorator.

In this book, the outcome of more than seven years' research, I have tried to present an objective study of the life, work and influence of this extraordinary man, accrediting him with neither more nor less than the evidence would permit, and considering his achievements, his successes and his failures alike, against the background of contemporary events in Europe.

The book is written in two parts. After a brief survey in the Introduction of the historical background, Part One is devoted to Mackintosh and his Scottish contemporaries. In Part Two, the field is widened to include the English and continental phases of the new movement, and Mackintosh's contribution is brought clearly into focus. An account of certain interesting events relating to the preservation of his work is given in the Epilogue.

xvii

The illustrations play an important part in this study and I have selected and arranged them with care. Every aspect of Mackintosh's work is, it is hoped, adequately represented, and numerous pictures of buildings and interiors by British and foreign architects have been included. It was impracticable to place the illustrations in chronological order and they are related to each chapter in the text. Their correct sequence is noted in the Table on pages 295–307 which, for purposes of comparison, includes a list of some significant contemporary buildings and other relevant information. Sources are acknowledged in footnotes throughout the text and a bibliography is appended. Although much has been written about Mackintosh since his death in 1928 reliable information is difficult to come by. I have found the articles and illustrated reviews published in early issues of *The Studio* and similar magazines of foreign origin to be of most value, but it has proved necessary to dig deeply into the files of journals of all kinds. Much of my information, however, has come from people who knew the architect and I have endeavoured to trace and interview, or to correspond with anyone who could claim acquaintance with him. For information about developments abroad (Chapter XI) I have turned more specifically to Professor Giedion's book *Space, Time and Architecture*, to Professor Pevsner's *Pioneers of the Modern Movement*,[1] and to *The Art Revival in Austria* (pub. *The Studio*).

During the course of my research, material has come to hand from places as far afield as Australia, Central Europe and America, and with few exceptions I have examined every work by Mackintosh of which a record remains. The quest has been full of incident. There has been the excitement of a new find— an original drawing perhaps, or a piece of furniture—which may have opened up a new line of enquiry, and there have been happy coincidences to relieve the monotony of routine investigation. I have found most rewarding, however, the pleasant, unforgettable hours spent in the company of Mackintosh's friends— Mr. and Mrs. Francis H. Newbery, Professor and Mrs. Randolph Schwabe, Miss Jessie M. King and many others—charming, gracious people who painted for me vivid word-pictures of a more leisurely, less materialistic age, and enabled me to better understand the complex personality of a truly remarkable man.

I gratefully acknowledge my indebtedness to the following:

The late Professor T. Harold Hughes for introducing me to a subject of such absorbing interest; Mr. W. O. Hutchison and the late W. R. Davidson for much help and encouragement in the early days; Professor W. J. Smith for his bene-

[1] Professor Pevsner was one of the first to draw attention to the historical significance of Mackintosh's work. Ref. Bibliography, Part One, p. 311.

volent interest in my research; Dr. George Pratt Insh, Mr. Paul Schaffer and Mr. Peter Jordan for assistance with foreign texts; Mr. David Blackhurst and others for help with line drawings; Mr. John Brandon-Jones for advice on the English phase; Mr. A. C. Sewter for invaluable criticism; Mr. W. A. Eden for a meticulous reading of the galley proofs; Miss Sabina Strich, Mr. Terence Jones and Mr. Lewis Keeble for assistance with proof reading and the index; Professor R. A. Cordingley to whom I have been able to turn at all times for wise counsel and penetrating criticism. And to my wife without whose patient co-operation this study could not have been undertaken.

I must thank also Mr. Geoffrey Grigson; Professor Nikolaus Pevsner (who found time to read my page proofs on the eve of an important journey); Mr. Burrell and the Staff of the Royal Technical College Library, Glasgow; Mr. John Dunlop and the Staff of the Mitchell Library, Glasgow; the Librarian and Staff of the R.I.B.A. Library, London; Mr. Edgar Kaufmann Jnr., of the Museum of Modern Art, New York; Mr. A. McLaren Young of the Department of Fine Art, Glasgow University.

Among Mackintosh's many friends and admirers who have submitted to cross-examination and tiresome correspondence, I am especially indebted to Miss Nancy Mackintosh and Mrs. Gibb, his sisters; Mrs. Mary Newbery Sturrock; Mr. A. Graham Henderson; and Mr. J. Herbert MacNair.

Manchester, England, 1952   THOMAS HOWARTH

To those whose special help and co-operation I acknowledged in the first edition of this book must now be added Dr. Eduard Sekler, of the Carpenter Center, Harvard University; H. Jefferson Barnes, Director of the Glasgow School of Art; Roger Billcliffe, Department of Fine Art, Glasgow University; Pamela Manson-Smith, Departmental Librarian, University of Toronto; Professor Douglas Richardson, Department of Fine Art, University of Toronto; George Banz, Architect, Peter Kolk and Patricia Taylor, all of Toronto.

I am especially indebted to Margaret Forrest, a native of Glasgow, who has worked with me in Toronto for ten years and has been of invaluable assistance in preparing material for the new edition.

Toronto, Canada, 1976   THOMAS HOWARTH

The author acknowledges his indebtedness to the Publications Standing Committee at Glasgow University, and the Carnegie Trust for the Universities of Scotland, for supporting the first edition of this book.

Further acknowledgments will be found on pages 321–2.

PREFACE TO THE SECOND EDITION

For reasons of economy the new edition of my book, first published in 1952, must be reprinted substantially in its original form and without the coloured illustrations we had hoped to include. However in this preface I will attempt to bring the Mackintosh story up to date and to comment on recent developments. I have given page references throughout to the original text and illustrations.

During the intervening twenty years or so, I have travelled extensively and lectured in many parts of the world; when Mackintosh has been the topic I have invariably been asked how I became interested in him and the early days of the modern movement, so some personal notes may not be out of place.

I began work on Mackintosh in 1940 as a result of an invitation to speak at a meeting of one of Glasgow's literary societies. The late Professor T. Harold Hughes, Head of the Glasgow School of Architecture at that time, had appointed me to his staff in 1939 and, I suspect, thought that this public appearance would be a good way of introducing his newest recruit, who like himself came from south of the Scottish border, to a critical group of Glasgow's intelligentsia. If so, he was right. He suggested as a suitable subject 'Charles Rennie Mackintosh'.

I soon found that very little reliable information on Mackintosh was available; moreover many people who had known him were curiously reluctant to speak about him. On the other hand a few of his close friends and clients spoke of him in messianic terms and considered him a man of genius.

During the three months I had in which to prepare the lecture I became engrossed in the Mackintosh story and unearthed a great deal of material. William O. Hutchison (now Sir William), the distinguished painter and formerly head of the Glasgow School of Art, presided at the lecture and in his closing remarks paid me the compliment of saying that I should continue my research and publish it. Professor Hughes and Professor Cordingley, my friend and mentor at Manchester University, gave quite remarkable encouragement; the subject was accepted by Glasgow University as appropriate for a doctoral dissertation (provided that I supplement it by graduate studies in world history and Italian), and so serious work began. I was carrying a full-time load of teaching (9 a.m. to 5 p.m. five days a week) at the School of Architecture, but Hughes released me to attend history and Italian classes and on two, sometimes three, evenings a week I taught architecture and interior design in Mackintosh's Glasgow School of Art. Research was confined largely to spare evenings, weekends (when I wasn't playing the organ at church), holidays, and this, of course, was only possible because of the enthusiasm and patient co-operation of my wife.

In the 1940s Miss Cranston's Ingram Street Tea-Rooms were still open and I used to have lunch there regularly. I was very surprised to find that the original Mackintosh furniture was in everyday use alongside common pieces that had been brought in over the years to replace breakages. Mackintosh's knives, forks and spoons were mixed up with commercial cutlery, and a place setting might include a Mackintosh fork and teaspoon along with an ordinary knife and dessert spoon. His murals, screens, metal work, fireplaces and lamp-shades were all in place.

As I became more aware of the significance of Mackintosh's work I realized the vital necessity of preserving what still existed before it was destroyed either through neglect, ignorance or, worst of all, sheer callous indifference. Ingram Street, the last surviving example of the tearoom series, was reasonably complete and unlike 'The Willow', which had been ruthlessly altered to serve as part of a modern commercial store, and the Argyle Street and Buchanan Street examples which had long since gone, still had an unmistakable *fin de siècle* character.

I determined, therefore, that the book would provide as accurate a record as possible of Mackintosh's life and times, and that I would endeavour to ensure that his furniture, drawings and paintings would be safeguarded. Although some substantial alterations to the great library windows and metal railings at the School of Art were then being considered, it was possible to prevent this. But it seemed inconceivable to me that any of his *buildings* would be endangered.

The Epilogue to the first edition (pages 291–4) describes the establishment of the two permanent collections, one of furniture at the Glasgow School of Art, and the other, of furniture and architectural drawings, that I catalogued for the first time in 1946, at Glasgow University. It ends somewhat naively on a note of triumph, the purchase in 1950 by the City of Glasgow of the Ingram Street Tea-Rooms complete with furniture for £23,000, a very large sum of money at that time. This achievement like the others was a result of long and patient lobbying, the support of the press, and the collaboration of many far-sighted people at the University and the School of Art as well as private individuals. Mackintosh, I claimed, had at last found honour in his own country!

I assumed that Ingram Street would be retained as a restaurant and our recommendation that it become a cultural centre for meetings of societies and so forth would be adopted. Soon after the purchase, however, it was closed down and remained closed for some years. The movable contents were placed in store where the majority still remain in 1975. The building was eventually leased to a firm marketing Scottish 'souvenirs'—kilted dolls, bagpipers and the usual tourist bric-à-brac—it was renamed 'The Rennie Mackintosh Gift Shop' and later 'The Mackintosh Discount House'! A great deal of damage was done and when I last visited this sad place in 1971 I found that amongst other acts of vandalism the Oak Room had been 'grained' and the large gesso panels ('The May Queen' and 'The Wassail', for which I have the original drawings) had been repainted. Some of the screens in the Chinese room, which was used as a storeroom, were badly damaged.

Since then the building has been demolished, and such interiors as could be salvaged have been removed and placed in storage pending a reconstruction of parts of the Tea-Room in an extension to the Glasgow School of Art. It is hoped that any such reconstruction will accurately reproduce the spatial relationships of the original rooms and the natural and artificial lighting. Unless this is done conscientiously and with complete understanding of the architect's objective, we will lose the last opportunity of capturing the unique atmosphere that Mackintosh and his wife created for Miss Cranston.[1]

In the mid-1960s I was informed that Hill House (Plates 36–42) might be offered for sale, and with others I tried to persuade the Scottish National Trust to purchase it as being of historical and cultural significance. We were told that although recognizing the importance of the building, capital funds could only be allocated by the Trust if an endowment of sufficient magnitude to cover future repairs and maintenance were guaranteed. Unfortunately no funds were forthcoming. However in 1971 Mr. T. Campbell Lawson, who had purchased the property in 1952 and carefully maintained it, generously announced his willingness to sell the house and its furnishings for £25,000 to any organization prepared to assure preservation. None of the official bodies—the government, the National Trust for Scotland or the Scottish Civic Trust—was able to accept the offer and for nearly a year nothing was done. Then the Royal Incorporation for Architects of Scotland raised a guarantee fund amongst Scottish architects and a formal offer of purchase was made and accepted. So, at last, Mackintosh has been recognized by the profession in Scotland, and Hill House is now safe, provided that funds are forthcoming for its continued maintenance; it is open to visitors and contributions for its upkeep will be welcomed.

I ended my Epilogue in 1952 with an optimistic exhortation hoping that 'Mackintosh's architectural work in Glasgow and its environs will be saved from further mutilation'. It is perhaps a measure of the insensitivity and unbelievable cultural starvation of our society that for the past four or five years a group of deeply concerned citizens has had to protest vigorously against a civic authority that threatened the very existence of Scotland Street School, the Martyrs' Public School and Queen's Cross Church, one or all of which were to have been sacrificed for the sake of traffic improvement plans. Already important sections of historical Glasgow—Charing Cross for example —have gone or been drastically changed. However the voice of public opinion has been partially effective and the Mackintosh buildings have been reprieved, for the time being at least.[2]

[1] The Mackintoshes' former house, 78 Southpark Avenue (pages 292–3), purchased by Glasgow University in 1945 has now been demolished, and the University has undertaken to reconstruct the interiors in a new extension that will be designed specially for the Fine Arts.

[2] It may be interesting to note that when appeals were being made to the Secretary of State for Scotland to save the Mackintosh buildings I happened to be fulfilling lecture engagements in Toronto, Winnipeg, Calgary, Vancouver and Victoria and obtained many signatures

In arguing for preservation, however, we must be fully aware of the major problems that face local authorities and planners, problems of rapidly changing urban conditions affecting transportation and traffic movement, housing and so forth, all of which have a social and economic base. Seen against the complex patterns of city and region the individual building or precinct often seems insignificant indeed. Moreover, changing local conditions may also render a building obsolete—churches and schools are particularly vulnerable—and make preservation difficult to justify on any but historic or architectural grounds. It is essential, therefore, that we evolve a value system in which the cultural aspects of social and urban development are given high priority and appropriate use is found for places that can be justifiably claimed to be an important part of our heritage. These should be recognized as legitimate constraints when planning is initiated because it is easy to destroy, and time is always one of the critical elements in matters of this kind. So many important buildings in Glasgow had been demolished already that the Mackintosh issue assumed even greater significance as a *cause célèbre*.

MACKINTOSH AT HOME

Since the publication of the first edition, and especially about the year 1968 (the centenary of Mackintosh's birth), several interesting papers and recorded interviews have been published that throw a little more light on the architect's life and work in Glasgow.

Mrs. Mary Sturrock, who provided me with much valuable information many years ago, has disclosed more intimate recollections of the Mackintoshes that help to round out the necessarily limited information available to me earlier.[1] She speaks of their house in Glasgow as 'always joyously attractive and fresh' and she describes them as 'awfully nice people'. She emphasizes Mackintosh's intense pride in his work and his independence; 'he would allow no one to touch his drawings.' She denies that flower studies bearing the familiar CRM/MMM initials were joint work, as I had speculated; and she

from right across Canada in support of my personal petition. I know that similar support could have been obtained from almost every city in North America and abroad, where architects and concerned people gather to study and debate cultural issues in general, and urban problems and the arts in particular.

[1] The transcription of a tape-recorded interview with Mrs. Sturrock was published in *The Connoisseur*, vol. 183, Number 738 (August 1973), pages 280–8.

believes they merely indicated that Margaret Macdonald was with her husband at the time the drawing was done. She goes on to describe how 'Mackintosh wore hairy tweed suits when everyone else was wearing blue serge. Margaret Macdonald made evening clothes for herself but she also had beautiful clothes from Greive and added braid, and beads, and embroidery.' Mrs. Sturrock's mother, Mrs. Jessie Newbery, wife of the head of the School of Art, taught embroidery and her pupils included the Macdonald sisters, Ann Macbeth and Jessie M. King, all of whom helped to make the school a lively social centre. She speaks of Sunday parties with peppermint creams, with actors and actresses, as well as the local artistic fraternity, in attendance. These goings on at School, the strange art work of Mackintosh and his friends, and their distinctive, unorthodox dress, were not acceptable to the ordinary citizens of Glasgow, who, Mrs. Sturrock says, were outraged. Mackintosh's identification with the School group, his continuing friendship with them and his growing associations in Central Europe, without doubt contributed to his isolation and his frustration with the existing order of things that he sought so desperately to change.

Reliable information about the Mackintoshes has always been difficult to come by, possibly because after about 1906 they lived very quietly in Glasgow and left the city in 1913. For example, I visited John Keppie (1862–1945), Mackintosh's partner, and his sister Jessie at their house in Ayrshire on several occasions in the 1940s, but unfortunately conversation about the early days was not easy; John Keppie did not have many charitable things to say about his former partner, who had been engaged to marry Jessie. From about 1890 Mackintosh had been a close friend of the family and he and John Keppie worked together frequently on competition projects at the Ayrshire house. However, about 1896, Mackintosh transferred his attentions to Margaret Macdonald and Jessie Keppie never completely recovered from the shock of losing him. She did not marry, and fifty years later she could not speak of him and the Art School days without dissolving into tears.[1] This was the beginning of the estrangement between the two architects that contributed to the dissolution of their subsequent professional partnership in 1913.

I have already described the developing situation (pp. 194–5) and its culmination in Mackintosh's resignation from the firm at the time of the

---

[1] Among other gifts Mackintosh presented to Jessie Keppie in the 1890s was an inscribed jewel box of beaten brass set with pieces of opalescent glass jewels. This was illustrated in *The Studio*, Vol. 11 (1897), p. 96 and in the catalogue of the Mackintosh Exhibition of 1968, Item 183, Plate 7.

Jordanhill competition. I am indebted to David M. Walker for additional information on what he describes as 'the Jordanhill crisis'. The competition was for a group of buildings including a training college, a hostel and a lodge and gates in addition to a 'demonstration school'. After months of work on the total project Mackintosh had little to show except some inadequately detailed drawings on tracing paper; it was evident to his partners that he could not handle the job and this incident, one of many, brought matters to a head. Walker says the partnership was dissolved just before the results of the competition were announced. The unenviable task of designing the demonstration school about a week before the due date fell to Graham Henderson, to whom I was indebted for the original description of the event. However the assessor decided that no single firm would receive the entire commission, and in *The Builder* on 17 July 1913 the winners were announced—the college, H. & D. Barclay; the hostel, Andrew Balfour; and the demonstration school, Honeyman, Keppie and Mackintosh.

On the evidence of the original partnership agreement found by the late Alexander Smellie shortly before his death, David Walker tells me that two years before his retirement in 1904 John Honeyman arranged for Mackintosh to join the firm as a partner. Knowing the younger man could not afford to buy him out, he took Mackintosh's share of the profits for 1902, 1903 and 1904. Legally, therefore, Mackintosh was a partner from 1902, although public recognition does not seem to have come until Honeyman's retirement in 1904.

During the course of his research for a superbly illustrated and documented book *Architecture of Glasgow*[1] David Walker gathered a great deal of information about Mackintosh's contemporaries in Glasgow—and elsewhere. In 1968 he wrote an article for *Architectural Review*[2] which supplements admirably my descriptive analysis of Mackintosh's early work and architectural sources, but he limits himself almost entirely to façade treatment and decorative details; no plans are illustrated. However, his paper emphasizes the young architect's continual search for inspiration from executed buildings by his British contemporaries and from projects illustrated in the pages of popular professional journals of the day. To my list of early projects Walker adds only two of interest —the competition for 'the rebuilding of Glasgow High Street' and 'The Manchester Technical Schools', neither of which was premiated. The former was a competition for workmen's dwellings sponsored by the City of Glasgow

[1] by Andor Gomme and David Walker, Lund Humphries, London, 1968.
[2] 'Charles Rennie Mackintosh', *Architectural Review* vol. 144 (November 1968), p. 355.

Improvement Trust (1891). I did not have David Walker's conviction that the five drawings in the University collection were 'entirely in Mackintosh's hand' nor did I consider the project to be of special concern to us. It may well be a joint effort by Keppie and Mackintosh and its orderly fenestration is typical of tenement dwellings in several parts of Glasgow and Edinburgh; the crow-stepped gables and other traditional elements may account for the appropriate competition pseudonym 'Scottish Baronial'.[1] The competition was won by Burnet and Boston.

The Manchester Technical Schools project[2] by Honeyman and Keppie did not seem to me to be of particular relevance. Walker detects the hand of Mackintosh in the figure sculpture and the *art nouveau* turrets of the internal courts and therefore it deserves mention here.

There is not space to comment on the many design currents and cross currents that David Walker investigates and the reader who wishes to pursue further the questions of origins and descriptions must be referred to his article.[3] However nothing he has written detracts in the slightest degree from the stature of the architect as described in this book. On the contrary, his paper serves to emphasize Mackintosh's dedication to the art of building, his knowledge of contemporary work, and the manner in which his mature style emerged. In summing up the work of the firm after the estrangement of 1896 Walker says quite rightly, 'Mackintosh moved on, Keppie left to himself did not.'

EXHIBITIONS

Before discussing Mackintosh's work abroad, on which some very interesting new facts have come to light, it might be well at this point to say a few words about recent exhibitions of the architect's work that have attracted a great deal of attention.

[1] A small part of the drawing of the façade of the Glasgow High Street was illustrated in David Walker's article (p. 355) and in the Mackintosh Centennial Exhibition catalogue (Plate 10).

[2] Illustrated in the *British Architect* 4 November 1892 and by Walker in 'Charles Rennie Mackintosh', *Architectural Review* vol. 144 (November 1968), p. 358.

[3] Reference might also be made to Robert McLeod's *Charles Rennie Mackintosh*, Country Life, 1968. This book extends our knowledge of sources with special reference to Lethaby, the English School and Mackintosh's few surviving written dissertations. There are also some excellent new photographs.

In 1953, the year after the publication of the first edition of this book, I was invited by the Saltire Society of Edinburgh and the Arts Council of Great Britain to design an exhibition of Mackintosh's work for the Edinburgh Festival, in collaboration with the late Robert Hurd. This was the first comprehensive showing of his work ever staged, if we except the presentation for sale of the residue of his effects after the death of his wife in 1933 as described on p. 291 under the heading 'Memorial Exhibition'. We arranged for part of the exhibition to go on tour after the Edinburgh showing and with the help of the Arts Council it was sent to schools of architecture at Newcastle upon Tyne, Manchester, Liverpool and Bristol, to the RIBA Headquarters in London and finally to Glasgow City Art Gallery. We prepared a modest catalogue using as a cover a reproduction in colour of one of Mackintosh's posters for the Scottish Musical Review of 1896 (p. 29).

The Exhibition was held in the Saltire Society's Edinburgh Headquarters in the Royal Mile; a fine seventeenth-century townhouse, stone-built, narrow and five storeys high. Our funds were limited to £250 and we decided that most of this should be spent on models of two unrealized architectural projects—the Concert Hall of 1898 (Plate 68) and the *Haus eines Kunstfreundes* of 1901 (Plates 61–63)—and on the School of Art (Plates 21–31), which, because of its difficult site, could not be comprehended in its entirety. We also constructed a large-scale model of the interior of the School of Art library.[1] All of this was made possible by the enthusiastic co-operation of some fifteen of my students both from Glasgow and Manchester Schools of Architecture. They built the models and the Glasgow group worked with me night and day in setting up the exhibition. It was a rewarding and exciting experience for all of us.

I asked Mrs. Mary Newbery Sturrock, who now lives in Edinburgh, to make the flower arrangements in the Mackintosh style (p. 136) and we invited Miss Nancy Mackintosh, the architect's youngest sister, to open the exhibition. We were able to obtain on loan from a famous Edinburgh store a quantity of superb Mackintosh tartan cloth, which I used as a pleated background to Newbery's large portrait of the architect as a centrepiece of the top floor display. However, on entering that room, Nancy Mackintosh came to an abrupt halt, stamped her foot and expressed her displeasure in no uncertain terms. Apparently her brother detested the clan tartan and always used instead the familiar black and white chequered fabric which his friends eventually named 'Mackintosh tartan'.

[1] All four models were given to the Glasgow School of Art when the Exhibition closed.

The exhibition aroused a great deal of interest wherever it was shown, and many students of architecture and the fine arts in several of the most important educational centres in Britain had an opportunity of seeing work by Mackintosh and his friends for the first time. It was particularly gratifying to take it to the RIBA because in 1933 negotiations for showing the Mackintosh Memorial Exhibition in London came to nothing and, so far as I am aware, the only occasion on which work of The Four had been shown previously in the capital was in 1896.

In 1955–6 I spent a year in the United States and Canada, with the aid of a Rockefeller Grant, studying architectural and planning education. I took with me a comprehensive collection of photographs, original drawings and easily transportable artifacts that I thought would interest North American students and others. During that year my family and I travelled over 17,000 miles by car and visited over thirty educational institutions. Wherever the tiny exhibition was shown, whether informally to small groups, or more formally, it was very well received, and again it provided a useful introduction to the work of the Glasgow designers.

The most elaborate and representative show of all, however, was staged in 1968 to mark the centenary of Mackintosh's birth. It was organized by my friend, the late Andrew McLaren Young, Professor of Fine Art, Glasgow University, and was generously endowed by the Edinburgh Festival Society and the Scottish Arts Council. Unfortunately I could not attend the opening ceremony at the Royal Scottish Museum, Edinburgh, but I was invited to give the Mackintosh Memorial Lecture at the RIBA in London in June 1968, and to repeat it at Edinburgh, so I had the opportunity of seeing the exhibition after it had been transferred to the Victoria and Albert Museum.[1] Not only was it superbly staged in London, but McLaren Young produced a catalogue that was a model of its kind—beautifully designed, well-illustrated and containing very useful notes. Among other important dates provided in the catalogue was that referring to Mackintosh's pencil and water colour drawing 'The Harvest Moon' signed and dated 1892. This was illustrated in the catalogue and would seem to be the earliest authenticated example so far discovered of the architect's imaginative work in what was to become 'The Glasgow Style'— excepting, of course, the painted frieze of cats which by circumstantial evidence I dated 1890 (pp. 120–1, Plate 5A). McLaren Young states that on giving

---

[1] Part of this exhibition was shown in Vienna from 7 June to 20 July 1969 at the Museum des 20. Jahrhunderts, Schweizergarten. The catalogue text was prepared by Dr. Eduard Sekler.

'The Harvest Moon' to John Keppie, Mackintosh dated it 1893 whereas the date 1892, partially obscured by the mount, should be assumed to be correct. The accuracy of these dates is important only in so far as they enable us to plot the emergence of Mackintosh's individual style and relate it to developments overseas.

Over the last fifteen or twenty years there has been an increasing demand for the inclusion in exhibitions of work by the Glasgow designers ranging from graphics, the applied arts and crafts, to furniture; some examples are housed in permanent collections in Europe and North America, but we have not yet had a major exhibition on the North American continent.

MACKINTOSH ABROAD

Although Francis Newbery sent an exhibition of work by students of the Glasgow School of Art to Liège in 1895 (p. 37) we have no positive record of subsequent contacts between the Mackintosh group and Belgium. This is unfortunate, since Brussels was already a recognized centre of progressive ideas in the arts. Victor Horta, now acknowledged as one of the pioneers of the *art nouveau* style, who had built No. 12 rue de Turin and Henry van de Velde, its most prolific propagandist, were both very active at that time. According to Mary Sturrock two Belgian artists taught at the School—'Jean Delville and a man called Artot', but we know little about them.[1] However, it would seem that the Mackintoshes found their contacts with Vienna much more congenial and productive; continental *art nouveau* as developed by the Belgians, and more particularly by the French, had no appeal for them. This needs restating, because, despite the evidence, many people still persist in classifying Mackintosh with the Guimards, Gallés and van de Veldes of *art nouveau* persuasion. Mary Sturrock is very positive on this issue. 'My parents didn't like *art nouveau*' she says 'and Mackintosh didn't like *art nouveau*. He fought against it with these straight lines against these things you can see for yourself are like melted margarine. . . .'[2]

Little new has come to light about Mackintosh's life and work in Scotland or in Western Europe, but some scholars, most notably Eduard Sekler, Horst-

[1] *The Connoisseur* vol. 183, Number 738 (August 1973), p. 283.
[2] *Ibid.* p. 282.

Herbert Kossatz and J. D. Kornwolf, who have had access recently to public and private archives in Vienna, have made possible a more precise documentation of the Scottish architect's influence on the important events that took place in that city at the turn of the century.

In a scholarly and detailed paper on Josef Hoffmann's Stoclet House[1] Sekler confirms my view that Mackintosh, more than any of his British contemporaries, made the deepest impression on the modern Viennese school of architects and designers. The two men met at the Secessionist Exhibition of 1900, and in fact shared two clients, Dr Hugo Henneberg and Fritz Wärndorfer, for whom Mackintosh designed the famous Music Room (Plate 60). Hoffmann designed Henneberg's house and the study contained a cabinet by Mackintosh from the Secessionist Exhibition.[2]

There is yet another description of the Wärndorfer Music Salon which indicates clearly the high regard in which the Mackintoshes were held in Vienna. It was written in 1905 by Ludwig Hevesi who describes a visit to the Wärndorfer house in rhapsodic terms.[3] He speaks of the salon as 'the well-known masterpiece of the Maeterlinck interior' which 'in the time of the Secession caused so much talk', and of 'the Mackintosh group in Glasgow' as 'great artists'. He goes on to say that 'a group of progressive friends of the arts wrote a letter to Mr. & Mrs. Mackintosh asking them to travel to Vienna, expenses paid, and to be their guests. The couple came and stayed six weeks'—unfortunately he does not say precisely when. One of the results of this visit was the Mackintosh salon in the Wärndorfer house. It was 'an artistic curiosity of the first order' and 'a place of spiritual joy' but primarily an elegant setting for the Mackintoshes' decorative panels depicting Maeterlinck's 'six princesses'.

In his catalogue of the Mackintosh Centennial Exhibition (item 325 p. 66), McLaren Young questions whether there would be room for the panels, but the surviving photographs (Plates 60A & B) show a deep frieze above the wall-panelling clearly prepared to receive such a decorative element. This was an architectural detail frequently used by Mackintosh, for example in the Ingram Street Tea-Rooms, gesso panels (Plate 50), in the Willow Tea-Rooms, plaster reliefs (Plate 56), and even in the Dennistoun bedroom, stencilled paper (Plate 5A).

[1] *Essays on the History of Architecture* (Phaidon, London, 1967), pp. 228–44.
[2] Illustrated *Das Interieur*, vol. IV (1903), p. 139.
[3] See *Altkunst-Neukunst Wien 1894–1908* (Vienna, 1909), pp. 222–3.

When Hevesi dined with the Wärndorfers he noted that all the silverware was 'of a singularly simple kind designed for the purpose for which it was used . . . formed according to the movements of the hand'. 'A sauceladle', he observed, 'could serve as a theme for a lecture on logic.' The silverware was designed by Josef Hoffmann and made in the workshops of the Wiener Werkstätte of which Wärndorfer was the most generous and enthusiastic patron. Hevesi noted, and his observations were written in 1905, that the 'upper wall surfaces' in the adjacent salon 'are still awaiting the pictures of the story of the six princesses' and he speculates as to whether these would be woven or embroidered, thus seeming to imply that they would be designed and made by Margaret Macdonald. It is interesting to see that a terse footnote was added to Hevesi's article, 'these have now arrived.'[1] Since the article was included in a book describing modern work in Vienna between 1894 and 1908 which was published in 1909, it would be reasonable to assume that although Hevesi visited the room four years earlier (1905) when he wrote his paper he just had time to insert the footnote before publication, say in 1907–8. This would seem to confirm my original deduction that the panels were installed between 1905 and 1907 (p. 157). Photographs of two gesso panels both signed by Margaret Macdonald, are in the Glasgow University collection. They are entitled 'The Opera of the Winds' and 'The Opera of the Sea'; the former is dated 1903. Notes on the back of both photographs indicate that they were to be placed in the Salon near the piano. Incidentally Hevesi says that each of the rods of the music stand on the piano (p. 156) was 'adorned with some symbol, with a pleasant emblem, or a monogram, all with an inscription. . . . In that way the room speaks to its inhabitants, calls them quietly by their names, whispers intimacies in their ears.' 'There is new poetry in the world not dreamed of before.' Hevesi enthusiastically describes the rich and evocative variety of Mackintosh's architectural detail which, he says, 'is not only to be viewed but must be touched in order not to miss any details.' This extension into the realms of tactile experience, although commonplace now, was not to the best of my knowledge advocated by any of Mackintosh's other critics.

Although no record of the Viennese excursions remains in the Mackintosh archives there should be no doubt that during their stay in Vienna the Scottish artists met the leading designers and architects of the day. All the evidence that has since come to light would seem to support my original contention that

[1] *Ibid.* p. 222.

the Viennese movement gained considerable impetus from their visit, and that the Mackintoshes were greatly encouraged and stimulated by their reception in the Austrian capital (pp. 267-70). In fact, Sekler tells us that Mackintosh was made a corresponding member of the Secession, and thereby joined the ranks of Hodler, Liebermann, Rodin, van de Velde and Whistler. It is also said that the Scottish designers received a pressing invitation to live and work in Vienna; in view of the contrast between their struggle for recognition in Britain and their welcome in central Europe this must have been a great temptation. It may be that Fritz Wärndorfer's confidential discussion with Mackintosh in Glasgow (1903) about a proposal to set up a metal workshop in Vienna—of which more later—may have included this possibility. The Wiener Werkstätte with Wärndorfer's financial backing was founded in 1904, and Mackintosh's skill as a designer in metal would seem to have been particularly relevant in that context.

My original statement that the Viennese episode unquestionably represented one of the most important events in the Scottish architect's life is now confirmed by the discovery of an undated letter to Josef Hoffmann written about 1908 or 1909 by Eduard Wimmer, the friend of the Wärndorfers who tried to salvage the contents of the Music Salon after their house was sold (p. 156); he says, 'Mackintosh appears to consider the visit to Vienna as the highpoint in his life.'[1]

The important archival work carried out in Vienna by Eduard Sekler and Horst-Herbert Kossatz help us to define a little more clearly the relationship between Hoffmann and Mackintosh, and between Mackintosh and the Secessionists, although there is a frustrating paucity of source material. Kossatz tells us that Hoffmann, in his diploma year at the academy (1894) under Otto Wagner, won the Austrian Prix de Rome (1895), and spent a year in Italy, where like Olbrich two years before him he was inspired not only by buildings in the classical tradition, but by the predominantly white cubical forms of the simple vernacular of the Mediterranean basin. Hoffmann was appointed by von Myrbach to the directorship of the School of Architecture in Vienna in April 1899, the year after the Secession published the first issue of *Ver Sacrum* and held its first sensational exhibition in Olbrich's Secession House. Kossatz says that Hoffmann 'progressively established himself as the exhibition designer of the Secession'. Apparently he refused a request by Adolf Loos for permission

---

[1] Catalogue of the Mackintosh Exhibition, Museum des 20. Jahrhunderts, Schweizergarten. Vienna, 7 June–20 July, 1969.

to design the council chamber, and thereby incurred his enmity. This hitherto unnoted incident would seem to account, at least in part, for Loos becoming a persistently hostile and vocal critic of the Secession and of Hoffmann himself (p. 282). It is regrettable that we do not have any record of Mackintosh's time in Vienna; a diary would have been invaluable. It would have been fascinating to know whom he met and how he responded to the leaders of the modern movement, but we can be sure that Loos would have had little time for him.

Strong links with Britain were established at the Fourth Secessionist Exhibition in the Spring of 1899, which coincided with Hoffmann's appointment as Director of the School of Architecture. It was at this exhibition that paintings by the Boys from Glasgow were shown—Macaulay Stevenson (whom I knew in Glasgow), Henry, Hornel, Walton and others.[1] If Mackintosh was not already known in Vienna either through *The Studio* articles or through Newbery's international contacts then I would agree with Kossatz that useful connections would have been established at the time of this exhibition. However, it is more likely that they would have been confirmatory, rather than initial, contacts. It is interesting to note that in the following year when Charles and Margaret Mackintosh went to Vienna to supervise the design of the *Ver Sacrum* room, for which they were responsible, at the 8th Secessionist Exhibition (November and December 1900) C. R. Ashbee, the distinguished English designer and founder of the Guild and School of Handicrafts, exhibited 52 works, the Glasgow group 33. In a letter from Vienna of 3 April 1971, Kossatz told me that a 'passageway' was designed to direct visitors through the exhibition via the Board Room, which was furnished by the Mackintoshes. This meant that all visitors would see the Scottish contribution. A special sheet was added to the catalogue explaining this arrangement.

The records show that the exhibition was an outstanding success; there were over 24,000 visitors and 241 works were sold. We do not know how many pieces by the Glasgow designers found purchasers, but it was from this source that Dr. Hugo Henneberg acquired a cabinet which was placed in his new house, designed by Hoffmann, then nearing completion.[2]

From the few letters that remain we know that von Myrbach, Wärndorfer and Hoffmann all visited Britain in the early 1900s and included Glasgow in their itineraries; von Myrbach in 1900, Wärndorfer in 1900, 1902 and 1903

[1] See Introduction, p. xxvii.
[2] Illustrated 'Mackintosh und Wien' by Eduard Sekler, the catalogue of the Mackintosh Exhibition in Vienna, 7 June–20 July, 1969, pp. 12–18.

and Hoffmann in 1902 when he met Hermann Muthesius[1] in London. In a letter dated 20 April 1900, Hoffmann refers to von Myrbach's forthcoming study tour and mentions C. R. Ashbee, but not Mackintosh. Fritz Wärndorfer was in England when preparations for the important 8th Exhibition of the Secession were underway. Karl Moll wrote to Mackintosh on 15 July 1900 inviting him to send material for a special issue of *Ver Sacrum*, but Mackintosh did not reply until 17 December, and he then sent photographs that were published. In this letter he referred to the warm reception he and Margaret Macdonald had received in Vienna, and congratulated all on the success of the exhibition, thus confirming indisputably the fact that they were both in Vienna at that time, most probably late October and early November 1900.

At this point it is important to correct my former description of the events surrounding the Haus eines Kunstfreundes competition of 1901 (pp. 157–63, Plates 61, 62 and 63). I am indebted to James D. Kornwolf for a more detailed description on which the following comments are based.[2] The competition was announced in the December 1900 issue of *Zeitschrift für Innendekoration* with 25 March 1901 as the submission date. There were thirty-six entries judged at Darmstadt on 16 and 17 May 1901 by a jury of J. M. Olbrich, Alexander Koch, von Berlepsch-Velendas, Hans Christiansen, F. Putzer, J. Gräbner, Hans Schliepmann and a local Darmstadt architect, Hofmann.

Kornwolf translates the objective of the competition as 'to contribute energetically to the solution of important questions confronting modern architecture'.[3] In the opinion of the jury this ambitious objective was not attained and the first prize of 8,000 Marks was not awarded; instead it was divided between about sixteen competitors. Baillie Scott received the second prize (1,800 Marks) and the jury said that if he had designed his exteriors in a more 'modern' way he would have won the first prize. Three third prizes were awarded to Leopold Bauer, Oscar Marmorek of Vienna and Paul Zeroch of Coblenz. Mackintosh's entry was disqualified because he did not meet in time the competition requirements for interior studies. However these arrived later and were published in the folio *Meister der Innenkunst* from which the illustrations (Plates 61–63) were taken.

[1] Hermann Muthesius, German architect and author of the important contemporary study *Das Englische Haus*, 1905.

[2] *H. M. Baillie Scott and the Arts and Crafts Movement*, J. D. Kornwolf, Johns Hopkins Press, 1972.

[3] *Ibid.* p. 216.

The jury was delighted with Mackintosh's design and awarded him a special prize of 600 Marks. It is regrettable indeed that he was unable to meet the time limits set for submission. Had he done so, he would almost certainly have won the competition. Only Baillie Scott's, Mackintosh's and Bauer's designs were published in folio form and this no doubt gave credence to the tradition that the order of merit was Scott, Mackintosh and Bauer. We know that Scott's design was preferred by the jury for its planning and spatial concepts and Mackintosh's for the originality of its massing and external treatment. It was unquestionably Mackintosh's design that had the greatest influence on the Viennese group, and on Hoffmann in particular. Hoffmann's Palais Stoclet in Brussels,[1] a major monument of the Viennese movement, was built between 1905 and 1907 and was obviously influenced greatly by Mackintosh's design.

Documentation for the year 1902 is a little more comprehensive. This was the year of the International Exhibition of Decorative Art in Turin and we now have evidence that Mackintosh was there also. On 29th April 1902 the indefatigable Fritz Wärndorfer wrote to Josef Hoffmann from Turin, saying that Mackintosh sent his best regards and expected to see him there. Francis Newbery, head of the School of Art, was responsible for the Scottish section at Turin, and his daughter Mary Sturrock confirms that Mackintosh went to Turin with him.[2] She describes how Mackintosh, the perfectionist, was highly incensed by her father's suggesting they order some flowers to complete the display. He is quoted by Mrs. Sturrock as saying, characteristically, 'no flowers in my room but my flowers'! Then the two men went into the country to pick brambles and twigs which he formed into the shapes with which we are now familiar (Plate 64B).

In the letter to Hoffmann Wärndorfer observed that Mackintosh had said 'the exhibition building'—presumably the one by D'Aronco (Plate 64A)— 'represents the meanest theft of things by Olbrich from Darmstadt'. There is also an amusing comment on the music salon in the Wärndorfer house then being constructed under the supervision of one of Hoffmann's students, N. Schmidt. Wärndorfer writes of the drawings Mackintosh had sent him from Glasgow: 'only one thing seemed to be difficult to understand, how Mackintosh imagines the construction of the chimney which is supposed to be carried on

[1] Profusely illustrated in Sekler's paper, *Essays on the History of Architecture*, Phaidon, 1967, pp. 228–44.

[2] 'Remembering Charles Rennie Mackintosh', a recorded interview for *The Connoisseur*, vol. 183, Number 738 (August 1973), pp. 280–8.

the outside of the house—but we consoled ourselves with the thought that you will find a way of doing it' and 'Mackintosh wants a giant fireplace and a lead roof over the projection (i.e. the portion of the structure projecting outside the building).'

In the autumn of 1902 Fritz Wärndorfer and his wife toured Scotland and went to Glasgow. They sent a picture postcard to Hoffmann from the Ferry Inn, Roseneath, on the Clyde Estuary. Wärndorfer said he saw Baillie Scott's White House at Helensburgh. Mackintosh's Hill House, Helensburgh, to be built close by for W. W. Blackie, would have been in the early stages of construction at that time, and most likely he took his friends to see the site.

It was shortly after this that Hoffmann visited Glasgow. He had been with von Myrbach in London and went north from there. Wärndorfer wrote to Hoffmann on 23 December 1902 and included this delightfully complimentary note: 'Mackintosh writes that he is furious because you stayed only two days in Glasgow and is more than ever delighted with you. This feeling appears to be mutual.'

The main purpose of Hoffmann's visit to Britain was to gather information and learn something about the peculiarly English form of guilds of handicraft. He was a lifelong admirer of Ruskin and Morris and was especially interested in Ashbee's Guild and School of Handicrafts at Camden Town, founded in 1888, which he evidently thought might provide a model for a similar experiment in Vienna. One of his principal reasons for meeting with Mackintosh was to discuss the establishment of a metal workshop in Vienna, and Sekler has discovered a letter in German from Mackintosh to Hoffmann concerning the project. This is an important document and may have been translated by Wärndorfer from the original by Mackintosh; it is most unlikely that Mackintosh had such a good command of German. The major part of the letter reads as follows:

I have the greatest possible sympathy for your latest idea and consider it absolutely brilliant. Moser is perfectly right in his plans to produce for the time being only items that have been ordered. If your programme is to achieve artistic success (and artistic success must be your first aim), then every object you produce must have a strong mark of individuality, beauty and outstanding workmanship. Your aim from the beginning must be that every object is created for a specific purpose and a specific place. Later on, when the high quality of your work and financial success have strengthened your hand and your position, you can walk boldly in the full light of the world, complete with commercial production on its own ground and achieve the greatest accomplishment ('Werk') that can be achieved in this century; namely the production of all objects for everyday use in beautiful form and at a price that is within the reach of the poorest, and in such quantities that the ordinary man on the street is forced to buy them because there is nothing else available and because soon he will not want to buy anything else. But until that time many years of hard, earnest, honest work by the leaders of the modern movement will be required before all obstacles will be removed either totally or partially. For a beginning the 'artistic' (excuse the term) [sic] detractors must be subdued and those who allow themselves to be influenced by them must be convinced through continuous effort and through the gradual success of the modern movement that the movement is no silly hobby of a few who try to achieve fame comfortably through their eccentricity, but that the modern movement is something living, something good, the only possible art for all, the highest achievement of our time.

Yes—the plan which Hoffmann and Moser designed is grand and brilliantly thought out, and if you have the means you risk nothing and I can only say: *embark on it today*! If I were in Vienna I would like to help with a big strong shovel ('Schaufel') and not waste another day.

(This humorous note was added by Wärndorfer who, apparently, was urging Hoffmann to make an early start.)

More poignant correspondence has been found by Eduard Sekler who quotes from two undated letters to Hoffmann written by Eduard Wimmer who was in London trying to find suitable material for an exhibition. Sekler says Wimmer visited the workshops of George Walton, and C. F. A. Voisey, C. R. Ashbee and others, and was greatly discouraged by what he saw—'my only hope is Mackintosh', he wrote, 'whom I intend to visit in a few days.'

Regrettably we have found no records of that visit but in the second letter he says 'the bad rumour about Mackintosh appears to be true. He seems like most Englishmen [sic] to drink too much but he cannot be called a drunkard. For instance at present he seems to be quite normal.'

Hoffmann wrote to Mackintosh about the exhibition but did not receive an answer. This information was passed on to Wimmer who said that it was regrettable and inexplicable and there the matter seems to have ended. But we do not know the date of these letters and it may well be that both were written after the Kunstschau of 1909 to which the Mackintoshes contributed.[1] However by that time Mackintosh was already in decline; four years later he resigned his partnership with Honeyman and Keppie and, with Margaret, left Glasgow.

Unfortunately events in Vienna were hardly more conducive to the continuing development of progressive and creative work. The Secessionists planned an exhibition in 1904 to which the Mackintoshes were invited to contribute. Although the original letter appears to have been lost Horst-Herbert Kossatz sent me a typed copy of Mackintosh's reply of 4 April 1904 to von Myrbach, 'President der Vereinigung Bildender Künstler Österreichs'. He apologizes, as seemed to be usual, for his tardiness in acknowledging the invitation and hopes they (he and Margaret) will have watercolours and panels ready. He says 'the panels from the Turin exhibition could be included if the owner agrees, and if Professor Moser deals with him not too roughly.' Work by Jessie King might be sent also. If furniture were included they would want to arrange the setting themselves.

The exhibition did not take place because of serious trouble within the Secession itself. This culminated in Klimt, with some of his friends, and von Myrbach and Hoffmann breaking away and forming their own group. Not unnaturally Mackintosh kept in touch with the Klimt–Hoffmann faction and when they, in collaboration with the Wienerwerkstätten, organized arts and crafts exhibitions the Mackintoshes' work again appeared in Vienna—at least on one occasion in 1909.[2] This, however, would seem to have been a flash in the pan, for by this time the work of Hoffmann himself was beginning to lose impetus and creative force and the reason is not far to seek.

Seen against the perspective of the latter half of the nineteenth century, the work of the English group whom Wimmer visited, with its emphasis on good craftsmanship and a fresh approach to design, had formed an inspiring model for Hoffmann and many of his European contemporaries. However, after

[1] The only other occasion on which the work of the Mackintoshes may have been shown in Europe is described on p. 168. Desmond Chapman-Houston says they exhibited in Moscow in 1913, a date challenged by McLaren Young in his foreword to the Catalogue of the 1968 Exhibition. McLaren Young says that Diaghilev arranged an exhibition of modern architecture and design in the Russian capital in 1903 and that an illustration of a stand by Mackintosh was included in *Mir Iskusstva*, 1903, No. 3, p. 17. This, however, does not necessarily invalidate Chapman-Houston's statement—which may refer to another undocumented event.

[2] In the letter from Vienna of 3 April 1971 Kossatz tells me that he reexamined the documents and found that the catalogue for the Kunstschau of 1909 included work by Mackintosh.

the promising development of the 1890s, the strong conservative element in England succeeded in inhibiting progress and resisting outside influence. We have noted the hostile reception given to the Donaldson gift to the Victoria and Albert Museum of *art nouveau* furniture in 1901 (pp. 262–3), and five years earlier to the work of the Glasgow designers at the Arts and Crafts Exhibition Society of 1896. It is quite evident that the followers of William Morris were determined to prevent the 'Scotto-Continental new art' from gaining a foothold in England. It was this kind of unremitting resistance at home in Scotland, too, that went a long way towards breaking Mackintosh's spirit. Hoffmann himself must have been more than a little demoralized by his friend's decline and by Wimmer's reports. Without the evidence of continuing enthusiasm for the 'modern movement'—to use Mackintosh's phrase—and the support of the English designers whom he admired so much, with Mackintosh no longer able to maintain his dynamic creative role, with the break in the ranks of the Secession, and with his friend and patron Wärndorfer's financial collapse and emigration to the USA in 1913, it is not surprising that the Viennese master himself began to lose faith.[1] His post 1914–18 war practice shows very little of the spirit of the new movement. It was in 1913 also that Mackintosh resigned his partnership with Honeyman and Keppie, and left Glasgow for good.

The curtain came down on this the final act in 1914 with the outbreak of the First World War.

CONCLUSION

In conclusion it must be emphasized that, despite Mackintosh's extraordinarily short period of intense activity from 1896, when the School of Art was won in competition, to 1906, when he redesigned the west wing (including the library)—little more than a decade which embraced all his important work and his continental excursions—he successfully established himself as a major force in the modern movement. If recognition of this fact has been long in coming, it is

---

[1] Mary Sturrock has a rather curious anecdote which would seem to confirm this, and although recollections of this nature are not always reliable, it must be recorded here. She says she visited Vienna in June 1913 and was shown one of Hoffmann's housing developments by Edward Wimmer. Although she does not say so, it would appear that she met Hoffmann who 'had turned entirely Biedermeierisch' and she quotes him as saying—'of course I was influenced by Mackintosh when I was younger but that was many years ago.'

due rather to the inability of the audience to appreciate his importance, than to any lack of conviction and significance in the work itself.

At the time of writing (1975) Mackintosh and the Glasgow School are recognized throughout the world. If material evidence were required it would be sufficient perhaps to say that when Margaret Mackintosh died in 1933, five years after her husband, the contents of their Chelsea studios, including watercolours, flower studies, architectural drawings, sketches, furniture and personal effects were valued at £88 16s. 2d., and little enthusiasm was shown in Glasgow when these things were exhibited and offered for sale later in the same year. Yet a single Mackintosh chair was sold by Sotheby's of London in February 1975 for £9,300—about $20,000.[1] In 1975, also, an Italian firm began to offer commercially copies of Mackintosh furniture, and by skilful advertising, especially in the USA, and the production of several exquisitely illustrated publications, found a market for it. These facts alone serve to demonstrate the remarkable change in public opinion over the past decade or so.

Quite apart from fashionable changes in taste, there can be little doubt that as we draw farther away in time we are better able to appraise the significance of new movements, and the contribution of those creative individuals who generate the intellectual force and provide the main impetus. Such a man was Mackintosh, and his work, rediscovered by a modern generation of students, is having a profound effect upon those who are now better able to comprehend and appreciate his objectives, and are capable of understanding those enduring principles of design that informed all his best work in whatever medium.

[1] The centre chair of the group of five illustrated in Plate 46.

INTRODUCTION

A<small>N</small> appreciation of native building traditions, and some acquaintance with the general trend of architectural development in Scotland, are essential to an understanding of Mackintosh's work, for many of the forms he employed and the methods he used are open to misinterpretation if judged solely by English standards. Let us survey briefly, therefore, the historical background to the Mackintosh period.[1]

In the Middle Ages the persistence of bitter feuds and internecine strife seriously retarded the transition from purely defensive building to more peaceful civic and domestic work in Scotland. Until well into the sixteenth century a strongly fortified tower of rectangular plan, often with the addition of a corner wing, proved to be the safest kind of dwelling, and, with modifications, this

[1] The best reference books are: *The Castellated and Domestic Architecture of Scotland*, 5 vols., 1887–92, and *Ecclesiastical Architecture of Scotland*, 3 vols., 1896–7. David McGibbon and Thomas Ross.

Some good later works are: *The History of Scotland in Stone*, Ian C. Hannah, 1934. *The Fortalices and Early Mansions of Southern Scotland*, by Nigel G. Tranter, 1934. *Shrines and Homes of Scotland*, Sir John Stirling Maxwell, 1937. *The Stones of Scotland*, edited by Geo. Scott Moncrieff, 1938.

form endured long after England and France had completed the transition from fortified manor to country mansion.

An increasing demand for comfort and for more spacious living accommodation was often met by extending and broadening the upper stages of old towers, meanwhile retaining the original substructure. Several daring and ingenious devices were employed to expedite this development—for example, ranges of massive corbels and oversailing courses of one kind or another, projecting boldly from the wall face; and greatly enlarged angle turrets. These features, used in conjunction with the ubiquitous crow-stepped gable[1] and sturdy chimney stack, frequently produced extremely picturesque and dramatic effects.

During the sixteenth and early seventeenth centuries the Scottish burgh, or market town, gradually assumed its characteristic form with a nucleus of kirk, tollbooth and 'mercat' cross. Round these clustered the burghers' houses with, of course, a complement of humble dwellings for ordinary folk, all more homely in character than the grim fortress dwellings of less propitious days, but still retaining something of the same forbidding aspect. By and large, these were unpretentious buildings of simple plan, stoutly constructed of stone, and harled (roughcast) externally; windows were few, small, and often irregularly placed, thus emphasizing the preponderance of unbroken wall surface. In the larger houses battlements and parapet walls were dispensed with, roofs were steeply pitched and gabled, with sweeping eaves-lines often interrupted by dormers lighting an attic. Angle turrets were used as rooms, sometimes rising through two or more storeys and occasionally enclosing a newel stair and descending to ground level, while massive chimney stacks and gables gave strong vertical emphasis. Often too, extensions were built to earlier defensive works, as for example at Fordyce Castle, where the contrast between the lofty sixteenth-century tower, and the later harled wing is most telling.[2] To this period also, belongs Lamb's House, Leith,[3] a typical merchant's house of the late sixteenth century, and a romantic composition of plain harled walls and red tiled roofs in which innumerable oversailing courses and an inconsequent pattern of windows lead the eye upwards to lofty crow-stepped gables, and an effusive sky-line. *Stenhouse*, Edinburgh (Plate 37B), is representative of seventeenth-century

---

[1] The characteristic Scottish gable parapet resembles a flight of stone steps, thus affording —in picturesque imagery—a convenient lodgment for the crow or 'corbie': hence 'crow-stepped' or 'corbie-stepped' gable.

[2] Illustrated in *Country Life*, December 1947.

[3] Illustrated in *Scotland*, a symposium (Nelson, 1947).

xliv

town dwellings, and Craigievar Castle (1620) and Barscobe House (1640), are typical country houses of the period.[1] All are dour and uncompromising and one can scarcely believe that they were built many years after the Elizabethan masterpieces of Longleat (1567–9) and Wollaton (1580–8), and that Stenhouse may well be contemporary with Roger Pratt's Coleshill (1650–64).

Such examples well represent the Scottish vernacular, an unsophisticated style reflecting the spirit of a hardy, unsophisticated people. Its character springs naturally from an appropriate use of the materials at hand, a stern climate, and an economy which left little room for the refinements and comforts of life.

The Reformation and subsequent enrichment of the nobility, followed in the early seventeenth century by the union of the Scottish and English Crowns, brought about a change in social conditions, and consequently in architectural design. Hitherto contact between Scotland and her southern neighbour had been limited in the main to border skirmishes and forays, and the geographical barrier of the Cheviots and the wild border country had made intercourse difficult and dangerous. Now, however, there was a more insistent demand in Scotland for standards of comfort approximating more closely to those enjoyed in the southern counties of England, and for a style of architecture more in keeping with contemporary fashion—the Renaissance. The first evidence of change appeared in furnishing and interior work generally, but gradually the planning and fabric of the building itself was modified, though the Scots clung tenaciously to many architectural features—turrets, corbels and the like—associated with their turbulent past. By the end of the seventeenth century, Renaissance details, pediments, balusters, cornices and so forth were introduced on the outside of Scottish buildings, and some attempt was made to achieve symmetry in planning. Slowly, and at first almost imperceptibly, the robust vernacular style was superseded and the old ways of building largely forsaken, except, that is, in rural communities and remote farmsteads where unpretentious domestic building was still practised. Eventually, however, the transformation was complete, and in the work of William Adam (1689–1748), and more especially in that of his distinguished sons, Robert and James, it is difficult, if not impossible, to recognize any distinctive national characteristics.

The Renaissance and the style of the Adam brothers was readily accepted, and rapidly achieved popularity in the north. During the eighteenth century Scotland succumbed completely to classicism, and within a remarkably short

[1] Illustrated in " Mackintosh and the Scottish Tradition ". T. Howarth. *The Magazine of Art*. Vol. XLI.

time several architects of distinction emerged, most of whom executed a great deal of their work in the south and have come to be associated more with England than with the land of their birth—Colin Campbell author of *Vitruvius Britannicus*, James Gibbs, and, of course, Robert and James Adam, to mention but four. To this period belongs Edinburgh New Town with its formal squares, crescents, and regimented façades—the antithesis of the Scottish style as exemplified in the 'Old Town'—and also, by way of contrast, the charming rural village of Eaglesham, and the small towns of Inveraray and Ullapool.

The first quarter of the nineteenth century saw the rapid growth of civic building and the flowering of the Greek Revival. William H. Playfair (1789–1857) was its leading exponent in Scotland, and his extensions to Edinburgh New Town and, later, his design for the Scottish National Gallery (1850), with Thomas Hamilton's Royal High School, and other notable buildings in similar vein, earned for the capital city the appellation 'Athens of the North'. To Ruskin's censorious eye, however, Edinburgh was 'nothing but square cut stone —square cut stone—a wilderness of square cut stone for ever and ever'.[1]

The limitations of the pure Greek style were soon reached and *circa* 1830, before the National Gallery was built, a modified style had been evolved—the neo-Grec—in which motives derived from Greek, Roman or Italian sources were combined. David Hamilton, the architect of the Royal Exchange, Glasgow —a building measured and drawn by Mackintosh when a student—was one of its more reputable Scottish advocates.

Scotland, and more especially, Glasgow, could boast one man, however, who had courage to defy convention and to embark on work of an unorthodox nature. This was Alexander 'Greek' Thomson (1817–75), though, as the sobriquet 'Greek' suggests, even he remained virtually within the academic fold. Nevertheless, in an age given over to pedantry, Thomson's work was fresh and stimulating: his dignified terraces, extraordinary churches, and fine city buildings—a curious blend of Hellenic and Egyptian forms—must be numbered amongst the most notable architectural monuments of the nineteenth century in Scotland; and his exotic interior decoration is paralleled in the south only by the brilliant polychromatic experiments of Butterfield. Thomson evolved a distinctive local style which had considerable influence upon the street architecture of Glasgow, but his work formed only a brief diversion, and he contributed little to the main stream of Scottish architectural development.

In England the Gothic revivalists had gained the ascendancy by the middle

[1] 'Lectures in Architecture and Painting', delivered at Edinburgh in 1853.

xlvi

of the nineteenth century but for secular purposes the style never achieved popularity in Scotland. There emerged instead a new and equally heterogeneous style—the Baronial. Under the spell of Sir Walter Scott (1771–1832) and of the Waverley Novels, the departed glories of Scotland were given new colour, and public interest revived in all things relating to her past, not least in her architectural monuments. In response to this impulse there came a demand for buildings of all kinds in the romantic manner, and practising architects quickly realized that a fruitful source of archaeological material had been neglected. William Burn (1789–1870) and his partner David Bryce (1803–76) led the field, and successfully inaugurated a new fashion to which considerable impetus was given by the publication of Robert Billings's *Baronial and Ecclesiastical Antiquities* (1845–52). Unfortunately the old mistakes were repeated. Billings's monumental work was used in exactly the same manner as Stuart and Revett's *Antiquities of Athens* which had been the copy book of the Greek revivalists. The characteristic features of the vernacular were seized upon, copied, and employed as fanciful trimmings to new work of all kinds. Thus, in the rapidly expanding towns of the central industrial belt of Scotland, curiously self-conscious buildings adorned with crow-stepped gables, machicolations, castellated parapets and Franco-Scottish turrets, appeared side by side with Gothic churches, Graeco-Roman banks and Italianate warehouses. Nor did the countryside escape the surge of perfervid romanticism, for to this period belongs Balmoral[1] and a host of ostentatious mansions and seaside establishments (Plate 32B) which, let it be admitted, often appear less incongruous, and at times even picturesque, against a background of mountain and forest. The bold functionalism of castle and keep, and the simple dignity of traditional farmhouse and cottage seemed to elude the Baronialists, however, and their work almost invariably possesses an air of fantasy which on occasion approaches the grotesque. In few instances prior to the advent of Sir Rowand Anderson (1834–1921), and later, of his pupil Sir Robert Lorimer (1864–1929), was any conscious attempt made to recapture the true spirit of the vernacular. Yet even these men concerned themselves primarily with the revival of craftsmanship, and with the reinstitution of old building methods; they had no solution to offer to the architectural problems of an industrial society.

Despite the material rewards that attended the gratification of popular demand—and this was the heyday of the great practitioner—there can be no

---

[1] Bought by the Prince Consort in 1848. The foundation stone of the new Baronial edifice was laid five years later by Queen Victoria.

doubt that the second half of the nineteenth century was a time of questioning and uncertainty for the serious student of architecture. He was confronted by many conflicting ideologies each with its influential champions—often, it should be remembered, men of culture and integrity—and its vociferous body of adherents. Nor was his path made easier by the professional journals which reflected the mood of the times, and devoted much space to academic papers and discussions, and to illustrations of buildings which for sheer diversity of character will probably never be equalled.

This unhappy state of affairs was perpetuated by the restrictive nature of the architect's initial training. As an apprentice and draughtsman he was given little freedom, and had few opportunities of developing his creative faculties. His first and most important task was to acquire a sound knowledge of the orders and classical elements, supplemented by measured drawings, and by reading from Rickman, Brandon, Pugin, Billings and others if his master were a Medievalist. As part of his normal office routine it was his duty to interpret preliminary sketches, and to provide mouldings, ornament and other details of correct antiquity—or to reproduce those of his master. 'Street, you know, would not let us design a key-hole,'[1] commented Norman Shaw to W. R. Lethaby when discussing his distinguished employer, and in this respect Street was by no means an exception.

To the apprentice, and to the great majority of draughtsmen, architectural design had become largely two-dimensional and divorced from reality: it had been reduced to a system—the arrangement of a given number of symbols to specified rules within a prescribed area, the limits of a façade. All too often thought was directed almost exclusively to the style of a building and to the archaeological exactitude of its details rather than to its planning, convenience and suitability. The successful architect of the Victorian era was the man who could manipulate historical forms with the greatest dexterity, or who could most skilfully adapt one or other of the fashionable styles to meet the needs of his patron, convincing himself meanwhile that the rules of propriety and good taste had been strictly adhered to.

'I was commissioned to erect the new University buildings at Glasgow,' said Sir Gilbert Scott, 'a very large work, for which I adopted a style which I may call my own invention, having already initiated it in the Albert Institute at Dundee. It is simply a thirteenth- or fourteenth-century secular style with

---

[1] *Philip Webb and his Work*, W. R. Lethaby.

the addition of certain Scottish features, peculiar in that country to the sixteenth century, though in reality derived from the French style of the thirteenth and fourteenth centuries.'[1]

It was into this world of studied eclecticism Charles Rennie Mackintosh was born—shortly after Scott embarked upon his quasi-medieval project for Glasgow University—and it was against this spirit that he rebelled some twenty years later.

We may well ask how it came about that a leader of the new movement should spring from remote, industrial Glasgow; yet the reason is not far to seek. From the middle of the nineteenth century onwards the Corporation and citizens of Glasgow showed a commendable interest in the fine arts, if not in architecture. In 1856 the city acquired the Archibald McLellan Galleries in Sauchiehall Street, together with McLellan's fine collection of pictures, which then became available to the public. Eleven years later the Galleries were extensively altered and the pictures re-hung to better advantage—and the Glasgow Art Club was founded.

The following decade witnessed a remarkable quickening of the artistic spirit in the West of Scotland, and in the early 1880's came the Glasgow School of Painters—the 'Boys from Glasgow'—a group of young men who met to discuss art in the studio of W. Y. Macgregor, and produced work of outstanding originality and independence. The paintings of these men—of E. A. Walton and James Guthrie, Macaulay Stevenson and John Lavery, E. A. Hornel, George Henry and others—attracted a great deal of attention both at home and abroad, and exhibitions at the Glasgow Art Institute (founded in 1879), and elsewhere, were the scene of much spirited argument and public enthusiasm. The work of the 'School', however, found its way not only into the galleries, but into city tea-shops, business premises and public houses. Business men—the patrons of the industrial age—stimulated by local pride (and the prospect of a sound investment) bought the pictures they liked—and Glasgow began to enjoy a minor renaissance.

Then, in 1885, when this enthusiasm was at its height, a new headmaster was appointed to the Glasgow School of Art—Francis H. Newbery. This was an important event, for Newbery was but thirty-one years of age, and an English-

[1] *Personal and Professional Recollections*, Sir Gilbert Scott.

man. He had trained as a painter and had taught at South Kensington, and he went to Glasgow fully informed of the significant events then taking place in the south.

As a teacher and administrator Newbery was superb. He was a strict disciplinarian, but he encouraged his pupils to develop their individuality and to adopt the art form for which they had most inclination. His liberal policy and unorthodox views caused the authorities a deal of misgiving, but so successful did his methods prove, that in little more than a decade the Glasgow School of Art was acclaimed internationally as one of the most progressive institutions of its kind, and Newbery's students had evolved a distinctive and extraordinary manner of painting and decoration, soon to be known throughout Europe as the 'Glasgow Style'.

Thus cosmopolitan Glasgow, the home of a school of impressionist painters, with a young and fearless administrator in charge of its School of Art, provided an environment singularly conducive to work of an experimental kind, an environment admirably suited to the development of Charles Rennie Mackintosh's peculiar genius.

1

PART ONE

MACKINTOSH AND THE GLASGOW STYLE

CHARLES Rennie Mackintosh, the second son of a family of eleven children, was born at No. 70 Parson Street, Glasgow, on 7th June 1868. His father, William Mackintosh, was of Highland stock from Nairn on the Moray Firth, a superintendent of police in the city and a man of integrity and high repute. Margaret, his mother, was a Lowlander, daughter of Charles Rennie of Ayr, an unassuming, homely woman of character, greatly loved by her children. The family occupied an unpretentious third-floor tenement flat in the east end of Glasgow, in a locality which subsequently degenerated as a result of the phenomenal growth of the city during the latter part of the nineteenth century. There is no evidence of any particular interest in the fine arts, much less an art tradition in either branch of the family and the theory of hereditary genius can be discarded at once in the case of the son.

As the family increased and William Mackintosh's position improved, they moved from the Parson Street tenement to a more attractive house, No. 2 Firpark Terrace, Dennistoun, when the boy Charles was about ten years old. Here the really formative period of his life began.

Dennistoun was a pleasant suburb of Glasgow in the 1870's and in more congenial surroundings William Mackintosh was able to enjoy and develop his favourite hobby—gardening. Even at the tenement in the early days, he had managed to keep a garden or an allotment, and such was his enthusiasm that he frequently rose at five in the morning and spent several hours working at his plot before going to the office—and he returned to it in the evenings. In Dennistoun he had the good fortune to obtain part of the garden of *Golf Hill House*, a large residence vacated by its owners, the Dennistoun family, and left in the hands of a caretaker. This was beautifully laid out and he tended it with great care; the children christened it the 'Garden of Eden'. Flowers were his speciality and he was particularly interested in the cultivation of hyacinths; every year large quantities of bulbs were sent to him from Holland, and he became a well-known figure and prizewinner at local horticultural shows. Flowers were always to be found in profusion in the Mackintosh household and from an early age the children were encouraged to take an interest in their father's hobby. They acquired, naturally, a profound regard for growing living things, a regard which, in the case of Charles, endured throughout his life and found expression in every work of art he created.

As a child, Charles Mackintosh was not very strong and two physical deformities added to his handicap; he was born with a contracted sinew in one foot which brought about an awkward limp as he grew older, and then as the result of a chill after a game of football, the muscles of his right eye were permanently affected, causing the lid to droop. The family doctor prescribed a remedy popular the world over—'the boy should be encouraged to take plenty of exercise in the open air and to have long holidays whenever possible'. This advice Charles found exactly to his liking. To the Mackintosh household, however, family holidays were always something of an adventure. Eleven children alone must have been a handful for the parents, but like most youngsters, they were fond of pets and at holiday times the pets went too. Miss Nancy Mackintosh recalls one amusing excursion to the Clyde coast where the family had taken a house—they boarded a steamer at Glasgow with a dog, several cats, a hedgehog, a tortoise, and a goat which had been acquired to provide milk for one of the children who was ill. Soon after their arrival Miss Nancy begged a lamb from a farmer to add to the collection, but after bleating all night in the kitchen the unfortunate creature was returned the next day, despite the tearful protestations of its young mistress.

Quite apart from the annual exodus, Charles saw much of Scotland in these early days. He delighted especially in wandering over the lovely countryside surrounding Glasgow, and, by sketching, greatly enlarged his knowledge of local architecture, wild flowers, plants and trees.

Charles's school days passed uneventfully and he does not appear to have achieved particular distinction at either Reid's Private School, or later at Alan Glen's High School, where he completed his education. Unfortunately records for the 1880's have been destroyed at both institutions and there is nothing now to be gleaned from either source. In other respects too—apart from a strong affection for cats—his early life appears to have been normal and without marked incident. He was a somewhat temperamental youth, however, capable of violent fits of rage, and he always insisted on getting his own way. But, even so, he was generous and kind-hearted and had an attractive personality which won him many friends.

From an early age Charles was determined to be an architect, and in spite of his father's attempts to dissuade him, he succeeded as usual in winning parental approval, but only on the understanding that he would 'put his mind to it' and work hard. So, on leaving Alan Glen's at the age of sixteen, he was articled to John Hutchison of Glasgow—a firm no longer in existence. At the same time he enrolled as an evening student at the School of Art (1884). In those days it was customary for an architectural apprentice in the city to serve for five years, though in the country the period was reduced to four. No remuneration was offered for the first twelve months; but the student received £10 for the second year, and then annual increments of £5 until, during the final year of his apprenticeship, he would earn the princely sum of £25.

JOHN HUTCHISON

Hutchison's office was situated at the back of a furniture shop owned by his brother James, at 107 St. Vincent Street, Glasgow. Here Mackintosh worked under the charge of the chief assistant, Andrew Black, an able draughtsman and a good teacher, who later became a partner in the firm of Miller and Black in the city. The proximity of the furniture shop is of some significance and no doubt accounts, at least in part, for the young architect's early interest in furniture design. Regrettably nothing now remains of Mackintosh's work in the office, but his place was taken in April 1889 by Mr. W. J. Blane, who was greatly impressed at the time by the vigour of his predecessor's draughtsmanship. Despite an interval of sixty years Mr. Blane distinctly remembers seeing

3

a drawing by Mackintosh of an Ionic capital which was to be executed in plaster for the premises of Messrs. Wylie Hill, Buchanan Street. This, he maintains, was brilliantly executed and showed surprising individuality. But Wylie Hill's store was completely destroyed by fire in the early 1900's and with it the tangible proofs of Mackintosh's early capacity. The architects at present responsible for the reconstructed premises do not possess drawings of the original building, nor has it been possible to trace other work by Hutchison to which he might have contributed.

On the completion of his apprenticeship, Mackintosh joined the newly established firm of John Honeyman and Keppie, the firm in which he eventually became a partner (1904). His name appeared for the first time in the office accounts for July 1889, when a single payment of £5 was recorded.

At the Glasgow School of Art where he studied from 1884 onwards Mackintosh figured with persistent regularity in the prize lists for some eight years, and there is reason to believe that his close association with the School did not terminate when he ceased to attend classes. Though few of his original drawings are extant, the School records and contemporary journals provide a valuable guide to his progress and, what is equally important, contain descriptions and criticisms of his work.

At the end of his first session (1884–5) he received a prize for 'Painting and Ornament in Monochrome from the Flat'. He also passed second-grade examinations in freehand drawing, modelling and geometry ('excellent'). In the following year (1885–6), he was commended in the advanced section, awarded a prize, and given a free studentship. His studies in sepia from the cast showed 'both care and fidelity'.[1]

The annual report of the School of Art for the year 1887 mentions an Architectural Section for the first time, although a certain Thomas Smith had been teaching the subject since 1884 at least, and classes in freehand drawing, geometry and perspective were attended by architects' and builders' apprentices. In 1887, however, the course seems to have been established on a firmer footing and classes in building construction, architectural design and measured drawing were instituted. Even so, the majority of pupils came from the building trades. Attendance at evening classes was not obligatory for the architects' apprentice and consequently only the keenest students took advantage of them. So poor was the response, in fact, that in order to stimulate enthusiasm, the Glasgow

[1] A drawing in sepia from the cast survives in the Glasgow University Collection (Plate 2A).

4

Institute of Architects awarded a number of prizes for which a student could compete by submitting work in three specified groups:—drawings of architectural ornament from the cast; measured drawings of existing buildings; and lecture notes on building construction.

In 1887 Mackintosh distinguished himself by gaining the Glasgow Institute's Book Prize for the best set of building construction lecture notes and the second prize of £2 10s. for measured drawings (of David Hamilton's Royal Exchange, Glasgow).

In company with similar institutions throughout the United Kingdom the Glasgow School of Art entered students' work for the National Competition held annually at South Kensington, and in 1888 Mackintosh was awarded a bronze medal for the 'Design of a Mountain Chapel', which received the following commendation from *The Building News*: 'A very clever design. . . . The plan is simple and well grouped. A low tile-roofed tower forms the vestry, attached to a vestibule and porch. A single-span tiled roof, hipped at end, covers the church; the walling is of a bluish grey "rag" making a pleasant contrast with the red tiles, and the details are simple and effective.' The examiners said the building was picturesquely designed and worthy of notice, but no illustrations survive. During the same year he also secured the Glasgow Institute's prize for the best set of three monthly designs and was awarded a prize of £1 for a 'Town House in a Terrace'. This project evidently showed signs of originality deplored by the local examiners. Their remarks admirably reflect the attitude of the profession at large: 'Under the Monthly Design Scheme sets of original designs were submitted, and the Examiners could wish that these efforts had more relation to the knowledge gained by a study of past work.'

At South Kensington in the following year (1889) Mackintosh was awarded a book prize—one of the National Queen's Prizes—for the design of a Presbyterian Church. The Cross Section and Plan only are extant,[1] but no characteristic details can be recognized, nor is the drawing signed. The examiners' report stated, 'The design though not quite satisfactory, is fresh and original, cleverly though roughly drawn and agreeably coloured, the shadows, however, being somewhat overdone.'[2]

The Building News (1889)[3] described it thus: 'Another design by Charles

---

[1] In the Glasgow University Collection.　　　[2] School of Art Report, January 1890.

[3] 2nd August 1889, p. 135. This design was submitted for one of the Glasgow Institute of Architects' competitions and Mackintosh shared first prize with John G. Gillespie a draughtsman in the office of W. Forrest Salmon.

Rennie Mackintosh, Glasgow, is picturesquely handled, has more originality, and is of brownish stone with red-tile hipped roofs, which are made pleasing features in the design. The plan is transeptal and better suited for a country service. A tower, the four rounded angles of which are carried up as pinnacles, supports a low, square, tiled roof, piquant in effect. The nave has at one end a large semi-circular window. A Renaissance doorway is shown and the whole is somewhat American in style.' 1889 proved to be a most successful School year. Mackintosh was awarded a prize in architectural design (Highest Grade), a free studentship (First Class Honours), a certificate and bronze medal for building construction, a first-class certificate and prize in architectural design, and second-class certificates in elementary modelling and painting in mono-chrome. In addition to the Glasgow Institute's design prize, he received a prize (15s.) for sketching ornament from the cast and £1 10s. for the best set of three monthly drawings.

Although an indefatigable worker at school and office, Mackintosh continued to interpret his doctor's orders literally and never neglected an opportunity of escaping from the city. Whenever practicable he spent week-ends in the country, or visiting places of architectural interest; on these excursions he was usually accompanied by his friend Herbert MacNair, a young draughtsman at Honey-man and Keppie's office whom we shall meet again and again throughout this study.[1] Mackintosh delighted in drawing from nature and soon acquired re-markable facility with the pencil; his ability for quick and accurate sketching proved a valuable complementary to his highly developed powers of observa-tion. Anything of striking colour or curious shape fascinated him, and notwith-standing the derisive remarks of his companions, he rarely returned home without a bunch of flowers, a few plants or perhaps a collection of twigs. These he would examine in minute detail and draw at his leisure, analysing and recording the form and structure of unfamiliar specimens.

The author will not easily forget a walk in Argyllshire with Herbert MacNair (1944); the conversation was, of course, of his old friend and the exciting days

[1] Herbert MacNair came of military stock, and his family lived at Skelmorlie on the Clyde estuary. He was educated at the Collegiate School, Greenock, and his father wished him to become an engineer. One gathers that some difference of opinion ensued, for at the age of eighteen or nineteen he spent twelve months at Rouen studying water-colour painting under a certain M. Haudebert. On his return to Scotland he was apprenticed to John Honeyman, a few months before the partnership between Honeyman and Keppie was formed (early in 1889). Mackintosh entered the office as a draughtsman shortly afterwards and the two young artists quickly became firm friends.

6

of the nineties. Suddenly the artist stopped, and pointing out a small tree of the fir species with remarkably brilliant orange coloured flowers, said with a sly grin, 'If Toshie'd been here he'd have gone to any lengths to get one of those branches.' The tree was growing in a well-tended private garden.

Mackintosh not only acquired an immense new vocabulary of line and form by his pleasant hobby, but also came to understand something of the inexhaustible riches of nature. Probably before he commenced to read Ruskin, one of his favourite authors, he had discovered that no two leaves on the same tree were identical, and that each petal on every flower had distinctive characteristics and could not be matched in texture, shape or colour. Such lessons he was not slow to apply in practice, and many of his later designs possess an elusive charm and vitality due entirely to subtle variations in detail achieved without impairing the balance or unity of the whole. Nor did he confine his attention entirely to flowers and plants but executed many architectural studies in pencil and wash, ranging from large subjects such as Glasgow Cathedral [1] to examples of less pretentious vernacular work. His interest in old Scottish buildings was stimulated by the publication of McGibbon and Ross's *Castellated and Domestic Architecture of Scotland* (1887–92) and he recorded with equal enthusiasm farmhouse and cottage, medieval castle and palace, thereby greatly increasing his knowledge of traditional materials and building methods. This, as we shall see, had a most important bearing on his subsequent work.

ALEXANDER THOMSON SCHOLARSHIP, 1890

Within twelve months of his appointment as draughtsman to Messrs. Honeyman and Keppie, Mackintosh gained one of the most coveted prizes available to architectural students in Scotland, the Alexander (Greek) Thomson Travelling Scholarship.[2] The result of the competition was announced in *The Building News* on 26th September 1890, and the competitors' drawings were exhibited in the Glasgow Corporation Galleries. According to the conditions published by the Glasgow Institute of Architects (*The Building News*, 15th November 1889), the competition was ' . . . for the best original design of a public hall to

---

[1] Sketches of Glasgow Cathedral dated 1886–8 are in the possession of W. Meldrum, Esq., of Glasgow.

[2] At this time too Mackintosh had work accepted for the R.I.B.A. Scholarship in Architecture, but the award was withheld as he was the sole competitor in the United Kingdom.

FRONT ELEVATION.

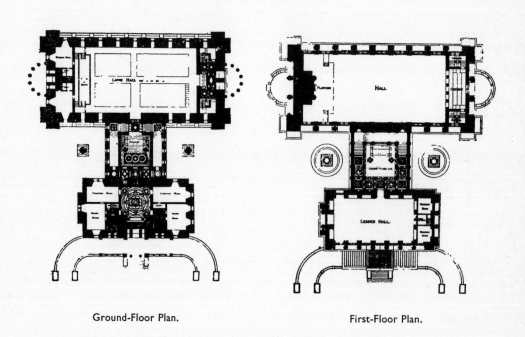

Ground-Floor Plan.   First-Floor Plan.

Figure 1. 1890. 'A Public Hall.' A design awarded the Alexander Thomson Travelling Scholarship.

accommodate 1,000 persons (seated), with suitable committee rooms, the design to be in the Early Classic style, and for an isolated site'. Mackintosh adopted the Ionic order and produced a symmetrical colonnaded building set on a high rusticated base (Fig. 1). The elevational drawing illustrated here gives a good impression of the project; the subsidiary views published in *The British Architect*, 1890, are less satisfactory. It is interesting to note that Honeyman and Keppie were at work on *three* monumental schemes for the New Glasgow Art Galleries Competition at this time; one in the classic style, one in the English renaissance manner, and one in the Scottish renaissance (Plate 19A). The first of these bears more than a superficial resemblance to Mackintosh's scholarship project.[1]

The Alexander Thomson award of £60 was a godsend: not only did it enable the young architect to spend several months abroad, but it increased his prestige immensely and gave him added confidence at the very outset of his career—matters of vital consequence to a man of his temperament. Full of enthusiasm, and well supplied with information from Ruskin and Baedeker, he planned an extensive tour of Italy. He left Glasgow in February 1891,[2] stayed a few days in London, and then sailed for Naples, where he arrived on 5th March after an uneventful voyage. His diary has survived, and so it is possible to follow his progress at least until 7th July, when the last entry reads, ' . . . left for Pavia'—no indication is given of his return home, though he travelled via Paris, Brussels, Antwerp and London. The diary contains many long and tiresome descriptions of buildings familiar to every tourist. Here and there, however, a paragraph reflects something of the enthusiasm with which he enjoyed each new aesthetic adventure; or, perhaps, a single sentence reveals the depth of some unexpected emotional experience.

Of the Ducal Palace, Venice, he says, 'Such an interesting combination of objects, such regal scenery, transported me beyond myself. The custodian thought me distracted.' And again, 'The various portals, the strange projections, in short the striking irregularities of those stately piles delighted me beyond idea; and I was sorry to be forced to leave them so soon especially as twilight, which bats and owls love not better than I do, enlarged every portico, lengthened every colonnade, added certain misticism, and increased the dimensions of the whole just as the imagination desired.'

[1] Honeyman and Keppie's three designs—none of which was premiated—were published in *The British Architect* in 1892.

[2] Mackintosh entered the wrong date on the manuscript of an essay on his Italian Tour at present in the Glasgow University Collection—the year should read 1891 not 1890.

Mackintosh revelled in the brilliant sunlight and deep shadows, the rich colouring, the form and texture of unfamiliar things. The reflections of light from gondola lamps in the Grand Canal fascinated him, and he passed in humility and awed wonder through the Uffizzi and Pitti Galleries where, he said, he could have stayed for ever. Nor was he oblivious to the less delectable characteristics of Italian life. He makes several pungent comments on the difficulties of sketching in the middle of a crowd of inquisitive, odoriferous peasants, and one of his most picturesque descriptions is of the road leading from the Capitol to the Colosseum, Rome, which in his opinion resembled the east end of Glasgow—it was, he observed, just 'as grimy, as filthy, as tumblesome, as forlorn, and as unpleasantly redolent of old clothes and old women who were washerwomen once upon a time, but who have long since foresworn (*sic*) soap. . . .'

Then again, in direct contrast, we find the sensitive, strangely melancholy youth casting a critical eye over the interior of Florence Cathedral and attempting to identify himself with the spirit of the building:

'There is something imposing about the decoration as it suggests the idea of sancity (sanctity) into which none but the holy ought to penetrate. However profane I might feel myself I took the liberty of entering and sat down in a niche. Not a ray of light enters the sacred enclosure but through the medium of narrow windows high up in the dome and richly painted. A sort of yellow green tint predominates which gives additional solemnity to the altar and paleness to the votary before it. I was conscious of the effect and obtained at least the colour of sancity.'

Mackintosh visited most of the cathedral cities of Italy and Sicily and inspected the principal art collections; he produced masses of drawings in several media, some half finished, others partly or wholly rendered in water-colour; and the majority, line drawings in pencil. His subjects were catholic in the extreme; with equal enthusiasm he turned to Pompeiian vases and pieces of sculpture, campanili and cathedral doorways, mosaics and pulpits.[1]

[1] Many years later a portfolio containing a large number of these sketches found its way into a Glasgow office, and in due course was thrown out with the rubbish. By a stroke of good fortune it was noticed lying on the top of a well-filled dustbin in one of the city's alleyways and was promptly salvaged. It is now safely housed in the library of the Royal Technical College, Glasgow. A fine collection of sketches was presented to the author in 1943 and these, with the Royal Technical College portfolio, constitute the major part of the work executed by Mackintosh in Italy.

10

Although some of these drawings are rather rough, many are finely executed and models of their kind. He made various experiments in different media—watercolour on tracing paper, or brown paper, for example—but one of the most striking methods he adopted was to sketch with a bold, rather heavy pencil line on 'Whatman' paper and then to render the shadows only in strong transparent washes—usually of cold grey-blue. He sent home a selection of these drawings for inclusion in the Annual Exhibition of the School of Art Students' Club and was unhesitatingly awarded first prize. In a letter to the *Glasgow Evening News* (17th February 1933) R. Eddington Smith, recalling the adjudication at which he was present, states that Sir James Guthrie, one of the judges, seemed to be impressed by the power and beauty of the drawings even more than the other artists present—Sir John Lavery, Alexander Roche and E. A. Walton—and, when told they were by an architectural student, turned to the Director of the School and said fiercely, 'But hang it, Newbery, this man ought to be an artist.'

Mackintosh's sensitive pencil and wash drawings are a measure of his appreciation of the Italian scene, and he was deeply conscious of the fundamental valuès represented by the buildings and *objets d'art* which he sketched. His subsequent designs, however, show that he was influenced little by Italian stylistic character, and mercifully we are spared a tiresome excursion into the neo-Renaissance. But on his return home his work in both the decorative and architectural fields soon became more confident and more mature—did not Dr. Johnson say that a man who has not been in Italy is always conscious of an inferiority?

The Alexander Thomson Competition drawings together with a design for a Science and Art Museum[1] were sent later to South Kensington, and in the autumn of 1891, Mackintosh was awarded the National Silver Medal. There are no published comments on the Public Hall, but the examiners' remarks on the second project are somewhat succinct. The design, they said, 'has many good points, but the effect of the larger features above smaller ones is disagreeable' —a criticism by no means unfounded. The elevation is an unimaginative essay in the French Renaissance manner, pedantic, ill-proportioned, and carelessly rendered in sepia. The project must have offended the purists greatly, or perhaps the jury disagreed, for over nine months later the matter was raised again by

[1] This project was illustrated in *The British Architect* supplement 31st October 1890. The original drawing of the principal elevation is in the Glasgow University Collection (see Plate 2B).

The Builder (1st August 1891) in an article violently attacking the work and policy at South Kensington in general, and Mackintosh's contribution in particular. The critic could hardly contain himself: 'We can only observe', he said, 'that if the department (of Science and Art) can secure no higher standard than the things to which they award prizes, they had better give up teaching architecture at all. There is a silver medal given to a Glasgow student, for instance, for a design for a classic building, which is bad in every way, clumsy and heavy in design and defective in drawing.' The project was referred to again later as ambitious, ugly and ill-drawn. No doubt comments of this nature in the professional journals of the nineties were treated with much the same disdain by competitors as they are in the twentieth century, but in all probability this angry protest represents the first direct public attack on the young architect, the first of many, for he was soon to become the target for much bitter criticism.

Despite this setback Mackintosh had little cause for complaint. His successes at South Kensington and in local competitions, and more especially the Alexander Thomson Scholarship, kept his name before the public and augured well for the future. It is evident too, that he was beginning to acquire a reputation in professional circles, for he had been invited to read a paper on Scottish Baronial Architecture to the Glasgow Architectural Association on the eve of his departure for Italy. A brief account of this is given in *The Architect* (20th February 1891) and fortunately his lecture notes survive.[1] Throughout the paper he stressed the importance of tradition in architectural design and eulogized the Scottish vernacular for its beauty of outline and picturesque grouping. He praised the sensible use of materials in old Scottish work—the frank and honest expression of purpose, and disdain of artificial symmetry. Significant too is his observation on 'the extraordinary facility of our style in decorating construction and in converting structural and useful features into elements of beauty'.

After a historical survey of architectural development in Scotland he concluded by saying that the national style was coming to life again, and expressed the hope that architects would not merely copy ancient examples but 'make the style conform to modern requirements'.

[1] In the Glasgow University Collection. On the back of one page there is a note—'very unkind of Mr. Walton to ascribe all the artistic features to France'. This would suggest that George Walton—of whom more later—was present, and raised a debatable point that was calculated to ruffle the temper of the lecturer—the real origin of many architectural features claimed as indigenous to Scotland.

This paper was the first of several he read to the Association—in the following year he discussed his Italian tour,[1] and in 1893 contributed a paper on 'Architecture'.

THE CHAPTER HOUSE, 1891–2

Immediately after his return from Italy Mackintosh set to work on the Soane Medallion Competition for which he submitted a design under the pseudonym *Griffin*. There were eight other competitors. The subject was a chapter house which he courageously attempted in the classical style in deference, no doubt, to the Alexander Thomson Trustees (Fig. 2). Apparently the standard of the entries was well above the average and though he did not succeed in gaining the award, the criticism of the jury was not discouraging. *The British Architect* (4th March 1892) commented thus: 'We must say that Gothic takes the palm for quality, the clever Renaissance of *Griffin* notwithstanding. The attenuated form of the sculptured dormers round the dome in this latter design very much detracts from the effect, though in some ways the design is very skilfully worked out.' The criticism of the dormers—if they can be so described—is well justified. Flanked as they are by kneeling angels and alternating with heavy open-work pinnacles, they form a broken and restless element in an otherwise dignified and by no means unattractive composition.

Though not acceptable to the assessors of the competition for the Soane medallion, Mackintosh's design came in useful when his employers required a dominant feature for their extension to Messrs. Pettigrew and Stephens's warehouse, Sauchiehall Street, some seven years afterwards.[2] The chapter house dome—with modifications—was translated into terms of wood and metal, elevated some 80 feet above one of Glasgow's busiest thoroughfares, and is now an important city landmark.

The drawings of the chapter house were submitted later in the year at South Kensington, and secured for its designer the National Gold Medal.[3] The report of the examiners (Professor C. Aitcheson, A.R.A., T. G. Jackson, A.R.A., and J. J. Stevenson) is rather amusing; of Mackintosh's work they said, '. . . a design showing considerable artistic power with details well drawn. It is a pity the author should have copied his candelabra directly from an ancient example'.

---

[1] September 1892. A brief report was published in *The Builder*, 10th September 1892.

[2] The project drawings were illustrated in *Academy Architecture*, 1899.

[3] The result of the competition was published in *Building News*, 29th July 1892, p. 122.

13

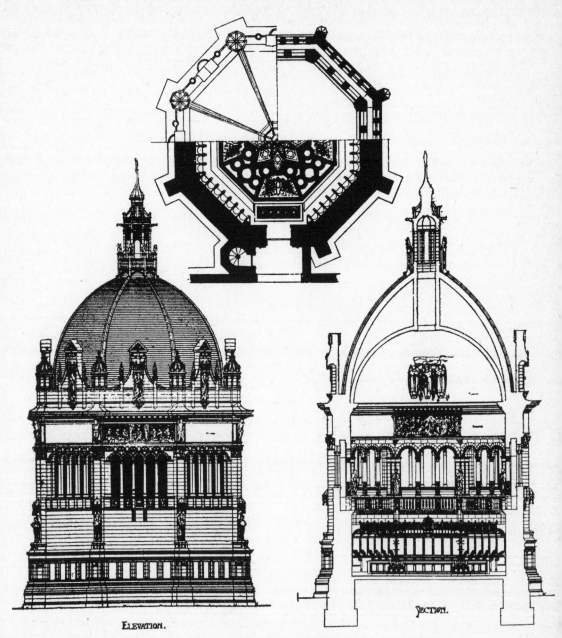

ELEVATION.

SECTION.

Plan at Cloister Level.

Figure 2. 1891. 'A Chapter House.' Elevation and Section. Unpremiated Design for the Soane Medallion Competition.

14

It has been claimed frequently that Mackintosh won the Soane Medallion and Haldane Scholarship during his student days at the School of Art, but he did not secure either prize. The Soane was not awarded in 1890, nor in 1891, and was won by Heber Rimmer in 1892. The Haldane Travelling Scholarship of £50 (open to all Schools of Art and Art classes in Glasgow) was won by Miss S. R. L. Dean, John Alsop and Miss Ella Alexander respectively during this period, and by Francis Dodd in 1893. Mackintosh, however, did submit a further design for the Soane in 1893, the year after his failure with the Renaissance chapter house. The subject was a railway terminus and this time he tried his hand at modernized Gothic (Plate 3).[1]

THE RAILWAY TERMINUS, 1892-3

The plan is simple and straightforward enough, but here Mackintosh came up against a very awkward problem, that of giving adequate expression to the enormous arched roof of the station proper, and correctly relating to it the many small administrative and public apartments. Like most of the competitors he avoided the issue by using a lofty two-storeyed entrance feature embodying a pair of high towers. The three centre bays of the main façade were raised above the parapet level of the rest of the block, and in order to obtain even more height, he employed an extravagant 20-foot screen wall which can clearly be seen on the section (Plate 3). Although well proportioned the main elevation is full of restless detail; arches of several kinds are used, semi-circular, pointed, flat, segmental and Tudor, in some cases they are superimposed for good measure. Buttresses and turrets also display striking variety—mostly octagonal in plan, they possess convex, concave, ogee and sloping roofs. The employment of so much unnecessary ornament, particularly the abundance of quasi-ecclesiastical window tracery, was singularly inappropriate for a subject of this nature, and there is little evidence here of the architect's later style—except perhaps in the bold treatment of the masonry in the side elevation.

It would appear from a report of the competition ascribed to the Honorary Secretary of the R.I.B.A., Mr. William Emerson,[2] that the standard of design was low, and that few competitors reached a satisfactory solution. The winner,

[1] Illustrated in *The British Architect*, 24th February 1893.
[2] Published in *The British Architect*, January 1893.

15

A. T. Bolton, A.R.I.B.A., however, was complimented for expressing the hall in elevation by means of a great arched opening which dominated the main façade.[1]

Mr. Emerson's general comments are particularly interesting: 'If the subject be a station,' he said, 'the principal feature of which is an enormous roof in one span, why mask it or altogether conceal it? If the design does not look like what it is intended for you may depend on it that it is wrongly conceived.' He also deplored ' . . . the addition of useless features or decorative details, however well they may be designed'. These pertinent remarks assume added significance when seen in retrospect, for expression of function and fitness for purpose became the catch-phrases of the modern movement in the 1920's, yet here we find such revolutionary principles advocated as early as 1893—and by the Honorary Secretary of the R.I.B.A.

Emerson's criticism seems to have made a deep impression on Mackintosh, for in February 1893, a month after it appeared in print, he again gave a paper to the Glasgow Institute. The subject was 'Architecture' and though the surviving notes are rather incoherent, his message is perfectly clear:

'Old architecture lived because it had a purpose. Modern architecture, to be real, must not be an envelope without contents.'

' . . . all great and living architecture has been the direct expression of the needs and beliefs of man at the time of its creation, and now if we would have great architecture this should still be so. How absurd it is to see modern churches, theatres, banks, museums, exchanges, Municipal Buildings, Art Galleries, etc., etc., made in imitations of Greek temples.'

'We must clothe modern ideas with modern dress—adorn our designs with living fancy.'

All this falls oddly from the pen of the architect who, in four preceding years, had designed in turn a Greek public hall, a French Renaissance museum, a Classical chapter house and a Gothic railway station. It should be emphasized, however, that these projects were competition drawings serving an academic purpose, in all probability executed under close supervision either at the School or office—and, unless human nature has changed, with an eye to the tastes and personal prejudices of a board of assessors. Then again, when he addressed the Institute, Mackintosh was little more than four years out of his apprentice-

[1] Illustrated in *The Builder*, 11th February 1893, also in *The British Architect*.

16

ship, and not yet twenty-six years old. The remarkable thing is not that he had shown scanty evidence of an original turn of mind in his academic studies before this, but that he, a mere draughtsman with no literary pretensions, should now have courage to read before the Glasgow Institute of Architects a paper which virtually condemned the work of every practising architect in Scotland—a paper which was at once a declaration and a challenge. One can well imagine the derision with which it would be received in professional circles.

Mackintosh's decision to break the bonds of convention was not reached hastily, however, and the first signs of his revolt are not to be found amongst his formal architectural drawings, but in his water-colours, sketches and craft-work, media in which he was able to express himself more freely.

Here he was not satisfied for long with straightforward pictorial representation, and side by side with his architectural sketches and exquisite flower studies —and sometimes superimposed on them—appeared curious drawings of less familiar objects. For these he found inspiration in the most unexpected places; in the delicate tracery of half a cabbage on his mother's kitchen table, in the section of an apple with its softly flowing curves and cluster of pips, in the grotesque fantasy of an onion gone to seed, in the bulbous roots of subaqueous plants, and even in a fish's eye seen under the microscope. Nothing appeared to escape his notice, and he seemed able to create fascinating, intricate patterns out of the most unlikely material. Moreover, experience brought the realization that line and form could express emotion as effectively as words and music, and this added to his insatiable desire for experiment. He would select a sonnet or a few lines of prose—almost invariably of melancholy timbre—and form linear patterns around it, usually finishing the design in wash: purples, yellows and greens predominating. The few examples that remain[1] enable us to identify and to date precisely the beginnings of the Glasgow Style.

CONVERSAZIONE PROGRAMME, 1894

He next attempted to express an idea, or to convey a message by symbolism alone, and designs in this category usually served some practical purpose—bookplates, posters and so forth. One of the earliest examples that has come to light is the cover of a Conversazione Programme illustrated here, which is

[1] In the Scrap Books—see p. 25.

C

intended to represent 'birds bringing harmony to the trees'.[1] The design was printed on coarse grey-blue paper and, notwithstanding the cheerful nature of the subject—music and song—possesses a curiously disconcerting air which, quite apart from colour, is implicit in the voluptuous curving lines and the malevolent half-bird, half-plant forms grouped at either extremity, not to mention the lettering.

Figure 3. 1894. C. R. Mackintosh. Conversazione Programme. In the Author's Collection.

Mackintosh was not the only student at the School of Art interested in work of this kind, and his friend Herbert MacNair was equally absorbed in the quest for new decorative forms. The work of the two young designers had much in common. According to MacNair himself, he first became interested in experimental design when, as apprentice to John Honeyman, he was thrown back upon his own resources during periods of idleness in the office. On such

[1] The original from which this illustration is taken was sent to the author from Australia by William Moyes who, *circa* 1900, worked as a draughtsman under Mackintosh's direction at Honeyman & Keppie's office.

occasions he used to take illustrations of objects which interested him—chairs for example—place tracing paper over them and try to improve on the original design, or better still, to evolve entirely new forms of his own invention. Whether or not this method is to be recommended, it was from such beginnings, born of a profound dissatisfaction with the existing order of things, that the so-called *Glasgow Style*—the Mackintosh style—emerged.

Figure 4. 1896. Herbert MacNair. Book Plate.
In the Author's Collection.

Of his decorative work Herbert MacNair affirms that not a line was drawn without purpose, and rarely was a single motive employed that had not some allegorical meaning. The whole design was contrived to embody 'the poetry of the idea'. A brief explanation of a single example will serve to illustrate the lengths to which this symbolic formalism was carried. The book-plate illustrated here was designed by MacNair for John Turnbull Knox; in it there is a falcon

19

—the Knox crest—hovering above the tree of knowledge which enfolds in its branches the spirits of art and poetry, represented by two sad female figures with long flowing tresses. The two spirits hold in their hands rose-buds which appear as cherub heads, and lilies, emblems of painting and sculpture. The heads embraced by the falcon's wings are breathing the dew of inspiration which falls on the tree of knowledge from above. The design is completed by a panel of lettering, the source of the artist's inspiration; it reads:

> *Nourished by middle earth,*
> *Breathed on by heavenly dew,*
> *Flourished a tree of worth,*
> *Flourished and grew.*

This example, with the Conversazione Programme, recaptures admirably the atmosphere of subtle, erotic symbolism that pervaded the last decade of the nineteenth century—the Beardsley period, the heyday of Wilde and Swinburne, and the followers of the Pre-Raphaelite brotherhood. In Mackintosh's case the phase was transitory; architecture remained his first love and, consequently, he was in closer touch with reality than Herbert MacNair who never took kindly to the practical limitations of the architect's office, and soon decided to embark upon the less prosaic, though somewhat insecure career of 'designer'.

This brief glance at MacNair's work raises an interesting though relatively unimportant point. If, in fact, he did commence experimenting in Honeyman's office (1888 or 1889)—and there is little reason to doubt the accuracy of his statement—it is obvious that he must have done so independently, that is before meeting Mackintosh. It is thus probable that he, and not Mackintosh, was the first of the Glasgow group to break new ground.

Authentic examples of Mackintosh's early work of an unorthodox kind are extremely difficult to come by, and the Conversazione Programme is one of the first so far discovered; it is clearly dated 1894. There is in existence, however, a photograph of the young architect's bedroom-cum-studio which shows several interesting pieces of furniture, and what is most important at this juncture, a decorative frieze of conventionalized cats (Plate 5A). In an amusing letter to the author,[1] Herbert MacNair suggests, amongst other things, that the frieze was probably executed in water-colour, for he says, 'At the same time I made a frieze of mermaids—the Mermaid being the MacNair crest—I also designed a cabinet. I was in "digs" in Glasgow at the time, and my frieze was in water-

[1] Dated 27th September 1947.

20

colour, juicily floated on, and on ingrain paper, my landlady allowing me to fix it on the wall with drawing pins. I remember it took a terrible lot of both water-colour and drawing pins.'

Before the author met Herbert MacNair this photograph presented something of a problem. Neither of Mackintosh's sisters could remember the room, and there seemed to be no means of discovering its whereabouts, nor of arriving at an accurate estimate of its date. MacNair, however, immediately recognized it as his friend's den at No. 2, Firpark Terrace, Dennistoun. The last date of William Mackintosh's occupation of this house is recorded in the Post Office Guide as 1891–2. Thus Mackintosh's frieze can be dated with some accuracy *circa* 1890, and it assumes added significance as the first design of its kind attributable to him. Moreover, many characteristics of his later work are clearly apparent here—the undulating sinuous lines and studied disposition of mass, the ingenious formalization of animal and vegetable forms, and the parsimonious use of strong colour. The subject, too, is not without interest as the cat motive was derived from the crest of the Clan Chattan of which the Mackintoshes are a branch.

The importance of the Dennistoun room cannot be over-estimated for it confirms the hypothesis that the two friends were experimenting with original forms by 1890 at least. The frieze of cats must have been executed before 1892 and it indicates that Mackintosh's peculiar style was already well developed by that time. Illustrations of contemporary work by MacNair are lacking, but the letter quoted above leaves little room for doubt that it was similar in character. If these facts are accurate, and they can hardly be otherwise, it is evident that Mackintosh and MacNair worked quite independently of the continental *art nouveau* movement with which they are often associated and, in fact, they seem to have anticipated it by some two years—a point that will be discussed in a later chapter.

Other than the frieze of cats, one of the most unexpected discoveries of an early work by Mackintosh was that of a pair of semi-detached houses built at Springburn, Glasgow, for the architect's uncle, William Hamilton, a haulage contractor of Dennistoun. It was possible in this instance to secure incontrovertible evidence of the date because Mr. Hamilton married in 1890, and he and his wife occupied one of the houses, *Redclyffe*, in December of that year.[1]

---

[1] This information was obtained from the late Mrs. Hamilton. The date was verified from the city archives but with considerable difficulty because Springburn was not brought within the Glasgow boundary until 1896.

'REDCLYFFE', 1890

Mrs. Hamilton told the author that Mackintosh set to work on this project with unbounded enthusiasm, but it is apparent that he immediately came up against two major problems which were to beset him throughout his professional career; that of dealing with a patron more or less indifferent to the claims of higher art, and that of curbing his fertile imagination so that his schemes should not exceed the limits imposed by his client's purse. It appears that Mackintosh's first design was far too unorthodox and costly to build; though, unfortunately, Mrs. Hamilton could not describe it, and the drawings were destroyed as valueless long ago. A revised design was soon forthcoming, however, and this proved to be more in keeping with current practice and far less expensive. The houses, No. 120 and 122, Balgrayhill Road, Springburn, were built in the summer of 1890 (Plate 4).

The site chosen for *Redclyffe* and its neighbour then commanded wide uninterrupted views over the city to the west. Mackintosh took advantage of this by making the block plan of the houses U-shaped. The short arms of the 'U' face west and comprise the drawing-room on the ground floor with the principal bedrooms above: in each case these spacious well-proportioned apartments terminate in wide bays. In order to achieve this layout the main entrance to each house was placed at the side, a convenient arrangement which, however, denies the householder the social prestige of a front door, and is seldom popular.

The houses were soundly constructed with sturdy walls of fine red sandstone, and slated roofs; no unorthodox structural methods were used. The plans are somewhat tortuous and the subsidiary apartments rather dark. It is obvious that the architect made some sacrifices in order to exploit the natural amenities of the site which, unfortunately, has now lost much of its former charm. Internally there is no indication that Mackintosh exercised any control over the permanent fittings; doors and fireplaces, which of all features most frequently bear the stamp of his originality, are of stock pattern; so also are skirtings, architraves and cornices, and they seem to have been chosen by the occupants (Plate 5B). That this was the case, has been largely confirmed by Mr. Alexander Orr,[1] a painter and decorator of Glasgow, who was called in to put the finishing touches to *Redclyffe*. He avers that Mackintosh supervised the colour schemes which he describes as 'unorthodox and very striking', but nearly sixty years have passed since Mr. Orr executed this work and he cannot now give precise

---

[1] At an interview with the author, 1946.

details. He clearly recollects, however, that Mackintosh insisted on brightly coloured doors to all the rooms, an innovation which must have caused the Hamiltons some consternation.

In several respects *Redclyffe* and its neighbour are rather disappointing, and although they show unmistakable signs of Mackintosh's handiwork they are not so revolutionary as one might have expected, and certainly are not so exceptional as, say, the frieze of cats. Had the project drawings for the original scheme survived no doubt they would have provided a more accurate measure of his intentions. Nevertheless, the houses possess qualities which distinguish them from the mass of pretentious middle-class villas of the period. They are neither Classical nor Baronial in character, yet their powerfully articulated wall masses and chimney-stacks recall unmistakably the Scottish vernacular. Their claim to distinction lies in their unpretentious dignity and pleasant proportions, and in the evidence they provide of Mackintosh's decision to put first things first, to take advantage of prospect and orientation rather than to sacrifice good living space to stylistic convention.

THE MACDONALD SISTERS

At about the time *Redclyffe* was built two new day students were enrolled at the Glasgow School of Art—Margaret (1865–1933) and Frances (1874–1921) Macdonald—with whom the future of Mackintosh and Herbert MacNair became closely linked. Information about the sisters has been extremely difficult to come by for both were English by birth—notwithstanding the deceptive national prefix 'Mac'—and were in their 'teens by the time they arrived in Glasgow. Moreover, no member of the family survives who might have been able to throw light upon the important question of their education and home environment in England—nor has it been possible to establish whether or not either of them had any previous art training. John Macdonald, their father, was the son of a Glasgow solicitor and spent most of his life in England where, prior to his return to Glasgow in the late 1880's, he was acting as a consulting engineer at Chesterton Hall, Newcastle, Staffordshire. The Macdonald family took a flat in the city for some years before moving to Dunglass Castle, Bowling (in 1899)—a house they acquired from Talwin Morris, the artist, then Art Director to Messrs. Blackie & Son, the publishers.[1]

[1] Talwin Morris (1865–1911), an important figure in the Glasgow movement, was born at Winchester of an old Quaker family. His mother died at his birth and his father died suddenly

The girls, Margaret and Frances, are first mentioned in the School of Art examination records of 1891. They studied freehand drawing, model drawing, ornament, anatomy and plant drawing. The few artists still living, all ardent admirers of Mackintosh, who remember their arrival, emphatically deny that either showed more than average ability, much less any marked originality at the time. But, of course, Mackintosh's dynamic personality so dominated the scene in later years that his friends and admirers almost invariably contend that he, and he alone, was responsible for all original work emanating from Glasgow in the 1890's. The early drawings of the Macdonalds in fact do bear a striking resemblance to those of Mackintosh and MacNair—they are similar in technique, in form and in emotional content—and, of course, it is possible that the sisters saw drawings by the two young architects at students' exhibitions and decided to work along similar lines. The earliest dated example of a watercolour by one of them so far discovered, however, is surprisingly mature, and hardly suggests an initial essay in a borrowed style. This work is entitled *Ill Omen* or *Girl in the East Wind and Ravens passing the Moon* (Plate 6A), and was executed by Frances Macdonald in 1893.[1] The subject is a young girl with streaming hair, silhouetted against a deep blue-black sky, and in the top left-hand corner, a flight of ravens passing before a full moon. Though rendered in ghostly yellow-green and blue washes, austere and cold, the drawing is dramatically presented and has mysterious charm. The style is well developed and technically the painting is more accomplished than, for example, Mackintosh's

a few years later. He was brought up by a spinster aunt, Emily Morris, a lady of strong Anglican convictions who wished him to enter the church. With this in view, he was educated at Lancing and was to have gone thence to Oxford. Morris had other ideas, however, and refused to continue his theological studies. He was articled to an uncle, Joseph Morris, architect, of Reading, and then worked for a time with a certain Martin Brooks of London. Morris was especially interested in the graphic arts and took a post as sub-Art Editor under M. H. Spielman of the recently launched journal *Black and White*. He married in 1892 and lived for a year in Field Court, Gray's Inn. Early in 1893 he answered a *Times* advertisement for an Art Director to Blackie's of Glasgow, was appointed to the position, and in May 1893 moved to Dunglass. Talwin Morris was never officially connected with the Glasgow School of Art either as a student or a teacher, but he and his wife became very friendly with the Newbery's and the Macdonald family and, of course, saw much of Mackintosh. They left Dunglass in July 1899 and took a small house, *Torwood*, on the hills above Bowling— Dunglass then passed into the hands of the Macdonalds. Morris executed some delightful designs for Blackie's and his work was given much prominence in *The Studio*.

[1] *Ill Omen* was reproduced in *The Yellow Book*, along with other work by the Macdonalds and MacNair, vol. X, July 1896.

Conversazione Programme of 1894. Then again, Herbert MacNair states that he and Mackintosh did not meet the girls for some time, for as he points out, they, as architects, attended evening classes and rarely came in contact with day school students. Moreover, he insists that they were not aware of the Macdonalds' presence until Newbery drew attention to the similarity of their work at a criticism. This was confirmed by the headmaster himself, who, having recognized the affinity of the four students, decided that they must be brought together; it was at his suggestion that they decided to join forces and work in close collaboration.[1] At the next School exhibition the coterie isolated their work with remarkable success. They were at once christened *The Four*, an appellation which they retained for many years.

In the light of this evidence it seems indisputable that the Macdonald sisters themselves had an important part to play in the evolution of the Glasgow Style, and that they cannot by any means be dismissed out of hand as mere plagiarists —an opinion that is further strengthened by a closer examination of their early work.

THE SCRAP BOOKS

Though many drawings survive, reliably dated examples of the Macdonalds' work are rare. Fortunately, however, Mrs. Ritchie of Edinburgh—formerly Miss Agnes Raeburn—though not an artist herself, was on intimate terms with the Glasgow group and kept a series of Scrap Books to which several of her friends contributed. Only four of these books remain, covering the years 1893–5, but they provide important evidence of the versatility of *The Four*, and of their ceaseless quest for original decorative forms. The earliest drawing by one of the sisters is a pencil and wash design for a book-plate executed by Frances Macdonald in 1893. Margaret's first contribution is dated 1894, and consists of a small water-colour about 9 inches high by 3 inches wide entitled *Nov. 5th* (Plate 6c). Two extremely attenuated female figures are depicted bowing towards each other with heads touching and long hair cascading to the ground. They represent rockets in flight; both figures are weeping and their tears fall in two streams of yellow light to meet above a sad mask-like face—a hill—at the foot of the sheet. Sadness and tears always seem to dominate the minds of the sisters,

[1] Mr. Newbery told the author of this, but unfortunately, he could not give any precise indication of the date at which the students came together for the first time.

but in spite of its melancholy, this drawing is by no means unattractive. The colours used are taken entirely from the cold palette—strong yellow for the hair and tears, and variations of yellow, green and blue for the remainder of the picture. The gently flowing curves are the curves of *art nouveau*.

Mrs. Ritchie's Scrap Book for 1894 contains another pencil and wash drawing by Frances, symbolizing November; it is a composition of two repulsive, emaciated human figures representing dragon-fly nymphs framed by aquatic plants, and crowned by a writhing group of tadpole-like masks. The subject is *A Pond* and admirably captures the atmosphere of a most unpleasant submarine world of stagnation, slowly undulating slimy vegetation and decay, the principal colours being mauve and green, now greatly faded—a most peculiar choice of subject for a young lady of the 1890's! It is interesting to compare this drawing with a contemporary design in the same medium by Mackintosh —the cover for the Spring Number of the Scrap Book (1894)—in which he also adopted an unorthodox viewpoint, but in this case subterranean (Plate 7A & B). The design is a characteristic piece of symbolism. Two female figures are depicted awakening from sleep below the surface of the earth, each has an arm extended so that the closed fist just breaks through the surface. They are surrounded by bulbs and root forms from which rises a pattern of stems and shoots. The colours employed are pale greens, yellows and blues on a white background; a small touch of purple is introduced where one or two shoots appear above the ground as crocuses. Although the general effect is somewhat bizarre it is by no means as unpleasant as *The Pond*. These two drawings are of particular interest because of the contrast between Frances Macdonald's hideous, angular, and greatly distorted females and the plump, well-proportioned nudes by Mackintosh.[1]

One of Mackintosh's earliest drawings in which the human form is used as the basis of a linear pattern, appears in the Scrap Book of 1894. It is in pencil and wash on coarse brown paper and is entitled *Autumn*.[2] In contrast to the designs previously described this is more highly stylized: the head of the figure —of oriental mien—is simply but clearly drawn, and surrounded by a large red

[1] Four nudes, identical in every respect with these figures, were used to embellish the clock faces of the Canal Boatmen's Institute, Port Dundas, a building designed by Honeyman and Keppie in 1893 (Plate 19B). A detail of the clock face was published in *The British Architect*, vol. XLIV, 22 Nov. 1895, p. 3.

[2] The earliest example of Mackintosh's conventionalized figure work forms part of the frieze of cats (1890) and it appears to resemble the drawing mentioned here.

nimbus; the limbs and trunk are dissolved into a pattern of lines and planes with little if any attempt at modelling.[1] It is quite different in character from the work of the Macdonalds, and belongs to another realm of experimental design into which Mackintosh alone seems to have ventured, and of which several examples are to be found in the Scrap Books. In the main, these consist of strange patterns based on flower and plant motives—stalks, leaves and roots— reduced to their most elementary form. The drawings are occasionally given a title, or are accompanied by a curious caption, for example, 'The Tree of Influence, the Tree of Importance, and Sun of Cowardice', (Plate 6B) and 'The tree of Personal Effort, the Sun of Indifference'—both of which are signed and dated January 1895. The subject in each case is indefinable, and though the colours are the customary limpid purples, greens, blues, relieved with red, the washes flow all over the sheet and practically obliterate the faint pencil lines below. Mackintosh's interest in this type of experiment persisted for many years and several much more ambitious drawings of a similar character are in existence.[2] However trivial and ill-conceived the Scrap Book drawings may be —and the majority of them have little real artistic merit—they establish beyond all shadow of doubt the fact that *The Four* were exploring many different avenues in an attempt to evolve an original style of drawing and decoration, and moreover, that the girls were as deeply engrossed in experiment as the two young architects. The Scrap Books also prove that, by 1894 at least, their peculiar style was already well developed.

POSTERS

Having achieved some measure of success by these methods *The Four* next proceeded to apply the same principles of design to subjects other than water-colour painting and book plates. One of the fields into which they advanced was that of poster design, and in 1895 and 1896 they produced a number of posters that excited no little comment.

Mackintosh seems to have led the way and from examples which survive, and from contemporary illustrations, the startling originality of his work can

[1] This design was developed later and used as the basis of a poster (Plate 9F), illustrated in *The Studio*, vol. XI, July 1897, p. 99.

[2] Mrs. Lang of Paisley (formerly Miss Elsie Newbery) possesses a large water-colour which was given to her by the Mackintoshes as a wedding present in 1906. As far as one can discern,

readily be appreciated. In the early 1890's commercial advertising was still in its infancy and voluminously draped Grecian ladies, naturalistic cherubs, columns and acanthus leaves were the order of the day. The most advanced French posters by Grasset and Toulouse-Lautrec, and the work of James Pryde (a friend of Mackintosh) and William Nicholson—known as the Beggarstaff Brothers—still betrayed the lingering signs of tradition, and was little known in Scotland at this time.[1] The grotesque half-human, half-vegetable entities portrayed by *The Four* were an entirely new departure and positively impinged upon public consciousness. A Mackintosh poster, once experienced, is not easily forgotten, and at this time, it must be remembered, comparatively few people had seen the work of the Glasgow School of Art group.

The large *Scottish Musical Review* poster published in 1896 and illustrated on Plate 9F was 7 feet 8 inches high and 3 feet 2 inches wide; the dominant motive being a tall human figure of oriental character outlined in black on a rich blue ground. The head was surmounted by a halo against which were silhouetted singing birds. The sombre hues of the scheme were relieved by the use of emerald green for the projecting discs on the birds' tails and the geometrical pattern above the figure. The small poster reproduced on page 29 is about 30 inches by 20 inches, and is much simpler in form. It is drawn in black on a white ground; the only colour employed is primary red in the large discs against which the singing birds are delineated. This design should be compared with the poster of like proportions for *The Nomad Art Club*, reproduced in *The Studio* (vol. XI, p. 98), executed by the Macdonald sisters. The motif and composition are the same in each case and the technique identical. In all this work the

it is an impression of small silver birches or larches against a background of tree-trunks and foliage—the shapes are so complex and the colours so intermingled that it is virtually impossible to distinguish the subject with any degree of certainty. For some time it was hung upside-down, but a group of trees of the same species in a similar setting on the Island of Arran gave its owner a clue to the probable interpretation of the painting. Mrs. Lang also possesses a second interesting 'painting' by Mackintosh, this one signed and dated 1906. It is about 12 inches by 4 inches and is formed from an elongated spot of colour on blotting paper which has been extended and embellished by hundreds of tiny red, orange and green spots—the caption reads, *The Old Yew Tree at Night.*

[1] James Pryde (1866–1941) and Nicholson joined forces in 1893, and in 1894 four posters of striking originality were exhibited by them at the Royal Aquarium, Westminster. In 1894, also, Dudley Hardy's Gaiety Poster and Beardsley's poster for the Avenue Theatre were attracting considerable attention in the south. (See *James Pryde*, Derek Hudson, 1949; *Picture Posters*, Charles Hiatt, 1895.)

designers employed broad, direct lines, and flat washes of colour; little if any modelling was attempted and primary colours were confined to small areas.

In professional circles Mackintosh's posters provoked the bitterest criticism, and only one voice appears to have been raised in his defence. The editor of *The Studio*, writing in 1897, said this:

Figure 5. 1896. C. R. Mackintosh. A Poster.
In the Author's Collection

'. . . It must never be forgotten that the purpose of a poster is to attract notice, and the mildest eccentricity would not be out of place provided it aroused curiosity and so riveted the attention of passers-by. Mr. Mackintosh's posters may be somewhat trying to the average person. . . . But there is so much decorative method in his perversion of humanity that despite all the ridicule and abuse it has excited, it is possible to defend his treatment . . . for when a man has something to say and knows how to say it the conversion of others is usually but a question of time'.

From Mackintosh's point of view the poster interlude was especially rewarding. It provided him with an opportunity of designing to a large scale two-dimensional patterns which of necessity had to be broadly conceived and strongly delineated. After this experience he was able to turn his hand with some degree of confidence to mural decoration and to wallpaper design.

CRAFTWORK

The highly-stylized linear patterns of *The Four* lent themselves admirably to execution in repoussé metal, gesso and stained glass. Their long flowing brush lines were easily transmuted into deeply incised grooves in brass or white metal; modelled in coarse string and plaster, or traced in lead. Whatever the medium, the character and interpretation of their subject remained the same. Candle sconces, mirror frames, clock faces, glass panels and so forth were added to the repertoire of the Glasgow designers. In these crafts, minute detail was of necessity subordinated to broad general effect; heads, faces and hands were usually drawn with care, but the rest of the human form resolved itself into a pattern of broad plain surfaces bounded by a multiplicity of strong vertical lines. In beaten metal especially, the girls seem to have delighted in emphasizing the contrast between surface and line, and subtle variations in tone were achieved by modelling the convex surfaces which usually represented exaggerated, sweeping drapery. It has been said that Beardsley revealed anew the expressiveness of the line and the value of black and white pattern; but Beardsley's art was confined to two-dimensional representation. The Glasgow group, on the other hand, applied similar principles to three-dimensional objects in an attempt to gain thereby added interest from the ever-varying effects of light and shade, and from the subtle beauty latent in the material.

Emphasis has been laid here on the similarity of the work of *The Four*, and broadly speaking, of course, they formed a singularly coherent group. In an age given over to vulgar commercialism on the one hand, and studied eclecticism on the other, their work appears homogeneous by sheer contrast. Individual traits are easily recognizable however—more especially in the work of the two men. Mackintosh in particular seems to stand a little apart from his friends and although subscribing to their aims and ideals, his art forms are more masculine, less sensuous and naïve, than those of MacNair and the girls who always remained content with a world of softly undulating lines, of brooding sadness, and death. He, on the other hand, appears to have been impelled by an urge to express growth—root, stem, branch and flower—and almost all his subsequent work can be analysed in these terms. Surging vertical lines invariably predominate, whether in the pattern of a Christmas card, or a poster, or in an exaggerated chair-back, and they find ultimate expression in the dramatic west wing of the new Glasgow School of Art.

Although Mackintosh never entirely escaped from the influence of the group, and all his work bears to a greater or lesser degree the impress of his early associations, he never lost sight of the fact that he was an architect first and foremost. He used his opportunities in the decorative field as a testing ground for the ideas and theories which later gave such distinction to his buildings. His friend Herbert MacNair, however, became more and more engrossed in the minor arts, and though nominally an architectural draughtsman soon transferred his attention entirely to design and craftwork.

FURNITURE DESIGN AND INTERIOR DECORATION

In addition to his reputation as a student and draughtsman of peculiar inventiveness, Mackintosh soon began to make a name for himself as a designer of unorthodox furniture, and as an interior decorator of exceptional promise.

Unquestionably the earliest piece of furniture which can be attributed to him is the cabinet that appears below the frieze of cats in his Dennistoun studio (Plate 5A).[1] This is rather heavily constructed, but nevertheless is well proportioned and the detail is admirably restrained. Even here he used a capping of *cyma recta* profile which later, in more refined form, became one of his favourite motives. The lower part of the cabinet is severely plain, the doors are not embellished, all unnecessary mouldings are omitted, and locks, handles and hinges are of the simplest kind. The cabinet thus possesses many characteristics of the architect's later furniture, and although not a particularly elegant piece, it compares favourably with much of the work produced by the English Arts and Crafts Society at this time.

Mackintosh had few opportunities of carrying out decorative work at home

[1] This can be seen also in Plate 15A.

and it seems that the family, or to be more precise, the father, had little time for his artistic pursuits, though he was idolized by his sisters—especially by Nancy the youngest, whom he wished to train as an architect. His mother, to whom he was deeply attached, died in 1885 and William Mackintosh married again. Thereafter, Charles seems to have gradually relinquished his domestic ties. In 1892 the family removed from Dennistoun to Regent Park Square, a street of formidable but fashionable stone-built early Victorian terraced houses, on the south side of Glasgow. Less than two years later the property was sold and they were obliged to leave. They then found an excellent detached house over-looking Queen's Park, Glasgow, with about a quarter of an acre of garden.[1] Here Charles's only notable contribution was a staircase carpet in two tones of green; he himself painted the stairs a pale yellow because he could not trust the decorator to get the exact colour he wanted. His own room was a badly proportioned high-ceiled attic, with which even he could do little. In disgust he said that next time the family removed he would have a cellar, a chance remark that proved to be prophetic, for within two years they were once again living in Regent Park Square, at No. 27 (1896), where he was given a room in the basement. This was more to his taste, though he immediately took a violent dislike to the built-up fireplace and despite the angry protestations of his father, set to work to dismantle it. To his delight he uncovered a simple cottage-type hob-grate with wrought-iron bars and a plain surround which, his sisters suggest, became the model for many of his subsequent designs. To the horror of the family, he next proceeded to cover the walls of the room with coarse brown wrapping-paper and completed the job with a stencilled frieze.

Charles occupied the basement for several years and used it as a studio-workshop. In this room he executed much of his beaten metal work with his sisters doing most of the beating, and that, to the spiritual discomfort of their father, usually on the Sabbath. At about this time, too, he acquired a studio in the city where he was able, after office hours, to work undisturbed at the various private commissions for furniture and so forth that came his way.

While Charles Mackintosh was still occupying his attic at *Holmswood*, how-ever, he was introduced (probably by Newbery) to the Davidson family of Kilmacolm—the parents of William Davidson, one of his greatest admirers for whom he later designed *Windyhill*. Mr. and Mrs. William Davidson, senior,

[1] *Holmswood*, No. 82 Langside Road.

and William Davidson, junior, his wife and young family, occupied a flatted house named *Gladsmuir*, to which Mackintosh contributed various pieces of furniture, water-colours and fabric designs from time to time.[1]

A photograph of the drawing-room is in the author's collection and though the apartment has no claim to distinction it is important as one of the earliest recorded interiors by Mackintosh. It is obvious that the architect played little part in organizing the room, but several characteristic elements are to be seen —notably a small square table, a built-in, high-backed wall seat upholstered in linen fabric on which a flying bird motive is stencilled, and a number of framed water-colour drawings sufficiently distinct to leave no doubt as to their author.

No other photographs of *Gladsmuir* seem to have survived though illustrations of a small cabinet and some curtains from the house were published in a continental journal in 1898.[2] The bow front and leaded glass doors of the cabinet give it a traditional air, but the frame to the top shelf has no historical precedent and is typical early Mackintosh. In outline it resembled the section of an apple, an impression strengthened by the presence of a centre support with small protuberances reminiscent of pips—a curious detail which appears greatly enlarged in the king-post of a roof truss he designed for the Martyrs' Public School in 1895. The two embroidered curtains were very charming and formed a striking contrast to work by *The Four* in other media. Both examples were simply and beautifully drawn; the artist succeeded in combining a variety of fascinating leaf and flower details in a perfectly balanced, though by no means symmetrical composition. The designs are quite fresh and original and though resembling to a certain extent the work of the William Morris school, they are much lighter in treatment and less formally presented.

The whole of the work at *Gladsmuir* of which any record remains may be dated *circa* 1894–5; the bow-fronted cabinet may have been the first piece of furniture executed for the Davidsons, the corner seat following a year or two afterwards. The curtains may well be later.

In addition to this work Mackintosh designed a number of pieces of furniture for Messrs. Guthrie & Wells, a well-known firm of cabinet makers in the city of

[1] Mr. Hamish Davidson, grandson of Mr. William, senior, told the author that Mackintosh executed a remarkable frieze of animals in the *Gladsmuir* nursery, and though he was a child at the time, he remembers the work distinctly. Photographs of the frieze were taken, but unfortunately they cannot be traced.

[2] *Dekorative Kunst*, November 1898.

Glasgow. Several illustrations survive which, with other examples that have come to light, form a valuable record. This furniture consisted in the main of linen cabinets,[1] wardrobes,[2] and the like, all of which were soundly constructed upon more or less traditional lines. The pieces are notable for their pleasant

Figure 6. Linen Press (cupboard).

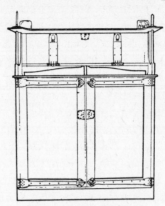

Figure 8. Linen Cupboard.

Figure 7. Chest of Drawers.

proportions, and the absence of superfluous ornament. Full advantage was taken of the natural qualities of the wood used—oak being a favourite material, with, on occasion, essays in the greenish-brown satin-like texture of cypress. Decoration was confined to small areas and consisted of either simple carving or beaten metal. Drawer-pulls, hinges (usually broad tapering bands ending in

[1] One each in the possession of Dr. Davidson and Mrs. Ritchie, Edinburgh.
[2] One in the possession of Professor Walton, Glasgow University.

Voysey-like leaf-shaped ornament), locks and so forth, were always designed with the greatest care, and are rarely obtrusive, nor do they display any of the flamboyant vulgarity common to so much late Victorian work.

Mackintosh detested glossy varnish and went to great lengths to discover stains and polishes which would reveal and enhance the natural beauty of the wood. He favoured dark brown, almost black hues, or deep olive-green, neutrals which provided an ideal background for repoussé metal, for his delicate harmonies of rose-tinted gesso and the stencilled fabrics which he introduced later. Few examples are to be found where warm brown intermediate colours were employed.

Unfortunately no records exist by which the Guthrie & Wells furniture can be accurately dated, although there are illustrations in the firm's catalogues—published *circa* 1894-5—and in *The Studio* (1897). By comparing their form and structure, however, it is possible to arrange the pieces in approximate chronological order. If the Dennistoun cabinet is assumed to be the first, probably the second is the linen-press (Fig. 6)—clearly an early example on account of the trivial candle-holders, the pendant-leaf motive below the apron, and the abundance of ornamental beaten metal—say 1893; the third, the ponderous hall settle (Fig. 9) with its somewhat crudely devised stencilled patterns and metal panels, 1894-5; the fourth, the chest of drawers (Fig. 7), the first piece entirely free from *art nouveau* and neo-classical detail, perhaps 1895. The linen cupboard (Fig. 8) may be placed fifth and last in the series. Here the candle-holders are more skilfully integrated with the main frame, and the subtle curve of the apron below the upper cupboard should be noted and compared with the inelegant rake of that on the linen press. The metalwork too is much superior and the whole design has an air of competence and efficiency—it may be dated 1895 or 1896 with some certainty.

It will be observed that none of these examples possesses any of the more unusual characteristics we are accustomed to associate with Mackintosh's furniture; none departs far from tradition, none of them is painted white, and not a single high-backed chair is included. Nevertheless, even if the linen cupboard is not so revolutionary as say, the Musical Review Poster, by contemporary standards—especially on the commercial market—it represents a bold step forward. This phase—from 1890 to 1896—is in fact a time of experiment in yet another medium, a medium in which Mackintosh had to meet strictly utilitarian requirements and to curb his restless, inventive spirit. Only when he began to design furniture for Miss Cranston's tea-rooms (1896–7) do we find a marked change in style, and not until he furnished his own flat in 1900 did that style reach full maturity.

LIÈGE EXHIBITION

The furniture that has been discussed here, and indeed the paintings and craftwork of *The Four* aroused little more than local interest. Most of their commissions were executed for relatives and friends but with the help of Newbery, they soon acquired a much wider reputation. Following a successful exhibition at the School, the headmaster received a letter from the Secretary of L'Oeuvre Artistique, Liège asking for examples of students' work to be sent to the City of Liège Arts and Crafts Exhibition. The letter, dated 10th May 1895, contained this interesting passage:

'Our schools of art are far, very far indeed, from being so advanced as yours and what has above all astonished us in your work is the great liberty left to the pupils to follow their own individuality which is so different from the ideas current in our schools of art that it is difficult for us to comprehend this freedom although we admire it very much. I think the exhibition of the works of your students cannot but cause serious thought and reflection to those here who direct art instruction. Many of us should like to have some of your posters which are very beautiful. . . .'

Three cases of exhibits, representing the work of all sections of the School, were sent, and the first link between the Glasgow designers and the continent was forged.

THE ARTS AND CRAFTS SOCIETY EXHIBITION, 1896

Shortly after this comparatively minor success, *The Four* were invited by the London Arts and Crafts Exhibition Society to send some 'modern style' furniture, craftwork and posters to the important exhibition of 1896.[1] Frances and Margaret Macdonald submitted notably a pair of narrow, beaten metal panels, *The Star of Bethlehem* and *The Annunciation* respectively, also a fine

[1] The Arts and Crafts Society arranged triennial exhibitions at this time.

37

clock case of beaten silver and a number of posters.[1] In addition to posters, Mackintosh's principal exhibit was the hall settle previously mentioned (Fig. 9), 'a most pleasant and decorative piece of furniture' according to *The Studio*, and a strange water-colour entitled *Part Seen, Part Imagined*.[2]

The unheralded appearance of the work of *The Four* evoked a storm of protest from public and critics alike. Everyone was shocked by their grotesque conventionalization of the human figure and strange linear patterns; everyone,

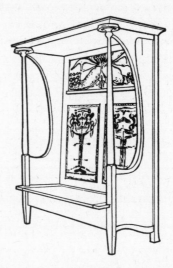

Figure 9. Hall Settle (exhibited in London in 1896).

it would seem, except Gleeson White, editor of *The Studio*, who wisely witheld judgment, and in commenting on the Glasgow Group used these significant words:

'Probably nothing in the gallery has provoked more decided censure than these various exhibits; and that fact alone should cause a thoughtful observer of art to pause before he joins the opponents. If the said artists do not come very prominently forward as leaders of a school of design peculiarly their own, we shall be much mistaken. The probability would seem to be that those who laugh at them to-day will be eager to eulogize them a few years hence. . . .'

[1] Illustrated in *The Studio*, vol. IX, December 1896, p. 203.
[2] Presented by Mrs. Talwin Morris to the Corporation Art Galleries, Kelvingrove, Glasgow.

The English Arts and Crafts Society, however, stolidly maintained its attitude of scornful derision, and the Scottish designers were not invited again to exhibit south of the border.

When the exhibition ended, White determined to visit Glasgow and meet the artists on their own ground, to discover if possible their aims and objectives, and to find the sources on which they drew for inspiration. He travelled north with an open mind and, no doubt, not a little curiosity, for he comments later on the 'legend of a critic from foreign parts' who attempted to deduce the character and appearance of the Macdonald sisters from their works—they were visualized as 'middle-aged sisters, flat-footed, with projecting teeth and long past the hope (which in them was always forlorn) of matrimony, gaunt unlovely females'. In all probability White too imagined the artists as a coterie of languid æsthetes, if not middle-aged, then at least effete sophisticates, surrounded by *objets d'art* from Egypt and the Orient, and brooding over Swinburne and Wilde. Instead, he found two 'laughing comely girls, scarce out of their teens' and a pair of serious architectural draughtsmen with a penchant for the decorative arts and craftwork.

White's views on the work of *The Four* and their sources must be relegated to a later chapter; suffice it to say here that he returned to London full of enthusiasm for the Glasgow designers. Like everyone who came into personal contact with the group, he was deeply impressed by their sincerity and astonishing versatility. He became one of their staunchest champions in the south and shortly afterwards published two well illustrated articles in *The Studio* entitled 'Some Glasgow Designers and their Work'. The first appeared in July 1897 and was devoted entirely to Mackintosh and the Macdonald sisters; the second, on J. H. MacNair and Talwin Morris, followed in September of the same year. The importance of these articles cannot be overestimated. At one stroke, Gleeson White disclosed the presence in Glasgow of a flourishing and well-integrated school of design with its own distinctive characteristics, a school, it seemed, that was completely independent of the English Arts and Crafts movement. Moreover, *The Studio,* one of the most progressive journals of the day, had a wide continental circulation, and the attention of all revolutionary elements in the European art world was immediately focused on Scotland, on Glasgow, and in particular on Mackintosh, whose personality clearly dominated White's articles. Alexander Koch, the publisher, of Darmstadt, editor of *Academy Architecture,* was quick to appreciate the significance of these events, and in the November issue of his periodical *Dekorative Kunst* (1898) there appeared a constructive and well illustrated article on the Scottish designers.[1] This was the first occasion on which work by *The Four* was reviewed in a continental journal and within a remarkably short time thereafter they were widely acclaimed leaders in the new art movement.

By the close of the year 1896 then, it is evident that *The Four* had achieved their primary objective. They had evolved a distinctively personal style of ornament and decoration independent of contemporary fashions, and with little if any archaeological bias. They had completed their training at the School, and were beginning to build up a useful business connection in the city. The names of Herbert MacNair and Charles Mackintosh appeared on the School of Art records for the last time in 1893, and that of Margaret Macdonald in 1894, but *The Four* retained their close association with the School and were at liberty to attend occasional classes and work there whenever they felt so disposed. On graduation, the girls opened a studio in the city and devoted themselves to the applied arts, to embroidery, repoussé metal, gesso, illuminating, book illustrating and leaded glass—the two young architects lending a hand, and on occasion providing designs for furniture and the like in which decorative panels could be incorporated. To their studio came many interesting personalities of the Scottish literary and art world—not least among whom were John Buchan and his sister; E. A. Taylor, the painter; James Pryde, Jessie M. King, Talwin Morris and his wife, and of course many of the younger artists who, under Newbery, were now making their contribution to the Glasgow Style. The Macdonald sisters were charming and attractive hostesses: Frances, petite, vivacious and pretty, Margaret tall, handsome, and majestic with a great mass of hair like burnished copper. They entertained not lavishly, but exquisitely, and tea taken at their studio was indeed a memorable event. The two architects were not slow to appreciate the advantages of such independence, and they too rented studios. Herbert MacNair, always restless and mercurial, had not taken kindly to the rigours of practice under John Keppie, and shortly after completing his course at the School of Art, resigned from the firm and opened an office of his own at 227 West George Street, Glasgow (1895). Although he

[1] This writer's comments will be discussed in a later chapter, but the illustrations are of particular interest. In addition to several familiar examples of craftwork, they included a glazed bookcase, a built-in cupboard and embroidered curtain design by Mackintosh—both early examples not published elsewhere—and a cupboard and wine glasses by MacNair. Some excellent book covers by Talwin Morris also appeared.

rejoiced in the grand title of 'architect and designer' he did not carry out any architectural work. Instead he too concentrated upon furniture design and the crafts. No one can remember the precise whereabouts of Mackintosh's studio, but it was in Bath Street, and presumably not far from Honeyman & Keppie's office. Here, frequently, he snatched a few hours' sleep after working all night on competitive drawings with Keppie; here, too, he and his cronies met to talk and to argue, to drink and to make merry. It was from this studio that the design for the first of his Cranston tea-room projects came; it was here, too, that *The Four* gave hilarious parties—for the nineties were gay, even in Glasgow, and the 'Mac' group was soon numbered among the brightest stars of the city's artistic constellation.

Several people, including Miss Nancy Mackintosh, remember visiting the studio which was decorated in characteristic fashion, and one of the more sedate parties is clearly recalled by Miss De C. L. Dewar who was then a very young student at the School of Art. Miss Dewar went with some trepidation to celebrate with the great ones the award of the Alexander Thomson Scholarship to Charles Mackintosh's friend, George Paterson. She recollects most vividly the studio curtains decorated by large appliqué heart-shaped motives, each of which had been hastily secured by a single row of stitches down its centre and had curled over. After 'a delightful tea' the company amused themselves by 'cock fighting', and blowing soap-bubbles and wafting them about with fans provided by their host!

Mackintosh, already a well-known figure in the city, was immensely popular with the younger architects and with Newbery's students. His supreme self-confidence, his devil-may-care attitude and indefatigable industry, made him at once admired and respected by all who knew him. The ladies in particular treated him with a certain amount of awe, tinged no doubt with sympathy for his lameness and admiration for his dark rugged features in which seemed to mingle the virile blood of the Highlander and the languid, easy sophistication of the Latin. To his friends he was a warm-hearted, genial soul with simple tastes and pleased by simple things. With strangers he was reserved and even aloof, especially if they were of the conventional sort—but he warmed at once to the sympathetic mind. He was a tireless, voluble talker and he would spring immediately to the defence of any man, work, or principle, which he thought unfairly assailed—a characteristic which remained with him throughout his life and in later, less propitious days, brought him in contact with the London 'Salon of the Independents', 'The Plough', the Arts' League of Service, and several other struggling causes in the south. His family and his friends remember many small acts of kindness which reveal a thoughtful and considerate mind, foreign, no doubt, to those who regarded him as an undisciplined young reprobate. For instance, Miss Agnes Raeburn, another Glasgow artist, tells with pleasure of an occasion on which the young architect brought to her studio a beautiful green vase filled with anemones which had caught his eye, and which he knew she would like to paint. A few days later he dropped in casually to see the finished picture and expressed his approval. Shortly afterwards, he came to the studio again, and this time introduced a friend, who bought the painting on the spot. A more ingenuous and delightful way of encouraging a student would be difficult to imagine!

And so *The Four* established themselves in Glasgow and, it seemed, their future was secure. Herbert MacNair and the two girls were kept fully occupied, and Mackintosh, now deeply engrossed at the office in the first of his major architectural projects, the new School of Art, somehow found time to beat metal, design posters and to paint—and indeed, it was at this point that he embarked upon the first of his tea-room projects for Miss Cranston. His capacity for creative work of this nature was phenomenal.

The fruitful partnership of *The Four* was soon to come to an end however. In the summer of 1898 Herbert MacNair was appointed Instructor in Decorative Design[1] at the School of Architecture and Applied Art, Liverpool University, and later in the year took the high-road to England. At the close of the University Session he hastened back to Scotland in order to marry Frances Macdonald. The wedding was a very quiet family affair and took place on 14th June 1899 at St. Augustine's church, Bowling, on the Clyde estuary. In the autumn, the MacNairs' set up house in Liverpool and remained there until about 1906.[2] During this period they sent work to exhibitions at home and abroad, and executed commissions—interior schemes, furniture, water-colours and the like—in the Liverpool area, and for friends and relatives in Scotland. To all intents and purposes, they cease to play any further part in the

[1] 'Instructor', not 'Professor of Design and Decoration' as claimed in the School of Art records.

[2] Reference is made to the MacNairs in Liverpool by Desmond Chapman-Huston in his book *The Lamp of Memory* (Skeffington, 1949). It would seem that their house became a mecca for the more adventurous architects in the North West when Mackintosh visited them. The author has come across two Manchester men who went to Liverpool on such an occasion especially to meet him and to learn something of his work and principles of design. Unfortunately neither can now recollect the substance of their conversations.

Mackintosh story, though we shall meet them again from time to time. Their marriage ended under tragic circumstances with the death of Frances some fifteen years later, and Herbert MacNair then lost all interest in the arts. He moved from job to job—for a time working in the Post Office—and eventually emigrated to Canada. He ultimately returned to Scotland and, unknown to all but one or two of his former associates, at the time of writing lives quietly in Argyllshire.[1]

Following the MacNairs' example, Charles Mackintosh and Margaret Macdonald became engaged, and they too were married at St. Augustine's—on 22nd August 1900—a fitting conclusion to the romantic story of *The Four*.

NO. 120 MAINS STREET [2]

Quite apart from its romantic interest, Mackintosh's marriage is an event of some importance to the narrative, for before the wedding he and Margaret Macdonald decorated and furnished a flat in Glasgow—No. 120 Mains Street —to which they returned after their honeymoon on Holy Island.

The Mains Street flat—now prosaically enough occupied by the Glasgow Corporation Parks Department—is of particular significance as the first clearly documented example of a suite of rooms decorated and furnished in Mackintosh's mature style, the first actual project he designed and executed unrestricted by the whims of a client, and limited only by the length of his own purse-strings —and the wishes of his future wife! Here, one may expect to take accurate measure of his progress.

It is notable that *The Studio* published several pictures of the flat in a special number, *Modern British Architecture and Decoration* (1901), but no comments were made in the text. One cannot tell, therefore, how Mackintosh's project was received by the critics, and no other British journal seems to have considered the work worth reviewing.

Four apartments are illustrated here (Plates 12 to 16); the white drawing-room and the studio, the sombre brown dining-room, and the principal bedroom

[1] The MacNairs had a son, Sylvan, who emigrated, and now lives in South Africa.

[2] Mains Street is now Blythswood Street. The flat occupied by the Mackintoshes was situated in a rather forbidding grey stone building near to Sauchiehall Street, one of Glasgow's principal thoroughfares.

(also in white).[1] This colour formula, incidentally, was used with slight variations in all the architect's subsequent domestic work.

By contemporary standards the drawing-room (Plates 12 and 13)—a spacious
apartment some 18 feet square—was positively bare, for in addition to half
a dozen chairs, all of different design, it contained but four other pieces of
furniture; a small oval coffee table, a square card table, a writing-desk,[2] a glazed
bookcase,[3] and a fireplace. The sense of freedom and spaciousness engendered by
the sparse furnishing was accentuated still further by the architect's treatment
of the dominating surfaces. The floor was covered by a plain grey fitted carpet,
the walls were divided into panels of light grey canvas with broad cover strips,
the deep frieze rail was decorated at intervals with richly designed square insets
of coloured gesso, and all the woodwork, the frieze, cornice and ceiling, were
painted white. Gas piping, which had to be pinned to the ceiling, was given
an elegant twist—a characteristic gesture this—and was carried to four clusters
of attractive lamps. Flowers, plants and twigs arranged in the prevailing oriental
manner were placed about the room, and a few framed water-colours standing
on the mantelpiece completed the ensemble.

Though entirely different in character, the dining-room was no less unusual
(Plate 15A), and here again one is aware of the astonishing versatility of the
designer, and of his ability to exploit the decorative value of the humblest
materials. The walls were covered to picture-rail level with coarse wrapping
paper—so heavy in fact that it had to be bought by the hundredweight. This
had a rough, uneven surface texture that Mackintosh found exactly to his liking
and its dark grey-brown hue formed a rich background against which flowers,
paintings and repoussé metal showed to best advantage. The woodwork
throughout was pine and with the fireplace surround—not a particularly note-

---

[1] These illustrations are usually assumed to belong to a house in Florentine Terrace, now
No. 78 Southpark Avenue, to which the Mackintoshes removed in 1906. Such a mistake is
understandable because they not only transferred the principal fireplaces, light fittings and
furniture to Southpark Avenue, but closely reproduced the colour schemes of dining-room,
sitting-room and bedroom in their new home.

[2] Mackintosh designed a number of writing-desks and cabinets similar in form to the
elegant piece at Mains Street; almost invariably beaten metal panels by Margaret Macdonald
were used as decoration with small insets of tinted enamel. The inner face of the doors too
were frequently embellished with inlay either of gesso, enamel, or of opaque glass.

[3] The glazed book-case is a finely constructed piece of furniture in two sections linked by
a central element of open shelves and magazine racks: unfortunately it has lost considerably
in reproduction.

worthy example—and the furniture, was stained black and bees-waxed. The ceiling and frieze were left white.

Mackintosh's objective here was to create a sombre, mysterious setting for what to him was a most important ritual—eating and drinking. By eliminating bright colours and light tones in the room itself interest was concentrated dramatically upon the table with its sparkling array of glassware and cutlery. The effectiveness of this arrangement was heightened in the evenings when the candles were lit—in such a sanctuary, of course, hissing gas-jets would have been unthinkable.

Here then, we have yet another aspect of Mackintosh's peculiar genius. Not only did he concern himself with the design of individual pieces of furniture, but in his hands the room itself became a work of art, delicately poised, harmoniously conceived and complete to the last detail—furniture and furnishings, napery and cutlery, fenders and fire-irons—nothing was overlooked. A work of art, moreover, in which the emotional content of the whole was as carefully considered as the practical element, and in which volume, surface, texture, line and colour, were skilfully manipulated to produce a predetermined aesthetic effect. Such work is an extension in three dimensions of his earlier experiments in painting and the crafts: it was followed by advanced spatial experiments elsewhere—at the School of Art and in the Cranston tea-rooms.

From the photographs available it is impossible to see the full extent of Mackintosh's scheme for the principal bedroom (Plate 16). If anything, however, the incidence of characteristic ornament was more pronounced here than in the other rooms, and the bird motive applied to the twin wardrobes, the carved totem-like centre post of the bed inlaid with jewels of coloured glass, and the affected curve of the mirror-stand, all point unmistakably to the late nineties. Even so, such details are less obtrusive in fact than the photograph suggests, and would detract little from the general pleasantness of the room.

Mackintosh seems to have had a predilection for four-poster beds and that designed for the flat was an enormous piece of furniture some 6 feet square and 6 feet 6 inches high, decorated with silk hangings embroidered by Margaret Macdonald. It is now in the Glasgow University Collection.

No other furniture is visible in the photograph, but it is safe to assume that the elegant linen-backed chairs, if not the attractive little tables, at Southpark Avenue (Plates 16B and C), were originally made for the flat. The assumption seems to be confirmed by the appearance of the former at the Viennese Exhibition of 1900. These chairs are among the best Mackintosh designed; they

45

are well proportioned, lightly yet soundly constructed, and comfortable to sit in.

In addition to the more familiar illustrations of the Main Street flat, a photograph survives of yet another white room—the studio (Plate 14A). The most notable feature here is the fireplace surround, made of roughly finished, six-inch boards, butt jointed and painted white.[1] This, no doubt, enclosed an existing mantelpiece which the Mackintoshes disliked. Despite its packing-case construction it is astonishingly modern in appearance—and the complete absence of carved or painted detail brings it closely into line with present-day practice. The fender, with its two slender candle-holders, was an old friend—it can be seen in the Dennistoun room with the frieze of cats (Plate 5A).

It is surprising that the Mains Street flat elicited no comment from British journals, and, in fact, it is necessary to turn to an obscure continental source for an independent opinion of the Mackintoshes' work. A certain E. B. Kalas, writing in a magazine entitled *De la Tamise à la Sprée! l'essor des industries d'art*[2] described his visit to the flat and his meeting with the designer. M. Kalas was enchanted by the interior decoration, he was captivated by the exquisite taste of the artists, and charmed by their masterly handling of form and colour. He commented especially upon the spatial quality and 'virginal beauty' of their unorthodox white rooms, rooms which appeared all the more startling and exotic in such unprepossessing surroundings. To M. Kalas, the Mackintoshes appeared as 'two visionary souls in ecstatic communion . . . wafted . . . aloft to the heavenly regions of creation . . .' etc., etc. This panegyric, couched in the flamboyant style of the period, may sound absurd in these days of studied understatement, but it conveys in no uncertain manner a vivid impression of the character and individuality of the house and its occupants as seen through the eyes of a foreign visitor. There can be no doubt that to enter the Mackintoshes' home was quite an adventure, a step into a new world, and an experience not easily forgotten.[3]

[1] On the illustration there is an electric lamp above the fireplace. It would appear that the Mackintoshes used gas, electricity and candles for lighting in this house—a most unusual arrangement. This picture was taken by Craig Annan in March 1900 and so were the three pictures published in *The Studio* Special Number, 1901. The dates of the photographs used here are not known, but they would be no later than this.

[2] Published by Michaud, Rheims, 1905.

[3] An all too brief description of a visit to the Mackintoshes' house at Southpark Avenue is to be found in each of Desmond Chapman Huston's books—*A Creel of Peet: Stray Papers*, (Adelphi Press, 1910), *The Lamp of Memory* (Skeffington, 1949).

46

The Mains Street interiors are a remarkable advance on any work previously discussed, and one might well ask how this change came about—where, for instance, was Mackintosh's first 'white' room, and where his first high-backed chair? The initial signs of change can be recognized in the *Gladsmuir* drawing-room where, despite the conglomeration of knick-knacks, there are plain walls and a simple picture-rail, an upholstered corner seat, and pictures standing on the mantelpiece—not hanging from untidy cords. The next comparable example of which a record remains, is the drawing-room at Dunglass Castle (Plate 11A). This can be accurately dated, for the Macdonald family moved to Dunglass Castle in July 1899, and this house, if anywhere, was the place most likely to lend itself to experimental work by Mackintosh, a future son-in-law.

The drawing-room was, and still is, a fine apartment, with an attractive bay formed of a corner turret, commanding extensive views over the Clyde estuary. Here Mackintosh cut away the ornate cornice and remodelled the ceiling, removed the old fireplace, and introduced one of his own design flanked by a corner seat. The corner seat was a new version of that at *Gladsmuir*, and, in fact, the linen back was stencilled with an identical flying bird motive —one of the rare occasions on which Mackintosh repeated himself. No other furniture appears on the photograph and apart from a glazed bookcase, a replica of that in the Mains Street flat, the room did not contain any other pieces by him. The family chairs were just re-covered with fabric embroidered by Frances and Margaret.

The *pièce de résistance* was the great white mantelpiece 7 feet long, 5 feet 6 inches high—in all probability the first of its kind, a mantelpiece of revolutionary design which, for elegance and simplicity, could not be matched by any of the contemporary masters of interior decoration. Although Voysey, Walton, Wood and others were giving much thought to fireplace design (Plates 11B, 17B, and 89B), and competitions in *The Studio* and elsewhere drew new ideas from an ever-widening field, nowhere does there appear to have been anything approaching so closely to the spirit of the new movement as Mackintosh's work at this time. At Dunglass Castle, as elsewhere, he achieved his objective with remarkable economy of means. The fireplace surround was of grey plaster, and the mantelpiece itself—containing square pigeon holes—was completely devoid of ornament. Interest was sustained by the form and proportion of its various members, and by the play of light and shade on receding and contrasting planes. Almost all Mackintosh's subsequent mantelpieces were painted white, no doubt in order to derive the greatest value from reflected light, and to provide a suitable background for flowers and plants without which none of his designs was complete. Little *art nouveau* ornament intrudes into this work and where it does occur, it is limited to small jewel-like inlays of enamel and glass, or to restrained carving. In fact, it is mainly the incidence of such details, and the appearance of an occasional flat, sensuous curve, that enables the casual observer to date a Mackintosh fireplace with any measure of success.

NO. 34, KINGSBOROUGH GARDENS

It may be well here to refer briefly to yet another white room which is contemporary with the Mains Street flat—No. 34 Kingsborough Gardens, a terraced house in Glasgow, owned by the Rowat family. Mrs. Newbery was Miss Jessie Rowat before her marriage and this, without doubt, accounts for the appearance of the young architect's work in the west end of the city at the time. The actual work carried out at the house comprised a built-in hall settle with a high back, forming a screen for the stairs, several light fittings and a number of fireplaces (and presumably the decoration of the rooms in which they occurred), all of which were still in position and fairly intact in 1944. For the first-floor drawing-room Mackintosh designed an excellent fireplace with an adjacent built-in wall-seat (Plate 17A). As at Dunglass, the high back to the seat was divided into broad panels each upholstered and covered with linen on which a floral motive was boldly stencilled. The panels, about 5 feet 6 inches high, terminated level with the mantelpiece in a narrow shelf for the display of small china ornaments: above this the wall, to picture-rail level, was decorated by a delightful stencilled pattern of conventionalized trees and flowers.[1] The fireplace is of similar dimensions to the example at Dunglass—about 7 feet long and 5 feet 6 inches high and consists of a small grate with a grey cement surround in which nine square, blue tiles are inserted. The hearth is raised some 12 inches above floor level and two adjustable ventilators are provided through which a regulated supply of air passes to the grate. A simple wooden mantel-

[1] This gay design has disappeared now and in the winter of 1943–4 the timber seating was broken up for firewood because the upholstery had worn threadbare. On entering the house for the first time the author was handed a splintered piece of timber and shown a few square feet of linen on which a faded pattern was still faintly discernible—all that remained of a most charming feature. The fireplace itself was undamaged, however, but looked singularly forlorn under a coat of thick brown paint which had obliterated its former glossy whiteness.

piece with square pigeon-holes encloses the fireplace and it is embellished with three characteristic motives, the centre one forming a bracket which serves to stiffen the deep fascia board. This design is, if anything, more successful than the Dunglass and Mains Street examples, and the room as originally laid out must have been most pleasing.

These commissions, of course, may represent but a fraction of the domestic interior work executed by Mackintosh at this time, but at the moment of writing they alone have come to light.[1] In attempting to bridge the gap between them, however, the lack of evidence of development is not of great moment, for in the meantime Mackintosh had gained valuable experience as an interior designer at the Cranston tea-rooms and as an architect, on the first section of the new Glasgow School of Art (1897–9). In fact, if one considers the prodigious amount of energy he expended on these projects—both of which will be examined in detail later—it is not surprising that so little domestic work was forthcoming, or that the Dunglass room was so different in character from all that had gone before.

The first evidence of a radical change in his furniture was to be seen, in fact, at Miss Cranston's Argyle Street tea-rooms, where he provided curious little stools, stocky arm-chairs and high ladder-backs (Plates 49B). In designing for the tea-rooms, he was able to exercise his imagination and creative gifts to a degree not possible in ordinary domestic practice. Moreover, on this scheme, he worked in conjunction with George Walton who had already made a name for himself as a designer of furniture. This alone provided just the incentive needed for a man of Mackintosh's temperament, and by the turn of the century he had produced a wide range of furniture—of chairs especially—that are quite original in conception. In the illustrations of the Mains Street drawing-room, for example, six different types are to be seen—and all but one, the large box-like wing chair, were designed for the tea-rooms.[2]

---

[1] The author has recently traced another furnished interior which belongs to this phase, though so far it has not been possible to verify the date: it is a bedroom at Queen's Place, Glasgow, a house now occupied by Professor Browning of Glasgow University. This interior was illustrated in *Dekorative Kunst*, March 1902.

[2] It would seem that Mackintosh kept for himself a replica of each chair he designed for Miss Cranston—a point that will, no doubt, bring some satisfaction to those who find his furniture inhumanly uncomfortable.

CHAIRS

Generally speaking, Mackintosh's chairs fall into two main classes: high-backed and low-backed. They all *look* equally uncomfortable and equally unorthodox, and rarely does their designer acknowledge tradition. His tall-backed chairs—often 4 feet 6 inches high—have been criticized frequently as unpractical and incomprehensible: unpractical they may be, but to anyone familiar with the architect's work in the minor arts, and especially with his water-colours and posters, they should not be incomprehensible. They convey the same message in a new medium, and the tall backs, the oval insets, the pierced patterns of squares and crescents, all tell the same story of growth, of upward surging vitality. Such chairs were always designed for a particular setting where vertical emphasis was required, as, for example, in the dining-room at Mains Street, and when used singly or in small groups, they provided invaluable decorative elements in a large, high room. Then again, they often had some particular significance, as in the Willow tea-room where the multiplicity of high, spindly backs was intended to resemble a forest of young willow trees. A less practical form would be difficult to devise for regular use, however, especially in a public restaurant, and the story of the tea-room chairs is one of continual repair. Many had to be reinforced with metal brackets and often the backs were reduced to a more reasonable height. There can be no doubt that in the majority of these designs Mackintosh was seeking primarily to create an aesthetic effect, to stimulate the observer spiritually rather than to provide for his bodily comfort—a point that was not overlooked by contemporary critics.

The low-backed chairs were, on the whole, much more soundly constructed, and approximated more closely to traditional types. They were of sturdy proportions, usually with very wide seats and sloping arms: sometimes they were lightly framed, and, on occasion, heavily built up with solid panels. A chair of this type in the author's possession is one of the first Mackintosh devised for Miss Cranston. It is constructed of oak with a solid wooden seat, panelled sides and an open back: an admirable restaurant chair.

Mackintosh favoured drop-in seats, lightly upholstered, and covered with linen or stout haircloth, usually of chequered pattern. He also used rush seats for dining-room chairs but never deep, comfortable upholstery. Even his fireside chairs are of extremely heavy box construction, with high winged backs sparsely upholstered. These chairs, of which only three types are known to the author, are reminiscent of farmhouse and cottage furniture—especially of Highland make. One example, 4 feet 6 inches high and rectangular in plan, is like a diminutive hall settle; another is the enormous wing chair which can be seen in the illustration of the Mains Street drawing-room, this is upholstered in unbleached linen, decorated with a drawn thread motive. The third, of much later date, is polygonal in plan. All these chairs, notwithstanding their clumsy appearance, are surprisingly comfortable.[1]

Mackintosh produced innumerable variations of these types; in all cases he preferred to leave the structure starkly naked and reduce the upholstery to a minimum. Only a single drawing for a completely upholstered chair, an un-distinguished cubiform tub-chair, has come to light—it is dated 1909.

The chairs, of course, boldly proclaim their originality and most readily attract attention, but the other pieces designed by the architect are no less unorthodox. The writing-desk and the book-case at Mains Street, for instance, should be compared with the linen press and the chest of drawers discussed previously (Figs. 6 and 7) if Mackintosh's progress is to be accurately measured. His tables also are worth noting. For dining-rooms, as the Mains Street example demonstrates, he favoured the simplest possible refectory type with four square legs, usually without stretchers. The rails were often decorated, as here, with small heart-shaped piercings. The wood was either oak or pine stained green or, more usually, almost black and wax polished. Tops were made of butt-jointed boards unframed and normally of slight section—about $\frac{3}{4}$ inch— with a wide overhang, yet another weak constructional form.

Occasional tables varied considerably and two characteristic examples are to be seen in the Mains Street drawing-room—one of these has a large square top; it is lightly built and rather unstable; the other, an oval coffee table, is more sturdily constructed and possesses an undershelf.[2] Sometimes, as in this instance, he used legs made of wide boards pierced or incised, and set diagonally or tangentially if the top were curved in form—a popular modern device.

Whether from the point of view of furniture design, or interior *décor* generally, the photographs of the Mains Street flat are of especial significance. They

[1] About 1904 Mackintosh evolved for Miss Cranston a charming ladder-backed chair, small and light, with flat curved rungs—two of these are in the author's collection. They seem to have been the starting point for fresh experiments with furniture of a more familiar type, and a group of interesting pieces with turned legs, arms and spindles, is to be seen at the *Grosvenor Restaurant*, Glasgow.

[2] Two of these attractive tables survive—one was presented by the Davidson family to Glasgow University, the other is in the possession of Miss Nancy Mackintosh.

prove incontestably that all the characteristics of Mackintosh's interior work which later became identified with *Windyhill* and *Hill House* were fully in evidence in the year 1900—the year in which C. F. A. Voysey built his own house *The Orchard* at Chorley Wood (Plate 88c). The Mains Street interiors were not tentative experiments, the work of an immature mind, but imaginative designs demanding a high degree of artistic perception and executive skill. Furthermore, they show that the architect's conception of the room as a whole, within which and to which, all minor elements were related, was clearly defined and had found expression at the turn of the century. It was this aspect of his work, together with his preference for broad, plain surfaces, and simple geometrical forms, that impressed continental observers and had far-reaching effects upon the trend of future developments abroad—and, eventually, at home.

APPRENTICESHIP AND PROFESSIONAL EXPERIENCE

Having observed the growth and flowering of Mackintosh's individual style in the crafts and interior design, and having studied his work in relation to that of his artist friends, it is necessary now to trace each succeeding step in his climb to power at the office of Honeyman & Keppie; and to follow as far as practicable the development of his architectural style between 1889, the year in which he joined the partners, and 1896 when the competition for the new Glasgow School of Art was held. Before embarking on this, however, it will be well to glance briefly at the work of local architects he is known to have admired, and more especially, to discover something of the two principals of the firm with whom he was closely associated, and by whom one might anticipate, he was most likely to be influenced.

The face of Glasgow changed and largely assumed its present cosmopolitan character during Mackintosh's youth, and an immense amount of new building took place in the last quarter of the nineteenth century. But there is no evidence of an original mind at work—no single figure of the stature of Alexander 'Greek' Thomson. Generally speaking the profession maintained its adherence to classicism, notwithstanding the diatribes of Ruskin and the national fervour of the baronialists. Innumerable nondescript buildings were erected here as elsewhere, but despite the eclecticism of the period the Glasgow street scene is remarkably uniform. It possesses scale and dignity foreign to most provincial cities, qualities due in no small part to the influence of Thomson, and to the work of the architects to be mentioned here—and, one might add, to the rhythmic, orderly fenestration of large tenement blocks, four or five storeys high, often set above ground-floor shops and warehouses.

Two practising architects in particular had considerable influence on the younger generation in Glasgow when Mackintosh was a youth—James Sellars and John James (later Sir John) Burnet—though neither man departed far from convention, and both were confirmed classicists; Sellars favouring the Italian Renaissance, Burnet readily turning his hand to anything from the Baronial to the Baroque.

James Sellars' most notable city buildings are St. Andrew's Halls and the New Club, West George Street (*circa* 1878), monumental projects in the renaissance manner; Wylie and Lockhead's Buchanan Street Warehouse (*circa* 1880); Belhaven Church, Great Western Road (*circa* 1880) and Anderston Church, Hillhead. Sellars delighted in good craftsmanship; wrought iron was one of his favourite materials, and as no stock patterns would satisfy him, he invariably produced his own designs, an example closely followed by Mackintosh. He was appointed architect to the first great international exhibition to be held in Glasgow (1888) and the similarity between his scheme—in the Saracenic manner (Plate 66B)—and Mackintosh's project for the exhibition of 1901 will be discussed in a subsequent chapter.

In the late 1870's John James Burnet returned from France to his father's Glasgow office with a first-class diploma of the French *École des Beaux Arts*, where he had studied in the atelier of Jean Louis Pascal. He initiated a popular phase of French Renaissance architecture with the scholarly Glasgow Institute of Fine Arts, Sauchiehall Street (1879–80), one of his most notable achievements. This was followed by the offices of the Clyde Navigation Trust and Charing Cross Mansions—both suffused with the spirit of French classicism—and the firm entered upon a new period of prosperity. Almost every thoroughfare in the city of Glasgow contains some work by the Burnets, father or son: they built the Stock Exchange, the great Merchants' House in George Square, the Barony Church (an essay in Scottish Gothic), Glasgow Athenaeum, and *circa* 1892, its dramatic Buchanan Street extension (Plate 18B), and a host of banks, insurance buildings and warehouses. John Burnet senior retired *circa* 1889, and

54

shortly afterwards John James came under the spell of the Romantic movement fostered in the Edinburgh region by Rowand Anderson (designer of Glasgow Central Station and Pollokshaws Burgh Hall) and Robert Lorimer—though Lorimer, the 'James Barrie of Scottish architecture',[1] did not return to his native heath to undertake the restoration of Earlshall, until 1892. Burnet's Scots traditional style at its best is exemplified in the new Pathological Buildings, Glasgow Western Infirmary (designed *circa* 1894) (Plate 18c), though on occasion his work in this idiom was mannered and flamboyant.

The Burnets dominated the architectural field in the West of Scotland during the last quarter of the century, and inevitably set a standard—and a fashion —to which all consciously or unconsciously subscribed. Though Mackintosh deprecated their classical enterprises, no less than they disapproved of him and his circle, he had a profound regard for their masterly handling of form, and he closely followed their work in the native idiom.

Sellars and Burnet—and to a lesser degree Lorimer—were the Scottish architects Mackintosh most greatly admired. There were, of course, many other notable figures who helped to mould the face and form of Glasgow, for example, J. A. Campbell, James Miller, J. T. Rochead, Charles Wilson, A. N. Paterson, W. Forrest Salmon & Son (designers of Lion Chambers, 1906, the first reinforced concrete building to be constructed in the city),[2] but none could measure up to the prolific John James Burnet, and few, in Mackintosh's opinion, could compare with James Sellars.

The illustrations given here (Plates 18 and 19) are fairly representative of the buildings erected in Glasgow at this time. They reflect the spirit of the age, and form a background against which the magnitude of Mackintosh's struggle for independence can be more readily appreciated.

Before discussing Honeyman & Keppie, one other person must be mentioned with whom Mackintosh came frequently into contact—Alexander McGibbon. 'Sandy' McGibbon was a brilliant draughtsman and despite the fact that he did little actual building, he eventually became Director of Architectural Studies at the Glasgow School of Art. At this time he earned his living as a free-lance

---

[1] See *The Work of Sir Robert Lorimer*, by Christopher Hussey, published by *Country Life*, 1931.

[2] James Salmon, the son—known locally as 'the wee troot'—and Mackintosh, became good friends. Mackintosh's influence is apparent in a number of buildings erected by the firm —notably the Savings Bank at Anderston, Glasgow (illustrated in *Academy Architecture*, 1900), and Alexandra Park Free Church, Glasgow (illustrated in *The British Architect*, 7th March 1902, p. 165) and 142–4 St. Vincent St., 1899–1902.

draughtsman, for a while with the Burnets, then with Keppie, then, perhaps, with Salmon and others, executing the perspectives for which he became famous and which were always in great demand.[1] He was a curious personality, small in stature, bearded, bespectacled and almost invariably dressed in a long dirty overcoat that reached to his ankles. Notwithstanding his unkempt appearance and notorious absentmindedness, he was a clever artist with a profound knowledge of architectural history: his pencil studies, executed in France and elsewhere, are among the finest of their kind. From McGibbon, whom he met frequently at the office and School of Art, Mackintosh learnt much about pencil and ink technique—and no doubt a great deal about architectural design —though the draughtsmanship of the two men is easily distinguishable. For instance, it is interesting to compare the perspective of Honeyman & Keppie's Royal Insurance Building project by McGibbon (Plate 19c), with the earliest drawing in this medium by Mackintosh that has come to light, the offices of the *Glasgow Herald* (Fig 10). The latter is the more dramatic and forceful; it is executed with a broad firm ink line, and the architect avoided the fashionable naturalistic street scenes introduced by McGibbon. His conventionalized linear sky, too, is worthy of note, for in all subsequent drawings he invariably formalized the setting—a radical departure from contemporary work of this nature, and to the best of the author's knowledge, quite unique in British nineteenth-century architectural draughtsmanship.[2]

JOHN HONEYMAN

John Honeyman, LL.D., R.S.A., (1831–1914), was born in Glasgow and educated at Merchiston Castle. He attended Glasgow University for a time, but left, without taking a degree, to become apprenticed to Alexander Munro, a local architect. By the end of his apprenticeship he was acting as chief assistant. At the age of twenty-three, after spending some months in London at the office of J. MacVicar Anderson, later President of the R.I.B.A., he began to practise alone. His first important work (1861) was Greenock Free West Church, won in competition; in the following year came Lansdowne Church, Great

[1] The majority of perspective drawings of Glasgow buildings, published in *Academy Architecture* in the 1890's, came from the pen of McGibbon.

[2] A similar technique of drawing was employed, however, by the Austrian architect Otto Wagner and his pupils, Josef Hoffmann, J. M. Olbrich and others (see Chapter XI).

Western Road, Glasgow—a building in the Gothic style remarkable for its slender spire which is higher than that of Glasgow Cathedral. From these beginnings Honeyman rapidly built up a fine practice. He entered the Sydney Houses of Parliament competition, and was placed on the short list—his perspective drawing was exhibited at the Royal Academy, and is said to have been used by Scott as the model for his new Glasgow University buildings.

In the secular sphere, too, he had a notable record—the Paisley Observatory (1862), Paisley Museum and Library (1868), the Municipal Buildings, Helensburgh (1868), Paisley Mental Hospital (1875) and a number of schools. Of his many domestic buildings the best known are, perhaps, Skipness Castle, Argyllshire (1878) and Auchamore House, Gigha (1882), large mansions in the baronial style.[1] The latter was illustrated in *Academy Architecture* in 1897. In 1872 he designed F. & J. Smith's furniture warehouse—now the *Cạ d'Oro*, Gordon Street, Glasgow (Plate 18A), a daring essay in cast iron and glass. The Smiths desired as much light as possible in their show-rooms and workshops, and Honeyman reduced the structural supports of the building to a minimum. The piers and arches to the ground and mezzanine floors are stone with iron window-frames, but the top three storeys are all cast iron—except for thin slabs of stone used as a facing to the narrow pilasters. Compound beams with a timber web and rolled iron top and bottom flanges were used for the major spans internally; this was a more logical and scientific arrangement than that of the conventional 'flitch' beam in which the plates were set on edge and bolted to a timber core.

Honeyman, then, was a versatile and accomplished designer, by no means adverse to experimenting with unorthodox materials and methods of construction. When he took John Keppie into partnership in 1889—the year in which Mackintosh joined the firm—he had to his credit about thirty churches, including the Scottish Church at Genoa (1877), and a host of public and domestic buildings.[2]

[1] Some features from the plans of these buildings can be recognized in Mackintosh's domestic work, and in the Glasgow School of Art.

[2] John Honeyman had many antiquarian interests. He was one of the founders of the Glasgow Archaeological Society and later its President, and a founder member of the Scottish Ecclesiological Society. He painted in water-colours and oils and at one time was Vice-President of the Royal Scottish Academy. But for failing eyesight no doubt he would have succeeded Sir George Reid as President. For this reason, too, he took less and less interest in the practice as time went on, until in 1904 he was obliged to retire. For the last ten years of his life he was totally blind. He died at Bridge of Allan, Stirlingshire, in 1914.

JOHN KEPPIE

John Keppie (1862–1945), the junior partner, had an entirely different personality. The son of a tobacco importer, he was born at Glasgow and educated at Ayr Academy and Glasgow University. Then followed a period of training at the *École des Beaux Arts*, Paris, after which he became chief draughtsman to James Sellars. It was after Sellars' death in 1888 that Keppie joined Honeyman, taking with him much of Sellars' business, and retaining the goodwill of a number of clients. Keppie was only twenty-seven years old—and more than twenty years Honeyman's junior—when the partnership was established. As far as can be ascertained, he had no outstanding buildings to his credit at this time, and despite the advantages of his continental training and valuable office experience, his subsequent work—mainly in the classical manner—was unimaginative and pedantic, often elaborated with carving and detailed with a heavy hand. Some of his larger projects however, display a breadth of treatment that is wholly admirable.

Keppie was only six years older than Mackintosh and the two men had a good deal in common in the early days; they worked together extremely well and were the best of friends. When competitive designs were being prepared Mackintosh was often invited to Keppie's home at Ayr, where they could work in more congenial surroundings. Herbert MacNair, who was also at the office, frequently went along too. At week-ends the Macdonalds, and other students from the School of Art, sometimes joined them, and to house his guests on such occasions Keppie rented two bungalows christened 'The Roaring Camp' at nearby Dunure. Usually the girls of the party, now well known in Scottish art circles, were Jessie Keppie, sister of John Keppie, Agnes Raeburn, Catherine Cameron, Janet Aitken and, of course, Frances and Margaret Macdonald. They adopted the title 'The Immortals'.

This happy phase of close collaboration between Keppie and Mackintosh did not last long, however. By the turn of the century relations between them had become strained—for reasons which will be discussed later—and although Mackintosh was taken into partnership on Honeyman's retirement in 1904, the situation did not improve thereafter.

Of the two men with whom he was in closest contact, there can be little doubt that Mackintosh was most influenced by the scholarly and dignified Honeyman from whom he acquired not only a profound respect for the architecture of his own country, but the courage to carry out structural experiments, and not a little knowledge of aesthetics. It is doubtful if Keppie contributed much to his professional education except, perhaps, in the practical fields of office procedure and building construction.

Between 1889 and 1896 it is not easy to isolate buildings designed by the firm in which personal characteristics—either of Keppie or Mackintosh—can be indisputably recognized. Had there been a well-established office tradition before Mackintosh joined the partners the problem of identifying his handiwork would have been simplified, or alternatively, if Keppie's personal style prior to 1889 could be clearly defined, the authorship of later work would not have been in doubt. Nevertheless, by studying buildings known to have been designed by Keppie after Honeyman's retirement[1] it is possible to divide the work of the firm prior to 1896 into two groups, one of which, with some degree of certainty, may be said to show evidence of Mackintosh's handiwork. The line of demarcation, however, cannot be drawn precisely, and certain motifs and details commonly occur on all the buildings considered here. The treatment of window architraves and pediments is a case in point—especially pediments with a curious tongue-like embellishment. Such features, often somewhat incongruous, no doubt represent the personal preferences or mannerisms of Mackintosh's employers—the Honeyman or the Keppie touch—a favourite motif that was virtually the hallmark of the firm. It is significant that after 1896 all such features were eliminated from buildings entrusted to Mackintosh's care though they persisted for many years in other work produced by the firm.

By and large, the projects emanating from the office at this time are not in any real sense different from those of other practising architects in Glasgow. They varied, for example, from a strictly formal classical design for the Glasgow Art Galleries Competition,[2] to the Canal Boatmen's Institute, Port Dundas, 1893, a modest building in the Scottish Renaissance manner (Plate 19B). These, with projects for the Royal Insurance Buildings, Buchanan Street, 1894 (Plate 19C), Paisley Technical School, 1896[3] (neither of which was executed),

---

[1] For example, Muir Simpson's warehouse, Sauchiehall Street, Glasgow; the Glasgow Savings Bank, Parkhead, and business premises in Sauchiehall Street—the two latter projects were illustrated in *Academy Architecture*, 1907, pps. 51 and 54.

[2] Published in *The Builder*, 25th June 1892. Interior perspective in *Academy Architecture*, 1898. Mr. L. H. Honeyman, son of John Honeyman, tells the author that his father and John Keppie were placed individually on the short list for this competition, but they combined forces to produce this design.

[3] Illustrated in *Academy Architecture*, 1896.

Figure 10. *circa* 1893. The *Glasgow Herald* Building. Perspective by C. R. Mackintosh.

and Pettigrew & Stephens' warehouse, Sauchiehall Street, *circa* 1896[1] all belong to the first—the Keppie group. With the exception of the Art Galleries project—a monumental design with a hexastyle portico of the Ionic order, raised on a high rusticated podium—the others have much in common; they represent sturdy, rather unimaginative buildings, combining neo-renaissance and romantic Scots features in a manner typical of the period.

In the Canal Boatmen's Institute, however, we can recognize the curious 'dormers' in the parapet of the tower—they were borrowed from Mackintosh's Chapter House Design of 1891-2—and the clock-face was designed by him (see footnote 1 to page 26). In any of the other buildings we may search in vain for a single characteristic detail.

The earliest of Mackintosh's professional drawings executed under the aegis of Honeyman and Keppie which has survived—it is now in the Glasgow University Collection—is a perspective of the *Glasgow Herald* Offices (Fig. 10). This represents the first of three buildings which were erected by the firm and with which he can be closely identified. In chronological order of design they are the *Glasgow Herald* building,[2] Queen Margaret's Medical College,[3] and the Martyrs' Public School.[4]

THE 'GLASGOW HERALD' BUILDING (designed 1893-4)

A perspective drawing of the water-tower and façade of the *Herald* building was published in *Academy Architecture* in 1894, and a rough pencil sketch of the tower also appears on the back of one of Mackintosh's Italian sketches (1891) in the Glasgow Royal Technical College Collection. Not too much importance should be attached to this latter date, however, for the young architect occasionally used the blank pages of old note-books, and the backs of earlier sketches for subsequent work which, more often than not, was undated.

There does not appear to be any prospect now of establishing with certainty exactly what part Mackintosh played in the evolution of this design; but there can be little doubt that it was prepared under the close surveillance of the

[1] Illustrated in *Academy Architecture*, 1899.

[2] Date on rainwater head of finished building, 1895. An illustration of the *Glasgow Herald* tower is included in a large portfolio of excellent photographs *Die Englische Baukunst der Gegenwart*, Hermann Muthesius, Berlin, 1900.

[3] Date on stone in wall, 1895. [4] Date on wall sundial in perspective drawing, 1896.

partners. It possesses many features common to the buildings already mentioned, and yet has characteristics strongly suggestive of Mackintosh. The attic storey, for example, contains details which occur again and again in work by the firm and which, in the case of the ornate pediments, dormers and corbelled sills, persist long after Mackintosh had developed his personal style. Moreover, this element bears little resemblance to the crowning stage of the *Daily Record* office, which was designed indisputably by Mackintosh in 1901 (Plate 69). The principal façade below the heavy string course, however, is admirably restrained and composed of window units which, slightly modified, appear in Mackintosh's later work: the recessed bays at ground, second and third floor level, are in principle identical with several windows in the library wing of the School of Art. The tall, narrow windows at first floor level have counterparts in the two other designs in this group, and so also has the tiny window at the top of the tower with its characteristic sill treatment.

The upper part of the tower is puzzling. It is most unlikely that Mackintosh would have condoned the swelling elephantine cartouches which clumsily mask the angles of the penultimate stage, and yet they follow sensuous curves which immediately recall the craftwork of *The Four*. Moreover, the coping to the parapet is swept up at the angles in typical Mackintosh fashion and the elegant ogee roof with its heavy weather vane can be identified as a favourite terminal feature which appeared in various forms on the railway station design of 1892, and on both the Medical College and the Martyrs' School.

Carved stone ornament and wrought iron almost invariably give a reliable clue to the authorship of a design by Mackintosh but in all these early buildings they are commonplace, and indeterminate. In the *Herald* project the stone embellishments bear little resemblance to his work in this medium at the Glasgow School of Art two years later, but, of course, it is probable that they were moulded to conform to popular taste under the watchful eye of his employers.

To sum up then, it may be said that the proportions and fenestration of the Mitchell Street façade—at least to the string course—and the form and character of the tower, are strongly indicative of Mackintosh, although his handiwork seems to have been heavily overlaid. It is most likely that he set out the main lines of the design under the guidance of Honeyman and Keppie, by whom he was obliged to make modifications and to introduce alien features—for example, the riotous dormers, and the arched openings at street level. Even Mackintosh's most ardent champions, who claim the *Glasgow Herald* building as his first public work, must concede that a commission of such magnitude would hardly be left in the hands of a young draughtsman, but would be controlled throughout by the principals of the firm.

QUEEN MARGARET'S MEDICAL COLLEGE, 1895

The next building in this group, Queen Margaret's Medical College, Hamilton Drive, was designed in 1894 as an extra-mural department to the University of Glasgow. It is said to have been the first school of medicine for women in Britain. Now it is linked to the ornate Florentine-renaissance palace—designed by John Honeyman in association with J. T. Rochead—known formerly as Northpark House, which at present is the Glasgow headquarters of the B.B.C. The two buildings form a strange contrast. Northpark House was built in the 1860's by two elderly merchants, John and Matthew Bell, with the magnanimous intention that after their decease it should serve as a private museum for their large collection of works of art. The brothers were an eccentric couple and staffed the house entirely by menservants. It was by an amusing turn of fortune that the building ultimately became a women's college. The art treasures were sold and dispersed.

The Medical College is situated behind the formal mansion and is constructed of red sandstone on traditional lines. It has an unusually informal plan, simple and efficient, with the principal apartments spiralling round a central hall—the hub of the scheme. In plan, the small galleried museum is similar to that of the original scheme for the new School of Art library (Fig. 15).

The interior has been entirely remodelled and the classroom wing—to the left of the doorway in Mackintosh's charming informal perspective (Fig. 11) —has been demolished and replaced by a massive studio block. The remainder of the building is intact, even the original iron gates are in position, and the staircase tower still sports its gay roof. In spite of the heavy and unimaginative ironwork, the traditional balusters and the meagre, banal stone ornament, the growing ascendency of the young architect is more clearly apparent in this work. The bold museum gable is similar in spirit to the east and west wings of the School of Art; the tall turret windows, climbing in sympathy with the rake of the stairs, appear later in his domestic work; and in subsequent designs he rarely departed from the steeply pitched, simple roof of traditional form employed here. It is surprising that the wrought iron gates should be so

Perspective view from the south-west.

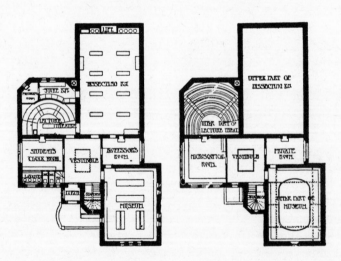

Fig. 11. 1894. Queen Margaret's Medical College, Glasgow. Perspective by C. R. Mackintosh.
Ground- and first-floor plans.

64

massively dull. At this point, if anywhere, might have been expected some indication of the inventiveness and delicacy achieved in his contemporary craftwork and, indeed, displayed in the perspective drawing of the Medical School itself.

Although Mackintosh's authorship of the original building may well be dis-

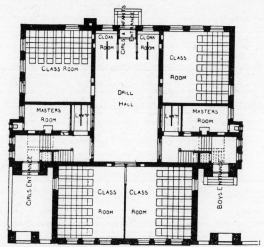

Fig. 12. 1895. Martyrs' Public School, Glasgow. Ground-floor plan. (See also Plate 20A.)

puted, no one can question the authenticity of the perspective which was published in *The British Architect* on 10th January 1896.[1] This drawing is in his mature style; meticulous, fanciful and charming. It is the first of a long series of competent pen and ink renderings in a manner peculiarly his own and in which, with few exceptions, architecture and landscape were carefully integrated. The design in which he did not introduce trees or flowers was rare indeed.

THE MARTYRS' PUBLIC SCHOOL, 1895

The third building in this group, the Martyrs' Public School, Parson Street, was designed *circa* 1895, and Mackintosh again produced an excellent perspective drawing which is now in the Glasgow University Collection[2] (Plate 20A). In this instance the setting was by no means conducive to lawns and shrubs,

---

[1] The original perspective is in the possession of Messrs. Keppie & Henderson, Bath Street, Glasgow—Mackintosh's old firm.   [2] Reproduced in *Academy Architecture*, 1896.

but the architectural background is full of interest and is no less characteristic than the cotton-wool trees and plants that decorate the earlier drawing.

The Martyrs' School is larger than the Medical College, and the plan is more formal (Fig. 12), but the similarity of the two buildings is immediately apparent, quite apart from the presence of common features such as the tall staircase windows, corbelled sills, relieving arches and so forth. A close examination of the perspective drawings reveal one or two new motives, however, and the building is crowned by three octagonal ventilators with the now familiar ogee roof, each terminated by a sturdy finial supported by four simple ring-like brackets—a shape frequently used by Mackintosh in later decorative work.

The most notable detail is a small section of roof above the staircase hall which is swept down boldly and carried on brackets projecting some three feet from the face of the wall—an idea first mooted over the porch at the Medical College—but here the treatment is identical with the eaves of the new Glasgow School of Art, not only from the point of view of appearance but constructionally also.   The internal roof structure above the staircase and galleried hall is particularly interesting (Plate 20B). The timber trusses over the well of the main hall are built up of heavy members held together by thick untrimmed wooden pins, projecting some two inches from the surface. Each king post has been moulded into a primitive tulip shape—a characteristic Mackintosh detail this—by the addition of four carved pieces of wood, one applied to each face; moreover, the silhouette of the truss itself has been modelled by the insertion of shaped webbing pieces, and the whole structural frame is carried on simple decorative corbels. Unusual trusses occur too over the staircase well, but these are much lighter in construction; the oxter pieces—or hangers from rafter to tie beam—are doubled and carried down to form elementary pendants which are pierced by an inverted heart-shaped motive.

The manipulation of structural members into a decorative pattern is a feature of Mackintosh's later work and, after searching in vain for distinctive detail in the two earlier buildings, the incidence of the small belcast roof and the presence of the unusual trusses is the first unmistakable, tangible evidence of his handiwork. Apparently this was the first occasion on which he was permitted a degree of autonomy; the next major design he attempted was that of the Glasgow School of Art.

Contrary to expectation, among the designs emanating from the office those for which Mackintosh can be assumed to be responsible—at least in part—do not show evidence of striking originality. There is no dramatic *volte face*, no exciting structural innovation, not even an infusion of unorthodox decoration, but, on the other hand, admirable restraint in the use of stylistic motives and ornament—no small achievement in the 1890's—and the emergence of forms with a strong traditional bias. All this seems at variance with the young architect's development in the applied arts, but the reason for his apparent inconsistency is not far to seek. Mackintosh was still a draughtsman, and no matter how fundamentally he might disagree with the ideas and principles of his employers, he was obliged to keep in step with his colleagues, curb his enthusiasm, and conform to office practice.[1]

Moreover, he had become deeply absorbed in the study of old Scottish buildings—encouraged no doubt by Honeyman—and it would seem that, as he secured more authority, he used every opportunity that presented itself to mould the alien features with which he was obliged to work into a form more in keeping with the architecture of his own country—as, for example, in the Medical College and the Tower of the *Glasgow Herald* building. The intensity of his feelings on the question of Scottish architecture was revealed by his lecture to the Glasgow architects in 1891,[2] and it is most likely that the preparation of this paper brought him up against one of the fundamental problems facing every young architect with an original turn of mind, and a strong sense of responsibility—the place of tradition in the scheme of things.

Subsequent events indicate that Mackintosh solved this problem to his own satisfaction there and then, for as we shall see, all his later architectural work, no matter how unorthodox, was unquestionably in the Scottish idiom, and could have been produced in no other country than Scotland. This is an important point largely overlooked in the past—not unnaturally, perhaps—for the sturdy functionalism of the Scottish vernacular had been neglected in favour of more sophisticated forms for a century or more when Mackintosh began to build, and even now is comparatively unknown beyond the borders of the country itself.

The period between 1889 and 1896 may be considered as a transitional phase; a time in which the young architect gained valuable experience in competition work, draughtsmanship, and the more mundane duties of field and office. His growing ascendancy can be felt rather than seen in the three buildings studied here; though in his paintings and craftwork, he had been able to give

[1] See reference at foot of p. 68.
[2] See page 12.

his imagination free rein. From now on these hitherto distinct spheres of activity merge, and his architectural style quickly reached maturity.

In 1896 two important events occurred which had a profound effect upon Mackintosh's career; the competition for the new Glasgow School of Art—ostensibly won by Honeyman & Keppie—and his meeting with Miss Catherine Cranston, the noted Glasgow *restaurateur* for whom over the next twenty years he produced an immense number of designs. In addition to these, and the work he personally executed in the office—Queen's Cross Church (1897), Ruchill Street Church Halls (1897-8), the competition drawings for the 1901 Glasgow Exhibition (1898-9)—he built up a useful private practice with schemes of decoration, furniture and the like. In 1899 his friendship with the Davidsons brought him the first of his important domestic commissions—*Windyhill*—to be followed shortly afterwards by *Hill House* for W. W. Blackie the publisher. Thus, within the space of a few years, Mackintosh came to the forefront as an outstanding designer and architect in his own right, and his identity could no longer be submerged in that of the firm.

From 1896 his activities became so varied and his output of work so prodigious, that it would be confusing to attempt a chronological examination. To simplify matters, therefore, a chapter will be devoted to each important subject—the Glasgow School of Art, domestic buildings, tea-rooms for example—and then the threads of the story will be picked up again in chapter IX, 'The London Phase'. Thereafter the question of sources and influences will be discussed and his work placed in its historical context.

The building of the new Glasgow School of Art, now to be considered, marks the opening phase of his dramatic rise to European stature.

For a superbly documented and illustrated study of Glasgow buildings which is of particular relevance at this point see *Architecture of Glasgow* by Gomme and Walker, Lund Humphries, 1968 and also *Glasgow at a Glance* by Young and Doak, Collins, 1965.

IV

THE GLASGOW SCHOOL OF ART

The new Glasgow School of Art has been acclaimed one of the first European buildings in the 'modern style' and a landmark in architectural history, but the exact date of the design—a question of no little importance—and the circumstances which led to the erection of such an unorthodox building have been largely matters of conjecture hitherto.

Under Francis H. Newbery's wise direction, the Glasgow School of Art rapidly increased in numbers until by the early 1890's it had obviously outgrown its makeshift home in the Corporation Galleries[1] where classes had been held for nearly thirty years. On the 6th September 1895, ten years after Newbery's appointment as headmaster, an extraordinary meeting of the Governors was called to discuss ways and means of raising funds for a new building. Thereafter events began to move quickly. A site of 3,000 square yards, secured for £6,000 by a body known as the Bellahouston Trustees, was offered to the Governors along with the sum of £4,000 on condition that they raised a further £6,000. The Corporation Parks and Galleries Trust then promised £5,000 on condition that £21,000 in all be subscribed—the estimated cost of a 'plain building sufficient

[1] Now a departmental store, Tréron et Cie, Sauchiehall Street.

69

for the present needs of the School'. Public appeals were made and friends responded generously. Within a few months the objective had been attained and a leading article in the *Glasgow Herald* on 26th February 1896, stated that with £21,000 in hand the Governors were in a position to build, and here followed a warning—'that sum will suffice to erect only a plain school; it will not even equip this bald erection in an adequate fashion'. Despite the need for more capital, however, the Governors decided to carry on with the scheme and appointed a building commitee under James (later Sir James) Fleming[1] to frame conditions for an architectural competition. They also agreed that an absolute limit of £14,000 should be fixed for the entire cost of the building, inclusive of all fees, lighting, ventilation, heating, draining and paving charges, but excluding assessor's fees, painting, and the cost of a retaining wall. Furthermore, any architect exceeding this sum by more than ten per cent was to be excluded from the competition. Mr. Newbery was asked to prepare a schedule of accommodation, to *indicate dimensions of classrooms and*—an important point this—*to make suggestions regarding the size and nature of windows*, and the provision of artificial lighting. It was also decided that not more than eight architects in Glasgow should be invited to compete, and that the assessors should be Sir James King, Bart., and Sir Renny Watson, with power to co-opt further professional advisers. The number of competitors was later increased to twelve, though actually eleven architects submitted designs.[2]

The parsimony of the Governors, coupled with Newbery's princely schedule of accommodation—and in particular his demand for classrooms of extraordinary spaciousness—set the competitors a most unenviable task. After having studied the conditions for some months they jointly declared that all the requirements could not possibly be met for the sum specified, whereupon the Governors asked them to state what portion of their designs could be carried out within the limit, and to estimate the final cost, stressing again somewhat naïvely, ' . . . it is but a plain building that is required'. The architects countered by saying that it was impossible to provide the accommodation even in the

[1] In addition to (Sir) James Fleming, Convener, the Building Committee consisted of Leonard Gow, Robert H. Leadbetter, David Tullis, Patrick S. Dunn, Seton Thomas and Baillie Bilsland.

[2] In addition to Honeyman & Keppie the following ten firms competed: T. L. Watson, W. J. Anderson, John A. Campbell & John James Burnet, H. & J. Barclay, A. N. Paterson, Malcolm Stark & Rowntree, H. E. Clifford, W. J. Conner & Henry Mitchell, A. McGibbon, James Salmon & Sons.

plainest manner without greatly exceeding the given figure. This controversy continued at some length until the Governors finally insisted that the competitor mark on their drawings the portion of the building that *could* be erected for £14,000 and submit an estimate of the cost of the entire scheme. The date for submission of the finished drawings was extended from 15th September to 1st October 1896, and two of the Governors resigned as they intended to take part in the competition—John James Burnet and W. Forrest Salmon.

The designs were duly sent in and after some deliberation the assessors made their award. At an extraordinary meeting of the Governors on 13th January 1897, the Chairman announced that the names of the successful competitors were Messrs. John Honeyman & Keppie.

The winning design—obviously drawn by Mackintosh—was on view to the public at the Annual Exhibition of Students' Work held in the Corporation Galleries in February 1897, and at once became the centre of a stormy controversy. It was forthrightly condemned from the architectural standpoint as a wholly reprehensible excursion into *l'art nouveau*. No one had the slightest doubt as to the real author of the project, and, moreover, it was well known that Newbery had done all in his power—short of flatly refusing to accept any design but Mackintosh's—to secure the only building he thought worthy to house his School of Art. However, the award had been made, the winners and the headmaster were delighted, and the Governors stood by the decision of the assessors. All had gone according to plan—Newbery's plan, that is—and it was decided that work should proceed on the first half, the eastern half of the building, although foundations were to be laid for the entire project.[1]

The Memorial Stone was laid on 25th May 1898, by Sir Renny Watson, and it is recorded that 'chief among the documents of interest placed in the cavity of the stone was a short history of the School illuminated on vellum by Miss Jessie M. King, one of the students. . . .' After the ceremony the company returned to the adjacent Corporation Galleries and regaled themselves on wine and cake, and toasted the future success of the School.

Thereafter architects and laymen alike watched apprehensively the gradual unfolding of Mackintosh's scheme. From a simple straightforward plan came a

[1] According to the architects, the ultimate cost of the new School would be £22,753, including gas lighting—£110 more if electricity were substituted—and the tender for the first section up to and including the entrance hall and staircase, amounted to £13,922 3s. 8d. The final accounts for the first section were greatly in excess of this estimate—for reasons to be explained later.

strange building completely devoid of recognizable historical trappings. It had no columns, cornices, pediments, or corbie-stepped gables—a *plain* building, as the Governors rather apologetically called it. Instead of a genteel façade befitting a School of Art, it had great windows 18 feet across with unmoulded mullions stiffened by curious metal brackets—these, in characteristic fashion, served a practical purpose as well as by their gaiety relieving an otherwise austere façade. The entrance itself was asymmetrical, a small island of masonry in a sea of glass, and instead of a parapet there was a wide overhanging eaves. In the end walls, by way of contrast, windows were reduced to a minimum and great masonry surfaces dominated.

A plain building indeed.

The first section of the School, up to and including the entrance hall (Plate 21), was opened in December 1899, by Sir James King, Baronet, of Campsie. Mackintosh's name was not mentioned at the ceremony—nor does the building appear to have been illustrated in any British or continental journal. A photograph of the first section was found in the library of the Graduate School of Design, Harvard University, *c.* 1960, but its source is unknown.

The School of Art then was designed in 1896—the year in which the Martyrs' School was built—between March, when the Competition was promoted, and 1st October, the closing date. The first section, up to and including the entrance hall, was erected between the end of the year 1897 and December 1899.

It would have been most instructive to follow the design through its various stages before it reached the adjudicators, but with the exception of a single rough one-sixteenth inch scale drawing on tracing paper (Fig. 13), all evidence has long since disappeared. Unsigned and undated, this fragmentary drawing is clearly a preliminary sketch by Mackintosh for the main façade and it bears little resemblance to that finally adopted. A broad central block of four storeys, flanked by five-storey studio wings, is crowned by an undulating parapet with wrought iron railings. Triangular gables surmount the wings, and an ogival parapet with a projecting coping superimposed over one of them is identical with that actually employed as a crowning feature to the eastern façade (Plate 24). Although the studio windows are much smaller than those finally adopted, the size of the panes is almost exactly the same.

This scheme must have been far too extravagant and it was drastically modified—the five storeys shown above street level were finally reduced to two, with the addition of a useful basement obtained by setting the building back some distance from the pavement and taking advantage of the sloping site. The attic storey, which now extends the full length of the building, was added when the second section was nearing completion (1908–9) and did not form part of the original competition design.

Nothing further is known about this drawing, and no complementary sheets exist, but even so, it provides interesting evidence of the architect's search for new forms in the early stages of the design. The qualities which are so admirable in the finished building, however, are conspicuously lacking in this preliminary sketch.

No trace can be found of the original competition drawings, and contemporary journals—usually a reliable source of information—seem to have

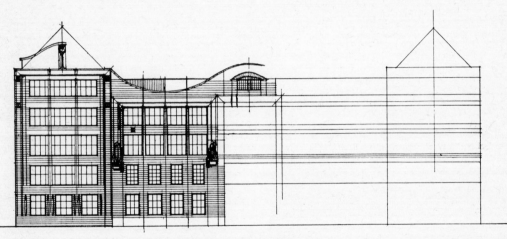

Figure 13. *circa* 1896. C. R. Mackintosh. Preliminary sketch for the North façade of the Glasgow School of Art.

taken no interest in the event, probably because the competition was limited, and purely a local affair. However, the illustrations given here (Fig. 15) and dated 1897, if not identical with the competition design, must have approximated closely to it.[1] They are of great importance.

It is now possible to comprehend fully the architect's original intentions, to see precisely how first he visualized the entire building, and to what extent his ideas were modified in the second section—the library wing—built between 1907 and 1909. To all intents and purposes the plan of the School has remained unaltered. It is 'E'-shaped with the arms pointing due south and the main stem —entirely occupied by spacious studios—facing north. The question of vertical

[1] These were the drawings approved by the Corporation and lodged in the city archives.

73

access, however, was singularly ill-considered in the original scheme and it was not possible to pass from the ground floor to the first floor except by the principal staircase—constructed of timber—in the centre of the building.[1] When the second section was commenced the architects were obliged to provide a fireproof staircase in each wing, and as a result, the curved western windows of the former Board Room in the east end are now enclosed in a staircase well (Plate 28B).

The east elevation, and half the south elevation of the School were built more

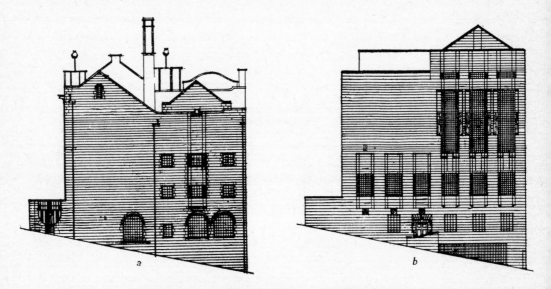

Figure 14. a and b. C. R. Mackintosh. (a) The West façade of the Glasgow School of Art as shown on the original drawings (1896), and (b) as redesigned in 1906–7.

or less as originally designed, but the west end, which shared the traditional character of the present east façade, was substantially remodelled, and now bears little resemblance to the first project. The date of this modification can be accurately estimated from two independent sources—a minute in the School records (September 1906) relegating the question of finishing the building to a special committee (on 25th September 1907 it is recorded that a letter was sent

[1] The city authorities apparently overlooked this dangerous arrangement at the time, but when the opening ceremony was performed elaborate fire precautions had to be taken: not only were buckets of sand and water placed in all the corridors, but a complement of firemen was stationed on each landing.

74

informing the 'Scotch Education Department' that the architect had completed his plans for the extension), and an ink drawing on cartridge paper, dated May 1907, showing the revised west elevation in its present form, with notes and enrichments in pencil added by Mackintosh.

Thus the west wing was redesigned between September 1906 and May 1907, and all the alterations indicated on Mackintosh's drawing—with the exception of the figure sculpture—were carried out as the architect intended. The change is very dramatic (Fig. 14). On the earlier drawing the west façade was dull and unimaginative. It was less well composed than the east front though somewhat similar in character. The library itself, though two storeys high, was expressed in elevation by diminutive windows of domestic proportions, the centre pair combined in a shallow oriel. The lecture theatre below the library was to have a pair of large, ugly, semi-circular headed windows which would have flooded the apartment with light. This illogical arrangement is as inexplicable as the inadequate library windows, and quite alien to the functional simplicity of the north elevation.

The revised west front, however, is one of the architect's most daring compositions—the very antithesis of the sedate, unenterprising earlier design. With its exciting horizontal rhythms and soaring verticals of glass and metal, its large plain surfaces of masonry, and rigid clean-cut angularity of form, this elevation represents not a step forward of a mere decade, but a stride of twenty or thirty years in British architectural development. And in fact few architects in Europe or America had produced a work of such uncompromising originality at this time.

It will be observed that Mackintosh introduced another floor and considerably increased the height of the south-westerly section when the new wing was added. His lecture room is still at the lowest level, but now has small windows. The six fine bays light studios in the Department of Architecture—architects of course being less particular than painters about north light. The three great windows above express clearly the presence of the galleried library. Their vigorous vertical movement is slowed down by the introduction of tiny horizontal windows in the composition room—originally the flower-painting room—and is finally brought to rest by the triangular gable of solid masonry. A fascinating composition that well repays careful study.

The library proper is one of the architect's best known interiors. It is shown as a much simpler apartment on the original drawings. Sturdy beams and posts are indicated, but from the aesthetic point of view the structural form was

75

not so skilfully exploited—the supporting pillars for instance pass through the gallery floor instead of rising free to the ceiling as they do now.

One of the most significant features of the west wing, however, is a small

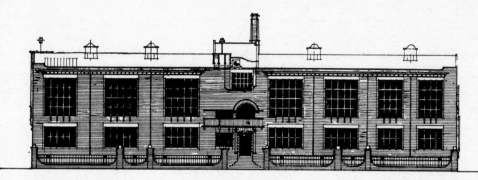

· FRONT ELEVATION ·

· SCALE ·   PLAN OF ENTRESOL OVER LAVATORIES ·   UPPER PART OF LIBRARY ·

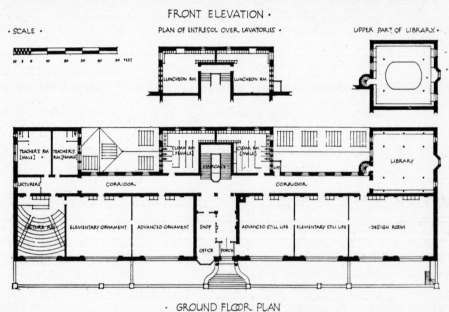

· GROUND FLOOR PLAN

Figure 15. 1896. The ground-floor plan and North elevation of the Glasgow School of Art as designed by Mackintosh in 1896.

cantilevered conservatory to the flower painting room above the library (which may be seen on Plate 26A). This glass-walled extension was thrust out into space some 15 feet from the wall surface, 80 feet or more above ground level—a most daring and exciting innovation unparalleled, to the best of the author's know-ledge, in architectural design at this time. But—and this is the important point —the conservatory appeared in Mackintosh's original drawings and, therefore, was conceived in 1896. Had it been designed with the new library wing in 1906 it would still have been a noteworthy contribution, but coming a decade earlier it is remarkable indeed—a striking anticipation of future trends.

From the historical point of view, however, the north front is the most important single element in the scheme, and it too stands today almost exactly as the architect conceived it. It is a thrilling composition with sweeping hori-zontal lines and vast, imposing windows. One can hardly imagine a more complete deviation from contemporary architectural practice.

On the original drawing illustrated here (Fig. 15), it will be observed that the great studio windows are linked by a debased form of cornice, or hood. This may have been incorporated by Mackintosh for diplomatic reasons, with an eye to the tastes and susceptibilities of the assessors, or perhaps to please his employers. Whatever the reason, this and other details of classical origin were discarded as building work progressed. In addition to the hood the parapet was omitted, and the roof cantilevered forward on simple wooden brackets, thus providing a far more effective termination to the façade; the applied pilasters flanking the doorway were rejected in favour of a simple, more Scottish archi-trave, and the heavy commonplace railings were entirely redesigned.

Mackintosh frequently expressed the view that an architect's drawings were but a rough indication of an idea. In his opinion the designer should be at liberty to modify them at will as work progressed; a building, like a piece of clay in the hands of a potter, should be moulded to its ultimate form by the architect-craftsman. To him the end always justified the means and if he thought his work could be improved, even when to all intents and purposes it was finished, he seldom hesitated to change it. The north front of the School of Art is a case in point, for when the first section was almost complete, he was dissatisfied with the appearance of the great windows and sent the mason back to round off all the sharp corners—a not inconsiderable 'extra' for the finance committee to meet.

Mackintosh was able to put into practice this delightful, but uneconomical theory for the first time when work began on the School, solely because at every point he had the headmaster's unqualified support. When the second section was commenced some ten years later, however, not even Newbery could prevail against the Governor's determination to stop his costly experiments. They absolutely refused to meet an interminable number of accounts for extras, and insisted that all drawings be signed by the Chairman of the Governors and the Convener of the Building Commitee, before they were passed to the contractor. Nevertheless Mackintosh fought hard and bitterly against all attempts to limit his authority—and it would seem he had a measure of success. For example the only surviving elevational drawing of the extension although in ink, signed and dated, has certain alterations roughly indicated in pencil, which in fact were carried into effect—most notably the elaborate mouldings round the doorway. And the window heads at ground-floor level are a different shape to those indicated on the drawing.

The School of Art is a building of absorbing interest—at first glance rather austere and forbidding, perhaps, like the line of Highland fortress-dwellings from which it springs—but, on closer acquaintance, a source of never ending delight.

Let us then examine the building in greater detail.

THE SITE

Mackintosh had to contend with a most awkward site. A long narrow rectangle in shape, it had a precipitous fall of about 30 feet from the north—Renfrew Street—to its southern extremity, which was bounded by a skating rink and overlooked, as now, by a conglomeration of nondescript buildings of various kinds.

At either end run cobbled streets of distressing inclination—Scott Street to the west and Dalhousie Street to the east. The problems created by the steep fall have been overcome to a certain extent by setting back the building from Renfrew Street, and by entering the ground floor at a fairly high level. Capacious studios and storage rooms are planned in the basement—the former lit by large light wells—and it is possible to obtain direct access to them at both east and west ends from Dalhousie Street and Scott Street respectively. It is interesting to note that even this site did not deter Mackintosh from considering the use of trees. Early in 1899, when the first section was nearing completion, he arranged for the draughtsmen in Honeyman and Keppie's office to present five trees, to be planted with suitable protection, at the corner of Renfrew Street and Dalhousie Street. No trace of them can be found, however, and it is doubtful if the plan ever materialized. The incident serves to emphasize the importance the architect attached to natural beauty as a foil to his rigid harmonies of stone, metal and glass.

78

PLAN

The Dalhousie Street entrance is flanked to the north by studios used for animal life drawing, and to the south by the janitor's house, which, incidentally, obtains east light only. The west end of the basement was designed to accommodate clay modelling and sculptors' studios, and also the lecture theatre.

At ground floor level and above, Mackintosh adopted the simple expedient of planning all the studios on the north side, and keeping the private rooms, cloak rooms, etc., to the south. Main acccess to the first floor is obtained by a large central staircase of timber, and to the upper floors by the fireproof staircases already mentioned, at either end of the long central corridor.

Few changes have taken place since the building was completed, the most noticeable being, perhaps, the Board Room, which was originally situated above the janitor's in the East Wing. This nobly proportioned, panelled room has four tall bow windows, two at either end, and a large stone fireplace— one of Mackintosh's first unorthodox fireplaces. For some reason—probably because the room was too large or the space too valuable—it was claimed as a studio, and the Governors met in the more intimate surroundings of the secretary's office. The old Board Room was used next for textile printing, and now houses an interesting collection of Mackintosh furniture and drawings.

The plan of the School—in the evolution of which John Honeyman played a not inconsiderable part—is notable for its directness and simplicity. A variant on the single-banked corridor type, it provides unusually spacious accommodation for a building of this nature. Flexibility is obtained by the provision of movable partitions between the studios instead of the customary solid walls, and mezzanine floors have been worked into the scheme to help compensate to some extent the lofty principal rooms which, on the first floor, have a ceiling height of 26 feet.

MATERIALS

The building is constructed of solid masonry and brickwork. The north, west and east façades are of masonry, a grey local 'Whitespot' and Giffnock stone being used, and the south façade is of brickwork, harled (roughcast) externally. All load-bearing internal walls are of brick. Steel lattice girders, or cast iron beams, encased in cement on metal laths are used for all major spans—

the lintels to the large northern windows, for example, 20 feet 2 inches long, consist of special cast iron box beams 24 inches by 30 inches, and the studios are spanned by rolled steel riveted lattice girders 24 inches by 12 inches, 37 feet long and stiffened at intervals of about 12 feet by cross members which carry the timber floors of the rooms above. The structural grid thus formed is not regular, and a bay of 20 feet alternates with a narrower one of 14 feet or 12 feet. The studios are separated by movable timber partitions which vary from about 11 feet to 15 feet in height; above these are light walls of plaster suspended from the ceiling. The entire studio floor area of both wings, to a depth of 35 feet from the north face, is thus perfectly free from structural load-bearing walls, and can be subdivided as desired.

With few exceptions, flat roofs are used throughout. The top storey which is set back about 11 feet from the north wall, is roofed in timber covered with asphalt; the remainder of the roof where not of glass, is similarly finished, except for the overhanging eaves which are covered with lead. Where pitched roofs are used, notably over the museum hall and on one or two of the basement craft rooms to the south, heavy timber trusses of unusual design are employed, and roof light obtained between them.

Concrete is used for foundations and all basement and sub-basement floors, and surprisingly enough, for the floor to the upper storey which is 6 to 7 inches thick. Otherwise, the floors throughout are of timber.

It is difficult to obtain a comprehensive view of the building because of the awkward site, narrow streets and surrounding property, and the visual effect is different from each approach.

THE EAST FRONT, 1897-9

In Dalhousie Street the end wall rises sheer from the pavement to a height of 80 feet or more, and the steep incline of the street accentuates the uncompromising severity of the large area of masonry and relatively small windows (Plate 24). One half of the façade—that forming the end wall of the line of studios to the north—is completely plain except for a tiny projecting shelf at parapet level surmounted by a gay pediment which serves no other purpose than to relieve the monotony of the wall surface, and to emphasize its scale.[1]

[1] Two large windows in this part of the wall at street level are later additions.

The southern portion of the façade contains a number of symmetrically disposed windows ranging in size from several of domestic proportions lighting the janitor's house, to a pair of tall narrow bow windows of the former Board Room.

The two contrasting parts, the unbroken surface of solid masonry and the section freely pierced by windows, are united by means of a polygonal oriel which projects slightly from the wall face and terminates well above parapet level. This is surmounted by a gay wrought iron feature representing the coat of arms of the city of Glasgow—a conventionalized bird and tree with four pendant bells (Plate 26D). The unhappy inverted salmon which also forms part of the Glasgow coat defeated even Mackintosh's ingenuity, and his bells were removed by venturesome students long ago.

Seen as a whole, the east façade—like the later west wing—embodies the surging vitality, the organic power and strength of a Dunderave or a Craigievar an impression derived from the architect's bold and forthright handling of form and materials. Nevertheless, it is surprisingly fresh in conception and no single detail is borrowed from a historical source.

THE NORTH FAÇADE, 1897–9 AND 1907–9

In direct contrast to the eastern façade, the north front (244 feet long) is entirely dominated by windows of enormous size and of completely unorthodox design (Plate 21). Newbery demanded the maximum amount of north light in his studios; the Governors appealed for 'a plain building'; and here, at least, Mackintosh must have satisfied everyone. The openings on the ground floor are 18 feet long by 12 feet high, and on the first floor 18 feet long by 22 feet high. The former are divided by broad unmoulded wooden frames 5 feet by 5½ inches into ten large rectangular panes about 5 feet 6 inches by 3 feet 3 inches and the latter into twenty panes of similar size. The glass is set well forward and this helps to preserve the surface of the façade, and consequently its unity, which might have been destroyed had deeper reveals been used.

The windows are asymmetrically disposed about the main entrance which is placed slightly off centre—there are four bays to the west and three bays to the east—a point that may be easily overlooked owing to the acute angle at which the façade must be viewed.

G

As already stated, there is no suggestion of a frieze or cornice as a vertical termination to the façade. The flat roof is boldly projected and the exposed rafters form a rhythmic, playful pattern against the rigid plane of masonry and glass which rises to meet them.

In relation to the vast studio windows, the main doorway seems small and rather insignificant on the drawing; actually it does not appear disproportionate, mainly on account of the preponderance of masonry at this point. The architect skilfully contrived to emphasize the door and central feature by reducing the window openings to a minimum and permitting a certain amount of decoration in and around the doorway itself—a modelled architrave, for example, with a large keystone embellished with one of his characteristic motives.[1] Additional emphasis is provided by a large semi-circular headed french window on the first floor, lighting the headmaster's room, and by the boldly projecting balcony with decorative metalwork. Above this again, there is a large unbroken mass of masonry, most of which constitutes a high parapet to a second balcony screening the window of the headmaster's private studio at second floor level —a feature largely invisible from the ground. To the left of the doorway is a projecting bay which develops at a higher level into the familiar polygonal oriel, with a wrought iron bird and tree motive used as a crowning feature. The tower houses a small stair from the headmaster's room to his studio, and at ground-floor level, the enquiry office in the main hall.

The somewhat uncompromising character of this façade has been cleverly relieved by the employment of decorative metal-work which characteristically serves a practical purpose (Plate 28A). Large iron brackets project at right angles to the wall from below the first floor windows, and from the extremity of each, a gracefully curved arm sweeps upwards and back to join the window frame in a ball of intricately intertwined metal, for all the world like the basket hilt of a sword. These brackets were intended to carry planks upon which window-cleaners' ladders could be erected, and at the same time they served as valuable stiffeners to the 22 feet high window frames. The architect employed them in such a way, however, that they form an indispensable part of the elevation, and a very necessary punctuation to the façade. The railings that protect the light wells on this side of the building serve a similar aesthetic purpose. They have an air of refinement, strength and gaiety which is achieved by the simplest

[1] William Moyes, then an apprentice with Honeyman & Keppie, tells the author that the keystone was modelled in plaster to full size by Mackintosh at the office. It was illustrated in *Dekorative Kunst*, March 1902.

possible means. For the most part they consist of perfectly plain cylindrical bars 7 feet high, rising to a broad horizontal capping. At intervals, there are sturdy groups of flat rolled strips 3 inches wide, terminating above the capping in a cluster of elongated spoon-like features surrounding a single member some 17 feet high carrying a pierced metal disc—the emblem of a tree.

Mackintosh makes able use of wrought iron throughout the School, and though it has been suggested earlier that he was inspired by James Sellars, the motives he employed in all this work owe little to tradition, and have their origin in the craftwork of *The Four*.

THE SOUTH FAÇADE

It would be difficult to find a greater contrast than that presented by the north and south elevations of the School of Art. The latter has relatively few and small windows, and cannot be comprehended in its entirety from any position at ground level—even at the east end of the site where there is a little open ground. Mackintosh, aware of this, made no attempt to follow the pattern of the east wing when work began on the second section of the School in 1907. (On his original design (1896) the south elevation was almost symmetrical about the centre block.)

Only from neighbouring windows and roof-tops is it possible to gain some idea of the form and complexity of the whole south façade, and at all points the grey roughcast walls tower grim and forbidding high above the adjacent property. Here, to a greater extent than anywhere else, the overwhelming impression is one of immense size rather than of architectural unity—an impression created largely by the irregular outline, and many small elements.

Suggestions have been made from time to time that the site between Sauchiehall Street and the School should be cleared and laid out with lawns and trees to form a worthy setting for Mackintosh's masterpiece. High land values would seem to make the realization of this scheme impossible, but if the objective were attained, the greatest care would have to be exercised in planning the site. Terraced gardens with skilful planting, however, would go a long way towards mitigating the austerity of the south front, and would provide a delightful foil to Mackintosh's dour, roughcast bastions.

THE WEST FAÇADE, 1907–9

Just as the Renfrew Street façade is remarkable for its unorthodox window treatment, so the elevation to Scott Street achieves its intensely dramatic effect by the use of glass, but in an entirely different manner (Plate 25). The northern half, the end wall of the line of studios, is again left completely plain except for three projecting windows on the ground floor. The southern half, on the other hand, is crowned by a gable, and is notable for three narrow projecting oriels 7 feet wide overall, which rise from strong corbels at ground-floor level to a height of 64 feet, terminating at the parapet. The panes are about 9 inches square and were framed in metal of remarkably slight section considering the enormous weight of the glass. The original iron frames were pronounced unsafe in 1947, and were replaced by bronze of slightly heavier section.

Scott Street, like Dalhousie Street to the east, falls very steeply, and the ground floor at this side is on the average 20 feet above street level, and the parapet some 95 feet high if measured from base to coping at the junction of the south and west walls.

The three very large windows on this elevation—25 feet high—light the library and internally start 3 feet above floor level, extending past the balcony into the room above. They are flanked by pairs of long, roughly hewed blocks linked together by an embracing moulding (Plate 96). These great half cylinders of stone, hanging it seems, like ear pendants from the narrow projecting window hoods, appear far too heavy and coarse even for this fortress-like façade. But in fact the west front was never completed. The blocks were merely prepared for the sculptors' chisel, and according to the architect, Cellini, Palladio and St. Francis were to have been the three principal subjects—a strangely assorted group. Mackintosh wisely proposed to introduce figure sculpture at this point to emphasize the importance of the library and more subtly to effect the transition from solid wall surface to window—to enable the eye to pass easily from plane to plane, texture to texture, in a horizontal direction—to counter, as it were, the surging verticals of the windows themselves. There can be little doubt that such an arrangement would have added considerably to the interest and architectural quality of the façade.

It is unfortunate that this work was not carried out under the architect's direction for he left no sketches or drawings—other than a few rough pencil notes—to indicate his intentions, and we have no large-scale examples of his sculpture elsewhere.

84

The west doorway (Plate 26c) which gives access to the basement floor and lecture room, is more ornate than either the east or the main doorway. It is surrounded by a heavy architrave and again by an elaborate secondary architrave, or hood, intended to enclose two carved figures—which, also, were not executed. The strength and vigour of this element is in keeping with the window treatment above.

On the adjacent façade—that part of the library wing facing south—the fenestration is entirely different. Here the architect incised his pattern of windows and allowed the plane surface of the great wall to dominate—an interesting and effective sculpturesque technique (Plate 96). Had he modelled this façade in high relief attention would have been deflected from the more important west front and the whole mass, seen three dimensionally, would have appeared restless and over-elaborate. As it is the eye passes quickly over the incised window pattern, merely noting and appreciating its close affinity to that of the neighbouring façade.

This skilful, daring, and imaginative composition is undoubtedly Mackintosh's most dramatic achievement.

THE INTERIOR

After the broad, dignified treatment of the front elevation of the School the vestibule and entrance hall seem cramped and gloomy, an impression which is mitigated little by the arched ceiling and predominance of white and cream panelling and plasterwork. Largely on account of this however—and as the architect intended, no doubt—the observer is drawn irresistibly towards the well-lit main staircase (Plate 29). Here the interplay of light and shade on intersecting and receding planes of open balustrading engenders a sense of freedom, spaciousness, and upward leaping movement which contrasts admirably with the crypt-like entrance hall. The staircase is remarkable for its high balustrading of simple vertical members of square section, terminated by unmoulded crowning cornices which run horizontally, and quite independently of the rake of the stair—a characteristic feature of Mackintosh's domestic work, and reminiscent of C. F. A. Voysey and George Walton. The square newel posts are carried up to various heights—from 8 feet 3 inches to 25 feet 3 inches—all taper from about 7 or 9 inches at the bottom to 6 inches and are crowned by square caps. The whole of the staircase is built of dressed yellow pine, originally stained dark brown, but the solid wall panelling is of sawn timbers set vertically and butt jointed.[1] In 1936 the stain was removed and the rich colouring of the natural wood emphasized by wax polishing—an act of vandalism which evoked a vigorous protest from a contributor to *The Scottish Daily Express*.[2] He does not appear to have obtained much support, however, and the staircase was not restored to its original colour. No other 'improvements' have been attempted, and, with its curious bird, tree, and bell centrepiece of wrought iron—another version of the Glasgow coat of arms—it remains one of the most striking features of the building.

The lofty corridors that run east and west from the staircase well are panelled in wood, and all the doors giving access to the various apartments were designed individually by the architect.[3] Each possesses a small stained and leaded glass window. The interior of the building abounds with such details—evidence of the care and attention Mackintosh lavished on the project.

The most impressive characteristic of the interior, however—and this applies to both wings—is the airy spaciousness of the studios, the most important apartments in the building. On the ground floor they measure 17 feet from floor to ceiling and on the first floor 26 feet: their average dimensions being about 35 feet square. With rooms of such proportions any other form of window opening than that adopted by the architect would have been unthinkable. By suppressing all small detail he achieved a breadth of effect that is wholly admirable. It is surprising, however, to find that a certain amount of roof lighting is provided in addition to these enormous areas of glass. The bold projection of the eaves on the north front is not obtained simply by extending the roof members as one might suppose, but by means of short rafters cantilevered from the external wall, and secured on the inside by brackets in precisely the same manner as in the Martyrs' School (Plate 20A). This form of construction—with the normal rafters terminating on an internal trimmer beam, and the verge of the roof cantilevered from the outer wall—enabled an almost continuous row of roof lights some 8 feet wide to be inserted parallel with the external wall. This elaborate and expensive arrangement was justified by the greatly improved

---

[1] In 1903 a relief panel portrait of Sir James Fleming, modelled by George Frampton, R.A., was built into the wall of the half landing over which is cantilevered the floor of the museum gallery. Mackintosh designed the polished steel surround in which the memorial is set. It was illustrated in *The Studio*, October 1911, p. 39.   [2] 30th September 1936.

[3] Several indifferent pictures of the studios, and an illustration of a corridor were published in *The Studio*, February, 1900, pp. 53–6.

86

diffusion of light throughout the apartment. Few Schools of Art, even today, can boast of such magnificent studios.

When the west wing was constructed in 1907–9 it was decided to increase the studio accommodation by adding an attic storey running the entire length of the building.[1] For reasons of economy and of structural necessity this was lightly built of timber, and set well back from the north front. By this arrangement the top storey is hardly visible from ground level, but in any case Mackintosh changed his window pattern to one of small regular squares which do not compete with the great panes of glass to the ground- and first-floor studios (Plate 23A).

The introduction of the attic storey, or second floor as it is called on the drawings, created several awkward planning problems, not the least of which was that of obtaining continuous east-to-west access, in other words of making a through corridor so that students and staff could pass from one end of the second floor to the other without the necessity of descending to the first floor by the terminal staircases. A reference to the plan (Plate 22A) will show that the lofty, top-lit museum hall prevented the architect from continuing his new corridor on the line of those already built and, moreover, the headmaster's studio rising high above the roof (Fig. 15) effectively blocked any east to west corridor above the main building.

Mackintosh tackled this problem in characteristic fashion. He built up the west wing to second-floor level, and added the attic storey to the east wing. Then from the curious 'loggia' with its heavy brick arches and thrilling canti-levered bays (Plate 27C) he built a light, elegant pavilion of timber resting partly on the museum parapet walls, and carried partly on iron brackets (Plate 26B). This by-passed the headmaster's studio, to which it was attached, and provided the necessary east to west link. The pavilion—or 'the hen run' as it is called by the students—is an extraordinary conception. It is framed in squares, and glazed from a height of three feet above floor level; it projects some 7 feet from the wall of the headmaster's studio and is carried for most of its length on triangular iron brackets—in much the same way as a shelf is supported (shown in section on Plate 23B). Quite apart from its utilitarian function 'the hen run'—and the loggia—provide a grandstand from which magnificent views over the city can be obtained. This alone would justify their existence.

---

[1] An excellent illustration of the interior of the attic storey appeared in *Modern Architecture*, by Bruno Taut (published by *The Studio*, 1929), p. 45.

87

THE LIBRARY

The west wing of the School is undoubtedly the more accomplished of the two sections, and of its many interesting features the library must take precedence. It is situated above the panelled lecture theatre—which, incidentally, has a curved stage with an ingenious sectional desk attachment that can be extended the full width of the room or removed altogether if desired. The library is about 35 feet square with a useful gallery and here Mackintosh went to some lengths to exploit the aesthetic possibilities of heavy timber construction. The soaring lines of the west windows are echoed internally by tall, square pillars of stained pine rising 17 feet from the floor to carry the coffered ceiling (Plates 30 and 31). Instead of bringing the front of the gallery forward to line with the pillars the architect set it back three feet on supporting beams, and filled the gap thus formed with tall balusters of square section, the edges of which were chamfered—or rather scalloped—at intervals and brightly coloured. The post and lintel construction of both gallery and ceiling is thus clearly revealed, and added emphasis given to the strong verticals.[1]

Solid panelling is used in the gallery front and alternate members are carried down about 12 inches as pendants and carved. The pattern is purely abstract, and no two pendants are identical in treatment. The walls are lined with built-in glass-fronted book-cases, and these, with the tables, chairs and magazine racks, were designed by the architect. The light fittings consist of small box-like shades suspended from the ceiling in clusters of a dozen or so. Each box almost completely encloses an individual lamp the light of which is directed vertically downwards, consequently the upper part of the room is left in deep shadow. However unpractical this arrangement may be, the visual effect of the clustered shades is very telling, and the sombre shadows were exactly to the architect's liking.

It has been stated that curves entirely disappeared in Mackintosh's later work at the School of Art,[2] but this is not so. The curves are there, but so subtly treated as to be almost unnoticeable. The front of the gallery, for example, is made of solid pieces of timber with overlapping joints, and all display a convex face—a refinement which gives an appreciable ripple of light and shade right round the apartment. Moreover, on closer examination it will be seen that

---

[1] It is interesting to compare the constructional features of the Library with the typical Japanese interior illustrated on Plate 8A—the resemblance is striking and will be referred to in a later chapter.

[2] Professor N. Pevsner, *Pioneers of the Modern Movement*, p. 160.

every minor decorative motive is curved, from the coloured notches in the balusters to the carved pendants, from the ogival apron of the bookcases to the pierced pattern on the table legs. Although the scale may be comparatively small, the cumulative effect gives just the right emphasis to the bold lines, and functional rigidity of the structural members—so much so in fact, that the refinements may be easily overlooked in admiration of the whole.

The library is an exotic apartment. The exciting verticals, the subtle harmonies of light and shade, and above all, the unrelieved sombre tones of the woodwork, engender a peculiar atmosphere of suspense and of mystery only paralleled in the authors' experience by the silent, brooding pinewoods of the Trossachs— nor is it inconceivable that Mackintosh went to this source for inspiration. Nowhere in the library do Mackintosh's *art nouveau* forms appear—there are no elongated females, no beads and wire, and no gesso panels. Gone too is the obvious symbolism, and the sweet sentimentality with which we have become familiar. Instead the structural form is emphasized, the lines are dynamic and masculine, and the architect's preoccupation with the manipulation and control of space is everywhere apparent. The Library, the very heart of this extra-ordinary building, is a remarkable achievement and in fact one of the most noteworthy interiors of the early twentieth century.

Of the remaining apartments two demand especial comment—the Head-master's Room and the Board Room. The former was undoubtedly one of Mackintosh's first 'white' rooms, and it contains a fine fireplace, this an early example with small wrought iron grate, plaster surround and wide spreading mantelpiece. The room is panelled to a height of about eight feet with single boards butt jointed; narrow cover strips extend from floor to crowning member, and the junction of timber and plaster is concealed by an attenuated cyma recta cornice of bold projection. At the base of the wall a simple cavetto cover strip about 2 inches high is used instead of the deep skirting then popular—both features, and the method of panelling, are characteristic of the architect.

Some useful built-in cupboards with doors decorated by small leaded-glass panels occupy part of one wall. Adjacent to these is a private stair to the studio screened by a light open framework of square balusters extending to the cornice, and panelled for part of its height in the form of a gay ogee curve (Plate 31A). The spacing of the balusters corresponds to that of the cover strips of the panelling; uniformity is thus preserved and the staircase included as an attractive yet unobtrusive feature of the room.

Mackintosh submitted estimates and drawings for furnishing the Head-master's Room in 1904. It would seem that his proposals were not greeted with enthusiasm, however, and Newbery was given the delicate task of persuading him to simplify his designs. The Headmaster either failed in his mission, or in turn delegated it to the Chairman of the Art Finance Committee, Mr. Patrick S. Dunn, who, three weeks later, reported that he had interviewed Mackintosh, and approved the style of the furniture 'with some slight modifications'. The furniture in question consisted of a fine circular oak table, a high-backed arm-chair and a number of small committee room chairs. A writing-desk in cypress was also designed but not carried out, and a haircord carpet was executed later —with the exception of the desk all these pieces are still in the building.

The Headmaster's Room—or Director's Room as it was soon re-named— is a charming and dignified apartment, admirably suited to its purpose; it is quite different in character from the new Board Room situated on the ground floor below.

When the Governors elected to vacate the original Board Room in the east wing, Mackintosh made a special apartment for them next to the general office, by erecting a permanent timber partition across an adjacent studio. The broad frame of the studio window provided adequate support, and enabled the struc-ture to be secured against the outside wall without affecting the external appear-ance of the building, yet permitting adequate light to both rooms. It is said that William Moyes, then a young draughtsman, had a great deal to do with this alteration which was completed just before work on the second section of the School commenced, but this is not so. In a letter to the author Mr. Moyes states that he had left Keppie before this work was finished, and had no hand in it, Mackintosh himself being responsible for the project. This is particularly interesting for, with the exception of a pedimented wooden doorway designed for the Lady Artists' Club, Glasgow, the new Board Room is the only example of neo-classical work executed by Mackintosh after the turn of the century. It may well have been intended as a subtle yet sardonic jest at the expense of the Governors, an august body of stylists who included in their number the great John Burnet and John Keppie, and who by this time, if not openly hostile, had little sympathy to waste on Mackintosh and his apparent idiosyncracies.

In the Board Room wooden panelling of a more traditional character is used—and there are fluted pilasters, each terminating in an imaginative Ionic capital (Plate 27B). These must have created no little consternation among the purists—Mackintosh appears to have taken as his model a normal Ionic capital

90

and virtually turned it inside out. The result is not unpleasing, though the form is rather attenuated and the transition from the cap to the heavy crowning cornice is not very skilfully effected. Then again, a peculiar type of decoration is employed below the capital, where, for a length of two or three feet, the flutes are interrupted at intervals by an irregular pattern of squares and rect-angles of varying sizes, reminiscent of musical notation. This unfamiliar cellular motive is allied to that employed in the balcony pendants in the Library. It is a form of decoration seemingly without precedent, though a regular motive of similar form was used by August Endell—an advocate of continental *art nouveau*—on the front of the buffet counter in his 'Buntes Theatre', Berlin, *circa* 1902.[1] The derivation of this pattern is difficult to establish, but Mackintosh no doubt employed it here to destroy the formality of the flutes, and to show his antipathy to the classical idiom.

The new Board Room is small and intimate, and fulfils its function satisfac-torily, but it is one of the least successful rooms that Mackintosh designed, and it cannot be compared with the magnificent apartment originally laid out for the Governors in the East Wing.

Quite apart from major features such as the library, the staircase, and the board room the School abounds in fascinating detail of all kinds. The attention is caught by wrought metal, by tiles set in grey cement, by coloured light filtering through jewel-like windows of leaded glass, or simply by the play of shade and shadow over richly stained and ingeniously modelled surfaces of timber. Everywhere one is conscious of the meticulous care with which the architect arranged each accent, each point of emphasis, to sustain the interest of the observer.

These comments, in conjunction with the photographs, will perhaps give some indication of the visual form and character of the School, and of the remarkable versatility of its designer. It is impossible, by such limited means, however, to capture the true spirit of the building. One cannot portray two-dimensionally the sweeping vistas, the ecstatic soaring lines of the staircase hall, or the vast, airy space of the magnificent studios. Nor can one paint in words the brooding mystery of the library, or the ironic gesture to orthodoxy contrived by the architect in the neo-classic board room. Like all works of art the School possesses many of the qualities of a living organism, and only by actual experi-ence can one obtain anything but a superficial knowledge of the building, and the creative genius of its author.

[1] Illustrated in *Deutsche Kunst und Dekoration*, vol. IX, p. 285, 1902.

The new Glasgow School of Art was by no means a superficial essay by an *art nouveau* decorator as the critics contended, but a building designed by an architect with a superb grasp of the three-dimensional nature of his art; a building designed primarily to fulfil its purpose well, with, of course, some artist's licence, for the time of the functionalist pure and simple had not yet come. It was and it remains Mackintosh's most representative work, and it is undoubtedly his most important contribution to the new movement.

V

HOUSES ON HILLS

In the last quarter of the nineteenth century domestic architecture in Scotland, as elsewhere, was notable more for its eclecticism than for its good taste; this, of course, applied particularly to the Clyde Valley region, which absorbed the full impact of the Industrial Revolution. The majority of practising architects, when they took an interest in domestic work, seemed quite content to follow the dictates of fashion which demanded either the Scottish Baronial style, ornate or otherwise according to the length of the client's purse, or more subdued essays in the classical idiom, especially that popularized by Alexander 'Greek' Thomson.

Towards the end of the century, however, a serious attempt was made to revivify the Scottish vernacular and to awaken public interest in old Scots buildings. The initiator of this movement, if movement it may be called, was Sir Rowand Anderson (1834–1921) and his influence was greatly extended by his pupil Sir Robert Lorimer (1864–1929) who returned to Scotland from Bodley's London office in 1892. Both men frankly adopted native forms—crow-stepped gables, angle turrets, dormers and the like—and used them with considerable skill in an attempt to produce a modernized traditional style. Often their work was delightful and charming, and invariably the craftsmanship is of the highest order, but their positive contribution to architectural development is questionable. Sir John Stirling Maxwell, in discussing Lorimer's work, has laid his finger on the crux of the matter, for he says: ' . . . his (Lorimer's) houses are so completely saturated with the spirit of the old builders and show so complete a mastery of their technique that those who come unexpectedly upon them for the first time . . . are for the moment completely staggered and where all is new, are left wondering how much is old.'[1] This contradiction is apparent in the work of both men, and however harmoniously contrived, their domestic buildings by and large are revivalist in the spirit and the letter.

The amount of Mackintosh's domestic work is insignificant in comparison with that of his prolific fellow countrymen. He executed but two commissions of importance, *Windyhill* (1900), built for William Davidson at Kilmacolm, and *Hill House* (1902–3), Helensburgh, for W. W. Blackie, yet both of these, while retaining traditional characteristics, belong unmistakably to the twentieth century, and the observer is not left in doubt for a moment how much is old, how much is new. Mackintosh's traditional features are derivative rather than imitative, and for the most part arise naturally from a simple plan. His façades, usually plain with little surface modelling, are pierced by small rhythmically disposed windows. He favoured an L-shaped plan, itself a traditional form, which gave him one dominant, sweeping roof with an unbroken ridge, and on the main elevation at least, an uninterrupted eaves line. His roofs invariably terminated in a gable which, whenever possible, embodied a sturdy chimney-stack. The ubiquitous crow-stepped gable, a legacy, it is said from a less opulent age when dressed copings were a luxury, does not appear in any of his executed work.[2] At both *Windyhill* and *Hill House* identifiable motives of a traditional character are rare, and the link with the past is expressed in the form and spirit of the buildings, not by the use of antiquarian detail.

Then, again, Mackintosh always paid close attention to siting, orientation and layout; his houses seem to form part of the landscape, they grow from the soil, and at *Hill House* in particular, the garden was arranged to the architect's instructions in order to enhance the long sweeping lines of the principal façade. At *Windyhill*, built on a precipitous open site, he used garden furniture and

---

[1] *Shrines and Homes of Scotland*, p. 206.

[2] The author has in his collection, however, a drawing by Mackintosh displaying this and other features beloved by the baronialists—it does not have a title and nothing further is known about it.

openwork screens to help unite man-made and natural elements. Seen from the south (Plate 33) his subtle play on the square is most noticeable—in the foreground it appears as a gay skipping rhythm cut from the grass, a two-dimensional pattern picked up in the vertical plane by the pierced back of a garden seat and then thrown, as it were, high against the building itself where window-bars echo the same theme.

Each of Mackintosh's houses was planned carefully to meet the requirements of a particular family—not as a showpiece demonstrating the archaeological knowledge of its designer—a point emphasized frequently by both his clients in conversation with the author.

It will be remembered that Mackintosh had already done some work for the Davidsons at their house *Gladsmuir*, Kilmacolm, about 1895, and he knew the family well. William Davidson Junior, in particular, became devoted to the enigmatical young architect in whom he recognized the same burning fires of evangelism that had animated the pioneers of the Glasgow School of Painters. By this time (1900), however, Mr. Davidson was a city business man of some standing, and a discriminating patron of contemporary art. He had already built up an interesting collection of work by *The Boys from Glasgow*—Hornel, Peploe, Hunter and the rest—and acquired several paintings by Pringle, the strange artist-optician of the Saltmarket, then practically unknown, but whose work has become greatly prized in recent years. Thus Mackintosh was fortunate in securing for his first major domestic project a client of unusual perception, a man who was not only benevolently disposed towards the new art movement, but who was willing to be guided by him in all things—and if necessary, to make some personal sacrifice to gratify his wishes. He was asked to undertake the design of a house for the Davidsons at Kilmacolm, Renfrewshire, in 1899.

Little information is to be had regarding the initial stages of the project—apart from the entertaining fact that when the architect's drawings had been approved and preparations made for building to begin, a small ceremony was performed on the site, Mrs. Davidson cut the first sod, a toast to the success of the scheme was drunk from a goblet designed for the occasion by Mackintosh, and the house was christened *Windyhill*. Work on the building and its furnishings proceeded satisfactorily, if somewhat slowly, and it was occupied late in 1901.

Mr. W. W. Blackie, on the other hand, made interesting notes of his impressions of the architect and of their close association during the early 1900's. It seems that in the spring of 1902, the Blackie family decided to leave their

95

home at Dunblane, Stirlingshire, and build a house more to their liking nearer the coast. With this object in view they acquired a magnificent hillside site at Helensburgh, overlooking the Clyde estuary. They were then faced with the problem of choosing an architect. It chanced that Talwin Morris—art manager of Blackie's firm—heard of the project and advised his employer to consult his friend Mackintosh who, he pointed out, was the designer of the new Glasgow School of Art. Mr. Blackie was somewhat taken aback at this, thinking that so important a person would be too big a man for such a trivial commission, but Talwin Morris persisted and promised to ask Mackintosh to call the next day. The meeting of the two men is described by Mr. Blackie in these words: 'When he entered my room I was astonished at the youthfulness of the distinguished architect . . . here was a truly great man who, by comparison with myself, I esteemed to be a mere boy.' The interview did not last long, agreement was quickly reached on fundamentals. To remove any lingering doubts as to his competence Mackintosh suggested that Mr. and Mrs. Blackie should see *Windyhill* which had just been completed. The Davidsons at once acquiesced in this proposal, and upon visiting Kilmacolm the Blackies were convinced that they had been well advised in their choice of architect. Mackintosh was instructed to proceed. Before preparing the preliminary sketches, however—and this is a most interesting point—he insisted upon spending some time with the family in order that he might, to use Mr. Blackie's phrase, 'judge what manner of folk he was to cater for'. And so he was invited to spend a weekend with the family at Dunblane. On entering their house for the first time, he was delighted to see an oak wardrobe in the hall which he himself had designed, along with other articles of furniture, for Messrs. Guthrie & Wells, of Glasgow. This was taken to be a good omen by all concerned.

In due course, plans for the new house were submitted and internal details discussed. Mackintosh would not prepare further drawings until the plan arrangement was finally agreed upon. Once this stage was reached, however, he soon produced the necessary elevations, and though his first design was not approved by his clients, in a few days he evolved a new set of drawings which were acceptable, and work on the building commenced. Everything seems to have gone well until a prolonged strike at the Ballachulish slate quarries caused considerable delay in the roofing. It was suggested to Mackintosh that he should find an alternative source for his material but he was obdurate, and refused to consider any other slate of whatever colour, texture or quality; the dark blue-grey hue of the Ballachulish quarries exactly suited his purpose and nothing would induce him to change his scheme. His clients had to wait patiently until supplies arrived, and they were not able to take possession of the house until March 1904.

Notwithstanding this, and other minor differences of opinion, Mr. Blackie pays tribute to the architect's skilful handling of the project; to his meticulous care of every detail both practical and aesthetic, to his minute attention to frequently overlooked incidentals such as fitted cupboards, linen stores, drawers for cutlery, china, etc., and in particular, to the trouble he took in planning the service quarters of the house.

'With him,' Mr. Blackie says, 'the practical purpose came first. The pleasing design followed of itself as it were.

'Every detail inside as well as outside, received his careful, I might say loving, attention.

'During the planning and the building of the 'Hill House' I necessarily saw much of Mackintosh and could not but recognize, with wonder, his inexhaustible fertility in design and astonishing powers of work. Withal, he was a man of much practical competence, satisfactory to deal with in every way, and of a most likable nature. . . .'

'REDLANDS', BRIDGE OF WEIR, circa 1899

Before examining the two houses in detail, a house *Redlands*, Bridge of Weir,[1] must be noted. This building stands in the same relationship to Mr. Davidson's and Mr. Blackie's houses as do the Martyrs' School and the Medical College to the School of Art. The house was built for a personal friend of John Keppie, and the design was controlled principally by him—he was especially proud of the spacious 'baronial' hall and great stone-built fireplace. The L-shaped plan and arrangement of rooms, and certain external features, notably a semi-circular staircase bay and sturdy gable, are, however, very much in the Mackintosh manner, and it is probable that he had a good deal to do with the project. Unlike *Windyhill* and *Hill House*, which are built of brick and are rough-cast externally, this building is constructed of red sandstone—in fact the elevational treatment recalls *Redclyffe*, Mackintosh's first commission, rather than either of the later examples.

[1] Illustrated in *Academy Architecture*, 1899.

'WINDYHILL' AND 'HILL HOUSE'

The plans of *Windyhill* and *Hill House* are similar in character though different in size, *Hill House* being the more ambitious project. In each case the building consists of a principal block running east and west with a service wing at right angles, the internal angle thus formed enclosing on two sides a diminutive ornamental courtyard. The *Windyhill* plan is the more simple and straightforward of the two: the service wing is better integrated with the main block and the only unpleasant feature is the juxtaposition of a semi-circular staircase and a semi-octagonal bay to the play-room at the west end—the latter however is only one storey high and consequently the staircase dominates on elevation.

Although Mackintosh employed the typical Scottish newel stair[1] on only one occasion—at *Hill House*—he always paid particular attention to the staircase as an important plan element. He favoured a spacious semi-circular bay, avoiding winders wherever possible by introducing a broad half landing—a simple expedient which gives surprising dignity to the staircases of *Windyhill* and *Hill House*.

Here too he used a tall, square newel post rising almost to ceiling level crowned by a square cap in the Voysey manner. On the first-floor landing, plain oak boards on end (of about 6 inches by $\frac{3}{4}$ inch section) were substituted for the familiar square balusters—a most attractive innovation. One is conscious too that the architect always studied carefully the play of light and shade in and around a stairway. At each house the staircase flows pleasantly into the hall, a channel, as it were, for indirect light, broken up and diffused as at the School of Art by ranges of lofty square balusters.

Despite its greater size, the *Hill House* plan differs from its predecessor only in detail; the entrance is to the west instead of through a small courtyard on the north and this necessitated a change in the position of the staircase, though

[1] Staircases expressed externally as a circular tower or turret have been a feature of Scots domestic work since the sixteenth century. They assumed added importance largely on account of the reluctance of builders to employ internal corridors; *Argyll's Lodging*, Stirling, for example, a notable town house built as late as 1632, possessed no internal passages, access being obtained to most of the rooms by means of four turrets, one at each corner of a small square courtyard. The transition to formal planning with internal corridors seems to have been made in Scotland *circa* 1700 in the work of Sir William Bruce of Kinross (d. 1710), the architect of Holyrood (1679), who was closely associated with Wren, and was familiar with English practice.

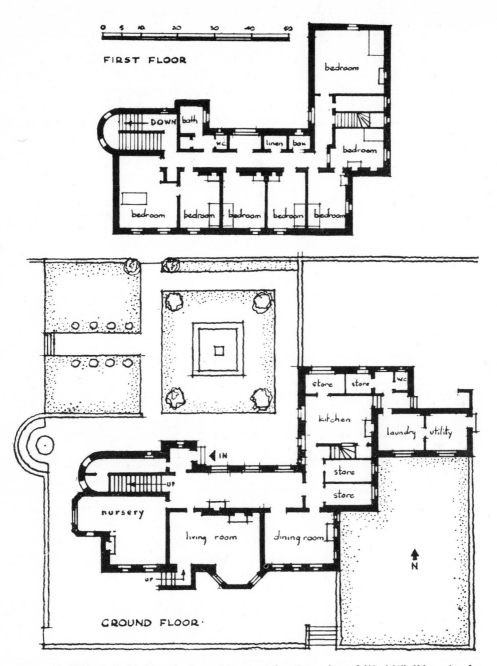

FIRST FLOOR

bedroom

DOWN bath

wc linen box

bedroom

bedroom

bedroom bedroom bedroom bedroom bedroom

store store wc

kitchen

laundry utility

IN

store

store

UP

nursery

living room dining room

UP

N

GROUND FLOOR·

Figure 16. 1900. C. R. Mackintosh. Ground-floor and first-floor plans of *Windyhill*, Kilmacolm, for William Davidson, Esq.

99

not in its form and proportions. The shape of the plan, however, is more restless and broken; the junction of the two wings is not so well considered and the architect introduced a circular staircase tower in an attempt to bind them more securely together. His difficulty with this angle can be appreciated better

Figure 17. 1902–3. C. R. Mackintosh. Plans of *Hill House*, Helensburgh, for W. W. Blackie, Esq.

when it is realized that the service wing is three storeys high and the main block but two storeys—at *Windyhill*, on the other hand, the service quarters were entirely dominated by the principal wing.

Grey or red sandstone was the popular material for large country houses in the Clyde Valley in the early 1900's, but like Voysey, Mackintosh achieved

100

character and individuality by using silver-grey rough-cast to unify his designs. Whether consciously or unconsciously, in this he reverted again to tradition, for harling, or rough-casting, was used in Scotland as early as the fifteenth century if not before, as a method of weatherproofing external walls built of rubble. In both *Windyhill* and *Hill House* the harling is returned into the window openings, a characteristic treatment in cottage building; in better-class work, however, it is customary to use dressed stone for sills, lintels and reveals, a method employed with reserve by Mackintosh. Only two small windows on the west façade of *Hill House* and the main doorway have stone dressings, on every other opening the rough-cast stops against the wooden sill and frame.

Generally speaking *Windyhill* has the unpretentious character of a Scottish farmhouse, with grey harled walls, steeply pitched roofs, and eaves of little or no projection. The southern façade is severe in the extreme. The plain wall surface is unbroken except for a small bay to the drawing-room, a few regimented windows and a rainwater pipe which assumes added importance by its central position and slight projection. Later, the Davidsons had wooden shutters fitted to the windows in an attempt to relieve the grim, forbidding appearance of this façade (Plate 33).

The house stands on the top of a steep hill and is approached from the north through a tiny courtyard containing a square pool flanked by trimmed yews (Plate 34A). Although on a small scale, the effect of enclosure is cleverly contrived and the result is quite charming. At this side of the house—a more sheltered position—Mackintosh used windows of widely varying shapes and sizes. On the service wing there are two triangular roofed dormers of traditional character, yet near to the doorway (Plate 35A) is a flat-roofed dormer containing an unusual horizontal window about 7 feet long and 2 feet high. The combined entrance feature and semicircular staircase bay with its tall, narrow lights belongs unmistakably to the twentieth century and is an innovation of some significance. Mackintosh seems to have been the first to employ this form— a form which was considered to be the last word in the 1920's.

Though we may admire the architect's imaginative treatment of the staircase, especially from inside the house, the exterior, nevertheless, is very much out of character with the rest of the building and appears rather incongruous against the traditional courtyard elevations. This raises an important issue. Originality and unorthodoxy in themselves are not always to be commended, though in our present unstable society they are usually considered to be so. Neither have anything whatever to do with the merit of a building—or a painting, or piece

101

of sculpture—as a work of art. It is always the unity, the wholeness of such a work, and the beauty of its form and proportions, the relationship of part to part, which proclaim its true worth. Unity and wholeness in the architectural context, of course, imply fitness for purpose, and the correct selection and use of materials. At *Windyhill*, Mackintosh lost for a moment his vision of the whole, his appreciation of the architectural form he was modelling, and, in consequence, the staircase feature is out of harmony with the more conventional main block. At *Hill House*, on the other hand, the relationship between the modern staircase unit and the traditional form of the house proper is more skilfully contrived.

Mr. Blackie's house is situated on a gently sloping open hillside, and Mackintosh laid out the garden with great care. The house is built on a terrace supported by a fine stone retaining wall which runs from west to east and terminates in a sturdy conical-roofed tool shed. To the south of this there is a terraced lawn, and finally a tennis court, all of which combine to emphasize the horizontality of the house itself, and form a contrast with the soaring vertical lines of the service wing. Mackintosh's preoccupation with landscape design did not escape notice and Fernando Agnoletti, Professor of Italian at Glasgow University, writing in 1905, observed that the charming character of the house is ' . . . less the result of the natural beauty of the situation itself than that of the artistic exploitation of every opportunity that offers itself.'[1]

In contrast to *Windyhill* the southern façade of *Hill House* is friendly and inviting, an effect due in no small part to the overhanging eaves and the interest created by the bold projection of the lofty three-storeyed gable. The western end of this elevation is punctuated by a curved bay containing the french windows of the library, and on the first floor, a small square window flanked by flat stone wings, originally intended as a field for low relief carving.

The pleasant horizontal lines of this elevation, the simple grouping of elements, and the complete absence of restless detail produce an air of ingenuous efficiency that is refreshing today, but which, in the complacent world of 1903, must have been quite startling.

Hill House is most impressive when seen from the short carriage-way which leads to the main entrance (Plate 36). The gable wall is modelled like a Nicholson sculptured relief. It is entirely plain except for three small slit windows, and the doorway is combined with a sturdy battered chimney to form an unusual asymmetrical element projecting from the wall some eighteen inches. This

[1] *Deutsche Kunst und Dekoration*, March 1905.

102

motive is reminiscent of the entrance of the School of Art—but here it is designed with even greater subtlety, and effectively establishes the importance of the doorway.

The view from the south-east is not so satisfying (Plate 38). There is a notice-able lack of cohesion between the service wing—which from this position appears as big as, if not larger than, the main building—and what for convenience might be called the dining-room block. The axes of these two elements are parallel, and the weakness of the angle formed by recessing the service wing is but thinly veiled by the interposition of a conical roofed staircase tower. The strong vertical accent provided by this feature is still further emphasized by the proximity of sturdy chimney-stacks. The interplay of simple geometrical forms at this point recalls seventeenth-century Scottish work, yet without any suggestion of superficial romanticism. Architecturally the grouping is not good.

After the huge expanses of glass employed at the School of Art, Mackintosh's predilection for small irregularly distributed windows may require explanation. After some investigation, the author discovered a craftsman who had actually discussed this point with him. The architect had explained that, in his opinion, a sense of enclosure, of warmth and security was the most desirable attribute of any dwelling. The house was primarily a place of shelter and refuge, in, but not of, the landscape. Furthermore, the entire conception of the house was quite distinct from that of a garden the one artificial and confining space; the other natural, free and virtually boundless. Each possessed distinctive characteristics which should be acknowledged and respected by an architect.

These views are particularly interesting in the light of subsequent developments, for one of the most persistent dogmas of the modern movement in architecture has been the desirability of eliminating the solid wall as a restricting factor in house design, and by using glass in place of bricks and mortar, to render obsolete the terms 'interior' and 'exterior', to make the garden an extension of the house itself. Mackintosh's point of view, however, is more logical and certainly more practical in the north country, and consequently it is not surprising to find his methods of building conforming closely to traditional practice (Plate 37A).

Apart from the principal façades to both houses in which the shape and disposition of windows is reminiscent of seventeenth- and eighteenth-century work, Mackintosh seems to have thrown discretion to the winds and used square, vertical and horizontal openings in close proximity, and bearing little if any relationship to each other. In this respect he diverged from traditional Scottish practice in which a window of pleasant proportions, the height about equal to twice the width, was commonly used. At *Hill House* some attempt was made to align lintels and sills on the façades overlooking the courtyard, but at *Windyhill* no such precautions were taken and the two intersecting wings lack unity. Another curious feature is the architect's arbitrary use of window bars; panes of four different sizes occur in the courtyard at *Windyhill*, and contribute in no small degree to the general air of restlessness. Here again, the traditional sub-division of six units to each sash seems to have been entirely ignored; four, six, eight, twelve lights of varying sizes appear. Nor did the architect take advantage of the pane as a valuable module in preserving scale, and ensuring some degree of unity between windows of different shapes—a factor long appreciated in old Scottish and English work, and rarely lost sight of by Voysey and Mackintosh's English contemporaries.

These points and others revealed in the accompanying illustrations demonstrate how the architect drew freely upon tradition, rejecting certain features, introducing new ideas of his own invention, or moulding old forms to suit his purpose; often, though not invariably, with notable success.

Mackintosh was able to supervise the interior decoration and to design fireplaces, built-in fittings, and some furniture for both houses. Neither of his clients could afford to give him a completely free hand, however, for his furniture was usually expensive—the penalty paid by anyone refusing to accept stock patterns.

Internally one of the most attractive features of both houses is a spacious lounge-hall of which the staircase forms an integral part. The *Windyhill* example (Plate 35B) is the less successful, largely because it lacks cohesion and scale. Each opening or recess—and there are many—in the white-papered walls is framed with narrow bands of dark oak, and the door architraves penetrate beyond the line of the frieze-rail in order to provide space for ventilation over the door itself. (Mackintosh considered it most desirable to provide egress in this position for foul air which, he contended, always collected near the ceiling and was most injurious to health.) The wall surface is thus broken up into irregular panels and the apparent height of the apartment reduced by the incidence of a dark frieze-rail which extends like a narrow thread from architrave to architrave. At *Hill House* on the other hand, although the same general scheme was followed, the effect is much finer and the relationship between wall

104

surfaces is more pleasing (Plate 40). Colour was introduced here, too, by a simple stencilled design in delicate tints of green and rose, repeating rhythmically right round the apartment.

The drawing-rooms were in the white tradition established by Mackintosh at the Mains Street Flat. At *Windyhill* the walls were entirely plain from floor to ceiling: at *Hill House* they had a delicate stencilled pattern of tall panels in silver, rose and pale green, a combination favoured by Margaret Macdonald. The *Hill House* drawing-room however, was a much more mature work, designed to meet the varying needs of the family. Especially delightful, even today, is the large bay window—virtually a sun room—from which the whole panorama of the Clyde estuary may be surveyed; it is charmingly decorated and equipped with a luxurious window-seat and book-racks (Plate 41). There is also a spacious alcove designed to accommodate a grand piano, and the architect provided a third centre of interest in the fireplace, cosily tucked away on the internal wall, and well screened from the door. The apartment is at once a summer and a winter room, easily adaptable to the rapidly changing climate of the north. Its windows are adequate on the sunniest day, and do not prove an embarrassment in winter; the whole character of the room can be changed quickly by directing attention towards the fireplace or to the musicians' alcove, or, of course, to the terrace and garden.

From the accompanying plans it will be evident that the *Windyhill* drawing-room is much simpler in conception, though it too has a small bay, the prototype perhaps, of the later sun-parlour. The fireplace, however, is the more attractive and here Mackintosh experimented with a surround of a new type (Plate 34B). Instead of the familiar grey plaster, he used a rich golden mosaic with five small circular rose-like motives of coloured enamel and glass. He employed insets of this type on many occasions subsequently. They were made from shallow zinc trays of the required shape—usually circular or square— filled with cement into which was pressed small pieces of mirror-glass, mother of pearl, enamel and so on, to form the design. When set, the trays were embedded flush with the surface of the surround. This fireplace is a charming feature and, but for its mantelpiece, would fit perfectly into a present-day setting. The example at *Hill House* is not quite so successful: bigger insets were used, and, consequently, the broad effect of the mosaic was largely lost.

The dining-rooms in both houses were similar in character to that at Mains Street, except that they were panelled to picture-rail level entirely in dark stained wood.

105

One of the pleasantest rooms Mackintosh designed was the library at *Hill House* (Plate 39). A small, cosy apartment facing south, it is lined with book-shelves and cupboards in dark oak, brightened at regular intervals by inlaid squares of white enamel or erinoid (a translucent plastic material). The fireplace and overmantel are admirable with restful horizontal lines and rhythmic squares taking the place of the sweeping verticals used in the other principal rooms. After the brilliance and sparkle of the drawing-room, and the dignified rhythms of the staircase-hall, the architect seems to have struck exactly the right note here.

Following the Mains Street pattern, the principal bedrooms at both houses were fresh and springlike: white wallpaper, ivory white enamel for the wood-work, and delicate stencilled patterns in mauve and green, combined to form an elegant setting for characteristic furniture. Mackintosh always made extensive use of luxuriously fitted, built-in wardrobes, and his bedsteads—other than the four-posters—are of exceptional interest (Plates 34C and 42B). These were of very heavy construction; the ends being of solid timber, not framed. Twin beds in the author's possession are built of butt jointed oak boards 13 inches wide by 1 inch thick, laid on edge. A simple moulding covers the top. At the centre of the foot and the head, this is modelled round inlaid coloured glass tesserae. The *Windyhill* bed (Plate 34C)—painted white—is a particularly fine example, and a remarkable precursor of twentieth-century developments. Owing to the generosity of the Davidson family, it is safely housed now at the Glasgow School of Art.

The bedroom at *Windyhill* was a considerable improvement on the Mains Street example, both from the point of view of general ensemble, and the design of individual pieces of furniture. The *Hill House* room is larger and more elaborate, a delightful apartment with little *art nouveau* detail and certainly one of the best interiors Mackintosh designed (Plate 42). All three rooms represent a notable advance on contemporary work in Britain, or abroad for that matter, and captivated all who had the good fortune to see them. Even Kalas' eulogy on Mains Street was not without parallel, and Fernando Agnoletti, lost in admiration, describes the *Hill House* bedroom as ' . . . the exotic bloom of a strange plant, not made but grown, not sensuous but chaste, not floating like a dream, but firm and decisive like the poetical vision of a fact that is expressed in the only possible art form. . . .' This beautifully illustrated panegyric, published by Alexander Koch in *Deutsche Kunst und Dekoration*,[1]

[1] Vol. VI, No. 1, March 1905, p. 337. *Windyhill* was well illustrated in *Dekorative Kunst*, March 1902.

greatly enhanced Mackintosh's prestige on the continent. At home, however, neither *Windyhill* nor *Hill House* excited undue comment in architectural circles. Apart from four small pictures of the latter in *Academy Architecture* they do not appear to have been noted in the professional press. It was left to Koch, Hermann Muthesius[1] and others, to sing Mackintosh's praises, and this they did with enthusiasm.

The conditions essential to the development of Mackintosh's peculiar genius were fulfilled both at *Windyhill* and *Hill House*, namely the enthusiastic and wholehearted co-operation of his clients—whenever his authority was questioned, however, the picture changed. In this regard it is interesting to compare his work for the Davidsons and the Blackies with the two houses of similar pretensions he designed subsequently (1906–7)—*Mosside*, Kilmacolm, for Mr. H. B. Collins, and *Auchinibert*, Killearn, for Mr. F. J. Shand. In both cases his clients had ideas of their own, and were reluctant to give him a free hand. By all accounts Mackintosh found Mr. Collins a difficult man to deal with, and apparently Mrs. Shand had very definite opinions on the style, internal arrangement, and decoration of her future home. It is hardly surprising, therefore, to discover that both houses differ in character from their predecessors, but, in fact, the difference is so marked that at first glance neither would be ascribed to Mackintosh.

'MOSSIDE', 1906

Of the two houses, *Mosside* (Plate 43)[2] is the more interesting. It is a large house of T-shaped plan, beautifully situated on the shore of a loch, about two

---

[1] Hermann Muthesius is an important figure who crosses the stage again and again throughout this study. He was attached to the German Embassy in London from 1896–1903 for the purpose of studying English domestic architecture and craftwork. He became, later, one of the most influential personalities in the German 'modern' movement. His publications include *Das Englische Baukunst der Gegenwart*, 1900 (see Chap. 3, page 61), *Moderne Landhaus* (1905), *Die Neuere Kirchliche Baukunst* (1901), and a voluminous treatise *Das Englische Haus* (1905), in which Mackintosh figured. None of these has been translated into English.

[2] Unfortunately the author's photographs of *Mosside* have been damaged beyond repair and the surviving example included here (Plate 43A), while clearly illustrating the masonry and unusual windows, does not do justice to the house.

miles north of the village of Kilmacolm. The meagre drawings that survive suggest that an old tower, or ruined cottage, was incorporated in the new structure though the author could not obtain confirmation of this locally. The walls of the house are of exceptionally thick random rubble, the bonding is irregular and the surface texture coarse to a degree not met with in any of the architect's other work. The splayed window openings, too, are unfamiliar and are used freely on the eastern side of the house. Elsewhere windows of all shapes and sizes seem to have been scattered at random.

The building looks like a converted mill, or as the villagers were quick to observe, a prison. Unquestionably it has a most forbidding aspect, especially when seen from the loch-side. As at *Hill House* the principal rooms are placed on the north side of the main corridor (overlooking the loch), but with the service wing at right angles forming the leg of the 'T'. The plan is tortuous, particularly in the kitchens and servants' quarters where awkward changes in floor level occur.[1] The service wing is roofed with finely coloured, variegated stone slates of a warm brown hue; the main block, for some inexplicable reason, is covered with red tiles. In 1944 the eastern wing was re-roofed with green slates and an inelegant red ridge. Thus each arm of the T-shaped plan is crowned by a differently coloured roof; an ill-considered arrangement which has by no means enhanced the appearance of the building.

The inside of the house belies its forbidding exterior. The rooms are lofty and well proportioned, and the small windows provide adequate, if not abundant light. Mackintosh must have exercised some control over the furnishing and decoration too, for every room originally possessed one of his fireplaces—a few of his narrow grates still survive.

Mosside is a strange building—a fairy-story house which Arthur Rackham might have peopled with gnomes and elves or Jessie King with bejewelled princesses. It is quite unlike any of Mackintosh's other buildings and its rugged charm is due in no small part to its austerely beautiful setting, and to the rich warm colouring and texture of the local stone.

[1] The plan reproduced on Plate 43 is copied from the architect's first sketch and was altered subsequently—the service wing is now more complicated as the photograph of the building indicates.

108

'AUCHENBOTHIE', 1901

Before building *Mosside* Mackintosh had executed several small commissions for Mr. Collins in or near Kilmacolm—mainly alterations to existing property. In 1901, however, he designed for him the tiny gate lodge to *Auchenbothie*, a massive red sandstone mansion on the main Kilmacolm-Greenock road. This is a curious little building reminiscent of Voysey, with very thick walls, rough-cast externally. It is square in plan with small deep-set windows, and a high, steeply pitched pyramidal roof terminating in a large chimney-stack which carried the flues from four fireplaces grouped back to back in the centre of the building. The four small apartments—living-room, two bedrooms and kitchen—are planned *en suite* round the central chimney-stack. There is no corridor, and the front door leads directly into the living-room and the back door opens into the kitchen—where, incidentally, the architect provided a fixed light in the solitary window; ventilation had to be obtained by the simple expedient of opening the door.

'AUCHINIBERT', KILLEARN, 1906

Like *Windyhill* and *Hill House*—and indeed like *Mosside* which stands on a low ridge overlooking the loch—this building also is situated on rising ground, but it is enclosed on three sides by trees. To the west well-wooded country rolls pleasantly away to Loch Lomondside and the straggling village of Killearn is just discernible about half a mile distant. Mackintosh's patrons always showed excellent judgment in their choice of site.

This house bears no resemblance whatever to any of its predecessors, and is Tudor in character—one must presume in accordance with the wishes of the Shands. Here Mackintosh must have subordinated his personal feelings to an extent not met with hitherto (Plate 43A).

The plan is a disorderly variation of the *Hill House* example, yet it works better than might be imagined at first glance. The roof pattern is complicated, with awkward interpenetrations and internal gutters—and of course the plan is reflected three dimensionally in the form of the building itself. In striking contrast to *Mosside* the masonry throughout is clean, tidy and of first-class workmanship—ashlar quoins were used in conjunction with irregular snecked rubble. The author was told by the mason in charge that when work on the site

109

began Mackintosh stood by him until he had obtained the precise bonding required. Thereafter he frequently lent a hand, and often selected the stones himself.

Mackintosh's quick appreciation of the problems encountered by the craftsman, and his readiness to work with the men on the job always won him respect

Figure 18. 1906–7. C. R. Mackintosh. 'Auchinibert', Killearn.
(Perspective drawing by A. G. Henderson.)

—even though his peculiar mannerisms were often heartily criticized by those who had to translate his drawing into terms of bricks and mortar.

At *Auchinibert*, however, there were few details to which the conventional craftsman could take objection. There is no carved ornament anywhere on the exterior, even the main entrance and deep covered porch is devoid of the familiar motives associated with the architect. All the windows are perfectly regular, well proportioned and pleasantly grouped—the antithesis of the fenestration at

110

Mosside. To the west, the drawing-room and dining-room project from the main block, and enclose a small paved terrace giving access to a charming formal garden with a broad lawn flanked by herbaceous borders and tall hedges.

As at Mr. Collins' house, the exterior reveals little evidence of Mackintosh's handiwork; the only identifiable features are the tall, sturdy chimney-stacks with widely projecting copings; a semicircular staircase bay, and a polygonal bay to the business-room, both of which are to be seen at *Windyhill*.

Internally, the house is disappointing. Not even the staircase conforms to precedent and a small mezzanine and fireplace are introduced, forming a kind of ingle-nook above the porch. This feature, of course, adds considerably to the spaciousness of the first-floor landing, but its practical value is questionable. Of Mackintosh's work, the staircase and several fireplaces alone remain to testify to his participation in the design.

Mackintosh was a frequent visitor to Killearn when the Shand's house was under construction but, it is said, he climbed the hill to *Auchinibert* all too infrequently. He had a favourite seat outside a public house in the village and, once ensconced there, could be dislodged only with the greatest difficulty. Not unnaturally, his clients objected to paying their architect fees for pleasant afternoons spent in this way with, perhaps, a garrulous interview afterwards. On this matter, as on several others, Mackintosh and the Shands did not see eye to eye, and though it has not been possible to discover exactly what transpired, before *Auchinibert* was completed, Mackintosh gave up the job and another architect was called in. This accounts for the absence of characteristic panelling and similar details in the drawing-room, business-room, and elsewhere.

The two houses, *Mosside* and *Auchinibert*—with the gate lodge—constitute the main body of domestic work executed by Mackintosh, in addition to *Windyhill* and *Hill House*. The list is by no means impressive. Drawings for several other projects survive but it is not known whether these were carried into effect. The most notable are two designs made in 1901 for a small town house and a country cottage for 'an artist' (Plates 44 and 45).[1]

[1] Illustrated in *Dekorative Kunst*, March 1902, pp. 211–13. Apart from these designs only two further projects are known to the author; a large unfinished drawing in pencil for a 'Country Mansion', and a few preliminary sketches for a house in the baronial style with crow-stepped gables and so forth, in the author's collection. The latter appears to be the only example of a flagrantly baronial design by Mackintosh. Neither scheme possesses either date or title, and it is impossible to say whether or not they were actually built.

The country cottage is the more interesting. It was to occupy a long narrow site—an island site apparently—and the plan is very compact. Here, as usual, Mackintosh paid great attention to the service wing and about two-thirds of the ground floor area is given over to storage space, the kitchen and its ancillaries. There is an intimate walled courtyard with pigeon-cote and trees, and on the west of the house a narrow garden approached through a vestibule from the entrance hall. A large studio, two minute bedrooms and a bathroom occupy the upper floor.

It is the elevations, however, that are of greatest importance. They conform to no stock pattern; they follow no recognizable precedent. Again, large plain rough-cast surfaces dominate, and openings are reduced to a minimum, but unlike *Windyhill* and *Hill House*, few of the forms employed are traditional in character. The large studio window recalls the School of Art, and the south façade with its long horizontal window, part of the architect's design for a pavilion at the Glasgow Exhibition of 1901. Beyond this it is impossible to draw parallels, except, perhaps, in the Voysey-like character of the shuttered windows in the north façade.

The town house is similar in feeling yet its dominant vertical lines give it a more traditional air. The plan is tightly compacted without an inch of waste space. It would appear that the house was to be either semi-detached, or at the end of a terrace—the west wall is windowless. Despite the inconsequential scatter of windows it is quite evident that in three dimensions the building would appear far more satisfactory than the project drawings suggest.

These designs seem to have no parallel in British work at this time, although they are similar in some respects to the artist's houses then being built at Darmstadt by J. M. Olbrich for the Grand Duke of Hesse. They are important for the evidence they provide of Mackintosh's sensitivity to changing conditions, sensitivity that amounts almost to precognition, for several of the forms he used here—as indeed at *Windyhill* and *Hill House*—are found again and again in the vocabulary of the most advanced European architects of the post 1914 war period. In this regard a notable instance is the south front of Mackintosh's cottage which to all intents and purposes is identical with the façade of a house at Platt in Kent designed in reinforced concrete in 1933 by Mr. Colin Lucas, of Messrs. Connell, Ward & Lucas (Plate 44D). The problems in each case varied considerably, and the materials were different, but it would seem that the architects had the same aesthetic objective in view—to heighten the dramatic effect of the façade, first by modelling it into an unusual shape, and then by cutting a small opening through it, or in Mackintosh's case, a series of small openings, which would contrast strongly with the plain, smooth wall surface. It is interesting, too, to note that Mackintosh used a long horizontal window— a form more appropriate to concrete construction than to brickwork—and, moreover, rendered the wall to produce a smooth, homogeneous effect, a concrete effect in other words.

The Belgian architect, Henry van de Velde, one of the most versatile exponents of continental *art nouveau*, was once accused of torturing his materials, of twisting and contorting wood in a manner alien to its nature. He replied that he had been convinced for a long time of the inadequacy of wood for his designs and was anticipating the discovery of a more suitable material that could be cast.[1] It seems evident that Mackintosh, too, felt the need for a medium of greater plasticity in which to express his ideas, and on several occasions he most certainly anticipated the character and form of later works in other materials. It is in fact his never-ending quest for architectural forms without historical bias, that is one of the most distinctive characteristics of his buildings. Thus, in recognizing and appreciating the traditional qualities of, say, *Hill House*, we are astonished, nevertheless, by its freshness and originality when compared with, say, C. F. A. Voysey's house, *The Orchard* (1900), (Plate 88c), Lorimer's *Ardkinglass* (1906), (Plate 32A), or even George Walton's *White House* (Plate 88D). It is indeed regrettable that circumstances prevented Mackintosh from developing his thesis.

Although this completes the survey of the houses Mackintosh designed in their entirety, there remain two interesting schemes of interior decoration that must be mentioned here—the *Hous'hill*, Nitshill, Glasgow, for Major Cochrane and his wife, formerly Miss Cranston,[2] and No. 6, Florentine Terrace, the architect's own house (now No. 78, South Park Avenue).

THE 'HOUS'HILL', NITSHILL, GLASGOW, circa 1903-19

It is usually assumed that Mackintosh designed and built the *Hous'hill*, but this is not so. A sketch of the building appeared in Charles Taylor's *The*

---

[1] *Modern Building*, W. C. Behrendt, pp. 78-9.

[2] Miss Cranston was the distinguished Glasgow restaurateur for whom Mackintosh carried out many commissions. To save confusion she will be referred to throughout this work by her maiden name.

Levern Delineated, published in 1831, and it was described then as 'the largest private house on the Levern'.

In 1903 when, according to the office records of Honeyman & Keppie, Mackintosh began work there, it was a large rambling place with a classical portico and crow-stepped gables—it had probably been altered and rebuilt several times before the Cochranes bought it. The fact that a bathroom had been constructed in the thickness of a wall between two bedrooms indicates that part of the house must have been of considerable antiquity.

In this instance Mackintosh did not attempt to alter the main fabric of the building. At the entrance he contented himself with paving the vestibule floor with square slabs of stone, some of which were incised with a flowing leaf pattern. The joints—about 1 inch wide—were covered with iron straps set flush with the surface. The square motive was echoed in a large wrought iron stand and trellis designed to carry a variety of plant pots which usually flooded the porch with a riot of vegetation and flowers. Dramatic lighting effects were obtained in the hall by means of large wrought iron, brazier-like lamps which stood on the floor. The walls were decorated with a stencilled tree pattern, and the floor and stairs were covered with brown horsehair carpet.

Apart from the entrance hall, Mackintosh was responsible for the drawing-room, card-room, music-room, billards-room, and several bedrooms in their entirety[1]—and for the decorations only, in the dining-room and the morning-room. He designed various pieces of furniture for a number of other apartments, and Margaret Macdonald designed the curtains and napery. All reports agree that the most original feature in the house was a large fireplace in the card-room which, instead of the customary plaster or mosaic, had a surround of thick plate glass set horizontally—that is, with the edge showing. The glass was broken in fairly large pieces, each of which was embedded *flat* in mortar, with one roughly straightened edge slightly projecting. The result of this extraordinary invention was a scintillating texture of liquid green, attractive enough in daylight, but especially so in artificial light when the full beauty of its colour was revealed. From the practical point of view, however, the fireplace had its drawbacks; for example, the edges of the glass were sharp and, when dusted, became covered with fluff and threads stripped from the cloth—and no doubt with skin from the housemaid's knuckles. But the aesthetic effect was considered to far outweigh the disadvantages, and the fireplace remained the principal object

[1] Five illustrations of the *Hous'hill* rooms were published in *The Studio Year Book of Decorative Art*, 1907, pp. 58–60, others are in the author's collection.

of admiration of those who visited the house. The walls of the card-room were finished in gold leaf, and the six tables and their complement of chairs were inlaid with chequered patterns of mother-of-pearl. Colourful accents were provided by a set of tinted gesso panels, *The Four Queens*, by Margaret Macdonald.[1]

The most important apartment from the historical point of view was the music-room, a large white room with a curved end wall, furnished in familiar Mackintosh style with fitted cupboards, high-backed chairs, small tables and a number of attractive wall-seats similar to those used at Kingsborough Gardens. The grand piano was painted by George Walton. The principal feature of the room was an exquisitely designed open timber screen, curved on plan, and built of light fins at about nine-inch centres, which extended from the floor to picture-rail level. The fins were stiffened at intervals by irregularly placed square panels which had a decorative rather than a structural value, but in any case did not detract in the slightest degree from the delicate transparency of the screen. The vertical lines were echoed in a circular electric light fitting suspended from the ceiling and also in the spindle-backed chairs (Plates 46 and 47B). It is not readily apparent from the photographs which survive that the screen formed a segment of a complete circle of about eighteen to twenty feet in diameter, described by the flat crowning member, to which the side walls of the room were tangential. The curved end wall, containing a large window, and this inner circle were concentric (Plate 47B). Mackintosh's objective here was to create a small, intimate salon, rich and jewel-like, within yet independent of the principal apartment itself. This he achieved with notable success. The circular form he adopted—virtually a continuation of the curved wall—merged admirably into its surroundings; and his screen gave just the right sense of enclosure to those within its orbit yet, by its lightness and transparency, did not materially affect the unity of the room itself.[2] The music-room represents a most interesting experiment

---

[1] Two of these, 'The Queen of Diamonds' and 'The Queen of Spades', were illustrated in *The Studio Year Book of Decorative Art*, 1917, p. 79. The original panels are now in the possession of William Ward, Esq., of Glasgow, to whom the author is indebted for much valuable information about the furnishing of *Hous'hill*.

[2] It would appear that the idea for the music-room came to Mackintosh after seeing a similar feature on a much smaller scale designed by Carl Witzmann, a Viennese architect—a salon for Sigmund Oppenheim. This included a curved bay window with luxurious fitted seats which was extended in the form of a circle by openwork screens almost identical with the *Hous'hill* example. This interior was displayed at the Turin Exhibition of 1902 at which Mackintosh exhibited, and was illustrated in *Deutsche Kunst und Dekoration*, vol. XI, Oct.–Mar. 1901–2.

in planning, an experiment which has much in common with the work of Lloyd Wright in America, and of Miës van der Rohe (Plate 47A) and others after the first World War.

None of the other rooms at *Hous'hill* is of major importance. On the first floor the 'Blue Bedroom'[1] and the 'White Bedroom'[2] were probably the most impressive apartments. Both had four-poster beds—that in the Blue Bedroom, with its complementary settee, closely resembles a similar piece in Princess Victoria's bedroom at the 'Treasurer's House', York. The slender bed-posts, the square cut hangings, and more especially the form of the settee, all seem to be derived from this example, which, incidentally, was illustrated in *The Architect*, 15th April 1904—about the time Mackintosh was designing the *Hous'hill* interiors.

The main apartments at the *Hous'hill* were completed in 1905, but for many years thereafter Mackintosh continued to design incidental pieces of furniture, and to prepare colour schemes for the Cochranes who proved to be two of his staunchest friends and most indulgent patrons. After the death of Major Cochrane in 1917, his wife remained at Nitshill for about three years and then decided to sell the property and estate. Even this sad duty she accomplished with characteristic *élan*. The house was left completely equipped with furniture, pictures, stocks of napery, bed linen, cutlery and china—most of which were designed by Charles and Margaret Mackintosh. Fresh flowers were placed in every room and a card of welcome presented to the new mistress on her arrival.

The *Hous'hill* changed hands several times after Miss Cranston's departure and, following a disastrous fire, it was bought by Glasgow Corporation and demolished to make way for a large housing estate. The furniture and equipment had been removed by the second owner and were sold by public auction on 18th August 1933. The auctioneer had difficulty in obtaining bids for many of the pieces; *The Four Queens*, by Margaret Mackintosh, were sold for 25s. each; heavy arm-chairs of exquisite craftsmanship brought between £2 and £3 each, and several beautiful cabinets were sold for £4 10s. each.

One cannot but deplore the fact that nothing but a few photographs remain of this interesting house. The fire may have done considerable damage, but the complete and merciless destruction of the interiors is unforgivable. Some of

[1] Illustrated *Artwork*, No. 21, Spring Number, 1930 (J. M. Dent), p. 25.
[2] The 'White Bedroom' was illustrated in *Modern Architecture*, Bruno Taut (published by *The Studio*, 1929).

the built-in fittings at least might have been saved, for an admirer of Mackintosh who happened to be passing the site when demolition was in progress saw a workman driving a pick-axe into one of the architect's charming fireplaces, and, intervening, was able to secure several of the small zinc trays—Mackintosh's jewel-like insets. He acquired also some specially made wooden blocks from a parquet floor which had been seriously affected by fire and water. These mementos appear to be all that remains of the Cochrane's house, apart from a few pieces of furniture and the gesso panels.[1]

NO. 78 SOUTHPARK AVENUE, GLASGOW

Shortly after completing the major part of the decorations at *Hous'hill*, and when *Mosside* and *Auchinibert* were being built, Charles and Margaret Mackintosh moved from their flat in Mains Street to No. 6 Florentine Terrace (now No. 78 Southpark Avenue), a narrow-fronted, grey house within a stone's throw of Glasgow University (1906). There was little they could do to improve the external appearance of the building, though Mackintosh did re-design the doorway. The interior was completely transformed. The ground-floor plan was modified by the provision of a cloak-room and the elimination of a tiny impracticable scullery; two rooms on the first floor were combined to form a spacious L-shaped drawing-room; two small front bedrooms on the second floor were made into a single apartment and the addition of a french window and balcony on the roof converted a small attic into an attractive bedroom (Fig. 19).

The Mains Street colour schemes were repeated here with even greater success for the Mackintoshes now had considerable experience behind them.[2] The drawing-room, a fine spacious apartment, was again the *pièce de résistance*, charming all who entered it—Desmond Chapman-Huston, sharing E. B. Kalas'

---

[1] It is said that the cellars of the *Hous'hill* were stocked with hundreds of iron-stone tea-sets which had been used by Miss Cranston for her restaurant at the 1901 Glasgow Exhibition. They are reputed to have been designed by Mackintosh and specially made for the occasion, but this is doubtful. No one seems to know what ultimately happened to them.

[2] To the best of the author's knowledge the rooms at Southpark Avenue were not photographed during Mackintosh's lifetime. The house was purchased by Glasgow University in 1946—see 'A Mackintosh House in Glasgow', T. Howarth, *Journal of the R.I.B.A.*, September 1946.

enthusiasm for the earlier room, describes it as 'an oasis, a revelation, a delight'.[1]

As at *Hill House* the L-shaped apartment virtually comprised three living areas. The toe of the 'L' pointed west and contained a fine new window—recalling the bay at Mr. Blackie's house. According to Charles Mackintosh this

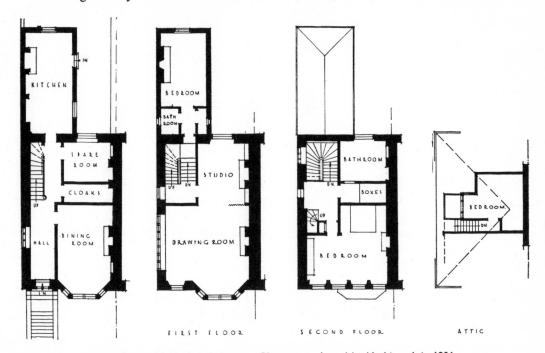

Figure 19. No. 78 Southpark Avenue, Glasgow, as altered by Mackintosh in 1906.

was provided 'for my wife, Mistress Margaret, so that she can watch the sunsets'.[2]

The dominant feature of the scheme was the great white fireplace from Mains Street placed against the inner wall, and now flanked by two exquisite cabinets (Plate 13c). The vertical stroke of the 'L' consisted of a studio-annex which, with its own fireplace, could be separated from the rest of the room by curtains.

[1] *The Lamp of Memory* (Skeffington, 1949), p. 125. Chapman-Huston became an intimate friend of the Mackintoshes—in this book he describes all too briefly his first visit to No. 78 Southpark Avenue, and his first meeting with Charles Mackintosh.

[2] Ibid., p. 126.

118

The entire apartment was painted white. It was flooded with light from Mackintosh's new window.[1]

The studio annex was used principally by Margaret who continued to paint and to design the many incidentals—curtains, napery, gesso and metal plaques and the like—without which few of Mackintosh's interiors were complete. Charles by this time had secured a partnership with Honeyman & Keppie (1904) and most of his work was carried out at the office where he had draughtsmen to assist him.

The other rooms at Southpark Avenue also followed the Mains Street pattern closely. The dining-room was decorated in precisely the same way. There was a charming white bedroom on the second floor with a deep recess to take the huge four-poster bed, and at the top of a narrow twisting flight of stairs, a delightful guest-chamber made from a disused attic. For this tiny apartment Mackintosh provided french windows opening on to a balcony with flower boxes and simple wrought-iron railings—'the loveliest lodging in the world' according to Lady Alice Egerton.[2] This was indeed a compliment from one who lived in Barry's Bridgewater house.

Since No. 78 Southpark Avenue was completed, white rooms and light rooms and rooms sparsely furnished have become so much the accepted accompaniment to modern architecture, that the advance represented by Mackintosh's interiors at this time may easily be underestimated. It is instructive, therefore, to compare his work with that of his most progressive contemporaries and representative interiors by several notable architects are illustrated here—architects who, at the turn of the century, were widely acclaimed at home and abroad as leaders in the new movement. There are, for example, the drawing-room at *Lead Cameron*, Bearsden (1898), by George Walton (Plate 11B); a dining-room by Frank Lloyd Wright (1899), (Plate 15B); project drawings by Baillie Scott for a dining-room and a music-room (1901), (Plate 62A and C);

[1] The author was told by the decorator who painted this house that Mackintosh covered the floor with heavy white sailcloth nailed to the boarding and sized. At the first attempt it shrank badly and burst from its moorings. A new piece of material was then obtained and treated before being stretched and secured into position. This proved to be entirely successful. Sailcloth stencilled with a chequered pattern, was also used as a stair covering and is said to have cleaned well and lasted for many years. These experiments may have been carried out some time later, for Chapman-Huston and others speak of a rich grey-brown fitted carpet in staircase, hall and drawing-room.

[2] *The Lamp of Memory*, Desmond Chapman-Huston.

and the dining-room and lounge-hall of C. F. A. Voysey's own house, *The Orchard*, Chorley Wood, which are exactly contemporary with the Mains Street interiors (Plates 14B and 17B). It will be observed that it is not Mackintosh's unusual furniture and ornament alone which distinguish his work, but his unequivocal insistence upon the unity of a room and its contents. He handled each element with the skill of a master musician, a composer in form and colour. Every subtle variation of light and shade, the precise point at which to introduce an accent, the value of a gay skipping rhythm or a sombre adagio, were exploited to the full; and when an interior was finished, it formed a complete and harmonious whole, from which little could be subtracted, and to which nothing could be added. In this regard it should be noted that a single Mackintosh chair or even a furniture group may provide an effective centre of interest in almost any carefully ordered room, but a piece of furniture by another designer introduced into a Mackintosh room at once appears alien and incongruous, a point soon observed and criticized by his more discerning contemporaries. Muthesius went so far as to say that Mackintosh's rooms reached such a high level of artistic achievement that even a book bound in the wrong kind of cover might be sufficient to upset the delicate colour relationships.

It is Mackintosh's consistency in the design of small and large elements, his exploitation of broad plain surfaces and rich points of contrast, and his striving for homogeneity that is so extraordinarily refreshing. Despite the symbolism, the gesso panels, the coloured glass and the peculiar chairs, his cool restful apartments, spacious and dignified, possessed an elusive beauty, a compelling stillness in striking contrast to the overcrowded interiors then fashionable.

VI

THE GLASGOW TEA-ROOMS

O F all Mackintosh's work in the decorative field nothing brought him greater fame than the tea-rooms he designed for Miss Catherine Cranston—most certainly none of his projects caused greater interest at home and abroad than these remarkable interiors.

The first of his commissions for Miss Cranston came in 1896, the year in which he sent work to the Arts and Crafts Exhibition in London, and designed the new Glasgow School of Art. Thereafter, over a period of twenty years, he executed for her an immense number of projects of all kinds, ranging from designs for cutlery and menu cards, to complete schemes of decoration and furnishing—projects which for originality, ingenuity and, let it be admitted, occasional eccentricity, would be difficult to equal.

Before discussing Mackintosh's work in this sphere, however, let us glance briefly at the background to the Glasgow tea-room movement, a phenomenon of the 1880's and 1890's.

The prosperity of ship-building and heavy industry in the Clyde Valley area brought about a complete transformation of Glasgow and its environs in the nineteenth century. Between 1830 and 1860 the population trebled and continued to increase at an alarming rate—the influx coming largely from the Highlands, from Ireland and the south. Not unnaturally the city magistrates were confronted with many new and disquieting social problems, one of which was an enormous increase in daytime drunkenness. Young clerks, many of whom were recruited from outlying districts, congregated at lunch-time in bars and public houses adjacent to the main shopping and business centres, and then sallied forth to make a general nuisance of themselves by interfering with traffic and passers-by. It was not until the late 70's that this situation was alleviated by the advent of the humble tea-shop which quickly began to rival the public house in popularity. Tea-shops were soon to be found everywhere, in side-streets, in alleyways, below warehouses, and in the most fashionable thoroughfares. Where rents were prohibitive cellars and basements were used. This new development coincided with, and no doubt was stimulated by Glasgow's art revival. Few, indeed, of the better class restaurants failed to display some paintings by the *Boys from Glasgow*, and many premises became veritable picture galleries.

By the turn of the century Glasgow was universally celebrated for the variety and excellence of its tea-shops: 'Nowhere else can one have so much for so little, and nowhere else are such places more popular or frequented', said a contemporary observer.[1] Miss Cranston, herself a native of Glasgow, was one of the pioneers in this new field. Much against the wishes of her family—especially the Cranston branch, already in business as tea importers and experimenting with a small restaurant—she decided to try her fortune in the city. In 1884, with the reluctant help of her father George Cranston, formerly licensee of *The Crown* and *The Crow*, two noted hostelries in George Square long since demolished, she rented part of a shop below Aitken's Hotel, 114 Argyle Street, and opened a tea-room. To everyone's surprise the tiny venture flourished. Miss Cranston personally supervised every detail of the business and kept a watchful eye on her customers and waitresses from the cash desk. She soon realized, however, that something more than a tea-shop was required to satisfy the needs of Glasgow's thriving commercial population, and she began to make plans for a veritable paragon among restaurants, a building in which her patrons would not only enjoy a good meal, but at any time of the day could drop in for a few minutes of quiet relaxation, a game of billiards, perhaps, or

[1] From *Glasgow in 1901*, a delightful little book by 'James Hamilton Muir'—a composite pseudonym disguising the identity of James Bone, Archibald Hamilton Charteris, and Muirhead Bone, the illustrator.

just to smoke. This dream was realized eight years later (1892), when she married Major John Cochrane, a well-known engineer of Barrhead, and acquired the whole of No. 114 Argyle Street—as a wedding gift, it is said. This building she soon transformed into a miniature community centre with a billiards-room, smoking-rooms equipped with lounge chairs, and small tables for chess, draughts and dominoes; a reading-room, and a separate tea-room for ladies. This restaurant, the first of its kind, created something of a sensation in the city. At midday it was virtually a business man's club, and in the afternoon a most popular rendezvous for both sexes. Thus Miss Cranston's reputation was established, and the public were curious to know what her next move would be. For two or three years she built up the Argyle Street business and perfected her organization, then in 1895 she acquired Nos. 205–9 Ingram Street and Nos. 91–3 Buchanan Street, the latter one of the city's most fashionable shopping centres. In the same year she employed a local firm of architects, H. & D. Barclay, to reconstruct the Argyle Street premises, which were renamed *The Crown Lunch and Tea Rooms,* and in 1896 she commissioned George Washington Brown, R.S.A., of Edinburgh, to rebuild the Buchanan Street establishment.

Within a few years Miss Cranston became one of the best known figures in the city of Glasgow. Like Margaret Macdonald she contrived to be original in everything. Tall and stately she affected picturesque superbly tailored clothes, described by a contemporary as 'a blend of bygone fashions and current styles, striking and elegant, but never *outré*' (Plate 86). Her restaurants were models of efficiency. She personally supervised the layout and arrangement of each room—napery, cutlery, china and glassware had to be impeccable. Three times a week she sent a large consignment of flowers from her own garden or conservatory, along with written instructions as to the precise positions they were to occupy. The flowers came to town in a donkey cart driven by a small boy in green uniform—a characteristic gesture this, for she was nothing if not a showman. Miss Cranston, too, interviewed the parents and visited the home of every prospective employee, and, after undergoing a rigorous course of training, each waitress had to attend upon Major Cochrane and herself before passing into service.

By such methods, by sheer force of character, by a phenomenal capacity for hard work, and painstaking care and attention to detail, Miss Cranston raised the tea-room business in Glasgow from the level of mundane commercialism to that of a profession, if not a fine art.

Charles Mackintosh was introduced to Miss Cranston in 1896—probably by Newbery—as work on her new premises in Buchanan Street was proceeding. At this time she already had in her employ as decorators George Walton & Co., J. & W. Guthrie, Alexander & Howell, and Messrs. Scott Morton of Edinburgh —in addition to the architects engaged on the reconstruction of the Argyle Street and Buchanan Street tea-rooms—thus Mackintosh was by no means first in the field. He was commissioned to share with Walton the decoration of the Buchanan Street restaurant, and from photographs which survive (taken in July 1897) it is evident that he played a minor role throughout—his concern being primarily certain mural decorations. At Argyle Street which, as far as can be ascertained, was decorated and furnished shortly afterwards (1897–8) the position was reversed; Walton being responsible for the fixtures and wall decorations, Mackintosh for the movable furniture.

Although pictures of the Argyle Street interiors were not published until 1906 (in *The Studio*) the records of Messrs. Annan's show that the photographs of the premises were taken in April 1897. From the records of Francis Smith & Son, cabinet makers, however, we find that a good deal of furniture designed by Mackintosh was sent to Argyle Street in 1898 and 1899. The importance of this lies in the fact that none of the furniture in the principal rooms at Buchanan Street shows evidence of Mackintosh's handiwork[1] whereas nearly all the chairs depicted in the Argyle Street interiors are of an unorthodox type and, one may assume, if not the first, then very early examples of his new style.

In 1897—perhaps before the furniture for Argyle Street was designed— George Walton moved to London, though his firm continued to function in Glasgow for some years.[2] For this reason, no doubt, Mackintosh was given complete control over Miss Cranston's Ingram Street tea-rooms when, *circa* 1901, they were extended and re-decorated. Then, three years later, he designed the last and most complete of her enterprises—*The Willow Tea-Rooms*, Sauchiehall Street. On this occasion he was not only responsible for the furnishing,

---

[1] It is probable that the billiards-room chairs were designed by Mackintosh. These are to be seen in *Modern British Domestic Architecture and Decoration*, published by *The Studio* in 1901 (Plate 196).

[2] The professional relationship between Mackintosh and Walton—who was one of the most original and influential designers working in Glasgow during the 1890's—has been the cause of much controversy in the north. In Chapter X the work of the two men will be placed in correct perspective, meanwhile it is important to note Walton's contribution to the Cranston Tea-Rooms.

decoration, and everything that went inside the building, but for the structure itself. *The Willow* was the most remarkable of the series.

THE BUCHANAN STREET TEA-ROOMS

At the Buchanan Street premises it is not possible now to trace exactly the limits within which each of the designers worked. The building subsequently passed into the hands of the Clydesdale Bank and the interior was entirely remodelled, in fact all that remains of the original scheme is two large fireplaces —designed by Walton—in the staff recreation room on the top floor. It would appear, however, that Walton was in charge of the whole project. Weight is lent to this speculation by the fact that, in addition to most if not all the furniture and equipment in the main apartments, he designed also the hoarding which was erected in Buchanan Street while the building was in course of construction —a most unusual field for the decorator.[1] The timber background was painted black, a brilliantly coloured exotic peacock motive was stencilled at each corner, and the scheme completed by a heraldic frieze of flowers, heart-shaped emblems, and appropriate lettering. This was probably the first occasion on which a utilitarian structure of the kind had been treated so ambitiously.

Externally the building had little claim to distinction,[2] and Washington Brown's essay in the Franco-Scottish renaissance is far more appropriate to a bank than a tea-room. The editor of *The Studio*, reviewing the project some twelve months later, tactfully referred to the building as designed by 'an eminent Edinburgh architect', and, he added, 'as several interior features are open to somewhat severe criticism, it will be best not to give the architect's name'.

Washington Brown planned the building in four floors with a spacious top-lit staircase-well at the rear containing broad galleries at each floor level, which could be used for dining purposes. There were the following independently decorated apartments: a ladies' tea-room and a ladies' dinner-room, a general tea-room and a general luncheon-room, a gentlemen's luncheon-room and adjoining gallery, and on the top floor, a billiards-room and smoking gallery.

[1] Illustrated in the *Journal of the R.I.B.A.*, vol. XXXVI, No. 11, April 1930, p. 540. *George Walton, his Life and Work*, Professor Pevsner.

[2] A perspective drawing of the exterior by T. Raffles Davidson, was published in *The British Architect*, 28th February 1896. Walton's hoarding was photographed on 6th March 1896.

To these apartments Mackintosh seems to have contributed nothing but the mural decorations in the general dinner-room, the dinner gallery and the smoking gallery. Gleeson White, writing in *The Studio* (1897) indicates that he decorated several floors visible from the staircase well—this presumably refers to the galleries. The predominating colours varied from green on the ground floor, through greys, and yellows, to blue for the upper floor, each basic colour intruding as a frieze on its neighbour. The whole scheme suggested the idea of transition from earth to sky. It is rather curious that White completely disregarded Walton's decorative work and furniture in his enthusiastic account of Buchanan Street—an unjustifiable omission which must have greatly offended the more modest, sensitive designer. To the uninformed reader it would seem that the credit for the entire project belonged to Mackintosh and, in point of fact, the first illustrations of Walton's murals did not appear in *The Studio* until 1901,[1] long after initial interest in Buchanan Street had waned.

Although far less imaginative, Walton's restaurant furniture was much more practical than Mackintosh's; he never went to extremes, and all the chairs at Buchanan Street were well proportioned and soundly constructed. Many of them are still in use, and in fifty years have required neither repairs nor modification. Mackintosh's chairs, on the other hand, rarely survived for long without attention from the cabinet-maker. Four principal types of chair were used by Walton in this restaurant; one with a high back and centre reeded splat, the second, a stocky spindle-back with turned legs and uprights made of oak from the grounds of Scone Palace; the third with a shaped back and rectangular reeded panel, and lastly an elegant rush-seated ladderback—the latter an especially attractive design on soundly traditional lines. All this furniture was designed in 1896, and records show that it was built and delivered in the following year.

THE MURALS

Mackintosh may have had little to do with the furnishing of this restaurant, but he certainly enjoyed painting the walls. Here for the first time he was able to put into practice on a large scale the technique he had perfected in poster work, and which was readily adaptable to this new medium. Identical characteristics can be recognized at once—the strongly delineated and highly

[1] A *Studio* Special Number, *Modern British Domestic Architecture and Decoration*, Plates 197–8.

conventionalized human and vegetable forms, colour applied in flat ungraded washes and bright colour of primary intensity confined to small areas. Always he avoided naturalism and never tried to penetrate, or to dissolve the wall surface by perspective—interesting points which distinguish his work from that of his contemporaries. His most imposing scheme at Buchanan Street consisted of a series of large white-robed figures entwined with an intricate pattern of branches and plants, and disposed in groups round the walls of the general tea-room on the first floor (Plate 48). In the luncheon-room, the murals had more in common with Egyptian decorative work—an impression conveyed by the employment of stylized trees reminiscent of the lotus, and the ubiquitous peacock motive. These are even more remarkable than the humanized patterns for their wealth of varied detail.[1] At first glance, the trees appear identical in shape, but a closer examination reveals that each design is different from its neighbour either in the form of the intertwined branches, or in the placing of small leaf or flower motives on, or around, the main stem. The sense of growth, of root, stem, branch and flower, is always maintained, however conventionalized the ultimate form becomes.

Mackintosh rarely used abstract pattern, and the inspiration of most of his decorative work is usually obvious and the symbolism apparent. One example at Buchanan Street, however, is incapable of analysis. It was to be seen in the smokers' gallery and consisted of a series of totem-like shapes linked by a wavy line, a symbol of smoke—or perhaps of cloud, for the end wall was decorated by a sun smiling benignly. The totem figures varied considerably though conforming to the same general shape, and may represent grotesquely conventionalized human forms.[2] The derivation of the patterns, however, is not of great importance; their significance lies in the evidence they provided of a highly original sense of design, and a remarkably fertile imagination. The smoke-room murals represent an even more daring innovation than the formalized ladies in the general tea-room, and were far removed from the tapestry-like work of George Walton (Plate 49c), the great easel paintings of Madox Brown, or the naïve allegory of John Duncan. They demonstrate that in this field too, Mackintosh was capable of venturing into new realms of visual experience, and they form an interesting diversion which, unfortunately, he did not pursue.

Mackintosh learned a great deal from the Buchanan Street experiment. Although he continued to use formalized trees, flowers and plants in his interior

[1] Illustrated in *The Studio*, vol. XI, No. 52, July 1897, p. 93.
[2] *Ibid.*, p. 94.

decoration schemes, the exotic and complicated forms employed here did not appear again. He realized that it was possible to obtain the effect he desired without recourse to intricate pattern, and by simplification, to achieve greater refinement.

Not only were his stencilled murals interesting from the aesthetic point of view, however, but also as examples of the reinstatement of a neglected and largely dishonoured craft. His ingenious patterns with their ever varying detail, bright colours and absence of hackneyed motives, gave a sparkle and life to a medium which, by its very nature, lent itself to dull, formal repetition. From the technical point of view also this work seems to have been noteworthy for Gleeson White commented thus: 'The plaster has been prepared in flat colours of singular quality: whether owing to the surface or to some clever manipulation, the effect is of flat but not even colour with a fine texture in it that imparts a surface not unlike that upon the "self-colour" bottles of Chinese porcelain'.[1] The value of the experiment was emphasized by White who later stated that the work at Buchanan Street must be regarded as a very important enterprise in the decorative field.

The opening of the Buchanan Street restaurant caused something of a sensation. Its success was instantaneous, though the strange and unorthodox decorations were the subject of much controversy. The attitude of the man in the street to Miss Cranston's first tea-room in the 'modern' style may be summed up in the following observation by a contemporary: 'It is believed (and averred) that in no other town can you see in a place of refreshment such ingenious and beautiful decorations in the style of the new art as in Miss Cranston's shop in Buchanan Street. Indeed, so general in the city is this belief that it has caused the Glasgow man of the better sort to coin a new adjective denoting the height of beauty . . . "quite Kate Cranstonish".'[2]

THE ARGYLE STREET TEA-ROOMS

Before Walton and Mackintosh were called in to transform the interior of No. 114 Argyle Street the building had been completely remodelled by the Glasgow architects, H. & D. Barclay—all mouldings were stripped from the façade, fanciful gables and dormers were built in the red-tiled, steeply pitched

[1] *The Studio*, vol. XI, No. 52, July 1897, p. 95.
[2] *Glasgow in 1901*, 'James Hamilton Muir'.

roof, a turret was added and the walls covered with rough-cast from eaves to first-floor level. The building appears today much as it did fifty years ago—except for the intrusion of 'modern' shop fronts. The same general layout of the interior was followed as at Buchanan Street. The ground floor was occupied by tea-rooms, the first and second floors by luncheon- and tea-rooms, the third floor and spacious attic by a billiards-room, reading- and smoking-rooms.

Walton was responsible for the panelling, the screens, the billiards-tables, the fireplaces, the wall and ceiling decorations, and electric light fittings; Mackintosh designed the chairs, tables, coat and umbrella stands. Walton panelled the ground-floor rooms in walnut, a timber rarely used by Mackintosh, and they were quite undistinguished. The luncheon-room on the first floor, however—a long low-ceiled apartment—was divided into two by a narrow panelled oak screen, the upper part of which was stencilled with a floral pattern on a light ground. The two rooms thus formed were sub-divided by low oak screens into small alcoves on either side of a central service passage—a very attractive arrangement.[1] A stencilled frieze by Walton in the shape of a conventional rose motive within a light pattern of small leaves and flowers—reminiscent of a Voysey wallpaper—encircled the room and forms an interesting contrast to Mackintosh's work at Buchanan Street and elsewhere. This treatment, however, broke up the wall surface above the panelling and emphasized the low ceiling. In similar circumstances it is almost certain that Mackintosh would have brought the ceiling colour down to the top of the panelled dado without introducing a decorative frieze—and probably would have painted the woodwork to match.

A large mosaic panel, *Eros*, later occupied the centre of one end wall. It was designed by Walton for the 1901 Glasgow Exhibition and was made of crystal, mother-of-pearl, green marble, slate and glass, with occasional pieces of silver. This was a perfect period piece with briar roses, doves, and an effeminate, adolescent Cupid—all unmistakably belonging to the Glasgow style, but completely different in character from the work of the School of Art Group.[2]

The smoking-room and billiards-room at Argyle Street were furnished entirely by Mackintosh, and the plain wooden panelling of the low screens would

[1] This and other rooms were illustrated in *The Studio*, vol. XXXIX, No. 163, October 1906, pp. 32–6.

[2] 'Eros' was reproduced in colour in *Modern British Domestic Architecture and Decoration* (1901), p. 202.

indicate that he had a hand in the design of the fixtures too. There were 'white' rooms, but here too Walton used a stencilled floral pattern, thin and spidery, right round the apartments and he applied stencilled patterns to the underside of the ceiling beams in the manner of Baillie Scott.

A most interesting and representative group of Mackintosh's new furniture was to be seen in a corner of the smoking-room (Plate 49B)—three sturdy ladder-backs, three small tub-chairs of solid planked construction, several stools, and four tables can be distinguished. All were very soundly built and of much heavier construction than most of the architect's subsequent furniture. The circular coffee-table on the left of the picture is an inelegant but remarkably efficient design that was repeated at Ingram Street some years later. The ladder-backs, tub-chairs, and stools did not appear again in this form.

None of the chairs has the grace and lightness of Walton's furniture at Buchanan Street, but nevertheless, they possess a down-to-earth, homely character eminently suitable for their particular purpose—they were chairs for men. All the evidence indicates that the small group of furniture illustrated here, designed *circa* 1897, was the first in the true Mackintosh manner, and it would seem that the architect's other forms were evolved from these early examples.

According to Herbert Smith, who made most of the furniture for the tea-rooms, Mackintosh designed a fine staircase for Argyle Street with tubular gunmetal balusters of square section, similar in character to the staircase still extant at Daly's, Sauchiehall Street—formerly *The Willow* restaurant. Nothing now remains of this, and it is unlikely that Mackintosh would be given such an important feature to design when Walton was virtually in command. The staircase may have been built in 1906, however, when Miss Cranston opened up the basement and commissioned Mackintosh to design the 'Dutch Kitchen' (Plate 49A)—designated by P. Morton Shand 'the prototype of innumerable Miss Hook of Holland Cafés' (*Architectural Review*, 1935). This was the last, and apparently the only scheme of decoration at Argyle Street entirely designed by Mackintosh, and the only one of which any reliable record remains.

The 'Dutch Kitchen' was a square, low apartment with a black open-timber ceiling. The fireplace was set in an inglenook and had a simple steel grate with a surround of Dutch tiles. The dominant theme was black and white with emerald green accents. The floor was covered with lino of a chequered design supplied by Herbert Smith, and despite the fact that the material was woven with the pattern set diagonally, Mackintosh insisted that it should be cut and laid on the square. It would be an exaggeration to say that Herbert Smith bears the marks to this day, but he still relates with some warmth the story of his struggle with the lino, which, apparently, was of battleship quality.

The Argyle Street project was rather disappointing. The interiors were pleasant enough, but they lacked the vitality of the later tea-rooms in which Mackintosh was given complete control and, apart from the furniture in the smoking- and billiards-room—and, of course, the 'Dutch Kitchen'—there was little evidence of his handiwork. The premises were eventually sold to Messrs. Manfield, and turned into a shoe shop. With the exception of a forlorn rusty firegrate in the attic, all vestige of Miss Cranston's charming tea-rooms has vanished, and a heavy mahogany staircase with turned balusters stands where Mackintosh's elegant stairway used to be.

THE INGRAM STREET TEA-ROOMS

After the reconstruction of the Argyle Street premises Miss Cranston directed her attention next to Ingram Street which, unlike the other buildings, consisted of a series of lofty, inter-connected apartments on the ground floor of a large block of offices.

It is difficult to establish, with any certainty, the precise date on which the first part of the premises was opened, but according to the Post Office Guide Miss Cranston took possession of Nos. 205–9 in the year 1895, and in 1901 added a third and fourth section, Nos. 213–15. From an illustrated brochure in the author's collection it is evident that Mackintosh had little if anything to do with the interiors prior to 1900, and curiously enough, the first section—No. 205— is termed, *The Pioneer Suite of Tea and Smoking Rooms in Glasgow*, information that would appear to contradict the evidence already given in relation to Argyle Street. The *Pioneer Suite* consisted of a gentlemen's tea-room, now the Chinese Room, a ladies' tea-room, and a smoking-room, all of which were designed by an architect, Kesson Whyte, and decorated by Messrs. Alexander & Howell. The apartments were narrow, dark and, as far as one can judge from tiny illustrations, rather depressing. The furniture consisted in the main of low spindle-backed chairs, with well-upholstered arm-chairs of clubroom type in the smoking-room. Heavy panelling, ornate gasoliers, ornamental busts on brackets and richly patterned wallpaper contrived to produce an effect of stuffy Victorian respectability.

131

Greater freedom was achieved by Messrs. Scott Morton of Edinburgh who were responsible for the second section, No. 207. The principal apartment—the lunch-room—was twice the width of the gentlemen's tea-room, and the designer took advantage of the 16 feet high ceiling by introducing a balcony—an attractive feature, notwithstanding its mechanical carved panels and turned balusters. Carving, turning and panelling of Victorian vintage seem to have been used indiscriminately here, and that precious legacy of a more elegant epoch, a frieze of mirrors, was placed below the gallery. Nevertheless, the Scott Morton Room was a considerable improvement on the earlier work, and remained more or less undisturbed for some years after Mackintosh appeared on the scene. In fact, the mirrors were still in position when the premises passed into the hands of Messrs. Coopers in the 1930's. The third and fourth sections, Nos. 213–15 were acquired *circa* 1901 and remodelled in the following year.[1]

Here for the first time, Mackintosh was given an entirely free hand. He opened up the party walls and combined the four sections in one suite of inter-communicating apartments. (In addition, there were, of course, kitchens and service counters, and the inevitable billiards-room, and smoking-rooms in the basement.) A main doorway was made in the centre of the block, and the former entrance to No. 205 retained. A new staircase was built, giving access to a small balcony over the servery and through an opening in the party wall, to the balcony of the Scott Morton Room; the original wooden staircase thus became redundant and was dismantled. The main stair, like all Mackintosh's stairways, is a fine luxurious feature. It has a well-proportioned wooden balustrade crowned by the customary cornice of wide projection; the sturdy balusters are square in section and rise to a height of about ten feet at the foot of the stair to meet the cornice, which is carried horizontally at balcony level. The entrance hall and staircase are separated from the main dining-room by an attractive timber screen 6 feet 6 inches high, with square leaded glass panels just above eye level (Plate 50A). The room itself is panelled vertically to a height of about 10 feet, and the lines of the broad cover strips are echoed in the front of the balcony, which in turn is decorated by a single row of square stencilled patterns. All the woodwork, including that of the staircase, is painted white. A particularly attractive beaten metal panel by Margaret Mackintosh occupies a conspicuous position at the head of the main stair; it is matched by a second one at the opposite side of the room and two large gesso panels, *The Wassail*, by

[1] *Post Office Guide:* This date was corroborated by a reference in *The Studio*, May 1903, where illustrations of Mackintosh's work appear as 'recently completed'.

Mackintosh, and *The May Queen*, by his wife, face each other across the apartment.[1] They make interesting comparison with Walton's *Eros*.

Both panels were designed by the Mackintoshes at the Mains Street flat in 1900, and were shown at the 8th Secessionist Exhibition in Vienna later in the same year. They are still to be seen at the Ingram Street Tea-Rooms.

The artists' method of working is worth recording. They used a base of coarse hessian or canvas laid on a stretcher. Over this a thin coat of gesso plaster was applied, through which the rough texture of the base clearly showed. When this had dried the pattern was drawn in charcoal on the surface, and outlined in thick string on which a few coloured beads were threaded—the whole being held in position by small pins. A second thin coat was then applied, and pieces of coloured glass, beads and metal were embedded in the wet plaster. When dry certain portions of the design were painted to represent hair, faces, flowers, and so forth. The rough uneven texture of the base was allowed to show clearly in the completed work. This technique lent itself admirably to the delicate linear patterns favoured by the artists and despite the rather sorrowful ladies, the panels were by no means unattractive.

As originally furnished and decorated Mackintosh's white dining-room was a spacious and dignified apartment. Nowhere was ornament obtrusive and the chairs were of a sober, square backed variety, soundly constructed and well proportioned—except for one or two which for some reason not now apparent, had excessively high backs. The gesso panels were fixed high against the ceiling, and unlike the gigantic ladies at Buchanan Street, provided a mere accent, a ripple of colour and texture above the hard white panelling. One discordant note was struck in this room, however, oddly enough by the fireplace, a heavy rectangular structure encased in beaten lead. This was one of Mackintosh's most inelegant and least attractive designs and seems quite out of place here.[2]

After completing the white dining-room Mackintosh and Miss Cranston turned to a new project—*The Willow Tea-Rooms*—in Sauchiehall Street, Glasgow's most fashionable thoroughfare. It was not until 1907—after this was completed—that the finishing touches were put to the westernmost section of Ingram Street—the Oak Room.

[1] The gesso panels and other details were illustrated in *The Studio*, vol. XXXVI, No. 122, May 1903, pp. 286–8 and were sent by permission of Miss Cranston to the International Exhibition of Modern Decorative Art held at Turin in May 1902. The original designs in water colour on tracing paper are in the author's collection. They were illustrated also in *Academy Architecture* 1901.   [2] Illustrated in *The Studio*, vol. XXXVI, No. 122, May 1903, p. 288.

THE OAK ROOM

The Oak Room (Plate 51A) is a narrow apartment lit from one end and one long side. Mackintosh constructed a balcony round three sides of the room, a balcony which recalls the School of Art Library, though on a much smaller scale. It is probable that the Library and the Oak Room projects were on the drawing-board at the same time (1906), and experience gained at Ingram Street no doubt came in useful when the larger scheme materialized some two years later. In the tea-room, however, the ceiling needed no further support and, unlike the School Library, the sturdy square posts carrying the balcony do not continue upwards to ceiling height. Instead they branch out into five slender uprights (3 inches by 1 inch) which pass through the balcony wall, and terminate at the ceiling against a moulding of slight projection. These members serve no structural purpose; they contain and define the balcony area, and have much the same significance as the *Hous'hill* screen. The balcony, too, is virtually a room within a room, separated from yet part of the whole.

This small apartment with its rich golden brown panelling and delightfully intimate atmosphere forms an admirable contrast to the sparkling dining-room, and is one of the most attractive of the Ingram Street Group.[1]

THE CLOISTER ROOM

Having thus remodelled the principal rooms to the west of the main entrance, the first section—the gentlemen's and ladies' tea-rooms, formerly decorated by Messrs. Alexander and Howell—was redesigned.

The records of Francis Smith & Son show that the two rooms were completed *circa* 1911—they were the last interiors of any importance that Mackintosh designed for Miss Cranston. The smaller of the two, known as the Cloister Room, has a low arched ceiling, and the walls are panelled in pine, planed smooth and wax polished. At one end there are groups of deeply recessed niches lined with leaded mirror glass and embellished with Chinese Gothic tracery (Plate 51C); and a strange wooden lintel over the doorway has a rich, scale-like

---

[1] A small oval room opens off the balcony; it was added much later, probably *circa* 1916, and contains a diminutive fireplace and an open screen similar to that in the music-room at *Hous'hill*, Nitshill. It is claimed that the screen and fabric panelling in this room were designed by one of Mackintosh's colleagues.

134

surface pattern. The walls are decorated with painted vertical strips of diaper pattern in garish colours—red, green, and blue outlined in black—the wavy lines of these are picked up by plaster bands running transversely across the ceiling.

In this room Mackintosh said he wouldn't have a straight line, and he nearly succeeded. But the multiplicity of elements, the broken wall surfaces, and the wriggling decorations, together produce an air of restlessness that is not found in any of the other apartments.

At the time of writing the Cloister Room contains a variety of nondescript furniture—with some pieces designed by Mackintosh. The original chairs had high square backs with a broad wavy central slat, but in August 1912, Francis Smith & Son were given the task of reducing the height of thirty-one of them —no doubt because they appeared out of scale with the low ceiled apartment, and added to the confusion.

THE CHINA TEA-ROOM

The last room at Ingram Street to be remodelled by Mackintosh was the former gentlemen's tea-room. It was rechristened the China Tea-Room; the name and decorative scheme continuing a tradition already established, for originally the room boasted several exotic oriental motives—notably a pagoda-like canopy over the doorway, and a pseudo-chinese chippendale screen. The surviving picture reminds one inevitably of this verse from *The Ballad of Bedford Park*:

> *Now he who loves aesthetic cheer*
> *And does not mind the damp*
> *May come and read Rossetti here*
> *By a Japanese-y lamp.*[1]

Mackintosh stripped the apartment, and then lined the walls with coarse hessian over which he applied a wooden lattice of $10\frac{1}{2}$-inch squares extending to a height of about 8 feet; all this was painted blue (Plate 51B). Some of the squares were filled with leaded glass and others were grouped and recessed to form small niches lined with pieces of coloured plastic material, or alternatively mirror glass. For his purpose the room was excessively high in relation to its width

---

[1] Published in *St. James's Gazette*, 17th December 1881. Quoted in full by Blomfield in his book, *R. N. Shaw*.

and he corrected its proportions by introducing three broad openwork canopies spanning from wall to wall, each with an intermediate support serving as a hat and umbrella stand. By dividing the room in this manner, instead of building a false ceiling, he secured the intimacy he required, meanwhile retaining the sense of spaciousness engendered by the high walls and existing ceiling (Plate 52).

It is said that Mackintosh designed bamboo furniture for the China Tea-Room, but this is most unlikely as no record of such furniture can be found. His built-in, tip-up settees are still in position, and the movable pieces consist mainly of round coffee-tables of the kind noted at Argyle Street (designed in 1896), and some excellent bucket-chairs with broad slatted backs—these are the most attractive and serviceable chairs he made for Miss Cranston. The settees were originally upholstered in blue corduroy to match the curtains.

The general effect of this room with its blue painted woodwork, dark oak furniture and subdued lighting is mysterious and bizarre—Mackintosh was delighted with it. Mrs. Mary Newbery Sturrock who, as a young student was shown round with pride by the architect himself, says that for some weeks after the opening he even arranged the flowers—a typical instance of the care and affection he was prepared to lavish upon any work that pleased him and over which he had entire control.

The Ingram Street Tea-Rooms thus contain examples of work by Mackintosh in many moods. The pleasant white dining-room in the Mains Street tradition; the Oak Room, sombre and restrained in the manner of the School of Art Library; the restless, indecisive Cloister Room; and the ingeniously contrived fantasy of the China Tea-Room, together reflect something of the complex personality of the designer.[1]

THE WILLOW TEA-ROOMS, 1903–4

After finishing the white dining-room at Ingram Street and *Hill House* for Mr. Blackie, Mackintosh commenced work on the most complete and

---

[1] It is believed that (*circa* 1920) Miss Cranston gave the Ingram Street tea-rooms to one of her manageresses, Miss Drummond. A decade later they passed into the hands of Messrs. Coopers of Glasgow, who, in a press announcement on 26th May 1930, undertook to retain the character of the premises as far as possible—a promise faithfully kept. Shortly after the expiry of Coopers' lease in May 1950, the tea-rooms, with their fixtures and fittings were acquired by Glasgow Corporation in order to prevent their destruction (see page 294).

accomplished of his tea-room projects for Miss Cranston—*The Willow*, Sauchie-hall Street. The site was acquired by Miss Cranston in 1901, but the new building was not finished until 1904.

On this occasion Mackintosh was architect for the entire scheme. He designed not only the interiors and furniture but the fabric, the structure itself, and it is interesting to observe that he followed George Walton's example at Buchanan Street by designing a protective hoarding for the contractors whilst the façade was being re-modelled. Part of this was carried forward on heavy beams as a canopy which was painted white and decorated with characteristic stencilled patterns and lettering.[1]

In spite of the limitations imposed by the narrow frontage and restricted site, Mackintosh produced a façade which would be considered modern by present-day standards and which, with its clean horizontal lines and refined detail, was extraordinary indeed in 1904 (Plate 53). He ignored the fenestration of the adjacent property—the windows in any case were not in alignment—and placed a simple unmoulded hood of about 18 inches to 24 inches projection right across the façade at second floor level, and below this curved the wall gently outwards. The windows on the two upper floors were of normal proportions, but the first floor was illuminated by a beautifully designed horizontal window with a clear span of 18 feet. This was sub-divided into tall, narrow lights of leaded glass each containing a single tiny leaf-shaped motive of mirror glass, and was flanked by wrought iron signs. The ground floor was lit by a large window enclosed in a slightly projecting architrave, and sub-divided horizontally at door height, the upper portion being deeply recessed and the lower part containing a row of narrow lights similar in proportion to those on the first floor. Two circular hoop-like features of wrought iron—tree symbols—linked the transome and lintel, and the lower portion of the façade was set back slightly from the building line so that small ornamental trees in cubiform tubs could be placed outside the restaurant without encroaching on the pavement.

Considered as a whole the façade is not well composed. The canopy divides it almost precisely into two equal parts, and thereby emphasizes the different treatment of the upper and lower sections. There are, in fact, virtually two façades here bearing little relationship to each other. One can appreciate the architect's wish to emphasize the importance of the first-floor room—the most important in the whole building—but it is difficult to understand why he changed the character of the upper storeys so completely—why, for instance,

[1] An illustration of the hoarding appeared in *Dekorative Kunst*, April 1905.

did he make the windows asymmetrical when they all serve exactly the same purpose, there being but one large room on each floor. The explanation may be that, by introducing larger windows on the left of the façade, he was expressing externally the presence of the main staircase deep within the building. This is an interesting theory for it would seem to account for the curved wall surface at this point—the merest suggestion, perhaps, of the familiar staircase bay, or traditional turret.

The lower half of the elevation, however, the only part that could be comprehended with any degree of comfort from the street, is one of Mackintosh's most elegant and attractive designs. Here his use of long horizontal openings, and plain unadorned surfaces brings him closely into line with the most advanced continental architects of the post 1914–18 war period. Once again Mackintosh seems to be reaching out towards a distant goal, as yet ill defined—towards an architecture of plain, smooth surfaces that can be deeply penetrated and modelled like sculptors' clay; and, as demonstrated by the sharply defined outlines of the ground-floor window, an architecture of clean cut, mechanical precision.

Yet here too we find wrought iron in the style of Mackmurdo and Voysey; the chequered borders of Josef Hoffmann, 'borrowed' perhaps from the Pürkersdorf Sanatorium, Vienna (1903); and the singing birds, the swinging crystal balls, and the coloured glass of Margaret Macdonald. The enigma of Mackintosh is clearly revealed in this façade. Nevertheless, despite its contradictions, this work alone would entitle him to a place in the forefront of contemporary European designers—and it would be difficult to find a greater contrast than that between *The Willow*, and the heavy carved sandstone façades which were the order of the day in Glasgow.

Mallet Stephens, the French pioneer of modern architecture, once wrote these words above the door of his studio:—'*Si j'étais Dieu*'. 'If you were God—what then?' he was asked on one occasion by E. A. Taylor. The reply came without hesitation—'I should design like Mackintosh.'[1]

There is a whole street in Paris built by Mallet Stephens!

Following their favourite practice of selecting an appropriate symbol or theme, the Mackintoshes based their designs for the interior of the restaurant upon the name 'Sauchiehall', which is derived from an old Scottish word signify-

[1] E. A. Taylor, the painter, a friend and contemporary of Mackintosh, told the author of this incident in 1945.

138

ing street, or alley of the willows. Thus the predominant motive throughout was the flat, pinnate shape of the willow leaf.

The general layout of the interior was similar to the Buchanan Street restaurant, but the rear half of the ground floor, a long narrow apartment, was only one storey high and was covered by a partially glazed, hipped roof. Mackintosh concealed the steel trusses by a timber ceiling framed in squares like an egg-box, and open in parts to admit daylight—a method very popular today (Plate 55A).

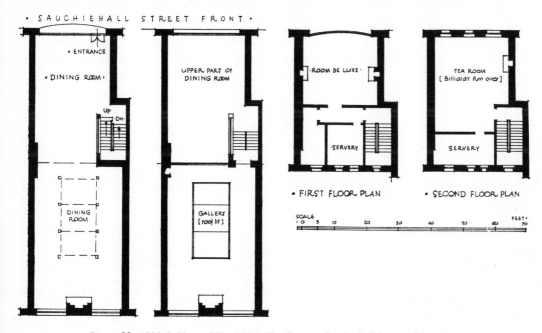

Figure 20. 1904–5. Plans of *The Willow* Tea-Rooms, Sauchiehall Street, Glasgow.

The ground-floor ceiling throughout was even higher than at Ingram Street—about 18 feet—and he introduced an airy balcony at the back of the premises, below the roof light.

A fine staircase leading first to the balcony, and then to the upper floors, was approached directly from the main entrance, and was separated from the principal apartment by a light balustrade of tubular metal rods of about three-quarter inch diameter. Each of these was secured to a tread of the staircase and carried up to the ceiling where it terminated in a twisted pattern of wrought iron, interspersed with green glass balls threaded on stout wire (Plate 54). This,

139

again, was a conventionalized tree form and echoed the motives embroidered on Margaret Macdonald's delicate silk curtains to the ground-floor windows.

The balcony reduced the ceiling level at the back of the ground-floor apartment and had the effect of dividing it into two sections, an illusion of which Mackintosh took advantage by contrasting the decorations. The front half, to Sauchiehall Street, was painted white from floor to ceiling. The walls were panelled to a height of about 7 feet and above this he inserted a curious frieze of plaster panels, worked in bold relief. One of these was used over the staircase in the Southpark Avenue house. The frieze itself is still in position and is quite extraordinary (Plate 56A and B). The willow tree motive is apparent, but it is used merely as a starting point for the architect's curious abstractions. His interest here lay, as always, in the creation of original linear patterns based upon, yet remote from natural forms. There does not appear to be any precedent for the frieze and it—and, indeed, the wrought metal of the staircase balustrade—seems to point forward unmistakably to the analytical work of painters such as Picasso, Mondrian or Kandinsky; to presage the abstract reliefs of Nicholson, and the constructivist experiments of Moholy-Nagy and his school. Though its merit as a work of art may be debatable, it served its purpose admirably, and provides still further evidence of Mackintosh's ceaseless quest for new means of expression.

In the white dining-room a strong dominant feature was required so the architect designed a fantastic timber contraption, a veritable baldacchino, 9 feet high, enclosing two tables. This supported a large transparent glass bowl, fully 2 feet 6 inches in diameter, in which were suspended test-tubes for holding flowers (Plate 54). Mackintosh was always attracted by the greenish hue of water and glass, and the curious effect of the test-tubes seen from beneath must have pleased him immensely. This extravaganza, however, was not in keeping with the simple refinement of the rest of the room, and no doubt attracted attention by its novelty, rather than its appropriateness and good form.

In contrast to the light and airy front apartment, the rear half of the ground floor below the gallery was panelled in dark oak (Plate 55B). The furniture throughout consisted of simple ladder-backed chairs and low square tub-chairs, all in dark stained oak. Unlike the galleries at the School of Art and Ingram Street, there were no pillars: the apartment was spanned by heavy wooden beams, two of which ran right across the open well of the gallery. Each carried a pair of tapered columns which did not continue down to floor level, but nevertheless, supported the principals of the false ceiling above. These can be

140

seen clearly on Plate 55A. The whole of the woodwork, columns, beams and timber ceiling was painted white, and by way of contrast, the panelled walls were stencilled in colour with Mackintosh's characteristic rose motive.

On entering the restaurant from Sauchiehall Street it was possible to see right through to the windows in the back wall 80 feet away below the mezzanine, and through an attractive wrought metal screen to the coffered ceiling above the balcony. Mackintosh thus achieved a surprising effect of space, light and freedom in very restricted circumstances; he provided three inter-related though virtually separate apartments of distinctive character without the use of a single partition-wall.

The second floor was used as a tea-room, and, in fact, still is, though the decorations have been altered considerably in recent years. The fireplaces alone remain of the original scheme. The third floor was designed as a billiards-room and panelled to a height of about 6 feet with dark stained timber, probably pine. One side was entirely occupied by comfortable built-in seats, raised on a low platform to give a better view of the play. The only decoration consisted of applied, stencilled or incised squares, and even these were used very sparingly. This was in fact a fine, dignified apartment admirably suited to its purpose; but now it has been turned into a workshop, and every trace of the former scheme has vanished.

THE ROOM DE LUXE

An innovation at *The Willow* restaurant was the *Room de Luxe* designed by the Mackintoshes as the very heart and centre of the whole project; an apartment which was to symbolize the grove, or alley of willows (Plate 57). It was rich and jewel-like in conception, a scintillating creation of crystal and glass painted entirely in white. It had a plain dado 3 feet 9 inches high above which a row of leaded mirror-glass panels 2 feet 9 inches deep extended round three sides of the room, their emphatic and insistent rhythm being continued on the fourth side by the vertical divisions of the charming bow window overlooking Sauchiehall Street. Each mirror was separated from its neighbour by a broad white fillet by which Mackintosh intended to convey the idea of a forest of slender tree-trunks—an impression further accentuated by the high chair-backs which were reflected again and again in great depth and diversity. The dazzling frieze was interrupted at one end of the room by a simple fireplace

141

enclosed in an enormous plain architrave, and at the opposite end by a large gesso panel similarly framed (Plate 56c).

The doorway which, like the panelling and mirrors, has survived, is of especial interest—not only because of its extraordinary patterns of leaded glass resembling the abstract designs of the ground-floor frieze, but on account of the narrow unmoulded architrave that was set, boxlike, at right angles to the wall (Plate 57c). This is a feature which has become popular in recent years but was rarely seen at the turn of the century, and never before in such a simplified form. Mackintosh's objective in using an architrave of this shape was to secure the maximum amount of space for his mirrors, to preserve their continuity, and at the same time, to concentrate interest upon the great double doors. A normal architrave lying flat against the wall, and correctly proportioned in relation to the door opening, would have seriously broken into the frieze, and, moreover, would have overemphasized the doorway. Now the frieze of mirrors seems to thread its way into and through the door surface, for a moment losing its form but not its substance, and the eye passes easily over the glazed surfaces of both elements which lie in the same vertical plane. By such means Mackintosh preserved the unity of the apartment and directed attention towards the fireplace and gesso panel.

To relieve the whiteness there was a luxurious, soft grey carpet, lined and patterned in squares of various sizes. The built-in settees and chairs were upholstered in rich purple, and tiny accents of rose pink and mauve enamel were incorporated with mirror glass in the frieze and doorway. On every table there was a pleasant ripple of blue in the Willow pattern tea services—a homely, healthy colour this, which, no doubt, re-assured those unfamiliar with the new art and overawed by the Mackintoshes' poetic harmonies. And then, of course, there were flowers, and sturdy knives and forks with black handles, and long, slender tea spoons with clover-leaf shafts, and sparkling glassware, all contributing to the brilliance of the ensemble.

In the evening the room was softly lit by a crystal chandelier suspended from the centre of the low arched ceiling (Plate 57B)—an intricate cluster of glass balls, spheroids and globular shapes, among which the lamps were hidden.

The *Room de Luxe* was indeed an exotic apartment and it became one of the show-pieces of Glasgow, a mecca for visitors to the city and the rendezvous of Miss Cranston's most elegant patrons. For all its brilliance, however, it had a strangely disquieting air, for the focal point of the whole scheme, the *raison d'être* of the mirrors and crystal, was the large gesso panel designed by Margaret

Macdonald and inspired by one of Rossetti's sonnets from *The House of Life*
—a sonnet, moreover, whose sensuous, sonorous rhythms epitomize the etherial
sadness of all her work:

> *O ye, all ye that walk in Willowwood,*
> *That walk with hollow faces burning white;*
> *What fathom-depth of soul-struck widowhood,*
> *What long, what longer hours, one lifelong night*
> *Ere ye again, who so in vain have wooed*
> *Your last hope lost, who so in vain invite*
> *Your lips to that their unforgotten food*
> *Ere ye, ere ye again shall see the light!*

How many of Miss Cranston's patrons recognized and appreciated the inner
meaning of all this, and were able to unravel the mystery of the mirrors and
willow leaves, is a matter for conjecture, but to the sensitive observer, and more
especially to the foreigner, the *Room de Luxe* seemed to be a miracle of applied
art—'the result of thoughts full of love', wrote an enchanted German visitor.

Oddly enough the professional journals in this country paid scanty attention
to the Sauchiehall Street tea-rooms—and even *The Studio* was strangely silent.
It is again to a continental source, to the indefatigable Alexander Koch, that
one must turn for a complete picture of *The Willow* restaurant. Practically the
whole of one issue of the journal *Dekorative Kunst* (April 1905) was devoted to
illustrations of the premises with an appraisal by an anonymous author—probably Hermann Muthesius. The writer was overwhelmed by the virtuosity of the
designers, and entranced by the beauty and elegance of the restaurant as a
whole. Some measure of the lyricism which his visit evoked may be gleaned from
his observations on the *Room de Luxe* where he speaks of 'the beauty of the
serene and pure colours of the panels, the lines moved by the breath of destiny,
and the star-like gems whose sparkling rays weave a veil of mysteriously glowing
light around the countenances and forms of women wandering silently under a
magic spell through the willow grove'.[1] Yes, Muthesius, if it were Muthesius,
was deeply moved by the work of the Mackintoshes, and he was astonished to
find such genius taken for granted by the citizens of Glasgow. 'Scottish artists
who are wise', he says, 'leave their native land early in life in order to make

---

[1] In contrast to this panegyric there is to be found an amusing account of a visit to *The
Willow* by a colourful local character in a book *Erchie*, by Hugh Foulis (Neil Munro),
Chapter 22, 'Erchie in an Art Tea Room'.

their fortunes in London.' Of far greater significance, however, is his statement that 'the existence in Europe of a real architect is an important fact in our time'.

Mackintosh, he claimed, was one of the few who could be called 'Masters of the art of architecture' and he upbraids Glasgow 'a thicket of unsightliness' for failing to recognize the genius in her midst—the School of Art, then only half built, *Windyhill, Hill House,* and 'two or three less important buildings' he considered quite inadequate to represent the capacity of so great an individual. Thus, through the medium of *Dekorative Kunst,* the fame of *The Willow* and the reputation of its designers, was broadcast throughout Europe. The architectural profession in this country was left to make what it could of an illustration of the lower half of the façade that appeared in *The Builders' Journal and Architectural Engineer.*[1]

The Willow Tea-Rooms were opened in October 1904. They fulfilled all expectations, and there is no evidence that subsequent alterations were carried out. During the 1914–18 War, however, the proprietress opened the basement as an additional tea-room to which she gave the topical name of *The Dugout.* The Mackintoshes, then living in London, made two notable contributions to this room; the first was a memorial fireplace (*circa* 1919) embodying the flags of the allied nations in coloured enamels; the second, a pair of large canvases about 40 inches square (Plate 81A), inspired by the words of the sixty-fifth Psalm: 'Thou crownest the year with Thy goodness . . . and the little hills shall rejoice.' This was the most ambitious work of its kind attempted by the artists. The complementary pictures are full of vitality and joyous abandon, in spite of a colour scheme dominated by sombre greys, greens and yellows. Fat cherubs sending forth a paean of praise take the place of the familiar weeping females, and the canvases are filled with a riot of flowers, jewels, ears of corn, butterflies and so forth—the emphasis throughout being on two-dimensional pattern with little attempt at perspective, or modelling.[2]

It has not been possible to discover details of the furniture, fittings and decorative scheme of *The Dugout* but an amusing story is told by the decorator who was responsible for carrying out Mackintosh's instructions. Apparently the architect wished to obtain a particular quality of glossy black for the ceiling and insisted that the painters should mix blacklead into a thick paste, apply it with a brush in the normal way and when dry, polish it. The workmen went on

[1] 28th November 1906, p. 263.

[2] Both paintings are now in the possession of Mrs. Dunderdale of Dunglass Castle, by whose permission they are reproduced here.

144

strike at this and refused to carry out the order in no uncertain terms saying that blackleading was a woman's job. Mackintosh was an adept at handling such situations, and the ceiling was finished to his satisfaction. By all accounts the result was superb—the workmen left the premises as black as chimney sweeps, convinced that the architect was mad.

The tea-rooms formed an interesting and rewarding diversion in Mackintosh's career; they provided an admirable outlet for his creative energy and compensated for the restrictions and formality of office practice which he often found irksome. Moreover, they kept his name continually in the public eye for, as we have seen, one or other of the tea-rooms was usually in the process of re-decoration or re-furnishing.

Mackintosh's association with Miss Cranston was not an unmixed blessing, however, and it is regrettable that he was obliged to devote so much time to decorative work in which the emphasis was always upon novelty or ingenuity. It would seem that his creative genius could have been directed into more useful channels and the care he lavished upon stencils, twisted wire, and leaded glass might have been used to better purposes. Here, however, we are on dangerous ground, for it is difficult to determine exactly to what extent the trivia of the tea-rooms can be ascribed to him, and how much of the new art *bric-à-brac* may be attributed to his wife. P. Morton Shand bitterly condemns Margaret Macdonald as one of the principal stumbling blocks in Mackintosh's path to greatness, and there is more than a grain of truth in his contention.[1] Her work shows little sign of development; she seems to have lived in a world of roses, love-in-a-mist, cherubs and falling petals—the quasi-dream world of Rossetti, Maeterlinck and the MacNairs—an amorphous paradise from which Mackintosh himself might well have escaped. It is very probable that Margaret Macdonald, however unwittingly, was responsible for limiting her husband's vision, for tying him more securely to the aesthetic movement, and encouraging him to dissipate his energies on work of comparative unimportance when he might have consolidated his position in the architectural field.

It would be easy of course to blame all the architect's failures on his wife, and to point to the beads and pieces of coloured glass suspended on the fine staircase at *The Willow Tea-Rooms*, or the crystal balls hanging at the fireplace of the *Room de Luxe*, as examples of her contrariety. But there is no evidence

[1] 'The Glasgow Interlude', P. Morton Shand, *The Architectural Review*, vol. LXXVII, 1935.

to show that she álone was responsible for such details—in fact the Mackintoshes worked more closely together on the *Room de Luxe* than on any other scheme. It is only when we brush aside the beads and wire, and look beyond the chinoiserie and the mystical symbolism of the willow wood—all of which are little more than the flotsam of the nineties—that we can appreciate the fundamental architectural qualities of Mackintosh's work for Miss Cranston.

In none of the tea-rooms of course was he able to model the form of the building itself—even at *The Willow* only the front and back elevations were visible. Thus denied one of the architect's principal delights, the composition and arrangement of mass, he concentrated upon spatial modelling within the shell. Instead of using bricks and mortar he employed openwork screens and balconies to divide and sub-divide the volume of the building. There is nothing unusual in this of course, balconies and screens are a practical necessity in many commercial buildings; in Mackintosh's hands, however, they were never used solely to solve a utilitarian problem but to achieve a specific visual or psychological objective—an interesting vista perhaps, a pattern in depth, or alternatively to create an illusion of space or an impression of intimacy. All these sensory experiences can be realized in the work under consideration here. The tea-rooms provided, as it were, a series of exercises in the control of volume and the organization of the plan, aesthetic and technical exercises comparable with advanced studies in music, and ultimately bearing fruit in the second section of the School of Art. It is the appreciation—subconscious at first perhaps —of this mastery of the inner form—which draws the observer again and again to Mackintosh's work long after he has tired of the ornament, the hanging lamps, and the stencilled decoration.

This, then, is the most important aspect of Mackintosh's work for Miss Cranston. In addition of course, it is necessary to stress again the unity of his designs, a unity seldom achieved by his contemporaries—even by Walton—and conspicuously absent from the interiors at Argyle Street and Buchanan Street in which the two artists worked together. Such unity was only possible when Mackintosh was in control, and where every detail was considered in relation to the whole.

Finally, mention must be made of the simple effectiveness of his colour schemes and decoration which, with few exceptions, set a remarkably high standard for work of this nature. Generally speaking, he followed the principles already outlined in relation to his domestic work. He had two main themes— light and dark, white painted walls or stained woodwork—and despite the use

146

of some *art nouveau* stencilled pattern, leaded glass, embroidery or beaten metal, in no instance, except, perhaps, in the Cloister Room at Ingram Street, was the decoration unpleasantly obtrusive.

Miss Cranston continued to preside over her four restaurants until 1917 when the death of Major Cochrane brought her career to an abrupt end. She had been devoted to her husband and after his passing seemed to lose interest in life. She disposed of the Argyle Street, Buchanan Street and Ingram Street premises and the *Willow Tea-Rooms* were sold to Messrs. Smith, Restaurateurs, in 1919 —they were re-named, ominously enough, *The Kensington*! Some years later the premises were absorbed by a large adjacent store, and the fine elevation to Sauchiehall Street completely and utterly ruined by the insertion of a commonplace shop-front. Fortunately, no alterations were made to the upper part of the façade, which still retains much of its original character, notwithstanding a thick coat of soot. Apart from the *Room de Luxe* little remains of Mackintosh's interior work; the staircase, a certain amount of panelling, the plaster frieze, several fireplaces and a large elliptical wrought iron light fitting are still to be seen, though they appear strangely out of place amid the shop fittings which have since been installed.

Thus Miss Cranston's courageous enterprises have come to a more or less ignominious end, and she herself, after selling her house and estate at Nitshill Glasgow (1920), returned nostalgically to George Square, where she had spent her childhood. She lived in comparative seclusion in the North British Hotel until her death on 18th April 1934. So Glasgow lost one of its most colourful personalities, and the past twenty years have witnessed the merciless destruction of most of her work, and that of the artists she employed.

VII

MACKINTOSH IN EUROPE

IT is generally assumed that Mackintosh executed a considerable amount of work in Europe at the turn of the century; in fact on one occasion the author was informed by a very knowledgeable person just back from Finland that he had built Helsinki railway station! The truth is that he carried out no architectural work abroad, and protracted and careful investigation has brought to light evidence of only three minor commissions, all in the decorative sphere, undertaken for private individuals.[1] This popular misconception—where not due to wishful thinking—has arisen, no doubt, because of the enthusiasm aroused by exhibitions of his work on the Continent, and the wide publicity accorded his designs in foreign journals.

As far as can be ascertained the first illustrated article on the Glasgow group appeared in November 1898, in Koch's *Dekorative Kunst*. It was similar to Gleeson White's essay in *The Studio* of the previous year, but the illustrations

[1] The author was told by Sir Stanley Cursitor some years ago of a house he had seen in Cologne during the 1914–18 War decorated by Mackintosh. At the time of writing it has not been possible to secure further information about this project, which does not appear to have been illustrated in the journals.

148

were few, poor, and confined to furniture and craftwork. In May 1899 the same periodical published photographs of a dining-room with furniture designed by Mackintosh, but neither the name of his patron, nor any indication of the whereabouts of the house is given. It is stated, however, that the room contained chairs by K. Bertsch, and this points to Munich as the probable location. Moreover, there are two early, but undated drawings of a cabinet and a cupboard in the Glasgow University Collection for H. Bruckmann of Munich, which may well have formed part of the same commission. The furniture consisted principally of two cabinets in dark oak; one, of large size, occupied an entire wall; the other, tall and narrow, probably a smoker's cabinet, was placed against the opposite wall. The larger of the two had a pair of glazed doors of characteristic design, and the doors of the smaller one were embellished with beaten metal panels by Margaret Macdonald. Above a projecting plate-rail on which stood a multitude of small vases, busts and the like, there was a curious stencilled frieze embodying a clumsy heart-shaped tree form found occasionally in Mackintosh's early work, but soon abandoned (Plate 58A).

None of the other furniture in the room was designed by Mackintosh, and, in consequence, the ensemble lacks the unity one expects of him. It is doubtful if he actually went to Germany at this time to supervise the work, and the fact that the room was overcrowded with innumerable *objets d'art*, not to mention heavy curtains and a commonplace gas-bracket, may be taken as sufficient evidence to the contrary. It is fairly certain that he would have insisted upon the removal of most of these impedimenta, and no doubt would have persuaded his client to accept designs for chairs, table, carpet and curtains in addition to the cabinets. Most probably the commission was obtained either through Newbery, or indirectly as a result of *The Studio* article. Drawings would have been sent from Glasgow, and the work executed on the spot.

There is no further evidence here, or elsewhere, to suggest that Mackintosh visited Europe before the turn of the century—except, of course, on his scholarship tour in 1891. Thus it can be said with a fair degree of certainty that before 1900 he was known abroad only through the medium of *The Studio*, and one or two relatively insignificant magazine articles—and possibly in educational circles by exhibitions of school work, posters and the like, arranged by Newbery. Thereafter, however, events moved swiftly. In the late autumn of 1900 *The Four* were invited individually to furnish and decorate an entire room at the 8th Secessionist Exhibition in Vienna—this was followed by exhibitions of their work at Munich, Dresden, Budapest and elsewhere. In 1901 Mackintosh submitted a scheme for the famous *Haus eines Kunstfreundes* competition, and designed a music salon in Vienna for Fritz Wärndorfer, one of the founders of the Wiener Werkstätte. In 1902 came the International Exhibition of Decorative Art at Turin, and thereafter a further visit to Vienna. Everywhere the Mackintoshes were greeted with enthusiasm and hailed as leaders in the new movement.

It may seem curious that the Scottish artists should have been invited to exhibit first at Munich and Vienna and the cities of Central Europe rather than, say, in France or Belgium; yet the reason is not far to seek. For some time Munich had been one of the most progressive art centres on the continent and, like Brussels, became a veritable storm centre of the revolt against academicism. The insurrection began after an exhibition of work by the Glasgow School of Painters in 1891. Here, as elsewhere, the fresh atmospheric canvases of the *Boys from Glasgow* caused a ferment in the art world, and a group of young progressives, eager to throw off the heavy hand of tradition, broke away from the Academy and founded a rival institution—the Munich Secession. But the tide of revolution was comparatively slow in reaching Vienna, a noted stronghold of conservatism. Ostensibly in order to preserve the home market for native artists the Viennese Academy had persistently discouraged exhibitions of work by foreigners and the public generally was unaware of contemporary developments in the west. In the spring of 1894, however, work by British artists was shown in the capital, and in addition to paintings by the English academicians Alma Tadema, Leighton and Herkomer there appeared for the first time canvases by the Glasgow Painters Macaulay Stevenson, D. Y. Cameron, Reid Murray and others. Here, as at Munich, the outcome was dramatic and far-reaching. Within a few months the more conservative element in the Academy had been out-voted and in December (1894) the previously ostracized Munich Secessionist Group was invited to the Künstlerhaus. Thereafter several young artists were elected members of the selection committee, and further exhibitions of modern work were held in the face of bitter opposition from the old school. An uneasy peace was maintained for about two years, and then serious differences of opinion began to show within the reformed administration. On 3rd April 1897 nineteen members withdrew and launched an independent society—the Viennese Secession. Among the founders of the new group were Josef Hoffmann (b. 1870), and J. M. Olbrich (1867–1908), architects, Gustav Klimt (b. 1862), Carl Moll (b. 1861), and Felician von

Myrbach (b. 1853), painters. The veteran painter Rudolf von Alt (1812–1905) was elected leader of the group.[1]

THE VIENNA SECESSIONIST EXHIBITION (1900)

It was at the invitation of these men—all artists who already had come directly under the influence of Scottish painting—that Charles and Margaret Mackintosh visited the Austrian capital in the autumn of 1900 to supervise the decoration and furnishing of an apartment allocated to them in the now famous *Secession House*, built by J. M. Olbrich two years previously. Their exhibits consisted of pieces mainly drawn from the Mains Street flat or borrowed from friends, and included the two large gesso panels from Miss Cranston's Ingram Street tea-room—*The May Queen* by Margaret, and *The Wassail* by Mackintosh himself. The MacNairs were in Liverpool at this time, of course, and although some of their work was exhibited they did not go to Vienna, and they played little part in the events which followed.

The Mackintoshes must have faced the prospect of the Viennese excursion with mixed feelings: apart from the support of Gleeson White and *The Studio*, they had received little encouragement from any but their immediate circle of friends and acquaintances in Glasgow. Moreover, they had had bitter experience of British conservatism at the Arts and Crafts Society Exhibition of 1896, and were well aware of the apparent futility of fighting against long-established customs in the art world. Their astonishment at the progress made by the Viennese Secessionists can only be imagined, for by this time the movement was securely established and the exhibition to which they were invited was the eighth of its kind held in the city, and the second to be staged in the new *Secession House*.

The lofty apartment allocated to *The Four* was prepared by Mackintosh in characteristic style (Plate 59A and C). The framed gesso panels formed the dominant feature, and were placed high against the ceiling facing each other across the room. Below them the walls were sub-divided into broad panels between freestanding tapered columns carrying the usual bold cornice. A slight variation was made by the introduction of a deep unmoulded rail pierced at intervals by square insets, each containing a linear pattern in brilliant colour

[1] The sequence of events in Vienna recorded here is that given by Ludwig Hevesi in *The: Art Revival in Austria*; *Studio* Special Number, 1906.

151

—an attractive detail used for the first time in the Mains Street flat. The entire room was painted white.

The MacNairs exhibited relatively few pieces. Their contribution consisted of an attractive wall cabinet and a clock, a few framed book illustrations, one or two water-colours and several examples of beaten metal. The work of the Mackintoshes dominated the apartment. Illustrations which survive [1] show two excellent cabinets in oak with decorative metal and leaded glass panels, two high-backed chairs, a tall white painted cheval mirror, a number of candle sconces and a pedestal flower vase of unusual design, in addition to paintings and embroidered fabrics. The flower vase which may be seen in the extreme left-hand corner of Plate 59A was an innovation. It consisted of a square metal tube, about 5 inches wide and about 2 feet 6 inches high, mounted on a flat weighted base; it was designed to conceal a large glass test-tube into which the flowers were placed. This was the first appearance of a type of container which Mackintosh used freely in a variety of forms and sizes in his subsequent work. In some instances the vertical section was cylindrical and sometimes the test-tube was held in an open framework—the latter, incidentally, was by no means an original idea, and may well have been borrowed from Josef Hoffmann who had many such designs on exhibition at Vienna in 1900. The tall cheval mirror with its elaborate white painted framework is a piece not mentioned hitherto; it is for all the world like a large sledge on end and came from the Mains Street bedroom (Plate 16A). It is a cumbersome but not unattractive piece of furniture, similar in some respects to two tortuous hallstands by M. A. Nicolai of Munich, and O. Richard Bossert of Leipzig, illustrated in the journal *Deutsche Kunst und Dekoration* in 1899. It is feasible that these came to Mackintosh's notice, and that he was influenced by them, but his design—despite its *art nouveau* curves—is considerably more restrained than either of the German examples.

The general ensemble of the Scottish room was very good. The all-pervading whiteness, the careful disposition of the furniture and its form and originality charmed and delighted the Viennese. Moreover the similarity between the work of *The Four* and the Secessionists was immediately apparent; obviously they were working towards a common objective—an objective which, no doubt, would have been difficult for either group to define lucidly in words, yet which found visual expression in the exhibits themselves. The Scottish room was by

[1] The best and most complete pictorial record of the Scottish contribution is to be found in *Die Kunst*, edited by Bruckmann, Munich, February 1901.

152

no means the only one in which plain wall surfaces dominated, however, nor were the Mackintoshes alone in recognizing the value of contrast in form and colour, and the charm of natural materials skilfully wrought. Illustrations of adjoining rooms and work by several English and Austrian artists show, on the whole, a surprising degree of restraint, notwithstanding the influence of *art nouveau* and the prevailing taste for bizarrarie and novelty (Plates 58B and C; 59B). Much of the furniture—notably a fine set of dining-room chairs—and many of the incidental pieces by Josef Hoffmann, for example, were as modern in spirit as anything produced by Mackintosh at this time.

A Secessionist Exhibition was always an exciting event in the Austrian capital, and on this occasion the presence of the Mackintoshes added more fuel to the fires of controversy. The work of a group of British exponents of the new style aroused considerable interest, and their contribution was singled out for especial attention by the critics. The art editor of *Vienna Rundschau*, for instance, commented thus on the Scottish room:

'There is a Christlike mood in this interior: this chair might have belonged to a Francis of Assisi. The decorative element is not proscribed, but is worked out with a spiritual appeal'. And again, 'In the strength, purity, simplicity and fervour of this work let us recognize the contrast between the vital expression of an idea and that affected dullness which for years past has been a source of tedium when encountered in certain alleged modern production.'

The artists' peculiar formalization of the human figure—always the *bête noire* of the art critic—was sympathetically examined and defended by Hermann Muthesius in a letter to the editor of *Die Kunst*, the German periodical which devoted considerable space to the Secessionist Exhibition in its February issue (1901). Muthesius' said:

'Can we distort the human figure and alter its proportions at will, to force it into an ornamental arrangement of lines, similar to the way we do with the plant? For this we find no parallels in the history of ornament; hitherto with each ornamental application the fundamental proportions of the human figure have been preserved, the figures have neither been drawn out into lines like baker's dough, nor compressed. But in Art there are no laws, the decisive factor is the artistic deed.'

However questionable Muthesius' thesis, and however abhorrent the Mackintoshes' seductive linear patterns to the painters of the old school, few voices

153

seem to have been raised in protest and their work fell into place naturally alongside that of Hoffmann, Klimt and the leaders of the Austrian movement.

And so Vienna welcomed the Scottish artists. It is said that students met them at the station on their arrival and drew them through the city in a flower-decked carriage. Here for the first time Mackintosh felt that his work was properly understood and appreciated; and he met and argued long into the night with some of the most progressive designers and architects in Europe, and found himself to be at one with them. Instead of grudging acknowledge-ment, or outspoken condemnation, he received unstinted praise, and his work was widely acclaimed by artists and public alike. Mackintosh had come into his own. He returned to Scotland full of new vigour, resolutely determined to convert his countrymen, and prepared to lead a rebellion against the established order of things in the art world.

But what of the material effects of the Viennese Exhibition? It has been said that all the exhibits were sold and that Mackintosh obtained many commissions as a result. But this is doubtful. Most of the pieces found their way back to Glasgow, and some were sent to the International Art Exhibition held in Dresden later in the following year (1901). The presence at the Turin Exhibition (1902) of a needlework panel by Margaret Macdonald lent by Herr Emil Blumenfelt of Berlin would suggest that some of the work had been shown in the German capital also, but it has not been possible to verify this—and of course, the example might have been acquired privately. Of commissions executed by Mackintosh little evidence is forthcoming. Two illustrations—one of a delightful bedroom shown at an exhibition in Dresden, *circa* 1903,[1] and the other of a charming white cabinet exhibited at Turin in 1902 [2]—appeared in later journals, but in neither case is any information given concerning their owners. The intimate nature of such work adds considerably to the difficulty of tracing it, of course, and commissions may have been received of which no word ever reached the art magazines. In view of the designer's reputation, however, this seems unlikely, for the single project of importance of which a reliable record exists—Fritz Wärndorfer's music salon—was widely publicized. Moreover, Mrs. Wärndorfer, in a letter to the author, states categorically that apart from the music salon and what she terms 'knick-knacks', Mackintosh did not execute any other work in Vienna—and if not in the Austrian capital where he was most popular, it is improbable that he would carry out much work elsewhere.

[1] Organized by the *Dresdener Werkstätten für Handwerks-Kunst* ; an illustration appeared in *Innendekoration.*   [2] Illustrated in *Deutsche Kunst und Dekoration*, September 1902, p. 578.

THE WÄRNDORFER MUSIC SALON

Sometime before the music salon was commissioned Mrs. Wärndorfer and her husband—a wealthy and influential patron of the new art movement in Vienna—came to Glasgow with the express purpose of meeting the Mackintoshes, and in fact, toured the Scottish lochs with them. Although the precise date of the Wärndorfer's visit is not known, it probably took place in the summer of 1900, and may well have been planned for the purpose of assessing the work of the Glasgow designers before inviting them to exhibit at Vienna. It was after Mackintosh's successful debut at the Secession House that he received the commission for the music salon.

The salon was yet another white room with lavender and rose-coloured accents. In conception it differed little from the work at Mains Street, *Hill House* and elsewhere—except for a deep frieze of twelve large decorative panels inspired by Maeterlinck's *Dead Princess*, six by Charles Mackintosh and six by his wife. As the panels are not shown in any of the surviving illustrations it is difficult to visualize the effect of this ambitious project, but they were executed, and by all accounts were greatly admired. The walls below the frieze were panelled in wood with the familiar broad, rounded cover-strips and wide cornice (Plate 60). At one end of the room there was a low-ceiled ingle-nook with built-in seats, a bejewelled fireplace, and a cupboarded mantelpiece. Into a large bay window at the opposite end of the room the architect built a pair of upholstered seats with high backs linked together by an inverted heart-shaped arch rising almost to ceiling height (this can be faintly discerned on Plate 60B). There can be little doubt that this curious feature was derived from a bay window and openwork screen of similar proportions exhibited by Otto March of Charlottenburg at Berlin in 1897, and illustrated in *Academy Architecture* (1897).

The movable furniture of the salon is interesting, and here Mackintosh used an attractive white arm-chair of pleasing proportion and the high-backed, broad-seated chairs of rather forbidding appearance which were illustrated on Plates 12B and 16B. These may have been copies, or perhaps the original models of the example at Mains Street.

One of the most difficult pieces of furniture to design—if an architect wishes to be original in everything—is the case of a grand piano, and there seems little excuse for attempting to alter the traditional shape of the instrument which itself is most decorative, and most functional. Mackintosh, however, made the Wärndorfer's piano case rectangular (Plate 60B). It was a massive piece of

155

furniture, heavily constructed, richly decorated with his flying bird motive in high relief, and supported by four enormous legs. By way of contrast the music stand consisted of eleven slender rods eighteen inches high, each terminated by a tiny cubic cap! Despite its elephantine proportions, the piano case does not seem to have provoked adverse criticism at the time, and no doubt its unusual form and ingenious decoration were much admired.

The music salon, the first complete work of its kind executed by Mackintosh on the Continent, caused something of a sensation in Viennese artistic circles, and according to A. S. Levetus, Vienna correspondent of *The Studio*, it became a place of pilgrimage for the connoisseurs. Of the room itself he writes:

'The composition forms an organic whole, each part fitting into the rest with the same concord as do the passages of a grand symphony; each thought resolves itself as do the chords in music, till the orchestration is perfect, the effect of complete repose filling the soul.'[1]

Although no record exists of interior work for the Wärndorfers other than the salon, there is evidence that Mackintosh designed several pieces of furniture for them shortly after the Secessionists' Exhibition. For example, a dark oak writing-desk and several gesso panels by Margaret Macdonald, were exhibited at Turin in 1902, 'by permission of Fritz Wärndorfer Esq.' Whether or not other schemes were prepared by the two artists it is obvious that the music salon was the *pièce de résistance*, and, as far as the intelligentsia were concerned, the last word in modern decoration.

The ultimate destiny of Mackintosh's work usually provides an interesting story, and this is no exception. The Wärndorfer's house was sold eventually to a couple named Freund, who shortly afterwards disposed of the contents of the music salon to a gentleman who wanted them for his daughter's room. Apparently the young lady soon tired of the furniture and removed everything —including the Maeterlinck panels—to her loft, and commenced to chop them up! Providentially a certain Herr Wimmer—who, it is believed, was associated with the Arts and Crafts Museum in Vienna, and had been searching for these things for some time—arrived on the scene and was able to save the panels from destruction. They were exhibited in the museum afterwards, but it is not known if they, or any of the furniture, survive. At the author's request several attempts have been made to find them, but without success.

The absence of reliable evidence about the frequency and duration of the

[1] *The Studio*, October 1912, p. 72.

Mackintoshes' continental excursions is at times exasperating, and makes the task of documenting their work extremely difficult. It has already been suggested that the Wärndorfers may have visited Scotland in the summer of 1900, that is just *before* the Exhibition in Vienna, and Chapman-Huston claims that the music-room was completed two years later. Yet Mrs. Wärndorfer, in a letter to a friend in New York (1942), states that it was finished in 1906–7, but admits she may be wrong. She then goes on to say that a few years after their visit to Scotland, the Mackintoshes spent several weeks with them in Vienna where —to quote her exact words—' . . . they completed the wall friezes in our Salon on the spot'. This implies that the furniture and other decorations had been executed previously, and only the finishing touches had to be applied. On this evidence the dates may be estimated as follows: in 1900, the Wärndorfers went to Scotland, and in the autumn of the same year the Mackintoshes exhibited in Vienna, and were commissioned to execute certain work, including the salon. This was designed in 1901 and in all probability finished before the Turin Exhibition opened in May 1902, because pieces were shown there from the Wärndorfer household. This would confirm Chapman-Huston's statement. The elusive Maeterlinck panels, of which no illustrations appear to exist, might well have been installed by the artists in either the year 1905, 1906 or 1907, but in any case these are relatively unimportant from the point of view of this study.

Within a few months of his triumph at the eighth Secessionist Exhibition in Vienna, Mackintosh was again making history on the continent and this time not only as a decorator, but in the architectural field also.

HAUS EINES KUNSTFREUNDES, 1901

In 1901 the *Zeitschrift für Innendekoration* promoted a competition for the design and decoration of a House for a Lover of Art (*Haus eines Kunstfreundes*), and although the competition was won by Baillie Scott, the distinguished English architect, it was Mackintosh's design which aroused the greatest interest and controversy.

The three projects accounted best by the assessors—those of Scott, Mackintosh and Leopold Bauer—were published separately in 1902 in portfolio form by Alexander Koch of Darmstadt under the title of *Meister der Innenkunst*.[1]

[1] With the exception of the Mackintosh volume none of the folios seems to be available

157

Mackintosh's scheme was prefaced by a critical discourse on his 'art principles' by Muthesius. The result of the competition was not altogether surprising for architects abroad, as well as in Britain, pursued an easy eclecticism based largely on traditional styles. Multifarious gables, high pitched roofs and dormers were the order of the day in domestic work, and England was the source to which all turned for inspiration. Baillie Scott's design was a romantic mixture of quasi-Dutch gables, Franco-Scottish turrets, Tudor half-timbering and mullioned windows: it must have delighted the assessors (Plate 62c and D). As one might anticipate from so accomplished a designer the scheme was well thought out, and had an excellent plan. It was symmetrical; neatly and precisely and charmingly symmetrical.

One can hardly imagine a greater contrast to this than Mackintosh's informal project in which all the niceties of convention were thrown to the winds (Plates 61 and 62). His uncompromising façades follow no set rules, windows are placed where required and not forced into a preconceived pattern. The house is asymmetrical, and the basic geometrical form emerges stripped of all fanciful elements; it is a building as sternly, austerely functional as Stenhouse, Edinburgh and a hundred Highland fortress dwellings.

'The exterior architecture of the building', said Hermann Muthesius in his preface, ' . . . exhibits an absolutely original character, unlike anything else known. In it we shall not find a trace of the conventional forms of architecture, to which the artist, so far as his present intentions were concerned, was quite indifferent.'

The astonishing originality of Mackintosh's project was emphasized, of course, by comparison with Baillie Scott's scheme, and in all its studied un-orthodoxy—the unorthodoxy of the Glasgow School of Art which at this time had not been illustrated anywhere—caused a deal of contention in architectural circles abroad. Although the scheme had little immediate influence on contemporary work, its significance was by no means overlooked. Here was recognized an original approach to domestic design and a new interest in planning and in the play of solid and void—an interest which foreshadowed a more rational approach to architectural design.

The most important problem involved in the competition was the harmonious

in Britain, but several illustrations of Scott's design appeared in his own book *Houses and Gardens* (Newnes, 1906), p. 170 et seq. Mackintosh designed the frontispiece for his folio and it was illustrated in *Deutsche Kunst und Dekoration*, vol. II, Book 6, p. 516.

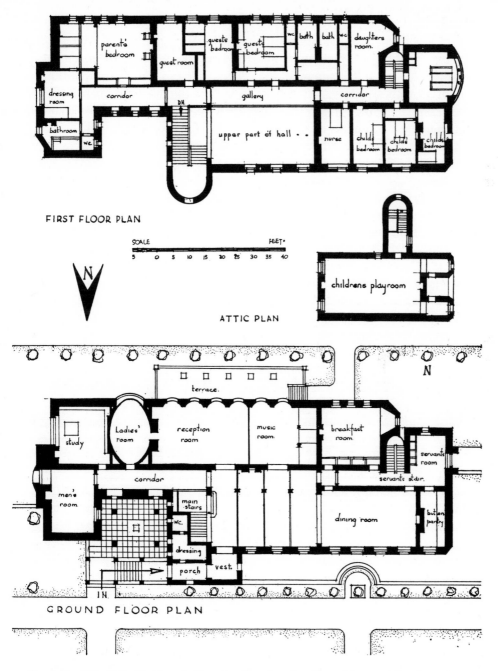

Figure 21. 1901. C. R. Mackintosh. *Haus eines Kunstfreundes*. Ground-floor and first-floor plans.

association of the main hall and the principal apartments, one of which had to include a small stage. Mackintosh made the hall the dominant element on the plan (Fig. 21) and, in the manner of the School of Art Library, carried it through two storeys with a gallery at first floor level. The dining-room opened directly off the hall from which it was separated by a light movable partition, and the two remaining apartments of consequence, the reception-room and the music-room, also partitioned, communicated directly with it by wide double doors. Thus the hall (32 feet by 22 feet) and dining-room (30 feet by 17 feet) could be combined into one magnificent apartment; and by throwing open the great double doors, and moving the screen between the reception-room and music-room, yet another apartment 50 feet by 17 feet could be added—altogether more than half the total area of the house of practically uninterrupted floor space. Here, too, Mackintosh modelled the apartments themselves with considerable subtlety. The porch and vestibule are tiny—almost cramped—the former long and narrow, the latter square. They give directly into the lofty galleried hall, and the effect is much the same as at the entrance to the School of Art—of confined, restricted space suddenly expanding; of a dramatic change of direction from slowly moving horizontals to leaping verticals. The hall and dining-room were to be lined in rich, sombre toned oak, dimly lit by the mysterious north light that Mackintosh loved. The reception-room and music-room on the south side of the house were to be gay, brilliant, and sparkling white, with fine bow windows and arched ceilings—thus contrasting in form, proportion and colour with the other apartments. By such means Mackintosh played upon a whole range of emotions. Each room was considered not as a box, a thing complete in itself, but as an element in a larger pattern, a pattern of related experiences.

As in his other domestic work the staircase is a fine feature, and it rises directly from the hall. After passing above the porch and cloakroom it emerges as the familiar semi-circular bay found at *Windyhill* and *Hill House*. With the exception of the children's suite, all the first-floor rooms of importance are placed to the south of a long corridor which extends the entire length of the building. A large playroom is planned above the nursery wing to the east, and is approached by a secondary staircase. Kitchens and servants' quarters are in the basement.

The simple plan form is reflected in the elevational treatment; the main ridge runs uninterrupted from end to end of the building and broad unbroken surfaces dominate (Plate 62A and B). Some modelling is achieved in the north façade by

160

the incidence of the courtyard and staircase feature, but the south elevation consists almost entirely of a great unindented wall surface. The fenestration, though informal, is carefully considered, and on the south elevation, from the small rhythmically disposed bedroom windows tucked away under the eaves, to the stolidly marshalled bays of the principal rooms below, the openings are unusually regular.

On account of the absence of shade and shadow the elevational drawings are not easy to interpret—especially is this true of the north elevation where the form is complex and the relationship between planes difficult to appreciate —even with the plan as a guide. The linear perspectives which Mackintosh produced, however (Plate 61), emphasize the bold modelling and show the true character of the building.

In addition to the architectural drawings the architect, assisted by his wife, produced a number of decorative schemes and designs for furniture. It is particularly instructive to compare these with Baillie Scott's interiors which are well within the William Morris tradition (Plate 63A and C). Scott was one of the foremost designers of his day, and certainly one of the most progressive individuals in the English Arts and Crafts movement. In 1898 he had been commissioned by the Grand Duke of Hesse to furnish part of the new Palace at Darmstadt—a project which received wide publicity in the journals, and greatly extended his influence in Central Europe. The two interiors illustrated here represent his style admirably—and for that matter the prevailing taste of the English school. The emphasis lies not so much upon unity of effect, as upon the excellence and quality of individual pieces of furniture, upon craftsmanship and upon ingeniously contrived backgrounds.

Scott's dining-room for the *Haus eines Kunstfreundes* is positively medieval in its richness of colour and ornament—and the proportions of the room are violently disturbed by the introduction of many unrelated elements—a heavy arcade of masonry (no doubt of plaster)—a peacock frieze, an enormous stone fireplace and a riot of decorative motives on carpets, furniture and ceiling. 'One of the greatest difficulties to be met by the decorator of a room which is to be lived in,' said Baillie Scott in 1898, 'is that he must needs tone down his effects so that there shall be nothing to unduly worry or distract.'[1] It would appear that Scott diagnosed the complaint accurately enough, but failed to find the remedy. How different is his approach from that of Mackintosh. Scott considers the decorator to be an enthusiast with paint-brush and chisel, a craftsman who

---

[1] *Houses and Gardens*, Baillie Scott (Newnes, 1906).

must be constrained—at least in habitable rooms. In Mackintosh's view beauty lay in the material itself—it was something to be extracted rather than applied —or it lay in the texture or form of a surface which might be given greater significance by stain or white paint. Complex pattern and colour, especially rich colour, were to be avoided except on small areas where they helped to give interest, and to raise the key of a scheme.

Thus we find Mackintosh's design for the dining-room (Plate 63B) almost painfully austere by comparison, with dark rhythmic panelling, small colourful accents, and a simple white curved ceiling. Every element here is carefully related, and nothing is permitted to destroy the unity of the room. Despite the intrusion of some *art nouveau* forms—especially in the chairs—this interior is far closer to the spirit of the modern movement than Baillie Scott's scheme.

The same may be said of Mackintosh's music-room (Plate 63D)—though attention is distracted from the fine qualities of the design by Margaret Macdonald's linen ladies, and the fantastic piano case with its ugly baldacchino— described rather naïvely by Muthesius as 'a fanciful composition'. Notwithstanding these symbols of the Glasgow style the room is still well proportioned, elegant and sophisticated—an apartment in which the music of Beethoven and Mozart could be enjoyed. Baillie Scott's room on the other hand has the rustic character of a village hall with low timbered ceiling, a cramped stage and much carved and polychromatic ornament—a room suitable for country dancing, perhaps. How thoroughly he had assimilated the teachings of William Morris!

The other interiors illustrated in Mackintosh's folio are not of particular importance; there are details of the balcony and entrance hall—almost identical with the galleries at Queen's Cross Church—the children's play-room in white, a drawing of a pair of fine built-in wardrobes, and a bedroom fireplace.

The importance of the *Haus eines Kunstfreundes* design lay not in the decorative schemes, interesting as they were, but in the fact that here for the first time a complete architectural project by Mackintosh—plans, elevations, perspectives and interiors—was made available to architects throughout Europe—a project, moreover, in which he had been completely free to express himself as he wished. To anyone unacquainted with *Windyhill* and the Glasgow School of Art, and to those unfamiliar with the Scottish vernacular, Mackintosh's design was as revolutionary as would have been Gropius' *Bauhaus*, or Lloyd Wright's *Taliesin*. In this single scheme he seemed to have swept away the stylistic conventions of a century. His set of drawings, like most of Alexander Koch's excellent publi-

162

cations, would find its way into the files of every progressive architect on the continent. Each plate was, in fact, framed and displayed by Koch at the International Exhibition of Decorative Art at Turin in 1902—a vast concourse at which practically all the countries of Europe were represented—and the apartment allocated to the German publisher was designed by Peter Behrens, soon to emerge as one of the most influential figures in the modern movement, the teacher and mentor of Walter Gropius.

Thus the influence of Mackintosh's project on future developments is incalculable. The publication of his drawings, prefaced by Hermann Muthesius' critical appraisal, firmly established his reputation abroad as an architect, not merely as an interior decorator and designer of furniture.

THE INTERNATIONAL EXHIBITION TURIN, 1902

No sooner had Koch's *Meister der Innenkunst* appeared than the Mackintoshes were again the centre of heated controversy, though this time in the south, in Italy.

Under Italian royal patronage an International Exhibition of Modern Decorative Art had been arranged to take place at Turin in the summer of 1902, with the object of drawing together the best examples of applied art and craftwork that Europe had to offer. Some indication of the growing reputation of the Glasgow School of designers may be derived from the fact that Francis H. Newbery was appointed a delegate by the organizing committee, and asked to undertake the supervision of a Scottish section. Needless to say, he at once passed on the responsibility of preparing the decorative schemes and layout to the Mackintoshes whose experience at Vienna now stood them in good stead. The resources of the School of Art were placed at their disposal in the meantime.

The architect of the exhibition was Signor Raimondo d'Aronco, and his lofty, barn-like galleries, with large windows 8 feet above floor level, provided a setting anything but appropriate to the delicate work of the Glasgow designers.[1] It is clear from contemporary accounts that Mackintosh's handling of this uncompromising situation attracted considerable attention. A suite of three galleries was apportioned to the Scottish section, but the rooms were linked by such wide openings that the suite had the appearance of a broad corridor with

[1] One of d'Aronco's pavilions is illustrated on Plate 64A, others are to be found in *Kunst und Handwerk*, vol. LII, No. 11, 1902, p. 294 et seq.

relatively shallow recesses on either side instead of three inter-connecting apart-ments. This Mackintosh corrected by reducing the width of the openings with pairs of narrow stencilled linen panels, 15 feet high and 1 foot 6 inches wide, attached curtain-wise on either side of the passage-way. This arrangement was not only satisfactory as a form of punctuation, defining each apartment, but one which added considerably to the aesthetic effect of the suite by emphasizing an otherwise unattractive vista, and most successfully drawing together the whole scheme.[1]

From the decorative point of view the rooms were treated alike in exactly the same manner as at Vienna; they were panelled in white painted woodwork and canvas, and the upper parts of the walls and ceiling were whitewashed. Although artificial light was not permitted, several lamps were shown either suspended from the ceiling in a flurry of crystal balls, or grouped at the top of tall masts. The architect's objective in all this was clearly understood and appreciated by at least one art critic, who, commenting on the Glasgow section, said that the rooms in themselves were worthy of close study, the exhibits being virtually added enrichments. He thus laid his finger on one of the principal reasons for Mackintosh's success at Turin, for it was his treatment of the dominating background surfaces that created the atmosphere of pristine fresh-ness and quiet repose which so distinguished the Scottish section.

Of the three apartments, the first was devoted entirely to work by Charles Mackintosh and Margaret Macdonald. One side of the central passage was designated *A Rose Boudoir* (Plate 64B); on the complementary side were dis-played framed plates of the *Haus eines Kunstfreundes* project, and a selection of drawings. One side of the second apartment, furnished as a writing-room by Frances and Herbert MacNair, had the wall surface painted grey with an ornate stencilled frieze. The exhibits here comprised furniture in black stained oak, decorative panels, and embroidered fabrics. Some pieces, especi-ally the chairs, were curious perversions (Plate 65c). The complementary side in this case was devoted to embroidery by Mrs. Newbery, Ann Macbeth, and their students. The third, and largest, apartment was occupied entirely by general exhibits ranging from book binding to fireplaces, executed by former and contemporary students of the School of Art. There were delicate fairylike drawings and water-colours by Jessie M. King, interior decoration projects by two little-known artists, Jane Fonie and George Logan; a grotesque fireplace

[1] For illustrations of the Scottish section see *Deutsche Kunst und Dekoration*, September 1902; *Arte Italiana Decorativa ed Industriale*, vol. XI, 1902, pp. 61, 68, pls 45, 46.

by J. Gaff Gillespie—an assistant in the office of Mackintosh's friend, James Salmon—and some attractive furniture and leaded glass by Ernest A. Taylor.[1]

In this part of the exhibition, too, were Mackintosh's charming show-cases, one of which is compared here with a similar feature by the Belgian designer Henry van de Velde (Plates 64c and 65d).

Although the work displayed by the artists of the Scottish section varied in materials and technique, the relationship between them was unmistakable. The watercolours of Jessie M. King, the flower-studded interior schemes of Jane Fonie and George Logan, the elegant furniture of E. A. Taylor, and the exquisite embroidery of Mrs. Newbery, all formed a coherent group which, in conjunction with the contribution of *The Four*, stood out in bold relief from the *concordia discors* of the exhibition as a whole.

By and large the aim of most exhibitors at Turin seems to have been to impress by quantity and variety rather than by quality and good taste (Plates 65a and b). Rooms, or stalls, were usually allocated to an individual, or perhaps to a group of designers, without first securing agreement on a general decorative scheme. Then again, the term 'modern' seems to have been interpreted somewhat freely, and exhibits ranged from stolid unimaginative reproductions of fashionable period pieces, to the most vulgar travesties of *art nouveau*. One Italian firm displayed an elaborately decorated bedroom suite with all the pieces circular in shape—bedsteads, wardrobes and cabinets—an interior which would be difficult to excel for sheer barbaric ugliness. There was, of course, some good work to be seen—especially in the Austrian and English sections—but the cumulative effect of gallery after gallery filled to capacity with furniture of every shape, size, and description, made objective selection well-nigh impossible for any but the most discerning observer, and gave little or no indication of future trends.

English work at Turin was not distinguished for its originality, though, as usual, the craftsmanship and finish were exemplary. Exhibits were provided mainly by C. R. Ashbee (the secretaire that had appeared at Vienna, Plate 58b), Walter Crane, C. Harrison Townsend, W. A. S. Benson and C. F. A. Voysey, and with few exceptions betrayed not the slightest tendency on the part of their designers to deviate from the safe path of tradition, the tradition established by William Morris and the Arts and Crafts Society. The German

[1] The best and most complete record of the Scottish Section was published in *Deutsche Kunst und Dekoration*, September 1902, but illustrations appeared in most contemporary journals—in *The Studio*, vol. XXVI, July 1902, p. 91 et seq.

section proved disappointing in view of the fact that Munich and Dresden, and to a lesser extent Berlin, had by this time influential Secessionist groups. Representative work was sent by Hermann Billing of Karlsruhe, Bruno Mohring and Richard Kummel of Berlin, Heinrich Kuhne and Wilhelm Kreis of Dresden and H. E. Berlepsch-Valendas of Munich. Except for several individual pieces of furniture and textiles by Kreis and Billing, and a suggestion of *art nouveau* in the interiors by Mohring and Berlepsch-Valendas, the entire section was unbelievably ponderous, with a background of ornate ceilings, columns, pilasters, grotesque masks, busts and statues. One observer remarked that it contained as many ideas as there were states in the German Empire, a criticism which could have been levelled equally at almost every exhibitor.

The work of the Scottish designers was by no means universally acclaimed, however, and here as elsewhere it either immediately captivated or repelled the onlooker. The *Milan Courier* led a violent attack upon the group in a leader entitled 'New Art at Turin'. The writer stated, somewhat tortuously, that the designs were false to all accepted art principles, and since their work consisted of imitations of 'the Japanese styles of Beardsley', they could have no existence from the artistic standpoint, and, moreover, could not possibly have any influence on art in the future. In contrast to this, Alfredo Melani, writing in the *Journal of Decorative Art and British Decorator*,[1] remarked that the Scottish section was 'the most quaint and curious in the whole exhibition' and, he says, 'The public in general passes through Mr. and Mrs. Macdonalds' (Mackintoshes') exhibits with a derisive smile, and sees in their work nothing but a pose and a caricature where we see a sincere and poetic attempt at profound art'; and again, 'Mr. Edward De Amices, one of the most popular of Italian journalists . . . accompanied me on one of my frequent visits to the exhibits. The conclusion arrived at by both of us is that we have in this husband and wife the two most interesting and original artists at the Turin Exhibition.'

Alexander Koch devoted practically all the September (1902) issue of *Deutsch Kunst und Dekoration* to a review of the Scottish work at Turin by George Fuchs of Darmstadt, and thus ensured a still wider dissemination of the Glasgow Style. Fuchs not only appraised their work, but tentatively pointed to one or two weaknesses which were already being recognized by their more discerning contemporaries. He stated categorically that Mackintosh's aims were not clearly defined at Turin, and he deplored the super-abundance of garlands of wire, artificial flowers and buds. He commented thus: 'It is a strange fact that

[1] Vol. XXII, 1902.

we feel ourselves among Poets when entering the rooms of Mackintosh. . . . It often seems as if the dream were a personal aim. . . .' He then observes that although one can imagine fairies reposing in the elegant high-backed chairs, they provide anything but a suitable setting for ordinary everyday purposes, for 'strong-boned Scots with auburn manes, threatening brows and defiant jaw-bones!' Although Fuchs mentioned the *Haus eines Kunstfreundes* design, and recognized its remarkable architectural qualities, he drew no distinction between the work of Mackintosh and that of his wife; between the broader, all-embracing mind of the architect-designer and the more circumscribed femininity of Margaret Macdonald with her predilection for small-scale pattern and mystical fairylike ornamentation. In this he overlooked an important point, the *raison d'être* no doubt of the capricious fantasy of the *Rose Boudoir*; for it was only when the artists joined forces that the dream unmistakably took precedence over reality.

Notwithstanding some difference of opinion between the critics, the Scottish representatives acquitted themselves with distinction: Fra Newbery was received by the King of Italy, and awarded the Cross of a Knight Officer of the Order of the Crown of Italy in recognition of his public service in connection with the Exhibition; Margaret and Charles Mackintosh were awarded diplomas of honour, Jessie M. King received a gold medal, and five silver medals and four diplomas of merit were obtained by other exhibitors in the Scottish section. The highest award of the Exhibition went to J. M. Olbrich, the designer of the Viennese Secession House of whom more will be said later.

The Mackintoshes do not appear to have secured any commissions in Italy as a result of the exhibition, but this is hardly surprising for the new movement had made little headway in that country, and there was no active body of secessionists to prepare the ground. Even at the Milan International Exhibition of 1907 the Italian correspondent of *The Studio* complains that the work of his countrymen in the field of modern decorative art still does not inspire confidence despite the stimulus of the 'memorable exhibition' at Turin five years earlier!

After Turin documented evidence of further continental exhibitions by the Glasgow designers is difficult to come by, but there is reason to believe that they sent work from time to time to several European cities. Desmond Chapman-Huston states in *Artwork* (1930) that they exhibited in Venice, Munich, Budapest and Dresden, and though no dates are given, this would appear to be substantially correct. Even supposing that they were not invited to send work directly to these cities, it is most likely that selected exhibits would go to Munich, Dresden and perhaps to Budapest after the Vienna Secessionist Exhibition of 1900, and to Venice from Turin in 1902. From yet another source, from B. E. Kalas, comes information that the Mackintoshes had exhibited at Berlin before 1905, but, strangely enough, there is no evidence to suggest that they ever visited the French capital. Chapman-Huston says that an exhibition of their work was planned for 1914, but had to be cancelled on the outbreak of war. Thus it would seem that Kalas' impassioned appeal to 'Paris, City of Light' to discern 'the glory of Mackintosh'[1] remained unanswered.

The last occasion on which they exhibited abroad may have been in 1913 and it is to Chapman-Huston's essay in *Artwork* that we must turn again for information:

'The Grand Duke Serge of Russia', he writes, 'visited the Turin Exhibition and was so enamoured of the work of the Mackintoshes that he became one of their most ardent admirers and invited them to give an exhibition in Moscow under Imperial patronage. This they did in 1913. Their work was received with acclamation by the Russian artists and public; it secured an instantaneous success. Everything was sold except the carpet, designed by Mackintosh, which had been specially made for the floor of the exhibition room.'

Repeated attempts to secure corroboration of this interesting event from Moscow and elsewhere have been unavailing, and it is impossible to determine what influence, if any, the Mackintoshes had upon contemporary design in Russia.

From this survey it is clear that for some years, from the turn of the century until about 1906, the Mackintoshes enjoyed a certain prestige abroad. Pictures of Margaret and Frances Macdonald and the Newberys' two small daughters even appeared in a book on contemporary fashions published at Krefeld in 1903.[2] And of course Charles Mackintosh's projects—*Windyhill, Hill House* and the Cranston tea-rooms—were widely publicized by Koch and Muthesius at this time. After 1906, however, we hear no more of continental excursions and enthusiastic receptions. There is no reason to suppose that this was due to any lack of appreciation on the part of the Secessionists and, in fact, Mrs. Newbery

---

[1] *De La Tamise à la Sprée* (Michaud, Rheims, 1905).
[2] *Das Eigenkleid der Frau*, Anna Muthesius.

in her introduction to the Mackintosh Memorial Exhibition Catalogue (1933) writes:

'At a banquet, held by the Künstlerbund, at the Decorative Exhibition in Breslau in 1913, at which were gathered all the most distinguished architects, decorative artists, sculptors, etc., one of the toasts of the evening was "to our master, Mackintosh, the greatest since the Gothic".'

It seems to have been assumed that Mackintosh was too busy in practice to venture abroad, and no doubt his continental friends would have been astonished to discover the real state of affairs in Glasgow.

Then came the first world war—four grim years in which old friendships were alienated, and valuable ties with the continent broken. During this time the main stream of the new movement abroad divided, and when peace returned, *art nouveau* was practically dead, and with it the world of William Morris, Baillie Scott and the Glasgow designers. New forces had been liberated, and a younger generation of architects rapidly assumed leadership, architects interested no longer in the arts and crafts, but in engineering and industrial design.

Josef Hoffmann survived the war and continued to work in Vienna, where, with a group of kindred spirits, he maintained the Secessionist tradition. Although Mackintosh played no part in subsequent events, he was not completely forgotten by his former friends. Some years ago the author was told by Major Alfred Longden, Director of Fine Art, The British Council, that early in 1929 he had been asked for Mackintosh's address by a group of Austrian architects who wished to invite him as their guest to Vienna in order to honour him . . . 'for his remarkable influence in their country upon the architecture and art of the time'.[1] But the letter arrived too late: Mackintosh had died a few months previously.

At the moment of writing no further information about Mackintosh's work and exhibitions abroad has come to light. As far as can be ascertained he did not exhibit in France, Belgium, or Holland, and it would seem that he had little direct influence upon the course of events in these countries before the first world war. However, we must be content here with a review of his work for which authentic evidence exists, and relegate to a later chapter the important question of his place in the European movement.

[1] In a letter to the author, 29th January 1945.

MISCELLANEOUS PROJECTS AND
LIVERPOOL CATHEDRAL

So far Mackintosh's work has been easy to classify, but in this chapter it is proposed to examine a number of widely differing projects, which for the sake of convenience have been grouped under a common heading but not in chronological order. It should not be inferred, however, that this work is in any degree less important than that discussed hitherto, and several major designs will be examined which, though relatively unknown, are especially interesting historically.

THE GLASGOW INTERNATIONAL EXHIBITION, 1901

In 1898 a competition was arranged for the design of the second great International Exhibition to be held at Glasgow—the first had taken place in 1888. The site again was to be Kelvingrove Park, an attractive *plaisance* laid out by Sir Joseph Paxton on the banks of the river Kelvin, and dominated by Sir Gilbert Scott's magnificently placed University buildings. In the proposed scheme had to be included the Corporation Art Gallery and Museum, an enormous building in the French Renaissance style designed by Simpson & Allen, a London firm of architects. (This can be seen in the background to the right of Plate 67A.)

The firm of Honeyman & Keppie submitted three designs for the competition, and though two of them were commended by the assessors—including, it is believed, that by Mackintosh—neither was premiated. The first prize was awarded to a local architect of repute, the late James Miller, R.S.A., F.R.I.B.A., and in consequence Glasgow was entertained by a jolly outburst of sugar-cake architecture in the Spanish Renaissance manner (Plate 66B for example).[1]

The result of the competition was published in *The British Architect* on 16th September 1898. This, it should be noted, more than two years before the exhibition was to take place, and at a time when the city authorities were still painfully conscious of the furore caused by Mackintosh's design for the School of Art, the first section of which in all its revolutionary unorthodoxy, was slowly taking shape. In these circumstances it is unfortunate—but hardly surprising—that Mackintosh's design did not gain the premier award. His drawings, of course, were always easily recognizable, and could not be disguised by any *nom-de-plume*.

The young architect's admiration for the work of James Sellars has been noted elsewhere, and it is instructive to compare Sellars' design for the Grand Hall at the Exhibition of 1888 with Mackintosh's project and to contrast both with Miller's winning scheme (Plates 66 and 67). The plans of all three are almost identical, and it will be observed that fundamentally the two later projects are re-statements of Sellars' original design. The great central area in each case is crowned by a cupola flanked by four towers differing only in detail; Sellars' in a restrained Saracenic style, and Miller's in flamboyant Spanish Renaissance. As usual Mackintosh's scheme cannot be placed in any of the convenient pigeon-holes of style; it is singularly free from ornamentation and, compared to Miller's design, positively austere.

Mackintosh's Grand Hall was a long, low building, terminated at either end by a pair of towers, and dominated by the great dome—similar to his Chapter House dome of 1892—above the entrance hall. The main exhibition space was flanked by low aisles roofed at right angles to the principal axis, their rounded gables providing a pleasant undulating rhythm which admirably offset the rigid lines of the hall proper. The principal towers were polygonal in plan and entirely

---

[1] Second and third places respectively were secured by A. N. Paterson; J. A. Campbell and A. McGibbon.

without ornament; they had neither string courses, windows nor terminal cornice, and rose sheer for a hundred feet or more above ground level. Those flanking the cupola carried light *flèches* supported by curious buttresses, and were similar in form and proportion to Sellars' towers—so much so, in fact, that it would appear that the architect had traced them from the original and merely omitted Sellars' oriental trimmings. Forward of the main building, however, Mackintosh had an advance guard of eight smaller towers arranged in pairs with gay roofs and inviting little windows. All of these are not shown on the perspective drawing illustrated here, but they emphasized the main entrance and provided an impressive approach to the doorway. The elevations are treated very broadly, and nowhere does the architect allow decoration to get out of hand: interest is provided by pairs of flags arranged rhythmically along each parapet, and by wrought iron motives above each bay division.

Seen in retrospect—especially against the work of Miller—and considering its early date, this building is remarkable, and one must admire the reticence with which Mackintosh handled the problem. The side elevations of the Grand Hall, perhaps more than any other, provide evidence of his independence, and we find him using motives which have since become identified with the new movement of the 1920's and 1930's. The bare polygonal towers have already been mentioned, but an even more interesting feature is to be observed at the extremity of the west elevation (Plate 67B) where the rectangular end wall of a small pavilion is pierced by a single horizontal window (32 feet long by 5 feet high), set low down and covered by a narrow projecting hood. Not only is the window shape itself unusual, but the position of the opening in relation to the vast area of wall surface is quite unprecedented; in fact the arrangement of solid and void is almost identical with the south façade of the artist's cottage (Plate 44), the significance of which has already been mentioned. And this project was designed in 1898—long before Olbrich, the Viennese architect, introduced similar 'modern' features at the artists' colony at Darmstadt.

Of the remaining exhibition buildings designed by Mackintosh one only is of particular interest. It is a project for the Concert Hall (Plate 68). The auditorium, planned to accommodate 4,221 people, was to be circular in shape with twelve great cast iron half-trusses designed to give a clear internal span of about 165 feet and a maximum ceiling height at the centre of 50 feet—in effect, a flat saucer dome. There was to be a gallery too, and a great platform backed by a Mackintosh organ-case. Externally twelve enormous buttresses sprang from the main wall, and between and through them ran an outer aisle to the

172

hall—virtually a series of vestibules—with a flat roof boldly cantilevered forward. Each 'vestibule' had two exit doorways, and a long horizontal window of the kind already discussed. Apart from a little decoration on and around the main entrance, the building was devoid of ornament; the architect relied for effect entirely upon the form and proportion of the structural elements themselves—the flat dome sheathed in lead and crowned by a gay ventilator, the great radiating buttresses, and the plain rough-cast wall surface and rhythmic window openings. Unquestionably this was one of his most remarkable and uncompromising essays, and one which bears a striking resemblance to the aluminium Dome of Discovery designed by Mr. Ralph Tubbs for the Festival of Britain exactly fifty years later.

Failure in the competition did not prevent Mackintosh from designing a number of exhibition stands—for the School of Art,[1] Messrs. Pettigrew & Stephen,[1] Messrs. Francis Smith[2] and Miss Cranston's White Cockade Tea-Rooms. With the exception of the first, none of them appears to have been of particular distinction, and they did not compare with his achievements at Vienna and Turin.

The School of Art stall was almost cubical in shape and sturdily proportioned; it had none of the catch-penny fineries of the usual exhibition stand and must have seemed strangely aloof in its gay setting. It had a deep, plain frieze relieved on each face by a wrought-iron tree emblem and a panel of lettering, and supported on a light wooden framework of squares, virtually a cage, enclosing the exhibits rather than displaying them.

Mackintosh had used a similar stand—but of more refined form—at Turin in 1902 (Plate 64c). Both served their purpose admirably, and are noteworthy examples of his telling use of simple geometrical forms at a time when fanciful elaboration was the order of the day.

Pettigrew & Stephen's stall was more ambitious, although by no means as successful. It was rectangular in plan with two open sides containing low showcases, and two closed sides against which were built glazed cabinets for the display of delicate lace and embroideries.

The only other stall, that designed for Messrs. Francis Smith & Son, was placed in an aisle of the exhibition hall. This presented a more difficult problem and left little room for experiment. Two bays had been allocated to the firm and Mackintosh linked them together by an elaborate moulded canopy and wall

[1] Illustrated in *The Studio*, vol. XXIII, June 1901, pp. 46–7.
[2] Illustrated in *Dekorative Kunst*, March 1902, p. 214.

173

panelling. The illustration in *Dekorative Kunst* (March 1902) shows the stand without its complement of furniture, and in 1950 part of the original fascia was still preserved by the late Herbert Smith.

Other than an indistinct general view in the official guide to the Exhibition, no record remains of Miss Cranston's famous *White Cockade* restaurant. Charles and Margaret Mackintosh designed the menus (one of which is in the author's collection), the cutlery, napery and, it is believed, the iron-stone tea-pots and jugs. It has been impossible to determine whether or not they had a hand in the structure also.

Mackintosh's contribution to the exhibition itself therefore was not particularly distinguished, but the project drawings which survive are sufficient to show that the story would have been very different had he won the competition.

THE 'DAILY RECORD' BUILDING, 1900–1

While preparations were being made in Glasgow for the exhibition, Mackintosh was at work on the publishing house of the *Daily Record*, a large building situated in Renfield Lane, a thoroughfare of canyon-like proportions, near to Glasgow Central Station. This was erected in 1901, but the interior has been much altered—it is now used as a warehouse. None of the project drawings are extant other than a large perspective in the Glasgow University Collection (Plate 69).

The *Daily Record* Building is interesting mainly as an example of the architect's handling of an awkward elevational problem. Renfield Lane is but 18 feet wide and the site, enclosed on three sides by very high buildings, is in perpetual shadow.

The façade Mackintosh designed is well proportioned with a stone-faced ground storey forming a sturdy base; above this white glazed brick is used. At fourth floor level there is a series of boldly projecting bays, and finally an attic storey enriched by gay dormers in red sandstone. Again one is conscious of the strong sense of upward-surging vitality noticeable at the School of Art and elsewhere. Here, however, this is emphasized not only by the transition from heavy base to light attic, but in the treatment of the intervening brickwork. Between the heavy bays the hard white surface is given an interesting texture by projecting occasional bricks in the form of a simple pattern, a ladder-like pattern, climbing up the wall face, and eventually branching into a geometrical

174

design at fourth floor level—yet another interpretation of the architect's tree motive. This is a successful sculpturesque treatment of a façade that otherwise might have been rather dull, it is a method commonly used in the Low Countries, and one which the architect might well have developed had other opportunities presented themselves. This is the only building known to the author, however, in which he used bricks as a facing material—apart from one or two minor commissions executed in England nearly twenty years later.

ECCLESIASTICAL WORK (1896–1905)

Mackintosh's ecclesiastical work was not extensive; he built one church and a suite of church halls in Glasgow, designed furniture for Holy Trinity, Bridge of Allan, Stirlingshire, and Abbey Close Church, Paisley, Renfrewshire; and submitted a project for the Liverpool Anglican Cathedral competition of 1903. He also did at least one scheme of interior decoration—and designed a number of gravestones!

QUEEN'S CROSS CHURCH, 1896–1899

As soon as the competition drawings for the School of Art had been completed (1896) Mackintosh transferred his attention to the design of a church at Queen's Cross, Glasgow. Entries relating to this building in Honeyman & Keppie's record are under the name of St. Matthew's Free Church, and the same inscription has been added to the original perspective drawing which is still extant (Plate 70)[1]—all this is rather misleading for the actual designation is, and always has been, Queen's Cross Free Church.

From information in the church magazine it seems that a Mission was established in the Maryhill district of Glasgow by St. Matthew's Free Church, Bath Street (hence the confusion), in the early 1890's. In January 1897, the minister, Dr. Stalker, announced to his congregation that one of his office bearers, a Mr. David Maclean, had offered to donate a large sum of money for the founding of a new church, that a site had been procured at Queen's Cross, and that plans were in course of preparation. No mention is made of an

---

[1] In the Glasgow University Collection.

architect, though it is most likely that Messrs. Honeyman & Keppie were formally asked to undertake the job—Honeyman, the specialist in such work, no doubt permitting Mackintosh to try his hand at, what to him, was an entirely

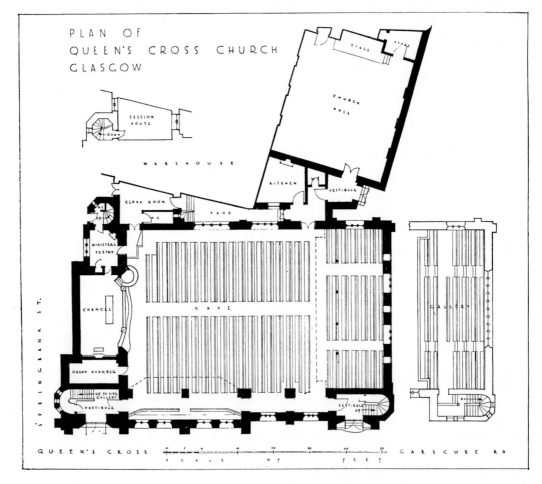

Figure 22. 1897. C. R. Mackintosh. Plan of Queen's Cross Church of Scotland.

new subject. Events appear to have moved slowly, and the foundation stone of the church was not laid until 23rd June 1898; the building was opened for public worship on 10th September 1899.

The corner site acquired for Queen's Cross Church lies at the junction of two busy thoroughfares—Garscube Road and Maryhill Road—in the middle of a seemingly illimitable expanse of crowded tenements fifty to sixty feet high. By placing a sturdy tower at the corner of the site, and boldly modelling the building itself, Mackintosh attempted to create some semblance of scale and dignity—a difficult problem in such surroundings, and one which he failed to solve satisfactorily.

The plan of the church is perfectly simple (Fig. 22). There is a rectangular nave and chancel with a single aisle extending from end to end, linking the north and south vestibules, each of which contains a semi-circular staircase giving access to a gallery. The minister's vestry is adjacent to the chancel, and is entered from a diminutive vestibule which, in turn, has a small stair leading to the session house above a cloakroom on the ground floor. At the back of the building, dwarfed by lofty tenements and approached through a narrow yard, is the hall and its appendages.

Externally the church is distinguished by its tower, an element of unusual design, with marked entasis, and an engaged polygonal staircase turret crowned by a wrought iron weather-vane. For some years the author was unable to account for the curious form and alien character of the tower which is certainly not Scottish in character. A reference to *The British Architect* (29th November 1895), however, disclosed two sheets of *Sketch Book Jottings by Charles R. Mackintosh*, one of which happened to include a rough drawing of the tower of the charming parish church at Merriott, near Crewkerne, Somerset (Plate 70B). All the main features of Queen's Cross tower are to be found there—the sturdy proportions, the entasis, the angle buttresses, the octagonal staircase turret with its enriched crenellations and wrought iron weather-vane, and the doorway and traceried window. Pictures of the Merriott church kindly sent by the vicar reveal that Mackintosh's tower is much taller and narrower than the English example, and in consequence the doorway and window are crowded into a smaller space between the angle buttresses. Despite these modifications, however, the proportions and general effect at Queen's Cross are very pleasing, and the tower is by far the most attractive external feature of the building.

The main façade to Garscube Road is irregular and indecisive in treatment; in fact, when viewed from the south it appears to have been conceived in two completely separate parts—the tower and twin gables forming one section and the secondary entrance and recessed portion the other—as though the architect had been forced to use semi-traditional motives for the first part, and had completed the southern half in his own way. Whether or not there is a grain of truth

N

in this, or whether the external form was sacrificed for internal effect, it is impossible to say. In any case there is an amount of original external detail that is worthy of attention. The southern doorway, for example, with its great flanking buttresses, curious window, and characteristic carving, is very well conceived and entirely without precedent. Though the windows throughout may be broadly classified as Perpendicular Gothic, they have assumed a new form in Mackintosh's hands, and the heart-shaped floral motives he affected can be recognized at once, particularly in the tracery of the large chancel window with its formal pattern of deep blue stained glass. Financial considerations probably limited the wider use of decorative motives, but where carving has been employed it is well placed and carefully executed.

Internally the church is sombre and restful. A sense of spaciousness out of all proportion to the size of the building is engendered by the lofty arched timber ceiling, pointed in section, and stained almost black. Naked rolled steel tie-beams with exposed rivets and plates, span the building at wall-head level—an unconventional method of utilizing structural members in a decorative manner typical of the architect—yet in no sense can they be said to limit the height of the building. Space flows between and beyond them and they become relatively insignificant against the dark background.

There are two galleries; one situated at the south end of the church, and a smaller one, adjacent to the chancel, approached by a spiral staircase in the tower. Both are built with heavy joists cantilevered forward a distance of about 6 feet, the entire structure being visible in each case—a daring innovation this, in a nineteenth-century Scottish church! And, it is interesting to observe, the gallery fronts are panelled with solid boards some of which are carried down as pendants and pierced in exactly the same manner as those in the School of Art library ten years later. The south gallery (42 feet wide) is supported by a deep wooden beam carried on four slender wooden columns only $7\frac{1}{2}$ inches in diameter, with broad square caps of delicate profile. During the 1939–45 War the minister and Church Session were anxious to obtain additional accommodation for Sunday School classes, and as new building was impossible, it was decided to utilize the space below the south gallery. Five rows of pews were removed and a light panelled screen erected right across the church. This was designed by the author, and was constructed almost entirely of wood from the old pews—a 'room' some 40 feet by 15 feet was obtained in this way, which, of course, could be subdivided by curtains. Because of this alteration the columns supporting the gallery are no longer visible from the church, but the main structure is in no way affected, and the screen could be removed easily if required.

Yet another attractive feature of the interior is the narrow low-roofed aisle linking the two entrance vestibules and separated from the body of the church by three sturdy stone piers (Plate 71B). In the late afternoon when the delicate pink stonework is illuminated by sunlight from the windows in the west wall, the effect of light and shade here is quite delightful. The chancel to the north, however, is sunless (Plate 71A). Originally it contained built-in choir stalls, but these were destroyed some years ago before any record had been made of them. The three centre bays of the panelling are enriched with a projecting hood carried on heavy carved brackets, the obvious intention being to use this feature as a background to some colourful decorative treatment.

The oak pulpit, too, is noteworthy: it is circular in plan with a high panelled back and a large projecting canopy; the curved front is decorated with low relief carving, as usual based on floral motives, in which the tulip form predominates. The back of the seat is upholstered in green plush below one of Mackintosh's highly conventionalized dove motives—which appears in Plate 71A as an oval panel. Other furniture in the chancel comprises a fine, sturdily constructed communion table and three chairs, all designed by the architect, and in one corner there is a peculiar angle cabinet on tall legs with doors decorated by Margaret Macdonald. The history of this piece is not known. It was presented to the church by the late William Davidson some years ago, and is similar to a corner cabinet with grotesque panels painted by the Austrian artist Gustav Klimt, and exhibited in Vienna *circa* 1903–4. There are, of course, many other interesting details of carving, leaded glass and so forth, throughout the building.

Quite rightly Mackintosh gave his church the dominant corner position on Garscube Road, but the awkward shape of the site imposed severe limitations on the plan, and accommodation behind the church is very restricted. The hall is quite inadequate: it is small and dingy, and only the heavy roof trusses and high panelled dado reveal the characteristic handiwork of the architect.

Queen's Cross Church is not one of Mackintosh's best buildings; it lacks unity and is interesting mainly for its ingenious details and bold constructional features. There is some competition between old and new forms, and it would appear that the architect was unable to get to grips with the problem, and to express himself freely—in this regard it is most likely that John Honeyman and he did not see eye to eye as work progressed. Nevertheless, the building possesses a warmth and charm conspicuously absent from many churches of the period due largely to the traditional simplicity of Mackintosh's architectural forms, and to the mysticism and spirituality of his decorative motives—albeit somewhat pagan in feeling—which have much in common with Celtic and Early Christian art. Given wider opportunities it is conceivable that he would have been able to express in modern idiom the distinctive character of the Scottish kirk, but here again circumstances decreed otherwise, and Queen's Cross Church remains the only completed example of his work in this sphere.

RUCHILL STREET CHURCH HALLS

The church halls in Ruchill Street, Maryhill,[1] designed at about the same time as Queen's Cross Church, are not of particular importance. The group—which, incidentally, was erected before the present church to which it belongs—comprises on the ground floor a large hall 40 feet by 26 feet with a useful annexe and an adjacent committee room and store. On the first floor, approached by a stone stair in an engaged conical roofed turret, there are a small hall and a second committee room, separated by a folding partition, a store and lavatory accommodation. The entire unit is well planned, and though each room can be used independently, it is possible, by means of connecting doors or movable partitions, to use them *en suite*. Although there are a few attractive leaded glass panels in the doors, the architect does not appear to have designed any furniture for the premises.

It is said that Mackintosh forfeited the chance of designing the adjacent church by the way in which he handled this commission, a statement which, if true, must be interpreted as a reflection upon his personal attitude, because under conditions then obtaining it is difficult to see how the plan could have been improved. One feature of the project however—the siting and arrangement of the caretaker's house—is open to criticism. When the church was built some years later the house was sandwiched uncomfortably between it and the halls, at the end of what then became a tiny, ill-lit courtyard. Not even Mackintosh's picturesque treatment of the elevations, nor the sweeping roofs, overhanging eaves and traditional staircase turret could compensate for the fact that the rooms were dark, and the accommodation very restricted. Mackintosh's building was faced in rough-cast with grey stone dressings; when the church was

[1] Illustrated *Glasgow at a Glance*, Young and Doak, 1965, pl. 143.

added the architect used red sandstone which, quite apart from the entirely different character of the building, destroyed completely any unity the group might have possessed.

ST. SERF'S, DYSART, FIFE

It is most unusual to come across work by Mackintosh far outside the Glasgow area, and yet, *circa* 1900, he carried out a scheme of decoration at St. Serf's Church, Dysart, Fifeshire. This information came from Mr. Henry Y. Allison, R.S.A., but the exact date is unknown, and all traces of it have long since disappeared. It was probably executed a little later than the Ruchill Street halls. The author believes, however, that a picture in Koch's *Dekorative Kunst* (March 1902, p. 210) of which no mention is made in the text, represents the completed work. This depicts a section of wall decorated by stencilled pattern very similar in form and character to that used in the early Tea Rooms. The design symbolized the dove of peace and the tree of knowledge, the latter consisting of three rings representing good, evil and eternity. The illustration naturally does not allow one to estimate the success or otherwise of the colour scheme, but the emblems arranged in groups of three between semi-circular headed windows, appear to have been most effective. Unfortunately a schism occurred in the church *circa* 1922; the original congregation is now scattered and it has not been possible to glean more information from this source.

HOLY TRINITY, BRIDGE OF ALLAN

Quite by chance the author came across a most interesting group of church furniture—a pulpit, communion table and chairs, organ screen and choir stalls —designed by Mackintosh in 1904 for Holy Trinity Church, Bridge of Allan, Stirlingshire. This appears to be the only occasion on which he used natural oak without resorting to stain of some description, and each piece is beautifully executed and abounds in original detail (Plate 74). The communion table is one of his best pieces of furniture, and his use of recessed panelling and rhythmic decorative motives of the simplest kind enhance its good proportions. The pulpit (not illustrated) is not so successful, mainly because the pierced legs appear too slight for the weight of solid panelling they have to carry.

181

The most extraordinary element, however, is the organ screen which also serves as a background to the communion table and furniture. It is divided into three panels, and is crowned by an elaborately carved and pierced canopy quite unlike anything previously designed by the architect. The intrusion of a flat ogival arch and heavy pendant in each section is rather ill-considered and destroys the clean lines of the fluting, but the richness of the foliated frieze is quite charming and most impressive when seen from the body of the church.

The pieces illustrated here—with the choir-stalls—demonstrate once again the virtuosity and exuberant vitality of their designer; one cannot but regret that they do not have a more spacious setting.

ABBEY CLOSE CHURCH, PAISLEY (circa 1906)

The author is aware of only one other example of church work by Mackintosh and, oddly enough, news of it came from Australia. It comprises an organ case and pulpit in Abbey Close Church, Paisley, Renfrewshire. In this instance the entire project is considerably inferior both in design and execution to the work at Bridge of Allan, and the architect did not design the communion furniture. The organ was installed in 1906 and this would seem to establish the date fairly conclusively. On the evidence of style alone, however, both the case and pulpit would appear to be little later than Queen's Cross Church, and certainly not later than 1900.

Abbey Close Church is almost square in plan, and the organ stands high against one wall at gallery level. The pipes are boldly cantilevered forward some 9 feet directly above the pulpit and the soffit serves as a sounding-board. In this instance the pulpit itself is not freestanding, but is built against the organ case, which is enclosed by well-proportioned panelling similar to that in the chancel at Queen's Cross Church. A rather thin corona, swept upwards, pediment-like, acts as a canopy to the minister's seat, and the pulpit steps are screened from the congregation by a high balustrade of grotesquely attenuated Roman-Doric columns on tall pedestals—Roman Doric in the Glasgow Style![1] The only other piece of furniture designed by Mackintosh is the font—a lightly framed wooden

[1] The canopy was similar in treatment to a feature in the former Manager's Room at the *Glasgow Herald* Building which was panelled in May 1899 (verified by Mr. A. M. Burnie). In the author's opinion, this date is more appropriate than 1906 for the church furniture.

182

case of triangular plan, about 3 feet 6 inches high, stained black, and carrying a shallow bowl of silvered pewter. The whole ensemble lacks the finesse of the work at Holy Trinity, and it is hardly conceivable that the two projects were executed at the same time.

GRAVESTONES

If gravestones may be included under the heading of ecclesiastical work—and they probably have as much right here as the Ruchill Street Halls—then Mackintosh had two interesting contributions to make. The first of these, a memorial to James Reid, was designed in 1898 (Plate 71c). It is to be seen in the tiny windswept cemetery at Kilmacolm, by a happy coincidence adjacent to the grave of the architect's old friend, the late William Davidson. The design—not altogether satisfying with its competitive rectilinear forms and broken outline —was modelled in clay to full size before being submitted to the mason. This, no doubt, accounts for the soft curves and rather glutinous *art nouveau* lines of the lower part of the stone—lines which are more suggestive of a softer material than the fine-grained local sandstone into which they were translated. The upper part, containing the inscription, is flanked by two beautifully drawn human faces in bold relief, swathed in the familiar long sinuous tresses which form a secondary frame to the composition. All detail is concentrated in this area and is emphasized by the flowing linear pattern of the hair and broad treatment of the remainder of the surface. The gravestone was illustrated in *Dekorative Kunst* (March 1902).

The second stone was designed some years later (1905–6) to the memory of Rev. Alexander Orrock Johnston, D.D., and is in the cemetery at East Wemyss, Fife. In this instance a large slab of sandstone, about 5 feet 6 inches long and 2 feet 6 inches deep, was laid horizontally on a low, broad base beyond which it projects some 18 inches at either end, forming a crude 'T' shape. The severity of the design is relieved to a certain extent by a large oval fillet which projects from the chiselled surfaces and circumscribes a rectangular block into which the inscription is cut. A highly stylized dove is carved in the lunette above the inscription, and is the only decorative motive employed. Without any suggestion of naïve reminiscence the stone is full of the Celtic spirit, a quality engendered by its primitive power and the expressive symbolism of the central motive. Unfortunately this stone weathered very badly in the strong sea air, and

Mackintosh was under contract to restore it at the time of his death. The inscription has been covered recently by a copper plate and though an attempt was made to copy exactly the lettering and spacing of the original, there are considerable variations. By chance it transpired that the craftsman employed to carry out the restoration had carved the original stone some thirty years previously, although the firm who formerly employed him had gone out of business during the 1914–18 War.

Mackintosh's two gravestones are most interesting not merely as objects in themselves, but because they reveal again his deep concern for good design in all things, and his willingness to devote himself to work of any kind in which his peculiar gifts could be employed. When the first tombstone was commissioned he had already designed the School of Art, the 1901 Glasgow Exhibition project, and Queen's Cross Church; when the second was executed he was a figure of international stature. Against either background a tombstone seems a trivial thing, yet by undertaking this work he was able to register a protest against the attitude of mind that had already made the British churchyard a disgraceful shambles of imported marble and polished granite. In fact, his first protest appeared in the columns of *The British Architect* in 1895 when two pages of his sketch-book were published—sketches of tombstones made at Chipping Campden and elsewhere in the south country in the previous year. These, he writes with some warmth, ' . . . all seem to be the outcome of the village mason's own ideas . . . ideas which would put to shame the designs of architects and others which make the modern graveyard hideous'. On the rare occasions when Mackintosh expressed himself publicly he did so with pungency, and the object of his attack was always the architect-designer who cared little about the traditions of his own country and less about the future of his art.

LIVERPOOL ANGLICAN CATHEDRAL COMPETITION (1903)

The practical work Mackintosh carried out in the ecclesiastical field appears rather insignificant when compared with the design he submitted for the Liverpool Anglican Cathedral competition of 1903—the competition which launched a third generation of the Scott family on a distinguished architectural career. At least two alternative schemes were sent in from Honeyman & Keppie's office. Fortunately Mackintosh's drawings—seven in all—are now in the Glasgow University collection, and a number of his preliminary studies in pencil can be seen at the Glasgow School of Art. His design was published in *The British Architect* on 13th March 1903, and though not premiated, was highly commended by the assessors. It was almost inevitable, of course, that a design of traditional form and in the Gothic manner would be selected by the assessors, and Mackintosh accepted these limitations. He adopted the so-called 'northeastern episcopal plan' with fully aisled choir and presbytery, double transepts and northern cloister (Plates 72 and 73). Unlike Scott who placed a tower over each transept—as at Exeter Cathedral—Mackintosh conformed to the best traditions of English practice by designing in addition to a great central lantern, an imposing west end, flanked by twin towers. In mass and proportion this fine arrangement is strongly reminiscent of Durham, but in detail recalls the work of J. D. Sedding and Henry Wilson. All three towers are slightly battered and have receding upper stages skilfully decorated with tracery and carved ornament. The ridge lines of nave, sanctuary and transepts are level and the length of the nave, seven bays, is but slightly greater than that of the eastern limb which has eight bays of reduced proportions—the rhythm quickening, the interest intensifying as the sanctuary is approached. This difference in bay width is expressed externally in the buttressing, and there is some loss of scale which detracts from the effectiveness of the north and south elevations, a weakness in the design which would have been less noticeable had the main transept occurred one bay further east, or alternatively if the nave had been a little longer.

The most striking external features, other than the towers, are the ranges of deep buttresses flanking nave and choir, which contrast with the stocky, wedge-shaped buttresses used elsewhere. These important structural members which are seen best in the perspective drawing owe little to tradition and Mackintosh deliberately set aside the universally accepted form of the flying buttress—the delicately poised arch of stone—and resorted to a series of solid masonry fins standing at right angles to the nave wall above the aisle roof; these are suggestive of modern concrete construction. Although highly dramatic, this form is very uneconomical; it would have imposed an immense load on the transverse aisle arches and inevitably have led to some loss of light in the nave—practical disadvantages which, no doubt, Mackintosh considered of little moment when compared to the magnificent external effect. Not only did the buttresses reflect the massive proportions of the great towers, but they also served as a valuable field for sculpture. Each was enriched with a deep band of carved figures, which, continued on angle buttresses and picked up by window tracery, stressed the horizontal lines of the building and gave added interest to the façades. Everywhere there are figures in niches—but the sculptured decoration throughout is kept under perfect control and is used with great skill.

The interior of the Cathedral as depicted on a longitudinal section would have been by no means as successful as the outside, and the discrepancy in scale between the east and west limbs already remarked is even more noticeable internally. The architect seems to have substantially diminished the nave arcade and triforium in order to introduce an excessively high clerestory—an error of judgment which would have destroyed the scale and dignity of the entire western arm, and which suggests that he could not have been familiar with the majestic ranks of Durham nave. The mistake was rectified more or less in the chancel and presbytery where the arcade is considerably higher. The clerestory was reduced at this point by an amount equivalent to the depth of the triforium which changes at the crossing from a module of twin arches in each bay—as at Lincoln and Salisbury, the form generally accepted as the best solution—to a continuous band of small arches in the manner of Wells. Nevertheless, the proportion of the presbytery bays is far superior to that of the nave, and though the vault shafts are carried on corbels at triforium level, instead of descending to the floor, the general effect would, no doubt, have been most pleasing.

The window tracery throughout abounds in original detail: Mackintosh's favourite tree and plant forms can be recognized again and again, and it is evident that he thoroughly enjoyed inventing innumerable variations on decorated Gothic. His admiration for the work of J. D. Sedding and Henry Wilson is reflected here too, for a good deal of the detail, notably round the south and west doorways, is borrowed from one or other of these architects—especially does this apply to the south porch with its flat arch and superimposed buttresses which pass right through the great transept window and terminate in a sculptured frieze. Wilson had used an identical treatment in his design for a new Cathedral at Victoria, British Columbia, published in 1893;[1] it was to this source also that Mackintosh had turned for inspiration when designing the tower of the Glasgow Herald Building a decade earlier.

The competition drawings Mackintosh submitted lost much in the rendering and the grey-green washes he favoured in this instance not only obscured his fine draughtsmanship, but materially detracted from the visual effect of the design—a contemporary remarked unkindly that the drawings appeared to be rendered in mud! Notwithstanding such criticisms, however, his project has magnificent architectural qualities; it is notable for its fine proportions, and

[1] In *The Builder*, 28th October 1893.

powerful massing, dignity and breadth of treatment. The impression of confusion and indecision which mar the tiny church at Queen's Cross is no longer apparent, and instead one feels that the architect had a sound grasp of the problem and drew each studied line with firmness and certainty. Had his design been accepted few, if any, major structural changes would have been possible, nor could there have been much variation in the general form of the building itself, but with the Glasgow School of Art in mind one may well speculate as to its ultimate appearance. To say the least a phase of Mackintosh Gothic would have been an exciting adventure.

It is interesting to note that the names Honeyman, Keppie & Mackintosh appeared on the Liverpool Cathedral drawings, though the new partnership was not officially formed until 1904 when Honeyman retired. In 1904, too, Mackintosh was elected a Fellow of the Royal Institute of British Architects and it was at about this time that he designed one of his most important buildings—Scotland Street School—the last work to be considered in this chapter.

SCOTLAND STREET SCHOOL (1904–6)

Scotland Street School was completed in October 1906–at a cost of about £15,000 (Plates 75A and B; 76A). The building is three storeys high and has a frontage of 148 feet to Scotland Street (on the north): it is built of the soft red sandstone common in the Glasgow region. The plan is extremely simple: a corridor runs the entire length of the building and to the south of it there are six classrooms on each floor. The two main entrances, for girls and boys respectively, are symmetrically disposed on the north side, below projecting semi-circular staircase bays with—at ground floor level—a drill hall 58 feet by 25 feet between them. There are three classrooms over the drill hall, the only ones without a southern aspect, and above these on the second floor, a cookery demonstration room. Cloakrooms and staff-rooms are provided at either end of the corridor adjacent to the staircase. The twenty-one classrooms, incidentally, were designed to accommodate 1,250 pupils!

The interior is light and airy: the finish and equipment are of the plainest kind, and nowhere, not even in the headmaster's room, is to be found any characteristic detail. Abundant use was made of glazed tiling as a hygienic facing for walls and piers—a necessary precaution—but this is mainly white with no attempt at patterning, except, that is, for a little chequered work on the drill-hall piers.

187

Externally the building possesses several important features not met with hitherto. The three-storeyed central unit of drill hall, classrooms and demonstration room, is confined between twin staircase bays of unusual design. These provide a strong termination to the horizontal rhythm of the windows, and at the same time help to unite this block to the east and west wings which contain five storeys of cloakrooms.

The great staircase bays with their tall windows and slim, stone mullions, appear at first glance remarkably modern, yet a staircase bay of this form had for two hundred years or more been a feature of Scottish domestic work, especially in tenement building. The significant point, however, is that Mackintosh took the traditional form and adapted it to new circumstances. His staircases had to carry a great deal of traffic, and he required the best possible illumination. Instead of the customary small windows, relics of a less settled age, he reduced the wall surface to a minimum and flooded the staircases with light—a step taken to its inevitable conclusion by Gropius in his Exhibition Building at Cologne in 1914 where staircases were enclosed in unobstructed walls of glass and metal (Plate 75c).

Mackintosh's bays, however, remain essentially Scottish in character and each is crowned with a traditional conical roof. He must have given considerable thought to the design of these elements, and the refinements he introduced are worthy of special mention. He seems to have been particularly anxious, for example, to secure an adequate and appropriate termination to the vigorous upward surge of the five tall windows, and at second floor level he introduced a deep horizontal band of reeded ornament which was picked up by a delicate motive in low relief on the face of every mullion. The lintels of the tall windows were slightly modelled, and it was his intention that a chequered pattern of three opaque coloured panes should be inserted in each window at this point. Above the lintels, which were continued as a string course across the classroom block, he placed seven small windows which were separated by deeply reeded mullions contrasting sharply with the square unmoulded members below. Thus, by progressively increasing the amount of ornament towards the top of the bays and by introducing a horizontal element, the architect succeeded in gradually bringing the eye to rest, and in steadying the whole composition. It is not easy to understand why, having gone so far, he failed to realize that the conical roofs, which appear so charming on the perspective drawing, would be considerably foreshortened when seen from ground level, and would render quite inadequate the narrow coping (compare Plates 75A and 76A). It would have

188

been easy to introduce a parapet here, and to raise the coping to align with, or to run just below that of the main block, thus giving a substantial band of stone above the topmost windows.

Mackintosh's ingenious refinements now have lost much of their subtlety, largely because of the poor weathering qualities of the stone. Moreover, the façade faces due north, and only on rare occasions are its finer details thrown into relief by direct sunlight.

In addition to the staircase towers, the north elevation possesses another feature which unmistakably foreshadows the new movement. This is a bank of five horizontal windows (lighting cloakrooms) set in receding stages at either extremity of the façade. The openings themselves are about 12 feet wide by 4 feet deep, and each is sub-divided by a simple wooden frame into six lights —a type of window that has become increasingly popular in recent years. In fact the cloakroom wings with their recessed upper storeys, concrete flats, well-proportioned windows and buttress wing walls might well belong to the 1930's or 1940's—they are certainly more modern in spirit than the ranks of small Wagneresque windows used by Peter Behrens at his famous A.E.G. Turbine factory at Berlin in 1909 (Plate 94c), and only the leaded panes are indicative of their early date.

The question of window sub-division and the architect's predilection for variety in shape and size of panes, has been mentioned previously, and Scotland Street School is yet another instance. The perspective drawing illustrated here shows that Mackintosh contemplated a much more intricate pattern of window bars than that ultimately adopted. For example, the drill hall windows were to have had fifty-five small rectangular panes each, and were to extend almost to ground level; as executed they possess fifteen panes and terminate about three feet above the playground. The two upper ranges of windows were to have had twenty-eight and twenty-four panes respectively; actually they have eight and four. This may appear to be a minor point, and of course the larger panes are much easier to clean—and more expensive to replace—but the window bars as executed look very fragile and inadequate, whereas in the original drawing they formed a stout, chequered pattern which helped to maintain the continuity of the wall surface and gave considerable vitality to the façade. Whether this change came about by accident or intent, to satisfy a finance committee or at the architect's behest, will never be known, but the fact remains that the building has lost both scale and character by the alteration.

In contrast to the north front, the south façade is simplicity itself, and the

189

three storeys of classrooms are clearly expressed in the fenestration. All the windows are similar in shape, and form a regimented pattern on a perfectly flat wall surface—three to each room. No attempt was made to group them or to vary their proportions, though the depth and treatment of the reveal in each row is different. The end windows, however, are framed in a linear pattern which stands out in bold relief—a most effective method of terminating and giving interest to a rather monotonous façade.

Apart from several minor modifications, including the omission of a row of poplar trees, the building as executed—and the adjacent Voysey-like caretaker's house—remains in all essentials exactly as the architect conceived it. It is unquestionably one of his best and most attractive designs.

Scotland Street School is the last of Mackintosh's projects to be examined in this chapter, it was illustrated in the professional journals in 1906[1] and thereby received a good deal of publicity—as indeed did his design for Liverpool Cathedral. But there is no evidence to show that either scheme had any influence whatever upon contemporary work in this country—though it is said[2] that Henry van de Velde, the Belgian architect, modelled the staircase towers of his school at Weimar upon those at Scotland Street.

What a different story might have been told if Mackintosh had won one or both of the competitions reviewed here. It is possible that success with the Glasgow Exhibition of 1901 would have changed the direction of architectural development in Britain; at the very least it would have given tremendous encouragement to others struggling to break the bonds of historicism. The design he committed to paper in 1898 must be judged as a preliminary sketch, and as such it is sufficiently clear to leave no doubt that the final scheme would have been as unorthodox and adventurous as his School of Art, yet its influence at home and abroad at this time could have been immeasurably greater. International exhibitions—a phenomenon of the last hundred years—have played a particularly important part in the evolution of the modern movement. They have provided useful vehicles for research and experiment, and their gay, transient nature enables an imaginative designer to investigate the possibilities of new structural techniques and untried materials; to venture into realms of

[1] *Academy Architecture*, 1906, pp. 76–7. *The Builder's Journal & Architectural Engineer*, 28th November, 1906, pp. 267–9.

[2] By P. Morton Shand in 'The Glasgow Interlude', *Architectural Review*, vol. LXXVII, 1935.

visual experience, untrammelled by the conventions of ordinary, every-day practice. The Great Exhibition of 1851, for instance, produced the Crystal Palace—now universally acclaimed one of the most significant monuments of the nineteenth century; Eiffel demonstrated the potentialities of cast iron at the Paris Exhibition of 1889; and Gropius and others revealed the architectural possibilities latent in steel, concrete and glass at Cologne in 1914. Not always, however, has progress been accelerated on such occasions and it is claimed with some justification, that the turgid, ostentatious classicism of the Chicago Exhibition of 1893 misdirected the genius of a generation of architects into the backwaters of revivalism, and thereby delayed indefinitely the emergence of a truly indigenous American style. And neither Sellars' nor Miller's essays at Glasgow in 1888 and 1901 had any profound historical significance. Had such a powerful instrument been placed in Mackintosh's hands, however, the outcome would have been dramatic and far-reaching, and it is not inconceivable that the foundation of a new movement in architecture—an essentially British movement—would have been laid in Glasgow in 1901.

The Liverpool Cathedral competition provided an opportunity of a different kind. Success here would have earned him the admiration and respect of architects everywhere, his future would have been secured, and his other work would have assumed added significance. The way of the pioneer is hard, however, and few attain such rewards. As we have seen neither of these schemes materialized and it thus came about that Mackintosh, recognized throughout Europe as one of the most progressive designers of the day and a leading figure in the new movement, was represented at an international exhibition in his own country by two or three insignificant stalls, and was not even placed in a competition that evoked universal interest.

This completes our survey of Mackintosh's work prior to the 1914–18 War. It seems incredible that, with few unimportant exceptions, the vast amount of work of all descriptions reviewed in these pages was executed in little more than a single decade, yet this is in fact the case. The Glasgow Style reached maturity in 1896—the year in which *The Four* exhibited in London and in which the School of Art competition was won: in 1906 Mackintosh finished his design for the second section of the School—though of course the building was not actually completed until 1909—and Scotland Street School was opened.

Thus within ten years, by sheer unmitigated hard work and an indomitable, burning idealism, this son of a Glasgow policeman rose to a position second to

191

none among the most advanced designers of his day—Mackintosh, 'master of the art of architecture'.

In less than ten years more he had disappeared from the European stage, and was remembered in his native city mainly as a designer of *art nouveau* tea-rooms. How did this come about? What caused such a gifted and versatile artist to cease work at the height of his career? And what ultimately happened to him? These are pressing questions which demand an answer even before his work is examined in its historical context. In the next chapter, therefore, we will complete the study of his life and achievements before discussing the wider issues and attempting to make an objective assessment of his contribution to the new movement.

THE LONDON PHASE AND AFTER

T HERE is no doubt that for some years after joining Honeyman & Keppie, Mackintosh was perfectly contented with the even tenor of professional life in Glasgow—with, of course, the stimulus of competitive work and exciting excursions into the field of decoration. This happy phase was extended by the succession of Cranston tea-rooms, by continental exhibitions and by the publicity accorded to him by Koch and Muthesius. As his horizon widened, however, and as his work assumed not only local, but national, and even international importance, he became less and less satisfied with his position at home. He soon discovered that the reputation he had acquired abroad made not the slightest difference to his status in Glasgow, and the applause of the Austrian Secessionists had no effect whatever on the stolid, unimaginative men-of-the-world with whom he had to do business. Moreover, his colleagues and professional acquaintances seemed oblivious to the great changes taking place in Europe, and no one shared his dream of an imminent Scottish architectural renaissance.

As time passed, the remarkable successes of his Austrian friends threw into still bolder relief his inability to make any notable impression upon the course

o

of events at home. While he argued, cajoled and struggled to get his plans for Scotland Street School approved and passed by the authorities Josef Hoffmann designed the Pürkersdorf Sanatorium (Plate 92), and before the Glasgow building took final shape, the Viennese architect had completed the Palais Stoclet, Brussels, both landmarks in the new movement. Then again, as the governors of the School of Art sought ways and means of preventing his costly innovations to the new west wing, J. M. Olbrich, secure under the benevolent patronage of the Grand Duke of Hesse, placidly continued his experimental work at Darmstadt (Plate 93). By this time, of course, both Hoffmann and Olbrich were well established; each had a flourishing practice and each possessed a large following—a 'school'.

Mackintosh thus witnessed the rapid consolidation of the Secessionist movement in Europe—a movement in which he himself had played a not inconsiderable part—yet in his own country he received little or no public acknowledgement. From abroad, too, came pressing invitations to emigrate; in Central Europe, he was assured, a lucrative practice awaited him. Such tempting offers he turned down on the grounds that he wanted to devote all his energies to a personal crusade in Scotland—the Glasgow Style, he was convinced, foreshadowed a revival in the applied arts and in architecture, a revival that would equal in importance the Secessionist Movement itself. 'It is indeed a great delight to oppose an all powerful enemy,' said an anonymous writer in *Dekorative Kunst* (April 1906), 'and this is precisely the reason why Charles Mackintosh is working in Glasgow . . .', the 'enemy' in this context being, of course, indifference to and ignorance of the claims of the new art. Mackintosh's youthful delight in opposing the all powerful enemy, however, gradually changed to bitterness and resentment when he realized the enormity of the task he had set himself. At one moment—at the completion of the Chinese Room at Ingram Street, for example—he could be exultant, proud and confident; then after a meeting with a client or committee less indulgent than Miss Cranston—and there were few Miss Cranstons in Glasgow—either he would be consumed with rage or be plunged into despair. Suggestions and advice he began to interpret as criticism, as a reflection on his ability and good judgment and he became more and more intractable. Even in his student days he had not been a temperate individual and now he turned frequently to drink, and in consequence began to lose interest in the practice. We are told by those who worked with him that his lunch hour often lasted from 1 o'clock to 4.45 p.m., then he expected the draughtsmen to stay on late into the evening. At times his directions became vague and purposeless; on one occasion he handed to a junior assistant a minute indistinct sketch of a rose—about three-quarters of an inch in diameter —and asked him to enlarge it to 2 feet 6 inches at once. This task was accomplished with some difficulty and Mackintosh then coloured the drawing, hung it upside-down behind the office door, and added a quotation. It remained there for eighteen months.

John Keppie's position became most unenviable. Some of his clients were beginning to object to the treatment they received, and threatened to take their work elsewhere; office routine was disorganized, and Mackintosh's financial affairs were in a hopeless muddle. There could be one end only to such a situation. The climax was reached when the firm entered drawings for the Jordanhill Demonstration School competition, Glasgow, *circa* 1912–13.

Mackintosh was given an opportunity of preparing the design but evinced little interest in the problem. According to Mr. A. Graham Henderson, P.R.I.B.A., who saw much of him at the office at this time, his preliminary sketches were unworkable, and some of his corridors terminated in mid-air. After spending several months on the project he had nothing to show, and at the last moment a design was submitted by Keppie and his assistants—it was awarded the first prize. This unfortunate incident gave rise to an allegation that Keppie stole his junior partner's design, the credit and the premium—but, in fact, he very generously sent Mackintosh a cheque for £250 in the following year as his share of the competition award.

Shortly after the competition result was announced Mackintosh resigned from the firm and the last regular entry of his name in the records occurs in 1913. The partnership was legally dissolved in June 1914.

Charles Mackintosh's movements after leaving Keppie proved to be something of a mystery until a chance discovery in the account books of Francis Smith & Son, cabinet makers, threw light on the problem. The entry reads:

'To removing large bookrack from shop to 140 Bath Street, removing effects from 257 West George Street to 140 Bath Street.'

This reveals that he returned to the premises in Bath Street originally occupied by Honeyman & Keppie, the very building in which he had designed the School of Art—what nostalgic memories this must have evoked! From this address he prepared some designs for tea-room furniture and, it would appear, endeavoured to continue in practice alone. But such a venture was foredoomed to failure. He

195

had no capital, no clients other than Miss Cranston, and few friends in the profession able to help him—certainly none who dared employ him. And so, in the summer of 1914, the Mackintoshes closed their house at Southpark Avenue and slipped quietly away to the village of Walberswick in Suffolk, where there was a small artists' colony. They stayed in rooms with a Mrs. King, next door to a house rented by the Newbery family, who spent some months each year in the district sketching and painting. Thus, in comparative seclusion, they were able to rest and to make plans for the future, Margaret Mackintosh meanwhile doing all in her power to restore her husband's self-confidence. They devoted their time exclusively to water-colour painting and flower studies and in due course sent work for exhibition to Liège, Ghent and Paris. Unfortunately the outbreak of war in August 1914 prevented once again an exhibition of their work in the French capital.

As soon as war was declared stringent security regulations were imposed on the East Anglian coastal areas. Every stranger was treated with suspicion and many artists immediately left the district; in any case the summer visitors usually departed by the end of September at the latest. The Mackintoshes, however, stayed on through October, November and December. They could not go back to Glasgow and as yet had no definite plans for the future. During the day they worked hard in a tiny studio by the river and in the evenings went for long walks into the country. The unaccountable presence of the two strangers, both speaking with a foreign accent—the pleasant vernacular of Central Scotland being a rarity in the marshlands of Suffolk—and wandering about the countryside at dusk, soon aroused suspicion, and brought them under observation as enemy agents. Mackintosh's taciturn manner, swarthy complexion, drooping eyelid and pronounced limp, and, most of all, his openly acknowledged friendships in Austria, added to this impression, and the police began to take an active interest in his movements. On returning from a walk one evening the artists found a soldier guarding their lodgings: all their papers had been examined and some correspondence with the Viennese Secessionists discovered. Their explanations were unavailing and, to his chagrin, Mackintosh was summoned to appear before a local tribunal. This he did, and only with difficulty was he able to establish his *bona fides*. In fact Professor Patrick Geddes of Edinburgh sent his daughter, now Lady Norah Mears, to the War Office to speak with the authorities on his behalf. Mackintosh, needless to say, was bitterly affronted at the injustice of the charge, and could hardly be restrained from taking the matter to a higher court.

196

When eventually cleared of suspicion the Mackintoshes moved to London and, not unnaturally, sought asylum in Chelsea. The precise date of their arrival in the capital is not known, but in all probability it was in the late summer of 1915.

The brief interlude at Walberswick, however, had not been unfruitful. Mackintosh's health had greatly improved and for the first time he was able to give his mind entirely to water-colour painting; the results were most gratifying. His subjects were, in the main, local riverside scenes, still life groups, and flower studies. The latter deserve particular mention. His youthful passion for wild flowers has been remarked already and it is interesting to observe that his enthusiasm for plant drawing never diminished. One of the earliest examples extant is dated Lamlash, Arran, 1893, and one of the last Mont Louis, France, 1925. These lovely lace-like drawings—Japanese in character—were executed very rapidly in pencil with a bold unhesitating line, and then delicately coloured with transparent washes—frequently by his wife, in which case the initials M. M. M. appeared beside the familiar C. R. M. They reveal a highly developed faculty for precise observation of detail, and a complete understanding of structural form. Mackintosh could capture the essential character of the subject without detracting in the slightest degree from either botanical accuracy or artistic quality. Many of these studies are housed in the Botany Department at Glasgow University, where they are recognized as among the finest botanical drawings of this kind ever produced. Desmond Chapman-Huston says that it was Mackintosh's intention to publish a book of flower studies in Germany, but the outbreak of war made this impossible. When peace came the cost of publication in Britain was found to be prohibitive and now many of these exquisite drawings have been dispersed (Plate 80).

CHELSEA

On their arrival in London the Mackintoshes took lodgings in Glebe Place, Chelsea, and rented two small adjacent studios. The one used by Charles Mackintosh was entered from a tiny high-walled courtyard (No. 43A Hans Studios); his wife's apartment had a separate entrance, though a mutual doorway linked the two rooms together. The studios were bleak and lofty, and the artists equipped them with furniture and decorative panels from their former Glasgow home.

197

For a time they lived quietly here, eating their meals in the studios. Dinner, however, they enjoyed invariably at *The Blue Cockatoo*, a nearby restaurant situated on the Embankment next to C. R. Ashbee's famous house the *Magpie and Stump*. *The Blue Cockatoo* was a noted artists' rendezvous in the Mackintoshes' day, and although the food was often unappetizing and the service erratic, there were many compensations. There was an upper room usually reserved for the habitués, friendly, eloquent folk of the artist fraternity, whose discussions and arguments lasted into the early hours. It was whispered that the proprietress's frequent absences 'in the country' were somehow connected with the non-payment of electricity bills and when the power supply was cut off, candles were brought in. The advent of the candles soon became an established ritual and in their light the small intimate rooms, the assortment of dark oak cottage furniture, the garish blue of the window frames, and the ugly yellow and black walls, were transformed. In addition to its candles *The Blue Cockatoo* was famous for another reason—the late Hettie Swaisland—a waitress of sterling character, picturesquely described by Allan Walton as having 'hair like a bird's nest'. Amusing and incredible stories are told about the unpredictable Hettie, yet despite her idiosyncracies—and they were many—or, perhaps, because of them, she was a law unto herself. All the artists who frequented *The Blue Cockatoo* were commanded to sign her autograph books, and she was an especial favourite with the Mackintoshes. In these surroundings Margaret and Charles found the warmth and companionship they needed. They delighted in the homely, informal atmosphere of the place, and soon made many friends, several of whom have since become artists of international repute—Randolph Schwabe, Augustus John, George Sheringham, Harold Squire, Derwent Wood, and of especial interest to the people of Glasgow, Margaret Morris, J. D. Fergusson, W. O. Hutchison, Allan Walton and James Stewart Hill.

For some time they seem to have lived quite happily in Chelsea and there is no evidence to support the popular assumption that they were in difficult financial circumstances—most certainly there is no truth whatever in the story that Mackintosh worked as a waiter in order to earn a living. Although kind and generous by nature, they were blessed with a natural dignity that discouraged confidences and little or nothing was known of their private affairs. They neither spoke of their former life in Glasgow nor discussed their future plans. Margaret managed the domestic situation with her customary grace and charm and, from the Walberswick period onwards, the sterling qualities of this remarkable woman became more and more apparent. She planned entertainments and diversions of

198

all kinds, and her parties—notably her children's parties (the Mackintoshes had no children of their own)—were among the most popular intimate social functions in the Chelsea colony. Her china tea and unusual sandwiches were especially celebrated. Even the most trivial social occasion assumed an aura of importance in the Mackintosh circle, and, as in Glasgow, minute attention was paid to every detail, to the arrangement of table-ware and napery, and to the position of chairs, pictures and flowers, all the artistry of the Cranston tea-rooms was turned to good account in the tiny Glebe Place studios. And the Mackintoshes still affected clothes of unusual appearance. Charles now favoured an enormous cloak of academic distinction which conferred on him the benign stateliness of a dignitary of the church. E. O. Hoppé's brilliant camera study (Plate 1) was made in Chelsea. He also had a collection of tweed shooting caps with ear-flaps in which he took the greatest pride, and whenever a holiday was in the offing all the preparations and packing were left to his wife—he himself just packed his caps! Margaret continued to make her own distinctive dresses, and in London, largely on account of her connections with manufacturers for whom she executed designs, she had access to ranges of materials hitherto undreamed of.

Notwithstanding the superficial gaiety of the Mackintosh household, there can be no doubt that they faced the future with some trepidation. By the time they had settled down in London the exigencies of war had brought architectural practice almost to a standstill and, of course, their work was practically unknown in the Metropolis. Charles was nearly fifty years of age; he had no influential connections in the city and the prospects of building up a good clientele in Chelsea were very remote. Then by a stroke of good fortune came a private commission. A friend, probably F. H. Newbery, on holiday at Ravenglass in Cumberland in 1916, met the late W. J. Bassett-Lowke, the well-known engineer of Northampton, who was contemplating the alteration of a small house. Mackintosh was recommended as just the man for the job, and was invited by Mr. Bassett-Lowke to undertake the structural modification and interior decoration. He accepted the offer with alacrity.

No. 78 DERNGATE, NORTHAMPTON, 1916

No. 78 Derngate, Northampton, proved to be a red brick house in a terrace of the Victorian bye-law type common to English industrial towns. The frontage was about 15 feet and the total depth, comprising parlour and living-room, 24 feet 6 inches. The front door opened directly on to the pavement and there was a long narrow garden at the back of the house. It is difficult to imagine a more striking contrast to the gloriously open sites of *Hill House* and *Windyhill*, but nevertheless, Mackintosh dealt with the problem with no little ingenuity. Only one external alteration was made to the front of the house—the parlour window was widened to 6 feet and projected out to form a bay. Internally the staircase was turned at right angles to its former position and the narrow stair-case hall combined with the parlour into a single apartment occupying the entire width of the house—a lounge-hall. An extension was built to the back (about 9 feet 6 inches wide by 5 feet deep) which substantially increased the size of the kitchen and the dining-room above, and provided attractive balconies to the owner's bedroom on the first floor, and the guest's bedroom on the second floor. This tiny extension is, in fact, of considerable interest. To the best of the author's knowledge, no other work in this country at the time bears so clearly the characteristics of the modern movement, though the feature is very similar in character to Auguste Perret's reinforced concrete apartment house, No. 25 Rue Franklin, Paris, built in 1903[1] which, perhaps, was known to Mackintosh. Its functional simplicity, the form, proportions and disposition of the open-ings, the concept of the enclosed balcony (or garden-room) on the second floor, and the use of flowering plants and gay sunblinds all belong to the post-war period. And yet it was completed in 1916. *New Ways*, Northampton, designed by the German architect, Peter Behrens (also for Mr. Bassett-Lowke), and usually claimed to be the first house in the modern style in England, was not built until 1925. Both buildings are illustrated on Plate 76 (B and C).

The alterations made to the plans are indicated on Fig. 23. It is necessary to point out, however, that the site sloped steeply, and although the hall was entered directly from the street and the dining-room was on the same level, it was necessary to descend a flight of stairs to the kitchen, which in turn gave access to the garden.

From the decorative point of view the dramatic lounge-hall and the guest's bedroom were the most interesting apartments in the house (Plate 77). In addition to the new bay window, the hall contained a large fireplace which Mackintosh remodelled in a manner reminiscent of the west doorway of the School of Art. The staircase in its new position occupied the inner wall, and was separated from the hall by a light timber screen framed in squares, some of

---

[1] Illustrated in *Space, Time and Architecture*, Sigfried Giedion, p. 251.

which were open and others solid—a favourite motive which the architect had employed on several occasions, notably in the Chinese Room at Ingram Street. The walls and ceiling were painted a dull, velvety black and all the woodwork and furniture was stained black and waxed polished. The walls were divided into narrow vertical panels by strips of stencilled white chequer pattern. The frieze (approximately 2 feet 9 inches deep) consisted of nine horizontal bands of small, triangular leaf-shaped motives stencilled golden-yellow and outlined in silver grey. These were interspersed by others of vermilion, blue, emerald green and purple, thus giving a rich subdued band of colour right round the apartment. Some of the square panels in the staircase screen were filled with

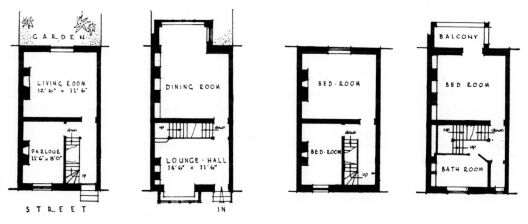

Ground floor.   First floor.

Figure 23. 1916. Plans of No. 78 Derngate, Northampton, before and after alteration by Mackintosh.

leaded glass in which the triangular motive again predominated. A horse-hair carpet, chequered in black and white with a broad, plain inner border was used, and the floor surround stained black and waxed polished. The stair carpet was grey.

According to a written description of the apartment by Mackintosh in the author's possession, his intention in using black on walls and ceiling was to obtain a sense of mystery and spaciousness, and he added, ' . . . it is claimed that the result has been achieved'. This was a modest statement for, without doubt, he wrought something of a miracle in the cramped, dingy parlour of No. 78 Derngate.

It will be observed (Plate 77) that the square which dominated all the

201

architect's decorative work during the Glasgow period, is here subordinated to the triangle—a form rarely met with hitherto, yet one which is characteristic of the London phase. The source of the triangular motive is not far to seek. It was used freely by Josef Urban, the Viennese designer, whose work was well known to Mackintosh if only through the medium of a special number of *The Studio, The Art Revival in Austria*, published in 1906. From the illustrations in this book it is obvious that he borrowed Urban's stencilled and inlaid patterns, and adapted them to his own use, and, in fact, from the same source came Mr. Bassett-Lowke's dining-room mantelpiece with its curious wall-lamps.

The other apartments were much more restrained than the exotic lounge-hall. The dining-room-lounge, for instance, was furnished throughout in walnut; the walls below the frieze were divided into narrow panels by flat strips of the same wood, and built-in china cupboards were placed on either side of a large tiled fireplace—the one with Josef Urban's lanterns. The principal bedroom was papered in light grey with a figured mauve edging and furnished in grey sycamore relieved by black inlay; the carpet was mauve. This room and its furniture were devoid of pattern and severely simple in form, but from the single indistinct photograph which remains it is not possible to assess their real merit.

The guest's bedroom on the second floor, however, was one of Mackintosh's most pleasant interiors (Plate 77). Here the triangle motive was conspicuously absent and, with notable success, the architect reverted to his former love—the square. The ceiling, walls and woodwork were painted white, and a plain grey Brussels carpet covered the floor. The furniture was of waxed oak decorated with narrow bands of black on which were stencilled ultramarine squares—a form of decoration favoured by Hans Offner, another designer of the Viennese School. The twin beds, linked together by a neat cupboard fitting, were flush panelled at head and foot, the only decoration being in the form of six square piercings in the top rail, and a chequered border. The fitted wardrobe was the most striking piece of furniture in the room and certainly one of the best single pieces Mackintosh designed. It was—and still is—an efficient and well-proportioned unit. The drawers and doors are close fitting and flush panelled, with knobs of truncated pyramidal form, each containing a square inlay of mother-of-pearl or white erinoid—a fine modern piece by present day standards. The rest of the furniture—two sturdy ladder-backed chairs, a square-framed stool, a mirror and a wash-stand with china *accoutrements* of Austrian character— were all designed by the architect. In this room the sinuous curves, the *art nouveau* elements of stained glass and rose-coloured enamel which were so

202

obtrusive in his earlier work, are no longer present. The only features reminiscent of the Glasgow period are the bedspreads and curtains—no doubt designed by Margaret Macdonald—the former in black and white striped silk with ultramarine blue centres, the latter in black and white cotton. The striped motive was picked up on the wall and ceiling with a patterned paper—a convention suggesting the architect's favourite canopy linking together and embracing the twin beds. This was edged with ultramarine harness braid, secured at intervals by black-headed drawing pins![1]

The bedroom furniture represents a marked advance on any of the architect's previous work and, at last, it would seem that he was able to discard the eccentricities of *art nouveau*. But by this time, of course, many others were working on similar lines and plain unadorned furniture was not so exceptional as it had been a decade earlier.

No. 78 Derngate was not illustrated in the press until 1920 when an article on the house appeared in the September issue of *The Ideal Home*. The editor made this comment on the guest's bedroom: 'The general effect and colour scheme are striking in the extreme and the most unique thing we have seen in bedroom decoration.' It does seem extraordinary that more than a decade after the architect's remarkable interiors at *Windyhill* and *Hill House*, projects which stirred the imagination of a continent, the bedroom at Derngate should be hailed by such a popular and informed journal as 'the most unique thing we have seen'. This single statement shows how completely Mackintosh had passed into oblivion, and how slight had been his influence on contemporary opinion in Britain.

Several minor pieces at the Derngate house are worthy of note but, unfortunately, all of them cannot be illustrated here. There was, for instance, an unusual mahogany table lamp about 12 inches high, circular in plan and cage-like—similar in shape to the wrought-iron chimney protectors used at Scotland Street School. It was a most attractive table decoration. There was a smokers' cabinet,[2] lacquered black, with brilliant yellow inlays, and there were also two charming clock-cases about 10 inches high (Plate 77) made of ebony and erinoid in various colours—red, yellow, purple and white. The movements were French bought

---

[1] Mr. Bassett-Lowke told an amusing story of a visit by George Bernard Shaw whom he introduced into the dramatically decorated guest's bedroom, saying, 'I trust the decor will not disturb your sleep.' G. B. S. glanced round the room, and retorted, 'No, I always sleep with my eyes closed.' Shaw came to know the Mackintoshes quite well during the Chelsea period.

[2] Illustrated in catalogue, Edinburgh Festival Exhibition, 1968, Pl. 30.

by Mr. Bassett-Lowke in London and the cases themselves were made by German prisoners of war in the Isle of Man (*circa* 1917). All these pieces were in the Bassett-Lowkes' possession in 1950.

Another minor commission he received at this time was to design adhesive labels for advertising purposes.

Several of these—and one of the original drawings—are in the author's collection (Plate 81c) and they are most attractive and colourful. Each consists of an ingenious pattern of conventionalized engineering forms—cranks, cogs, levers and so forth—and makes interesting comparison with the architect's linear patterns of the Glasgow period. The softly flowing curves have disappeared—in all except one—and the melancholy purples, greens and yellows are superseded by masses of primary red and blue. Only the lettering gives a clue to the identity of the designer!

Despite the local interest aroused by the Northampton house Mackintosh had great difficulty in securing further commissions of an architectural nature, though he did execute a scheme of decoration and design some furniture for the late F. Jones, Esq., of *The Drive*, Northampton, Mr. Bassett-Lowke's brother-in-law. It will have been noted that four years elapsed before No. 78 Derngate was illustrated in *The Ideal Home*, but the designer's name was not mentioned in the accompanying article. The long interval, and this singularly unfortunate omission, denied Mackintosh a deal of publicity at a time when it would have been invaluable to him, and nothing of importance came of his promising introduction to the Midlands.

Between 1916 and 1919 the Mackintoshes directed their attention mainly to designing printed fabrics of one kind and another, and to water colour painting. Through friends in Chelsea they had work accepted by two well known textile firms in London, Foxton's, and Sefton's. Mrs. Sefton, the artist who sketched for *The Tatler* under the pseudonym of *Fish*, greatly admired their work and was instrumental in securing useful introductions for them. Their experiments in this new field achieved some measure of success, and during the year 1920 alone—the only period for which a reliable record exists—they received about £200 in fees from the two firms mentioned. Mr. Foxton wrote to the author in 1945 of his happy association with the designers, but all his records had been destroyed in the German air raids some three years earlier and with them the only remaining examples of the Mackintoshes' work. A number of their original drawings have survived, however; some are in the Glasgow University Collection, several are in the author's possession, and two were illustrated in *The Studio Year Book of Decorative Art* of 1917. In this work the sensuous rhythms of the Glasgow Style are superseded largely by a more vigorous, dynamic *tempo*, and the undulating stalks, and yellow-greens and mauves give way to gaily coloured flowers of all kinds. Occasionally simple geometrical patterns are used —zigzags, triangular and chequered figures, and so on, but most of the designs are of highly conventionalized floral forms, and bouquets of cultivated blooms, dahlias, pansies and peonies, take the place of the wild flowers of former days (Plate 81B). On the whole these designs are charming and, having seen them, one is not surprised by the brilliance and originality of Charles Mackintosh's water-colour paintings of the later 1920's, which reveal a similar interest in two dimensional pattern and rich colour.

Once they had settled down to their new life in Chelsea the Mackintoshes began to play an active part in the social life of the artist community. They could be relied upon to enter with enthusiasm into any movement, or to take part in any demonstration, against conservative elements in the art world. One of their favourite resorts was the studio of Margaret Morris who at this time was attracting considerable attention as a teacher of dancing. Miss Morris—now well known in the north as the founder of the Celtic Ballet—had opened a small theatre at the corner of Flood Street, Chelsea in 1914 and started a school of dancing. Her pupils were encouraged to invent and stage their own ballets—to design the decor and to evolve new dance figures. Everything was very informal and very unconventional; pupils, teachers and friends met on equal terms to discuss the problems of contemporary art and, as a matter of course, to express their contempt for orthodox methods of training and orthodox methods of painting, dancing and making music. Thus the Mackintoshes found themselves in pleasant and congenial company; they took a lively interest in the work of the students, and soon were on intimate terms with Miss Morris and her husband, J. D. Fergusson the painter. It was at J. D.'s suggestion that Charles Mackintosh became actively engaged in the reorganization of the *London Salon of the Independents* (founded 1908) after the 1918 armistice. This society of artists sponsored 'open' exhibitions of Painting, Sculpture and Craftwork in opposition to the 'closed' academy exhibitions—it claimed a membership of 200. There was no selection jury and—for an annual subscription of £2 2s.—an artist was at liberty to show three works without any restriction whatever, and without the intervention of a middleman. Wall space was arranged by

205

ballot. The aims of the society were closely allied to those of the *Salon des Indépendants* in Paris, which enjoyed the support of the French Government. The *London Salon*, however, had no such good fortune, and no accommodation could be found in the city for its first exhibition. Fergusson and Mackintosh hit upon the idea of using army huts with glass roofs in Hyde Park—but this scheme fell through because the necessary permission was not forthcoming. After a year of fruitless searching the Management Committee—which included Malcolm Arbuthnot, Frank Dobson, Charles Ginner, Alexander Jamieson, Frank Rutter, Randolf Schwabe and E. McKnight Kauffer—decided to wind up the Society, and the subscriptions were returned. London, they concluded, was not yet ready for an Independent Salon.

And then there was *The Plough*—a society formed 'for the purpose of stimu= lating interest in good art of an unconventional kind'. According to E. O. Hoppé, the distinguished photographer, Charles Mackintosh was a founder-member serving, with Hoppé himself, on a committee including Lady Lavery, the Baroness d'Erlanger, Clifford Bax, Eugène Goossens, and George Sheringham. The society presented little-known musical, dramatic and literary works of merit and originality which for one reason or another, had been neglected by the ordinary theatre. Plays by Miles Malleson, Antonio Cippico, Emile Verhaeren, Torahike Khori, d'Annunzio and Machiavelli were included in their repertoire. One of the main objects of the society was to encourage close collaboration between author—if a contemporary work—composer, painter, actor and producer. It was hoped thereby to attain a unity of aesthetic effect impossible under the less ideal conditions then prevailing in the commercial theatre.

The Mackintoshes' particular interest, of course, lay in stage settings and costumes. As students at the Glasgow School of Art, they had assisted frequently with the staging of Masques and similar entertainments. This experience was found to be invaluable, and they designed the decor for at least one of *The Plough*'s productions—Maurice Maeterlinck's *Joizelle*, played in 1917. It seems that the society went from strength to strength; and by 1921 its productions were attracting large audiences. Soon, however—in the words of E. O. Hoppé —the venture 'died of its own vitality' and the group disintegrated as, one by one, its gifted members were offered wider opportunities elsewhere.

Largely as a result of his close association with *The Plough* and similar organizations, Mackintosh received several commissions which must have given him no little encouragement and turned his thoughts again towards serious architectural practice.

206

The first work he undertook was an extension to a gamekeeper's cottage on an estate at Little Hedgecourt, East Grinstead, Sussex, purchased (*circa* 1919) by E. O. Hoppé. This building he converted into a studio-house and the original drawings are now in the Glasgow University Collection. Mr. Hoppé confirms that the project was carried out according to Mackintosh's design, but it is quite undistinguished and lacks the character of the architect's earlier work.

Mr. Hoppé's house was followed in rapid succession by a number of other commissions, and for some time Mackintosh was fairly busy. He kept a diary for the year 1920, and mercifully it has survived—the only one to escape the destruction thoughtlessly meted out to all his private papers, account books and the like shortly after his death. Though entries are few and far between, they confirm evidence gleaned elsewhere and are most valuable. On 8th January he was asked to design a studio house on a site in Glebe Place, Chelsea, for Harold Squire the painter, and a few weeks later, to prepare similar schemes for F. Derwent Wood and A. Blunt (an artist who specialized in the design of glass chandeliers, mirrors and the like). It is most likely that Mackintosh and Derwent Wood were already acquainted, for the sculptor was at one time Director of the Modelling Department at the Glasgow School of Art and he made monthly visits to Scotland during the session 1897–8. Then 'in March 1920, Mackintosh commenced work on a project for a block of studio flats for the Arts' League of Service; in June on a small theatre for Margaret Morris, and in August on a cottage at Burgess Hill for a certain Miss Brooks. Only two of these schemes materialized, however, and in all cases he encountered serious opposition from the local authorities who objected to his unorthodox designs in no uncertain terms.

The proposed studios for A. Blunt and Derwent Wood (Plate 78) kept the architect occupied for some time: plans were completed and submitted to the L.C.C. and estimates received, but no further progress seems to have been made. Entries in the diary throw little light on the matter and no reason is given for the abandonment of the schemes—but Mackintosh's elaborate designs were probably uneconomical, or the opposition of the L.C.C. too strong.

HAROLD SQUIRE'S STUDIO, 1920

Harold Squire seems to have been made of sterner stuff, and work on his scheme proceeded. The first design Mackintosh submitted was very ambitious.

207

The studio-house was to occupy three floors and to include a roof garden—the site was narrow and deep with a 30-foot frontage to Glebe Place on the north. Living quarters were situated on the ground and first floors at the rear of the block (to the south), to which access was to be obtained by means of a narrow paved passage at the side. More than half of the first floor was taken up by a large studio, 32 feet by 22 feet, passing through two storeys and lit from the north. Two bedrooms and a bathroom were placed behind this, and a wide staircase led up to the second floor which contained another studio, 27 feet 6 inches by 13 feet 9 inches, facing south, and a gallery to the upper part of the main studio. A spiral staircase gave access to a small sun room and garden on the roof.

The elevation to Glebe Place (Plate 78)—a dramatic composition—was dominated by a large studio window 15 feet high and 12 feet wide, and crowned by a simple wrought-iron balustrade. The southern elevation on the other hand was small in scale and entirely different in character from any previous work by Mackintosh (Plate 78). It had three rows of windows of Georgian proportions, equipped with shutters—a type common in the Chelsea district—and no attempt was made to express the presence of the second studio by varying the window treatment.

Apparently Mr. Squire was well satisfied with the scheme, but estimates proved far too costly. Mackintosh was then asked to prepare a statement showing how the price could be reduced to about £6,000! His client meanwhile suggested that the accommodation might be provided on one floor. Revised plans were eventually prepared and the architect was instructed to proceed, keeping the cost as near to £4,000 as possible. Work commenced on 25th June, 1920, but was suspended for some months on account of legal difficulties over the purchase of the site; it was resumed on 27th September. A month or so later an additional storey containing two bedrooms was designed; the estimated cost of this alteration amounted to £650 and the amended plans were approved by the local authority. This scheme is fundamentally different from the first project. There are two principal blocks, the 'house' at the front, separated by a small enclosed courtyard 20 feet long by 8 feet wide, from a studio of palatial dimensions, 40 feet by 27 feet by 17 feet high at the rear. Access to the studio is obtained only through the living-room—which opens directly on to Glebe Place—and across the yard. The roof of the house was designed as a steeply pitched lean-to so that as much north light as possible would be admitted to the great studio window which, of necessity, overlooked the courtyard.

Harold Squire was delighted with the finished building, and in a letter to the author,[1] he says that the studio ' . . . had a magnificence which no other in London possessed'. Very soon, however, he found that it had several less desirable attributes.

The Glebe Place site originally formed part of the large garden of a curious house which was sold for development purposes after the death of its owner, a Dr. Phené. The doctor appears to have been a strange individual whom the local inhabitants regarded with some suspicion. It was rumoured that he indulged in mystic rites of a most unpleasant kind, including that of snake worship! The doctor's house occupied the Oakley Street corner of the garden, and at the Upper Cheyne Row end there was a second mystery house in which, according to Mr. Squire, a wedding breakfast remained untouched for years in the authentic Dickens manner, the bride for whom it was prepared having died on her wedding morning. When building work started, the studio site was found to be littered with the remains of an old church and numerous pieces of carved stone, presumably from an altar, were unearthed. When the studio was finished and had been occupied for some months, Mr. Squire noticed that the servants were uneasy and reluctant to be left in the building alone at night. On making tactful enquiries he found that they claimed to have seen the spectre of a man on horseback in the studio on several occasions and were certain that the place was haunted. Notwithstanding his reassurances they adamantly refused to stay in the building alone, and eventually gave notice. Nor was he able to keep new servants for more than a few weeks. Some time later Mr. Squire himself saw the apparition in broad daylight, and was sufficiently convinced to have the case investigated by a medium who gave him a description of the ghost, and an explanation of the occurrence—'without anyone giving her any previous details'. The authenticity of this story was vouched for also by the late Professor Schwabe, who mentioned the ghost to some carriers in the vicinity at the time, and was told that Dr. Phené had been fanatically attached to a horse which on one occasion had saved his life. The animal was buried in his garden directly beneath the spot chosen for the studio, and its remains had been unearthed during the preparation of the building site. The late Professor Harry Price of the Society for Psychical Research had no record of the case, however, and it has not been possible to discover whether the spectre was successfully exorcised. Harold Squire himself did not occupy the building for more than two years: quite apart from the difficulty of keeping servants, and the disturbing

[1] 26th January 1946.

P

influence of the ghost, he found the studio far too expensive to maintain—the cost of heating alone was enormous.

The author examined the building in 1945—it was then being used by the local authority as an emergency A.R.P. store and had been uninhabited for a number of years. Mackintosh's original scheme had been materially altered by increasing the height of the living quarters to two storeys which completely overshadow the great studio window. The studio itself was dismal and gloomy in spite of its whitewashed walls, and not a single detail remained by which the architect might be identified—yet the proportions and vast airy space of the apartment inevitably recalled the studios at the Glasgow School of Art.

THE ARTS LEAGUE OF SERVICE

When Mr. Squires' work was in hand, an ambitious scheme for building studio flats was evolved by a group of artists with whom the Mackintoshes were closely associated—members of the Arts League of Service. The Arts League, like *The Plough*, and the Salon of the Independents, was yet another altruistic enterprise that flourished in the aftermath of the first World War. It was founded in 1919 with the object of 'bringing the Arts into everyday life'—into the life of the people of the provinces, and of remote country districts, as well as into the life of the metropolis itself. The organizers planned to have mobile exhibitions of painting and sculpture and the things of everyday use—and a travelling theatre.

The initiators of this ambitious project, which was virtually a forerunner of C.E.M.A., were Miss Anita Berry—a jovial Chilean lady of immense vitality, who in the words of Alan Walton was 'made up of circles'—and Miss Eleanor Elder who before the war was a pupil and then a teacher at Margaret Morris's school of ballet. The irrepressible Miss Berry had been working in London for some years before the founding of the League, and was well known as a staunch champion of the cause of the neglected genius. She ran exhibitions, theatrical and musical performances in order to introduce unknown artists and their work to the public. Among the many people who benefited from her generosity and have since become internationally famous, Miss Elder names Frank Dobson, Henry Moore, Paul Nash and Edward Wadsworth.

Eleanor Elder returned from India in 1918, determined by some means to realize her dream of a travelling theatre.[1] She outlined her plans to Margaret Morris and J. D. Fergusson, who suggested that the basis of her scheme should be extended to include the fine and applied arts. They introduced her to Anita Berry and things began to move quickly. Several public meetings were held in Chelsea in 1919 and the Arts League of Service was finally launched with Lord Henry Cavendish-Bentinck, M.P., as President, an enthusiastic committee, and Miss Berry and Miss Elder as organizing secretaries. The League drew its income mainly from subscriptions, but to help obtain funds, an Arts League shop was opened by Miss Berry in John Street, Adelphi, for which Harold Squire and Malcolm Milne and others designed rugs, metal candle-holders and the like. For some years this venture proved to be very successful.

One of the main problems facing the artist community after the war was that of finding suitable studio accommodation. Many former studios had been converted to domestic use during hostilities: rents were high, and, of course, commissions were difficult to come by. The Arts League devised a scheme which, it was hoped, would go a long way towards solving this problem—the building of a large block of studio flats financed on a co-operative basis, each artist-tenant being a shareholder in the property. Randolph Schwabe and J. D. Fergusson were to have been two of the first tenants and both took an active part in the initial moves. Charles Mackintosh—for whom, needless to say, the objectives of the League had an irresistible appeal—was invited to design the building.

A site occupied by Old Cheyne House and adjacent to Harold Squire's studio, was selected, for which Mackintosh advised Miss Berry to offer £1,850. On 31st March 1920, he was instructed by her to prepare preliminary sketches. For some weeks he worked extremely hard and produced a series of interesting designs which, after being approved by the Arts League Committee, were submitted to the local authority in June (Plate 79A). Trouble began at once. The drawings raised a deal of controversy, and the project was scathingly described as factorylike and 'not architectural enough'. Two months later Mackintosh was informed that the Ecclesiastical Commissioners also objected to the studio block and to his design for Margaret Morris's theatre (Plate 79B) as unsuitable buildings for the locality. In a stormy interview with their architect, he was advised to make his elevations more elaborate, and according to a friend, the climax was reached when the man took his drawings and exclaimed, 'My dear sir! This isn't architecture!' and proceeded to insert pediments, swags and other classical details. Mackintosh afterwards vowed to J. D. Fergusson that he

[1] For an excellent account of this enterprise see *Travelling Players*, Eleanor Elder, 1939.

211

would give up the profession altogether and resort to painting if his scheme were rejected. He refused to alter his design, or to compromise in any way. After a delay of some weeks, however, it was provisionally approved (13th December) and a week later (19th December) permission was given 'by Archdeacon Bevan'[1] for the work to proceed.

It has not been possible to obtain a clear picture of subsequent events, but despite this favourable decision the project came to nothing. It is most probable that the scheme miscarried because the requisite capital was not forthcoming, but whatever the cause, the fact remains that the plan was abandoned.

The accompanying reproductions of Mackintosh's drawings for the three buildings which were to occupy contiguous sites—Derwent Wood's studio, Harold Squire's studio and the Arts League flats—give a clear indication of his intentions and are worthy of study (Plates 78 and 79). The projecting and receding masses of the north elevation in particular produce a highly complex and most diverting pattern of solid and void, of shade and shadow, with the squat flat-roofed centre block of Squire's studio—the hub of the scheme—and the great rectangular window openings steadying and resolving a ferment of gables and inter-penetrating planes. The triangle, it will be observed, again dominates and the eye leaps from one gable to the next, and then is led back into the heart of the composition by receding wall planes. This, of course, is not architecture if by architecture we imply orderliness, dignity and repose and adherence to the canon—it is sheer romanticism, the artist playing with form and pattern and creating intricate, complicated harmonies of his own choosing. Here, perhaps, we see reflected something of the spirit of the Margaret Morris ballets, and of *The Plough* but, in architectural terms, no indication of the shape of things to come. It is salutary to remind ourselves that less than five years later Gropius was to build the Bauhaus at Dessau, and that already Le Corbusier had embarked upon his career as architect.

The less important elevations to Cheyne House Gardens (the south front) and Upper Cheyne Row were not as interesting as the Glebe Place façade. The back of Squire's studio overlooking the gardens was to be Georgian in character and brick faced—a treatment that can hardly be reconciled with the architect's decision to build the adjacent walls in concrete. It must be assumed that the shuttered windows, the arcading and the wrought-iron balconies were provided at his clients' request—and yet there is one familiar detail in Derwent Wood's studio, a variation on the south front of the country cottage designed in 1901

[1] From a note in Mackintosh's diary.

212

(compare Plates 44 and 78). Here, however, the material used *is* concrete—the logical conclusion to the earlier experiment. This, it would seem, answers the question posed in Chapter 5. The architect was in fact searching for a material of greater plasticity in which his peculiar forms could be more easily expressed—but how completely he failed to rise to the opportunity presented by the Arts League building!

Nothing else of importance emerges from a study of the surviving drawings. When it is realized that Squire's studio—by far the smallest of the buildings depicted in the scheme—had to be drastically modified and completely redesigned to bring the cost below £6,000, some indication may be obtained of the prodigious expense Derwent Wood and the Arts League might have incurred had they embarked on the scheme laid down here by the architect.

THE THEATRE, 1920

Mackintosh's project for Margaret Morris' little theatre is one of the few formal designs he produced (Plate 79B). The plan is rigidly symmetrical with carefully balanced, spacious lounges, ante-rooms, and axially placed corridors. Two long narrow lounges flank the auditorium and extend through two storeys; at first floor level they are overlooked by a balcony. A 'cinematograph projection box' is provided, and a revolving stage, though the auditorium was designed to accommodate an audience of only 470. The scheme is compact, economical, and well arranged within a rectangle 120 feet by 90 feet.

From the two surviving drawings it is not possible to determine the materials. The structure may well have been concrete, though the front elevation was to have been faced with brickwork. There are no startling innovations and no dramatic constructional features. Only one elevation is shown and this expresses clearly the internal arrangement. The façade is well composed on the drawing but would be far less satisfactory in three dimensions as the rectangular entrance feature is stepped forward clumsily—concertina-like—and the junction between it and the sloping sides of the contiguous towers would be most awkward. Even on Mackintosh's drawing the architrave bites with a saw edge uncomfortably into them. The unification of the three elements—the octagonal towers and the sturdy rectangular centre block would have been effected more easily had the outer fringe of steps been omitted; the eye demands to see more of the attractive pepper-pot towers, and instinctively one seeks to free them from the grip of

213

the powerfully modelled centre block—to push them outwards. But a reference to the plan will show that all kinds of other problems are involved here—not the least of which is that of accommodating the twin staircases, apparently the *raison d'être* of the stepped architrave which houses them. Unlike the majority of Mackintosh's designs this project will not bear close analysis; perhaps it was for this reason, or because of the strange oriental character of the building, the absence of windows and other familiar features, that the local authorities objected so strongly to its erection. How Mackintosh would have overcome the problems involved must remain a matter for conjecture; he did not produce a revised scheme, and the proposal was abandoned.

The drawings of the theatre reproduced here represent the last architectural work of moment that Mackintosh attempted. Squire's studio was built, of course, on modified lines, and it is believed that the Burgess Hill cottage progressed satisfactorily, but no further commissions were forthcoming to compensate for the loss of the Arts League Building, the theatre and the other studios. In view of all this it is surprising to find an entry in Mackintosh's diary, dated January 1921, to the effect that he engaged an assistant—Miss Hero Elder, sister to Miss Eleanor Elder of the Arts League. In a letter to the author Miss Elder confirms that there was no work to be done other than Squire's studio and the cottage—
—'a very small job'. She herself had been trained at an art school and had had no practical drawing-office experience, consequently she was of little help. She stayed but a few months, and though the architect and his wife were very kind to her she did not get to know them well.

From time to time the Mackintoshes received commissions of a minor nature from loyal friends in Glasgow, notably from Miss Cranston: and, of course, they continued to design textiles and to paint. Mr. Blackie too came to their aid, and in 1921 engaged Charles Mackintosh to design covers for a series of booklets, 'Rambles among our Industries' and 'Rambles in Science'. At least two were approved—*Our Railways* and *Wireless*.[1] These were published in 1922 and 1925 respectively and were bound in dark green limp cloth on which the design was printed in black—not a very happy combination. Unlike Bassett-Lowke's gay labels, the covers were dull and unattractive and, what is more, Mackintosh reverted to his former linear and chequered patterns which seem most inappropriate for a series of this nature. At least one further commission came from Mr. Blackie for in January 1922 he wrote to Mackintosh regarding

[1] Copies of these books are in the author's collection.

covers for some of Henty's books, but it is not known whether they were executed.

Thus with little work in hand, disappointed at the failure of his architectural projects, and frustrated by the opposition of the local authorities, Mackintosh again became truculent, morose and apathetic. It is significant that his friend Bassett-Lowke found him quite impossible to work with, and when (*circa* 1922) he wished to build himself a house in the modern manner, turned to Professor Peter Behrens, the German architect, who designed *New Ways*, Northampton (Plate 76c), claimed to be the first house in the modern style to be built in England.

Confirmation that all was not well with the Mackintoshes came from an unexpected and independent source. A Glasgow architect, employed in Sir John Burnet's London office at this time, came across a painting by Charles Mackintosh in an exhibition and secured his address from the catalogue. He had been an admirer of his work in Glasgow and, assuming that he had a flourishing practice in London, made up his mind to seek an interview and, if the prospects were good enough, to offer himself as an assistant. A meeting was arranged in the Glebe Place studios, but to his disappointment Mackintosh greeted him coldly and was obviously in a state of acute depression. Notwithstanding Margaret's attempt to make her visitor welcome, her husband hardly spoke a word during the interview, and in some embarrassment, the prospective assistant was glad to escape from the studio.

From this time onwards things went from bad to worse and on the advice of friends the Mackintoshes decided to take a long holiday abroad. In 1923 they sub-let the studios in Glebe Place and left the country. After a short stay at Mont Louis in the Pyrenees they finally settled at Port Vendres, a tiny hamlet on the Mediterranean side of the Franco-Spanish border. Here they took rooms at the Hôtel de Commerce.

At this juncture Mackintosh resolutely decided to give up all thought of architectural practice and to devote himself to water-colour painting—a decision not altogether unforeseen in view of his remarks to J. D. Fergusson mentioned already. His flower studies and early water-colours indicated that he possessed undoubted talent, and during the Walberswick and Chelsea periods he had had several opportunities of working in this field.[1]

---

[1] In July 1920, for example, in company with his wife, Randolph and Mrs. Schwabe and their daughter Alice, he enjoyed a month's holiday at Worth Matravers, Dorset, where he produced at least three masterly water-colours *Abbotsbury*; *The Village, Worth Matravers*; and *The Downs, Worth Matravers*—two of these are now in the Glasgow School of Art Collection.

THE WATER-COLOURS

At Port Vendres, however, he applied himself seriously to the task of perfecting his technique as a water-colourist, and of establishing his claim to recognition as a painter. His work during the following three or four years is as extraordinary as it is unexpected, and he seems to have plunged into this new form of creative enterprise with unbounded confidence and enthusiasm. The water-colours produced between 1923 and 1927 are entirely different from any of his previous essays in this medium; they are as diverse and full of character, as vigorous and original as his youthful experiments in the field of decoration and craftwork.

The paintings fall into two main groups; still life, invariably comprising flowers or plants; and landscapes with a strong architectural bias. Of the former an excellent example, *The Grey Iris*, was purchased by Glasgow Corporation in 1933 and is to be seen at the Kelvingrove Galleries; another, entitled *Pinks*, a perfectly delightful study of a mass of flowers in a jade green vase, was reproduced in colour in *The Studio* (December 1923), and was highly commended. In none of these later studies do we observe the brooding melancholy of the Glasgow period; they are brilliantly executed, colourful and full of vitality. Incidentally Margaret Macdonald does not appear to have ventured into the realms of landscape painting and all the water colours of the Port Vendres series known to the author are signed by Mackintosh himself.

The landscapes may be divided into two groups; that in which a comparatively small over-all pattern of buildings, fields and so forth dominates—for example, *Port Vendres*, *La Ville* also purchased by Glasgow Corporation in 1933 and reproduced in colour in *The Studio* (June 1933); and a second group in which the attention is caught and held by a single dominant feature—a building perhaps, or a mass of rocks. Two paintings in this category are illustrated here, *Le Fort Maillert* (Plate 83)[1] a dramatic composition of cliff and castle in greys and blues, and *The Rocks* (Plate 82). In all this work it is evident that Mackintosh's interest lay primarily in design—as indeed one would expect—in mass composition, pattern and texture. He made little attempt to achieve depth or atmosphere, and subtle relationships between near and distant places are seldom expressed. Instead the geometrical form of rocks, fields, hills and buildings is emphasized, and these elements are juxtaposed and woven together into fascinat-

[1] *Le Fort Maillert* was illustrated in the French periodical *Revue du Vrai et du Beau*, 25th March 1929, p. 13; it is now in the Glasgow School of Art Collection.

216

ing patterns, unmistakably architectural in conception. In some examples—notably in a picture *The Boulders* reproduced in *The Studio*, June 1933, a swirling spiral composition of jagged rocks and equally serrated gables, cubist influence is apparent. This painting too bears more than a slight resemblance to one of Cezanne's landscapes in Provence,[1] though the contrasts are harsher, and the artist is more concerned with the solidity of the forms themselves than with the shimmering lights and spatial values exploited by the French master. Always his subjects were translated into architectural terms, and we recognize in *Le Fort Maillert*[2] much of the character of the Glasgow School of Art (compare Plates 83 and 96), and the complex overlaid rhythm of *The Rocks* echo again the restless formal contrasts of the Glebe Place studios (compare Plates 82 and 78). In this medium, as in all others, Mackintosh accepted no conventions and followed no rules.

The third of the paintings illustrated here—*The Little Bay* (Plate 85),[2] a restful evening soliloquy with smoothly flowing tide, sun-soaked walls and deep, deep shadows—and *La Rue du Soleil* (Plate 84), an astonishing study in reflections, are two of·his most delightful and accomplished paintings. They were acquired by Sir John Richmond from Desmond Chapman-Huston in 1948, and presented to Glasgow University.

According to Chapman-Huston Mackintosh was a slow worker and during the four years he spent at Port Vendres, he completed only about forty pictures out of the fifty considered necessary for an exhibition at the Leicester Galleries —the objective for which he was striving. He had work exhibited at the third, fourth and fifth Chicago International Exhibitions in 1923, 1924 and 1925 respectively, at the Duveen Invited Artists' Show in Paris in 1927, and at the Leicester Galleries in 1928.

Once again, however, he failed to reach his objective, and the fifty pictures were never completed.

In the autumn of 1927, the year in which he executed many of his best and most interesting water-colours, he complained of a sore throat, and on the recommendation of the local doctor, was persuaded to return to England for specialist advice. On reaching Dover, he and his wife sent an urgent message for help to the Newberys who were then living in retirement at Corfe Castle, Dorset. Mrs. Newbery met them in London, and largely through her influence Mackintosh was admitted for treatment to a city clinic. He was quickly trans-

[1] Notably that in Lord Rothschild's collection exhibited at the Royal Academy in 1949.
[2] Now in the Glasgow School of Art collection.

ferred to Westminster Hospital, however, where, for some months, he endured the agony of radium treatment for cancer of the tongue, and practically lost his power of speech. But he never doubted that he would pull through. It is said that on one occasion medical students were taking notes and sketching the position of the apparatus, when he signified that he wished to see their drawings. Then he borrowed a pencil, made a correct anatomical sketch of his tongue and throat, and clearly demonstrated the best way of depicting the apparatus.

Mackintosh made good progress and to all intents and purposes recovered from the disease. He was discharged from hospital, but of course, a long convalescence was imperative. During his illness he frequently expressed a wish to sit again in a garden, and preferably under a tree. After a great deal of fruitless searching, Margaret Macdonald discovered a furnished house in Willow Road, Hampstead Heath, a house with a small garden *and* a tree. Here he spent his convalescence, nursed devotedly by his wife and visited constantly by his friend Margaret Morris, who taught him to express himself in sign language, and was instrumental in helping him to regain his power of speech. He wrote to Mr. Blackie about this time and spoke of the suffering he had endured in hospital, which, in his opinion, was well worth while because he had been restored to health, and was able to work again. This was followed shortly afterwards by a second letter accepting a commission to paint a picture for Mr. Blackie which, unfortunately, was never executed.

The Mackintoshes were not permitted to enjoy the peace of Hampstead for long, and after some trouble with the landlady they were asked to leave the house. Again a good friend came to their assistance. Desmond Chapman-Huston, whom they had known in the old days at Glasgow, offered them the use of the two upper floors of his house, No. 72 Porchester Square, during his absence abroad. This was a large, early Victorian building with the principal rooms overlooking the gardens in the square. For a time Mackintosh was extremely happy there. He enjoyed browsing through his host's collection of books and pictures, and walking in the garden. Soon, however, he found the stairs too exhausting and arrangements were made for him to occupy the ground floor dining-room which possessed a balcony, so that he had only to go upstairs to bed. Eventually even this became too much for him and in the autumn of 1928 he was moved into a nursing home at No. 26 Porchester Square. At about this time *La Rue du Soleil* and *The Little Bay* were shown at the Leicester Galleries, and Chapman-Huston bought them. As they were unsigned he took them to the nursing-home, where Mackintosh sat up in bed and printed his name on each—the last occasion on which he held a pencil. After a brief illness he died on 10 December 1928.

To Desmond Chapman-Huston also fell the responsibility of arranging for the funeral, and on 11th December a cremation ceremony was held at Golders Green in the presence of a few friends. The ashes were taken home to Mrs. Mackintosh who had expressed a wish to scatter them at Port Vendres where the happiest years of their married life had been spent—a wish that was never gratified.

Margaret Mackintosh was deeply affected by her husband's death, and for a short time remained at Porchester Square. She then went back to Chelsea and lived quietly in lodgings in Royal Avenue and later at No. 10 Manor Studios, Flood Street. Little is known about her life at this time, and she died in comparative obscurity some four years later. She also was cremated at Golders Green—on 10th January 1933. Only six people were present—Professor Randolph and Mrs. Schwabe, Mrs. Talwin Morris, Lady Alice Egerton, a Mr. Hardeman (a cousin of Margaret's) and, representing Desmond Chapman-Huston, Miss Todd his secretary.

Thus ends the last phase of the Mackintosh story, an unhappy and disquieting finale to a curious and fascinating history—an ending as melancholy as one of Margaret Macdonald's first drawings, to a story as enigmatical as an early water-colour by Charles Mackintosh himself.

PART TWO

SOURCES, INFLUENCES AND BRITISH CONTEMPORARIES

In considering the question of sources and influences it is important to remember that the Glasgow movement was not an isolated phenomenon. It was, rather, a local symptom of a widespread revolt against convention in all the arts, the seeds of which had been sown early in the nineteenth century neither by architects nor even by painters, but by men of letters who left behind the solid ground of tradition and ventured into new and seductive fields. By Baudelaire the French poet, for example, who in 1851 wrote *Les Fleurs du Mal*, and by Gautier his compatriot, to whom is accredited the aphorism 'l'art pour l'art', the foundation on which the aesthetic movement was built. Accepted ideas of beauty, propriety and good taste were challenged openly—art, it was claimed, might be found in the root no less than in the flower, and in vice no less than in virtue.[1]

The philosophy of art for art's sake, however, was late in assuming visual form for this was the hey-day of the subject picture and the Academies, a time

[1] For an excellent and entertaining survey of this subject, Whistler and the decadent nineties see *The Aesthetic Adventure*, William Gaunt (Cape, 1945).

of sentiment and moralizing in oils. Even Whistler had difficulty in breaking away from the firmly established tradition of the salon, and it was not until the early 1860's that painters chanced upon a new source of inspiration—Japan. The accidental discovery of woodcuts by Hokusai and other Japanese masters, used for wrapping up small *objets d'art* imported from the Far East, aroused great enthusiasm. Here, it seemed, was the visual expression of Gautier's philosophy. The work of these artists was strangely, mysteriously alive, and of compelling naïveté; symbolic, rather than realistic in its representation of nature. Women with parasols, beasts and fishes, buildings, plants and flowers were woven together into delicate harmonies of line, form and colour with an engaging nonchalance which implied no other object—at least to Western eyes—than that of aesthetic satisfaction; the very epitome of art for art's sake. This revelation of a new, unexplored world had far-reaching consequences—especially in the field of painting; it was under the influence of Japan that Whistler embarked upon his extraordinary career, and quickly became one of the most significant figures of his day; to Japan also went Hornel and Henry of the Glasgow School of Painters, and many others. Books were written on every aspect of Japanese life, and in the decorative field, too, *Japonisme* became the vogue—*objets d'art* and *bric à brac* from the Far East began to flood the European market. Even Japanese flower arrangements were carefully emulated, and the 'Ko', 'Hana no moto', 'Seizan' and other styles, discussed at great length in *The Studio*, became fashionable—the Mackintoshes seem to have taken especial delight in this aspect of oriental art, and their interior schemes usually had several vases of flowers and twigs arranged in the Japanese manner.

During the 1880's, when Charles Mackintosh was commencing his studies, several important works on Japanese domestic architecture and decorative art appeared, among these were Christopher Dresser's *Japan, its Architecture, Art and Art Manufactures* (1882) and E. S. Morse's *Japanese Houses and their Surroundings* (1886). The former contained many illustrations of native drawings in black and white, drawings which reveal unmistakably the source of Aubrey Beardsley's inspiration, and suggest the origin of Mackintosh's linear presentations and analytical plant studies. Morse dealt more specifically with the ordinary Japanese house, a building lightly framed in timber with foundation stones resting *on* the ground, and no walls in the Western sense—a building fantastically remote from the stolid Victorian house in Britain, with its agglomeration of box-like rooms and heavy draperies. The Japanese dwelling was built entirely of wood with square cut, slender pillars and beams and open timber roof. Internal divisions were made of opaque paper screens so that at will several apartments could be made into one. There was neither furniture nor fireplace, and decorations were of the simplest kind. The outer walls consisted of sliding wooden shutters which were stowed away in the daytime so that the building was completely open to the four winds, and virtually became part of the garden (Plate 8A). All this, of course, reflected an entirely different way of life, and a conception of physical comfort that could have little general appeal in Scotland.

To those with eyes to see, however, and especially to Mackintosh, the Japanese house presented a new challenge. Could the delightful freedom and spaciousness of the open plan be translated into Western terms; could its remarkable flexibility and exciting aesthetic potentialities be exploited under the climatic conditions prevailing here? These questions Mackintosh attempted to answer in his own way by the use of openwork screens, balconies, and square post and lintel construction. The influence of Japan is evident throughout his work, especially in the Cranston Tea-Rooms, and in the library at the Glasgow School of Art—even the boldly cantilevered galleries of Queen's Cross Church have at least one counterpart in the Far East, the balcony of an old inn at Mishima, illustrated by Morse.

In domestic buildings, however, Mackintosh had few opportunities for experiment and the Hous'hill Music Room remains his most advanced spatial study. It fell to others, notably to Frank Lloyd Wright in America (*circa* 1907)— developing the traditionally free layout of the American house[1]—and later to Miĕs van der Rohe in Germany, to evolve the sophisticated, Western equivalent of the open plan—taking full advantage of course of modern constructional techniques, reinforced concrete, plate glass—and central heating (Plate 47A).

AUBREY BEARDSLEY (1872–98)

In the graphic arts the man who, without doubt, most faithfully captured the spirit of the age was Aubrey Beardsley the illustrator. While still a clerk in an insurance office Beardsley had come under Whistler's spell and, in fact, visited in 1891 the famous *Peacock Room* designed by him for Mr. Leyland's Princes

[1] See *The Shingle Style*, Vincent Scully, Yale, 1955 and *The Prairie School*, H. A. Brooks, Toronto, 1972.

Q

Gate residence.[1] He also had a passion for the writings of the French School, and was deeply versed in Flaubert, Gautier and the rest—and he collected and studied Japanese prints. By a happy coincidence he was commissioned to illustrate Joseph M. Dent's edition of Malory's *Morte d'Arthur* in 1891–2, and Joseph Pennell, the American author, wrote a well illustrated article on him in the first number of *The Studio* (1893). His claim to fame was securely established by his brilliant drawings for Oscar Wilde's *Salome* in 1894, the year in which he became art editor of John Lane's quarterly, *The Yellow Book*.[2] Thus, it will be observed, Beardsley came into his own just as the style of *The Four* was beginning to emerge, and his influence on them is clearly apparent. His strange drawings abound in fascinating detail and his work possesses many of the characteristics we have come to associate with the Glasgow group—broad plain surfaces contrasted with relatively small areas of rich pattern, sensuous vertical rhythms, and a highly conventionalized treatment in the Japanese manner of trees, plants and flowers. He also made 'patterns out of people' and reduced the human figure to a symbol, a decorative motive (Plate 9c). At first glance it would seem that here lies the answer to the question of style, and that we need search no further for the origin of the curious perversions of the Glasgow designers. But the sad dream world of *The Four* is not the malignant world of Beardsley, and though in many respects their objectives seem to be identical and their technique similar, the whole answer does not lie here.

THE PRE-RAPHAELITES

Yet another source that merits investigation is that of the Pre-Raphaelite Brotherhood, founded in 1848, with romantic Dante Gabriel Rossetti, poet and artist, its high priest. Rossetti's message too was one of dissatisfaction with the existing order of things, but a message more amiable, more gently persuasive than Beardsley's. It has been said that his mind reached out towards

[1] Illustrated *J. McNeill Whistler*, Pennell, pp. 204 and 207 and in *The Studio*, vol. XXXII, pp. 243–6, 1904. This room, remodelled by Henry Jeckyll of Norman Shaw's office, had many shelves—similar in character to some of Mackintosh's tea room details—for Mr. Leyland's china collection. The walls were lined with Spanish leather which, to the owner's horror, Whistler painted blue, with gold peacocks. The room is now in the Freer Gallery of Art, Washington D.C.

[2] Drawings by *The Four* were published in *The Yellow Book*, vol. X, July 1896: *The Dew* and *Ysighlu*, by MacNair, p. 89. *A Dream* and *Mother and Child* by Margaret Macdonald, p. 162. *Ill Omen* and *The Sleeping Princess* by Frances Macdonald, p. 173.

226

'a world of symbols, winds, dim moonlit waters, strange, rich colours, seen in the half-light, not the material world at all but the breath of space'![1] Round him, attracted by his mysticism and magnetic personality, gathered the Pre-Raphaelite Brotherhood; Millais, Holman Hunt and the rest, each of whom tried to recapture the spirit of medievalism—to 'escape from the present into a world of beautiful regrets'.[2] The circle soon disintegrated however, some of its members like Millais and Hunt, turned for inspiration to Christianity and the painting of scriptural themes; others—Rossetti and Burne-Jones—went rather to literature and took their subjects from the Renaissance, from medieval legends, or, alternatively, endeavoured to represent some abstract idea in human form—Faith, Hope, Charity. They created a new type of female beauty with dreamy eyes, pallid features and masses of heavy hair—figures dressed invariably in long flowing robes. Throughout their work one is aware of a skilful and systematic use of the vertical line as a means of expressing emotion and of concentrating interest upon heads and faces—as indeed in Byzantine and Early Christian decoration. The soft folds of drapery and the simple rhythms of trees and foliage are all called to the task, and help to create an atmosphere of strange, melancholy beauty; a beauty nevertheless which is singularly pagan and far removed from the dramatic subject pictures of Hunt and Millais. It was the second—the Rossetti—group which captured the imagination of the Scottish designers. In the work of *The Four* the mysticism and spirituality of the Anglo-Italian poet is combined with the sardonic malignancy of Beardsley, and the Macdonald sisters' weeping females stand somewhere between the tragically innocent figures of Burne-Jones, and the depraved women of Beardsley's imagination.

From the technical point of view, however, the Glasgow group owe more to Beardsley, and if, in the light of this survey, we examine again their early work the point is clearly demonstrated. There is, for example, a marked change in style between, say, Frances and Margaret Macdonald's water-colours in the scrap books of 1893–4 and their beaten metal exhibited at the Arts and Crafts Exhibition of 1896. During the interval *The Studio* article (1893), *Salome*, and the first edition of *The Yellow Book* (1894) had been published. Beardsley's influence is at once apparent in the arrangement and ordering of line and mass, in the broad sweeping dresses and the concentration of detail about the head. The *Salome* illustrations in particular seem to have captivated the Scottish artists and *The Peacock Skirt* (9C) and *John and Salome* find an immediate echo not

[1] Professor B. Ifor Evans. [2] Osbert Burdett.

227

only in the illustrations and craftwork of the Macdonalds, but in the work of George Walton and in Talwin Morris's peacock firescreen and repoussé metal cats at Dunglass.[1] At no time, however, do the Glasgow artists approach the technical virtuosity of the Pre-Raphaelite painters, and the tiny bejewelled water-colours of the Macdonalds cannot be compared with the majestic canvases of Hunt and Burne-Jones, nor can their wispy linear patterns stand comparison with Beardsley's incisive draughtsmanship.

Beardsley, the Pre-Raphaelites and Japan are the most obvious sources on which Mackintosh and his friends drew, but there are others no less important. In a foreword to the Mackintosh Memorial Exhibition Catalogue of 1933 Mrs. Newbery points specifically to two continental artists who, she claims, through the medium of *The Studio*, contributed to the Glasgow style—Jan Toorop and Carlos Schwabe.

Toorop was of Indo-Germanic descent, born in Java in 1859; he studied art at Amsterdam and Brussels. One, and one only, of his paintings was illustrated in *The Studio—The Three Brides* (Plate 8B). This 'odd, fantastic, sibylline production', as it was described by W. Shaw Sparrow, was reproduced in the first volume of that journal (1893). The Dutchman's weird allegory of the church, 'The Bride of Christ', set between the earthly powers of good and evil, and surrounded by disincarnate entities, thorns, and tolling bells evoked an immediate response from *The Four*. Herbert MacNair 'borrowed' a pair of Toorop's women, complete with writhing ectoplasmic hair, for a bookplate illustrated in *The Studio* four years later (September, 1897, p. 235), and the hideous, sharp-featured females of Frances Macdonald's drawing *The Pond* (Plate 7B) and of Charles Mackintosh's Diploma of the School of Art Club (Plate 7C) have many sisters in this strange painting.

Although the phase of grotesque conventionalization soon passed there can be no doubt that *The Four* were deeply affected by *The Three Brides* and the emotional, or spiritual content of their subsequent work approximates far more closely to that of the Dutchman's painting than to any work by contemporary British artists.

With the exception of a theatre programme published in 1897,[2] it is most unlikely that the Glasgow group had seen any more work by Toorop until 1899 when a number of his paintings—including *The Sphynx* and *Les*

[1] Illustrated in *The Studio*, vol. XI, pp. 231–3.
[2] *The Studio*, vol. X, No. 50, May 1897, p. 240. A programme cover for Le Théâtre de L'Oeuvre.

Rodeurs—were reproduced in *Deutsche Kunst und Dekoration*.[1] By this time, of course, the Glasgow style had fully developed.

It is difficult to see how Carlos Schwabe could have influenced *The Four* to any marked degree, unless they saw an exhibition of his work of which no record appears to survive. Schwabe was an illustrator who lived in Paris, and one of the leading figures in a strange society known as Le Salon Rose + Croix. Mrs. Newbery states that he illustrated *Zola's 'Le Rêve'*, but this book is not known to the author. The first and only drawing by him to be published in *The Studio* appeared in May 1897, with that by Toorop in the article on French illustrated programmes—it was for *Le Théâtre Libre*—a demure little design that would make not the slightest impression on Mackintosh and his friends. There is one drawing by Schwabe, however, that must have been known to *The Four*; it was published in Charles Hiatt's excellent survey of contemporary poster design *Picture Posters* (1895), which contained also some of the best work of the French masters—Toulouse-Lautrec, and Bouchon, for example— and Greiffenhagen, Beardsley and the 'Beggarstaff Brothers'.[2] Apart from a superabundance of archaic lettering and a large title 'Audition d'Oeuvres de Guillaume. Lekeu Salon d'Harcourt', the poster contained a single human figure, a sad-faced female kneeling in a bed of irises! Every line of her transparent veil, every fold of her dress, and the voluptuous form of the flowers exudes malevolence, the strange disquieting malevolence of Beardsley and Toorop, and the ethereal melancholy of *The Four*.

Here again, however, it is the spirit of such work rather than the form and technique which is reflected in the early drawings of the Glasgow designers, and in the work of their European contemporaries Munch, Hodler, Klimt, and the rest.

Undoubtedly one of the most potent stimuli in the evolution of the Glasgow style, and one that has been generally overlooked, was the incipient Celtic revival in Scotland. This was heralded, according to Holbrook Jackson,[3] by W. B. Yeats' publication in Dublin of *The Wanderings of Oisin, and other Poems* (1889) and was given considerable impetus by Grant Allen, who, writing in

---

[1] Vol. IV, pp. 541 et seq.

[2] William Nicholson and James Pryde. Later Mackintosh and Pryde became firm friends. Cf. *James Pryde*, Derek Hudson. A poster by Maurice Greiffenhagen also appeared in this book. An illustration of an interesting drawing by Pryde, *Pierrot*, from the Arthur Hickman Collection is reproduced on Plate 9B.   [3] In *The Eighteen-Nineties*, Holbrook Jackson, 1927.

The Fortnightly Review (1891), claimed that the Celt dominated in all fields of artistic activity—he speaks of 'the return wave of Celtic influence over Teutonic or Teutonized England'.

The resurgence of the national spirit in Scotland is reflected also in the researches of Romilly Allen into the origins of Celtic art and in the writings of Patrick Geddes and his followers in the 1890's, writings in which merge the Ossianic mysticism of the Celt and the sensual morbidity of the aesthetic movement.

Geddes (1854–1932)[1] scientist, socialist, philosopher, and town planner, founded in 1895 a publishing firm in Edinburgh with the help of William Sharp, and launched a small illustrated quarterly journal *Evergreen*—a kind of Scottish *Yellow Book* which ran for one year. The articles ranged in content from the strange philosophical meanderings of Geddes himself to spine-chilling island fantasies by J. H. Pearce. Geddes' dissertations on, for example, 'The Scottish Renascence' in the Spring number (there were four seasonal issues) possessed all the vague, disquieting mystery of a Macdonald painting:

' . . . in some young soul here and there the spirit of the hero and the poet may awaken, and press him onward into a life that can face defeat in turn. Such is our Scottish, our Celtic Renascence—sadly set betwixt the Keening, the watching over our fathers dead, and the second sight of shroud rising about each other. Yet this is the Resurrection and the Life, when to faithful love and memory their dead arise' (end of the first volume).

Precisely the same mournful sadness is caught in the poems of 'Fiona Macleod' and the forbidding mists of the islands seem to swirl and eddy round the words of the living dead in one of Pearce's stories:

' "It is cold," muttered the master, as she led him to the door.
' "It is colder where we are going," said the girl.
' "It is dark."
' "It will be darker where we'll have to sleep together."
'And out they went into the wild, mirk night.'

And in the Autumn number there was a lengthy dissertation on 'The Moral Evolution of Sex' and a rather unpleasant poem 'The Unborn' above the pseudonym 'Vita'.

[1] For a full and informative study of the life and work of this remarkable man see *Patrick Geddes*, Philip Boardman (University of North Carolina Press, 1944).

230

Although the whole character of *Evergreen*, with its emphasis on nature and the seasons, and on birth, flowering, harvest and death, is the precise literary equivalent to the Macdonald sisters' craftwork and painting, the sombre melancholy of Geddes' journal was relieved throughout by many black and white drawings—a few of excellent quality (notably those by Helen Hay and

Figure 24. 1891. Book Illustration, 'Natura Naturans', by Robert Burns.

by Robert Burns in the Japanese manner (Fig. 24)). Notable, too, are the embellishments of Celtic style, the headpieces and tailpieces, and small figures in the text. These again point to the revival of interest in Celtic design whilst the convolutions of strapwork and the grotesque imagery of the Book of Kells —that most wonderful of Celtic documents[1]—are reflected clearly, but more

[1] An initial from the Book of Kells is reproduced on Plate 9A by kind permission of the Librarian, Trinity College, Dublin, and Urs/Grafverlag, Berne. The fighting animals whose grotesque elongation resembles the stalks and roots of a strange plant, have much in common with Mackintosh's graphic work.

231

subtly, too, in the work of Mackintosh and his friends as a comparison of Plates 8 and 9 will demonstrate.

Contemporaries of *The Four*, however, usually ascribed their peculiar mannerisms simply to Egyptian influence, and they claimed to discern the lotus flower and anthemion in Mackintosh's stylized linear patterns, and, no doubt, to see a similarity between his formalized women at Buchanan Street and the sculptured warrior kings of Karnak. This is hardly surprising, especially in Glasgow where the exotic Graeco-Egyptian decorative schemes of Alexander Thomson had scarcely ceased to be a source of wonder and astonishment. But Gleeson White, when he visited *The Four* in 1897, seems to have settled the matter—as far as a matter of this kind can be settled—by his subsequent *Studio* article in which he states:

' . . . those sons and daughters of Scotland, who appear to be most strongly influenced by Egypt affect to be surprised at the bare suggestion of such influence, and disclaim any intentional reference to "allegories on the banks of the Nile." . . . With a delightfully innocent air these two sisters disclaim any attempt to set precedent at defiance, and decline to acknowledge that Egyptian decoration has interested them specially. "We have no basis," they say, in tone of demure contrition, "that is the worst of it"; nor do they advance any theory, but enjoy the discomfiture of an enquirer who had expected the intensity of their work to be the produce of "intense" artists.'[1]

White then goes on to say that their studios contain no casts, reproductions, or photographs of Egyptian art—a point which he suggests is of some moment because the designer inevitably gathers round him examples of work from his favourite period. In this regard one wonders whether he failed to notice Mackintosh's Japanese prints and Pre-Raphaelite reproductions—evident also in the earliest of his studios, the Dennistoun bedroom (Plate 5A)—or the abundance of flowers and plants that invariably graced the rooms of the Macdonald sisters. These, perhaps, were too commonplace, and in seeking the profound he overlooked the obvious.

Seen from the vantage point of the 1950's, however, the Glasgow Style merges perfectly into the background of the decadent nineties; it belongs unmistakably to the Beardsley period, to the world of Wilde and Swinburne, of Rossetti and Burne-Jones, and *Evergreen*; it owes something to Japan and much to the Celtic tradition. But, even so, its main source of inspiration lay

[1] *The Studio*, vol. XI, No. 52, July 1897, pp. 88–9.

232

in nature—'where else indeed should we go', Mackintosh had said in 1893—and if we wish to find the origin of Charles Mackintosh's elementary decorative forms we must turn to the potting shed at Dennistoun, and to his mother's kitchen table, rather than to Egypt and the Far East. It was more than fortuitous that the bulb and bud, leaf and petal, rose and tulip, became and remained throughout the characteristic emblems of the Glasgow Style.

If then, we accept the contention that Mackintosh's forms were derived principally from nature, and that the spiritual content of work by *The Four* was the outcome of time and place, what of his furniture and interior decoration?

Here, again, it is necessary to stress the fact that Mackintosh was not alone in his attempts at simplification, nor was he by any means the first to try to break the bonds of historicism.

GEORGE WALTON (1867–1933)

In Scotland, indeed in Glasgow, there was at least one man whose work deserves especial attention here—George Walton.[1] Walton was born in Glasgow on 3rd June 1867 (the youngest of twelve children) and thus was almost exactly a year older than Mackintosh. His father, Jackson Walton, was a painter. He left school at fourteen to work as a junior clerk in the British Linen Bank and attended evening classes in art. It has not been possible to determine whether he went to the Glasgow School of Art though this is most likely; in any case there can be little doubt that as students, Mackintosh and MacNair were well known to him.

At the age of twenty-one, the year in which Mackintosh completed his apprenticeship with John Hutchison, Walton gave up his comparatively secure position at the bank and opened a business at 150–2 Wellington Street, Glasgow, under the grand title of 'George Walton & Co., Ecclesiastical and House Decorators'.[2] Professor Pevsner has said that 'we shall probably never know exactly what made him take this step', but an article in *The Studio* (1906), written by a certain J. Taylor, seems to provide the answer; this is the relevant paragraph:

[1] An excellent monograph on George Walton by Professor Pevsner was published in the *R.I.B.A. Journal*, 19th April 1939—it is from this source that some of the following personal details are taken.

[2] First mentioned in the Post Office Guide, 1888.

'It is not easy to imagine what would be the position of modern decorative art in Glasgow today, apart from the group of teahouses controlled by Miss Cranston, for it is a remarkable fact that while George Walton was yet a bank accountant, he accepted a decorative commission connected with a new smoking room for one of them and when he abandoned finance to carry out this, his first commission, decorative art may be said to have entered a new phase at Glasgow. . . .'

As we have observed already, the first tea-room was opened in Argyle Street in 1884, and one can imagine Miss Cranston inviting the young, unknown designer to decorate and furnish her smoking-room more or less as an experiment, thereby launching him upon his new career in much the same way that she introduced Mackintosh to the public some seven years later.

Unfortunately nothing is known now of Walton's first work for Miss Cranston and no photographs have come to light; thus an important link in the chain is missing. Nevertheless it is possible to measure Walton's progress by reference to subsequent designs of which reliable dated evidence remains. His principal commissions in the Glasgow region were photographed by his friend the late J. Craig Annan from 1891 onwards—that is, before any of Mackintosh's executed work had been published.[1] All the photographs taken between 1891 and 1896—with the exception of one, a gown shop, are domestic interiors in which no consistent principle of design or arrangement can be detected.

None of these interiors is conceived as a whole, and with few exceptions, the furniture is quite without distinction, revealing little evidence of the refined and elegant forms he eventually achieved. Moreover, Walton seemed content to follow the prevailing fashion of highly decorated wall surfaces, and in nearly all the examples wallpapers and stencilled mural decoration played an important part. These were usually of vigorous but inoffensive floral patterns with acorns, pineapples, leaves and so forth—and if an opportunity occurred similar patterns were applied to ceilings. Generally he drew with broad precise lines which were never allowed to get out of control, but in some cases, notably in the hall at Sir Frederick Gardiner's house (1891), they approach the vigour of Horta's threshing, vermicular scrolls at No. 12 Rue de Turin, Brussels (1893), which, it is often claimed, announced the advent of continental *art nouveau*. Walton's

[1] Through the kindness of Mr. Thomas Craig Annan the author has been able to examine many original negatives of this work and to secure dates and so forth from the records of the firm. Furthermore a large selection of photographs is housed in the R.I.B.A. Library, but at the time of writing these are neither catalogued, classified nor dated.

234

candelabra, too, often writhe and twist with the acanthus leaves in a wild dance reminiscent of Van de Velde's work ten years later, a concession never made by Mackintosh even in his most exuberant moments. At this time, however, neither Horta nor Van de Velde had produced work of this nature and in Walton's wall decorations, as indeed in Macmurdo's flame-like designs of the preceding decade, we can recognize many of the forms which later became identified with the continental movement.

Before 1896, the date of the Buchanan Street Tea-Room interiors, all Walton's work that has been recorded consists of piecemeal decorative schemes of this nature. The first published illustrations of interiors by him appeared in *Academy Architecture* in 1898—the staircase hall and drawing-room of a house *Lead Cameron*, Bearsden, near Glasgow, for J. B. Gow, Esq.[1] In both apartments the predominant colour was white and the principal features were fireplaces of which the hall boasted two, a small one with a delightfully simple architrave enclosing the tiled surround, and no mantelpiece; the second one, an enormous structure comprising a deep tile-lined recess with a canopied basket grate and a great plain architrave fully 7 feet high. For Walton this was a bold achievement, and apart from a terminal cyma recta moulding not a single decorative motive of traditional form is employed. The staircase is notable for its unusual balustrading of square unmoulded members and lofty newel posts, a detail reminiscent of the School of Art staircase with which it was probably contemporary.[2] Both Walton and Mackintosh seem to have derived this popular form of balustrading from Voysey, whose staircase at No. 14 Hans Road, London, one of a pair of most interesting terrace houses, was illustrated in *The Studio* in September 1893. From a photograph of the drawing-room at *Lead Cameron* (Plate 11B) it is still not possible to assess Walton's style of furniture; two upholstered chairs with tall backs are visible but nothing more of consequence. His stencilled friezes in both hall and drawing-room, however, are much more pleasing than any previous examples—in the former he employed a Whistler butterfly motive, and in the latter a graceful floral pattern in which ogival stems form the principal rhythm. Both mark a radical departure from the acanthus leaves and scrolls of Sir Frederick Gardiner's house (*circa* 1891) and elsewhere.

It would seem that Walton's style, like that of Mackintosh, underwent a con-

[1] Photographed 10th June 1898. Annan's record.
[2] Mackintosh had employed an identical form in metal for the candle-holders on his study fender at Dennistoun—see Plate 5A.

siderable change *circa* 1896–7: before this date, neither designer had achieved a white room, and although Mackintosh's furniture appears to have been the more imaginative, neither had made substantial progress, and their work was on the whole heavy, and lacked refinement. In 1896, of course, they worked together on Miss Cranston's Buchanan Street Tea-Room and, of even greater significance, in the autumn of that year Mackintosh sent work to the Arts and Crafts Society's Exhibition at a time when Walton, if not himself an exhibitor, was making preparations to transfer his headquarters from Glasgow to London, and thus would be in close touch with events in the south. Here the Glasgow designers were able to measure their strength against the best work the country had to offer, the work of the acknowledged contemporary masters of design. At the New Gallery, Ashbee, Crane, Lethaby, Lorimer and a host of others were represented, and above all, C. F. A. Voysey, who demonstrated his versatility by exhibiting not only delightful wallpapers, craftwork and furniture, but a street lamp-standard, an invalid chair painted light green—remarkably similar in shape to Mackintosh's oak settle—and an enormous white painted mantelpiece on which Walton undoubtedly modelled the *Lead Cameron* example. As *The Studio* pointed out, some of Voysey's contributions were at once the most restrained and the most original in the Exhibition; furthermore, said the reviewer, 'It is especially good that his influence, which tends to simplicity and severity should be made prominent at this time. . . .'

After Voysey's work at London the unusual fireplaces and fresh interiors at *Lead Cameron* are more easily accounted for, and Mackintosh's ingenious essays in white become less inexplicable. It would seem that each designer learned much from the Exhibition and from the Buchanan Street experiment, but though their subsequent work has many points in common—particularly in their handling of metal and wood—neither varied one degree from the course he had already embarked upon. Walton's interiors and furniture show much greater refinement and more coherence than hitherto; they are lighter, more adventurous and gay; his stencilled patterns and wallpapers, too, are used with greater discretion, and as at *Lead Cameron*, they partake of the freedom and character of his rival, but he never ventured far from the traditional fold. Mackintosh, too, discarded many of the coarser features which had marred his earlier work. His mural decorations were substantially modified—the frieze at Kingsborough Gardens, for example, is far removed from the *art nouveau* convolutions at Buchanan Street, executed four years earlier. But he plunged with increasing enthusiasm into experimental work and in this respect differed

236

radically from Walton who pursued a more amiable course closer to that of the English school.

Whatever opinions may be held now as to the relative merits of the two designers, craftsmen who worked with them had no doubt as to who was the greater artist. The author has been able to find several such men and they agree that Walton was a designer of good taste and something of a connoisseur, but it was Mackintosh who fired them with enthusiasm, and astonished them with his capacity for invention. Walton always remained dignified and aloof, insisting that his designs be executed with mechanical precision; Mackintosh was rarely absent from the job for long, and often worked with the decorators, varying his designs, and adding touches of colour here and there to give sparkle and vitality as the scheme materialized. It was his complete grasp of the problem in hand, his delight in using simple materials, and his inexhaustible creative genius that captivated all who came in contact with him.

If further contemporary evidence is needed to show that Walton and Mackintosh worked independently and had little in common, it is provided by Gleeson White, who, writing in 1897 states:

'In Glasgow the newest and most individual manner is undoubtedly that which is seen in the work of the Misses Macdonald, Mrs. F. H. Newbery, Mr. Charles Mackintosh, J. Herbert MacNair, and Mr. Talwin Morris. Mr. Oscar Paterson, in his very original stained glass, must not be placed quite in the same group, nor can Mr. George Walton, whose work is entirely devoid of the qualities which make the first group so prominent.'[1]

And again:

'These two craftsmen (Paterson and Walton) have nothing in common with what might be called the "Mac" group . . . indeed it would not be fair to Mr. George Walton to link him with any other workers. . . .'[2]

Thus it would seem that Walton and Mackintosh came under Voysey's spell, especially after the Arts and Crafts Exhibition of 1896, and though each assimilated something of the older man's spirit, each in turn expressed himself in his own way. Walton, as we have seen, was in closer touch with the English designers than Mackintosh and, in fact, he and Voysey later became firm friends —a point which, no doubt, accounts for his finesse and greater soberness, both

[1] *The Studio*, July 1897, p. 87.
[2] *Ibid.*, September 1897, p. 234.

237

characteristics of the southern school.[1] Mackintosh, on the other hand, though subscribing to Voysey's ideals and closely emulating his methods, remained always the individualist and applied himself to the development of his own personal style with Voysey as his initial inspiration but not as his master.

Where then do Walton and Mackintosh stand in relation to the English Arts and Crafts movement?

There is no need to enlarge here upon William Morris's great contribution to the development of English craftwork; his chintzes and carpets, wallpapers and furnishings are justly famous for their simplicity of form, rich colouring and exquisite workmanship, characteristics all the more remarkable in an age given over to vulgar commercialism. But we may remind ourselves that Morris founded the famous firm of craftsmen that bore his name—'Morris, Marshall, Faulkner & Co., Fine Art Workmen in Painting, Carving, Furniture and the Metals'—by which he was determined to reform the applied arts in this country, in 1861, seven years before Mackintosh was born.

Morris was an indefatigable worker and a militant propagandist, and there were few contemporary designers not profoundly influenced by his teaching. The Morris 'movement' grew into a general revival of the handicrafts, with, as one of its most interesting manifestations, the emergence of numerous guilds or societies—the Century Guild established by A. H. Mackmurdo in 1882 and

---

[1] In 1897 Walton moved to London though retaining his workshop and showroom in Glasgow, and in the following year opened a shop at York. His friendship with George Davison, head of Kodak's European Sales Organization, brought him a series of commissions for the decoration and furnishing of showrooms for the firm in London, Glasgow, Brussels, Milan and Vienna (1898–1901). These were beautifully illustrated in *Dekorative Kunst*, vol. VI, No. 6, March 1903. In 1901, apparently without any previous experience, Walton turned his hand to architecture and designed *The Leys*, Elstree, for Mr. J. B. B. Wellington (Plate 88B)—a house the size of, and contemporary with *Hill House*. In this work, perfectly symmetrical about a curved entrance feature—'borrowed' it would seem from Ernest Newton's *Red Court* at Haslemere (1897)—Walton owed little or nothing to Mackintosh, although the interiors belong unmistakably to the Glasgow Style. The influence of Voysey is apparent, however, and more especially in *The White House*, Shiplake (1908) (Plate 88D) —but here the parts of the building are less well integrated and the façades are broken up and restless, faults rarely found in Voysey's work.

Walton's other buildings need not concern us here. He executed a number of domestic commissions prior to the first World War, but less interesting than either of those mentioned here. Like Mackintosh, he did not find work easy to come by thereafter and turned to the design of fabrics and stained glass. He died on 10th December 1933.

the Art Workers' Guild, 1884, for example. But Morris and his followers were not satisfied with this; for if, as they maintained, art is indivisible and handicraft its fundamental basis, then the schism between the fine arts and the applied arts —or rather between the practitioners of the fine arts and of the arts not so fine —should be healed, so that all might advance together towards a grand Renaissance. The Royal Academy was approached with a view to extending its orbit to encompass the minor arts, and it was suggested that joint exhibitions be held at which work by craftsmen in wood, metal and glass might take its place along with paintings and sculpture; where Webb, Morris, Gimson, Ashbee and Lethaby might be represented equally with Leighton, Alma Tadema and Landseer. This heresy, however, was emphatically rejected by the academicians and all attempts at conciliation failed. The protestors then came together and decided (in 1888, the year in which George Walton opened his Glasgow workshop) to form an independent society—the Arts and Crafts Exhibition Society, with Walter Crane as President.

The real objective of the new body could not be comprehended easily in a title: it far transcended the arrangement of annual or triennial exhibitions and, in the words of William Morris, was rather 'to help the conscious cultivation of art and to interest the public in it'—or, as another member claimed, 'to extend the conception of art, and to apply it to life as a whole'.

In order to achieve this ambitious objective lectures and demonstrations formed part of the Society's programme. At the first exhibition (1888) illustrated lectures were given by Morris on Tapestry, by George Simmonds on Modelling and Sculpture, by Emery Walker on Printing, by Cobden Sanderson on Bookbinding and by Walter Crane on Design; unfortunately, no verbatim record was kept, but each year notes were appended to the Exhibition catalogues, and in 1893 they were collected and published.[1]

Thus the aims of the Society, and the personal views of its members were widely disseminated. But by no means all the members subscribed to the view Morris expressed in his preface to the book, namely that their objectives must be achieved: ' . . . by calling attention to that really most important side of art, the decoration of utilities by furnishing them with genuine artistic finish in place of trade finish'. Nor, for that matter, with his condemnation of machine production as a condition of life as wholly evil. Even Cobden Sanderson objected to this, and he writes: 'Surely things there are, the production of which by machinery may be wholly right, things which, moreover, when so produced

---

[1] *Arts and Crafts Essays* (Rivington, Percival & Co., 1893).

may be wholly right also, and in their rightness even works of art.'[1] This represents a considerable advance upon Morris's conception of the movement, and reveals a more rational approach to contemporary problems of design and production—an approach analogous to that of the Deutsche Werkbund founded in 1907.

Of all dissenting elements in the early days, however, the most dramatic note was struck by J. D. Sedding (1837–1892), an architect and craftsman, a builder of unorthodox churches,[2] and one of the most respected and admired figures in the profession.

'Our designers can design in any style,' he said. 'Every old method is at our finger ends. . . . We are critics: we are artists. We are lovers of old work: we are learned in historical and aesthetic questions and technical rules and principles of design. . . . Yet our work hangs fire. Why?'

And then this:

'Think of the gain to the "Schools" and to the designers themselves, if we elected to take another starting point! No more museum-inspired work! No more scruples about styles! No more dry-as-dust stock patterns! . . . But instead . . . designs *by* living men *for* living men. . . . We must clothe modern ideas in modern dress, adorn our design with living fancy and rise to the height of our knowledge and capacity.'

A new starting point! Design by living men for living men! By these words Sedding brought into sharp focus the problems besetting many of his colleagues at this time—but he himself had no solution to offer, nor could he define the new starting point. Nevertheless, it was this outspoken address, echoed and re-echoed in lectures by Newbery, that gave *The Four* courage to break with convention, and largely determined the course of events in Glasgow. Strangely enough Sedding's words to the Arts and Crafts Society nearly sixty years before came immediately to the lips of Herbert MacNair when discussing the origins of the Glasgow Style with the author—Sedding who had inspired *The Four* with his assurance that ' . . . there is hope in honest error: none in the icy perfections of the stylist'.

---

[1] In *The Arts and Crafts* (1905), p 25.

[2] For example, St. Peter's Church, Ealing, illustrated in Muthesius's *Die Neuere Kirchliche Baukunst in England*, pp. 48–9, and Holy Trinity, Sloane Street, London (1899); *ibid.*, Plate XXIV, and p. 46.

Thus we find that the Arts and Crafts movement was well established in England before the Glasgow designers started work and that they, like their European contemporaries, drew inspiration principally from the discourses of men like Sedding, Lethaby, Voysey and others, architects who sought a broader interpretation of the precepts of Ruskin and Morris.

If at this point we turn from the minor arts to building it will be observed that the most discussed personalities in the architectural profession were no longer the great stylists, the Scotts, Bodleys and Streets, but a new generation that came more directly under the influence of William Morris, and won its reputation almost entirely with domestic buildings and craftwork.

It is hardly surprising, therefore, to find that one of the first buildings to show evidence of the new spirit was designed for Morris himself, *Red House*, Bexley Heath (1860)—the architect being Morris's friend and mentor in Street's office, Philip Webb, then twenty-eight years old. In marked contrast to most contemporary work,[1] this building was quite unpretentious and devoid of stylistic motives: it had a simple straightforward plan, red brick walls and a tiled roof: no attempt was made to force symmetry, and every advantage was taken of the texture and colour of ordinary materials. It was as though the designer had taken to heart Ruskin's lesson at Edinburgh some seven years earlier:

'The first thing to be required of a building—not, observe, the *highest* thing, but the first thing—is that it shall answer its purpose completely, permanently, and at the smallest expense. . . . The sacrifice of any of these first requirements to external appearance is a futility and absurdity.'[2]

Philip Webb, whose work and influence on British architecture has been greatly under-rated, was born in Oxford in 1831. It has been said[3] that he was the first architect since the Renaissance to select materials with real sensibility to colour, texture and surface—a statement that contains more than a grain of the truth. He was undoubtedly one of the first to turn for inspiration to the unsophisticated vernacular buildings of his own country, and to delight in

---

[1] Webb's early work was a continuation and simplification of that of Street and Butter-field, and *Red House* does not represent a complete break with the past as frequently claimed.

[2] *Lectures in Architecture* (Edinburgh, 1853).

[3] By Noel Rooke in a paper read before the R.I.B.A. on 21st February 1950.

exploiting local building methods and materials. 'Architecture to Webb', wrote W. R. Lethaby,[1] 'was first of all a common tradition of honest building.'

This new approach—an ethical approach—to the problems of architectural design and practice, with its emphasis on rational building, the dignity of labour, and the value of good craftsmanship, laid the foundations of the revival in English domestic architecture which, at the turn of the century, won the admiration of Europe.

Joldwynds, Surrey (1873), *Rounton Grange*, Northallerton (1872–6), and *Clouds*, East Knoyle, Wiltshire (1886) (Plate 87A and B), all illustrated in Lethaby's book, well represent Webb's style of building and his sensitivity to regional character. They are more ambitious than Morris's *Red House*, but evidence the same care in the use of materials, the same interest in good planning, and simple, orderly fenestration. Webb's little school at Rounton (1876), (Plate 88A), is an excellent example of studied elimination, and is obviously a precursor of the romantic gabled cottage with low sweeping roof and plain rough-cast walls made popular by Voysey twenty years later—and indeed often employed by Mackintosh.

Philip Webb's only serious rival in the domestic field was Richard Norman Shaw, who, it has been said, was one of the first to build again on English lines on English soil. Shaw had taken Webb's place at Street's office in 1858, and for a time became a confirmed Gothicist. Four years later he began to practice in London with William Eden Nesfield and gathered round him a brilliant group of assistants and pupils. Within a few years he built up one of the finest practices in the country, and was at work on many important public and private commissions.

At first Shaw favoured a style based on sixteenth- and seventeenth-century domestic architecture with many gables, half timbering and lofty chimneys; then in 1873 at New Zealand Chambers, Leadenhall Street, London, he introduced the style for which he became famous—his so-called 'Queen Anne'—and which found expression most happily in a series of town houses, notably *Swan House*, Chelsea, 1875 (Plate 87D), and 170 Queen's Gate, 1890.

Shaw's office became the centre to which many of the most progressive architects of the day gravitated. To Shaw in 1881, for example, came W. R. Lethaby (1857–1931), Webb's friend, who had been trained at Barnstaple and had spent his time there designing farm buildings and cottages; he was made chief assistant and remained at the office for twelve years—during which

[1] In *Philip Webb and his Work* (Oxford University Press, 1935).

242

he helped to found the Art Workers' Guild (1883) and took an active part in the Art and Crafts movement. He was persuaded, after leaving Shaw, to become joint-principal of the L.C.C. Central School of Arts and Crafts with George Frampton the sculptor, and thereby he, too, was able to exercise a considerable influence upon the younger men of his day.[1]

The similarity between Lethaby's philosophy of life and style of building, and that of Webb is clearly revealed in the illustration of *Avon Tyrrell*, Hampshire (1891), (Plate 87c)—a fine country house with rhythmic gables, bay windows, and excellent brickwork—traditional in construction, yet modern in conception. It was by such work that Webb, Shaw and Lethaby laid the foundations of the revival of domestic architecture in this country.

Two other architects in particular played an important part in giving direction and impetus to the new movement—Arthur H. Mackmurdo (1851–1941)[2] and C. F. A. Voysey, both of whom have been mentioned already.

Mackmurdo was apprenticed to T. Chatfield Clark in 1869, and then worked under James Brooks, a Gothicist. He read widely and became interested in socialism and the teachings of William Morris. In order to attend Ruskin's lectures he graduated at Oxford, and later accompanied him on a tour of Italy. To Mackmurdo, Italy was a revelation; he spent over a year in Florence, sketching, measuring, and drawing from life, and even then was obliged to leave under duress after his appeal to the Italian Minister of Fine Arts successfully prevented local enthusiasts from 'restoring' the exterior of the Duomo and Giotto's Campanile with acids.[3] About 1876—presumably after his return from Italy—he set up in practice at 28 Southampton Street, London. One of his first buildings of which record remains is a house at Bush Hill Park, Enfield, built *circa* 1876,[4] with lofty chimneys and half-timbered gables, clearly influenced by Shaw. A second house in the same locality built in 1878, however, is of entirely different character and unmistakably foreshadows the twentieth century. From the single illustration available, it appears to have a flat roof hidden

[1] Frampton did not play an active part in running the school and soon resigned from the position.

[2] See *The Architectural Review*, Vol. LXXXIII, 1938. *A Pioneer Architect—Arthur H. Mackmurdo*, by Professor Pevsner.

[3] Mackmurdo's prolonged visit to Florence and his subsequent interest in the formation of the Society for the Protection of Ancient Buildings—1877—is dealt with by Aymer Vallance in *The Studio*, vol. XIV, April 1899.

[4] 'The first house I designed, 1871.' Mackmurdo wrote this note on a rough $\frac{1}{2}$ inch scale drawing of an elevation of this building (now in the William Morris Museum, Walthamstow).

behind a parapet wall, and the second storey of the façade is divided horizontally into three broad bands approximately equal in depth, by two narrow string courses between which the architect placed long horizontal windows. The details, like so many of Mackmurdo's details, are deplorable. (This feature —horizontal windows linked together at sill and lintel level by string courses— became a popular affectation of the modern school, and was used *ad nauseam* in the 1920's to 1930's, but it had no precedent in the world of Richard Norman Shaw).

Had it not been for further evidence of the architect's original turn of mind, this single building might well be passed over as an isolated example that coincidentally possesses features which later assumed new significance. But on his return from Italy, Mackmurdo set to work on a book, *Wren's City Churches*, for which he designed a striking cover (1883); the dominant motive was a vicious, swirling composition of flame-like leaves and exotic flowers, flanked by a pair of tall attenuated birds, so emaciated that they are hardly distinguishable from the linear border. The same pulsing vitality is apparent in the carved back of a chair which he designed in 1881,[1] and in an embroidered screen (1884),[2] and is the embodiment of the spirit of continental *art nouveau,* yet preceding it, Mackintosh, Toorop and Beardsley by a decade. In 1882, along with his partner Herbert Horne—a former pupil—and Selwyn Image, Mackmurdo instituted the Century Guild, a society similar in conception and objective to Morris's firm, and in April 1884 launched its mouthpiece *The Hobby Horse.*[3] Mackmurdo, however, was remarkably inconsistent and though on occasion his furniture reveals a fresh and imaginative approach to design, all too often it is heavy, over-elaborate, and out of scale.

Mackmurdo seems to have become more and more interested in philosophy and the applied arts, and only one later building is of particular interest here, a town house—No. 25 Cadogan Gardens—designed in 1899 for Mortimer Menpes, the Australian painter (Plate 87E). Menpes had made a special study of Japanese decoration and before the interior of his house was finished, he visited Japan taking with him Mackmurdo's drawings, and arranged for a complete

---

[1] *The Studio*, April 1899, p. 186.   [2] *Ibid.*, p. 184.

[3] Professor Pevsner points out that in this work modern printing was treated as an art for the first time; the type was carefully selected and spaced, and hand-made paper was used. It was largely as a result of this venture and of Emery Walker's illustrated lecture to the Arts and Crafts Society on Letter-Press Printing, that William Morris decided to turn his attention to printing, and founded the Kelmscott Press.

244

range of fittings to be designed and constructed under his supervision by native craftsmen. This extraordinary house achieved considerable notoriety, and good illustrations of the interior were published in the August number of *The Studio*, 1899, the year in which the first section of the Glasgow School of Art was completed. The house itself, now dwarfed by Peter Jones's Store, Sloane Square, occupies a corner site, and is constructed of red-brown, two-inch bricks: tall, elegant windows extend through the first and second floors, and the façades are terminated by a coved plaster cornice and a slated attic storey with pedimented dormers. The windows recall Mackintosh's treatment of the library windows at the School of Art; on one elevation—to Cadogan Gardens—they are recessed, and on the adjacent elevation they project as oriels from the wall surface. Mackintosh must have known this building well, if only through the medium of *The Studio*, and he may have used it as a starting point for his own experiments at Glasgow. Compared to the dramatic west elevation of the School however, Mackmurdo's house seems diminutive and insignificant, although its proportions are such that photographs inevitably falsify its size. But, for all its originality, No. 25 Cadogan Gardens is well within the Shaw tradition, and, coming as it did, some fourteen years after *Swan House*, Chelsea, evoked little comment in the architectural journals.

Mackmurdo is an interesting and enigmatical figure but he is of far less importance than his friend C. F. A. Voysey who worked independently of any group, and who alone seems to have had his objective clearly in view from the first.[1] Voysey went back to first principles and in rejecting ready-made styles as such, evolved an idiom that was at once modern and yet traditional, at once personal and yet generic:

' . . . the value of Mr. Voysey's art', wrote a contemporary, 'is not in the use of any material, or of any mannerism, but in his evident effort to seek first the utilitarian qualities of strength and firmness, and to obtain beauty by common honesty.'[2]

Although Voysey confined himself almost entirely to domestic building and the minor arts, the effect of his work and philosophy was profound. He was

---

[1] Voysey was born in 1857, the son of the Vicar of Healaugh, in Yorkshire. He became a pupil of J. P. Seddon in 1874 and in 1880 joined George Devey, who specialized in the design of large country houses and farms. He commenced practice alone in London in 1882. Voysey's work, and the significance of Devey as a formative influence, are to be discussed in a forthcoming book by Mr. John Brandon-Jones.   [2] *The Studio*, 1897.

idolized by the younger element in the profession, and great prominence was given to his designs in the professional journals. His influence, and that of Webb, can be seen in the work of many architects of the southern school—most notably perhaps, in that of Baillie Scott—and also in the north-west, where Edgar Wood (1860–1935) established an outpost of the new movement in the 1890's. Wood was articled to Murgatroyd and Mills, architects to the Manchester Royal Exchange (1868), and became particularly interested in the work of Burges, Godwin and J. D. Sedding. In 1885 he began to practise on his own and *c*. 1895 to design and exhibit furniture. Wood and another local architect, J. H. Sellers,

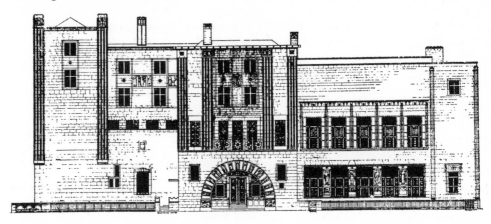

Figure 25. 1891. J. A. Slater. 'A Town Mansion.'

who had built a flat-roofed extension to a house in Oldham in 1901, formed a loose partnership in 1904–5; they worked independently but shared experience. Sellers designed a strikingly unorthodox office building, flat-roofed, and decorated externally by coloured tiles, for Dronsfields of Oldham (1906), and in the same year Wood built his first reinforced concrete, flat-roofed tile-decorated house at Hale, Cheshire. His 'Upmeads', Stafford (Plate 89A), came two years later. One of Wood's most representative buildings, with many good arts and crafts details, is the First Church of Christ Scientist, Victoria Park, Manchester (1903). Neither Wood nor Sellers did any work of consequence after the First World War.[1]

Not all experimental building was confined to the domestic sphere, however, and several unorthodox schemes had been illustrated in the journals, and some

[1] The authority on Wood and Sellers is John Archer, of the School of Architecture, Manchester University.

246

actually carried out, before Mackintosh startled Glasgow with his design for the School of Art. Before considering this work though, two more projects of domestic proportions must be mentioned which could hardly be classified with any of the preceeding examples. One is a design by J. A. Slater for 'A Town Mansion': it was dedicated to W. R. Lethaby and published as a supplement to *The Architect* on 20th February 1891—the issue which, significantly, contained a report of Mackintosh's paper on 'Scottish Baronial Architecture'.

The second is an extraordinary design for a studio (Fig. 26) by Voysey. This drawing would be notable if only for its eccentricity, but there can be little

Figure 26. *circa* 1893. C. F. A. Voysey. 'A Studio.'

doubt that Mackintosh found inspiration here for his great studio windows at the Glasgow School of Art (cf. Plate 23A).

The long rambling elevation of Slater's project (Fig. 25) is strangely akin to the Glasgow School also, but more especially to the *Haus eines Kunstfreundes*, yet it betrays a certain affinity with the exotic Graeco-Egyptian work of Alexander Thomson. There is all the studied inconsequence of Mackintosh in the play of solid and void, superimposed upon the inflexible, dominating rhythms of a Thomson-like fenestration. Stripped of its ornament, this design might easily be mistaken for a work by Mackintosh, and yet it ante-dates the School of Art by five years, and the German project by a decade or more. It would, without doubt, find its way into Mackintosh's files.

Evidence of a new spirit of enquiry comes from many sources during the

247

1890's and a number of new names appear in the journals, for example, Sydney Greenslade, Leonard Stokes, Henry Wilson, C. Harrison Townsend, A. Dunbar Smith and Cecil Brewer. In much of the work executed by these architects the influence of Shaw is clearly apparent, and in few instances do they depart far from tradition. Henry Wilson, a pupil and admirer of J. D. Sedding, specialized in ecclesiastical work and continued the experiments of his master—but principally in the neo-Gothic manner. In 1892, the year in which Sedding died, he designed a tower for St. Mary's Church, Lynton, an elegant, simple structure with a gay roof; in the following year he submitted in competition an unorthodox design for a New Cathedral, Victoria, British Columbia—from which Mackintosh borrowed freely for Queen's Cross Church and the Liverpool Cathedral schemes—and his project for the west front of St. Andrew's Church, Boscombe, as depicted in *Academy Architecture* (1895), represents a bold step towards the twentieth century.

Secessionist tendencies are not easy to detect in the ecclesiastical field where tradition inevitably plays an important role, yet a drawing for 'The West End of a Town Church' (1898) (Plate 90A) by Sydney K. Greenslade, is one of several which indicate that even *art nouveau* and the Glasgow Style were not without their adherents in the south. The façade depicted here is, in fact, a tower of imposing proportions, and with its riot of *art nouveau* detail at parapet level, and about the doorways—and its voluptuous flêche—was considered a daring innovation.

In the secular sphere many tentative experiments were made. *Circa* 1894 Leonard Stokes[1] designed Nazareth House, Bexhill, a big three-storeyed building of simple character and pleasing proportions: the ground storey was faced in brick; the second and third storeys were rendered, with windows rhythmically disposed in the Shaw manner; and there was a roof in the style of Voysey. Altogether the building had an air of refinement and efficiency which makes it the natural precursor of Smith and Brewer's Mary Ward Settlement, Tavistock Place, London (1895). This building has been described by Professor Pevsner as 'the most remarkable example of twentieth-century feeling reached by English architects before 1900'.[2] The settlement is four storeys high, and constructed of brick with the top floor contained within a mansard roof, and lit by large dormers. The windows throughout are of Georgian proportions and, in fact, not a single element, except the porch—derived from Voysey's

---

[1] Leonard Stokes became President of the R.I.B.A. in 1910 and Gold Medallist in 1919.
[2] *Pioneers of the Modern Movement*, p. 158.

houses Nos. 14 and 16 Hans Road, Chelsea—and the railings, is of itself unusual. The principal elevation, however, is notable for its bold modelling, and extensive plain surfaces; its dominant horizontality is accentuated by a deep rendered frieze, and widely projecting eaves recalling the Glasgow School of Art.[1]

The Mary Ward Settlement is a building of some importance, not only because it was erected before the Glasgow School of Art and thus might have influenced Mackintosh, but because it points the way to future development in this country. It is at once modern in spirit, yet well within the fold of Shavian romanticism—Shaw incidentally was the assessor of the competition for the building and this may account, perhaps, for the dignified 'Queen Anne' of the other elevations.

This experimental stage was carried a stage further by C. Harrison Townsend (1850–1928), who succeeded in shaking off the last remnants of revivalism. His most notable contribution, the Whitechapel Art Gallery (Plate 90D)—a curious little building—was erected in 1897–9. His first project[2] was an ambitious symmetrical scheme with a large central doorway surmounted by a heavy semi-circular hood—a feature he had employed in somewhat modified form in terra-cotta at Bishopsgate Institute (built 1882–4).[3] Above the doorway ran a series of five semi-circular windows and above these again, an enormous mosaic frieze 65 feet long and 17 feet high, to be designed and executed by Walter Crane. A pair of strange towers flanked the main central block, and gave the building a toy-like air of unreality. Probably for financial reasons this scheme was considerably modified, and the building as erected occupies a site little more than half that originally intended. Townsend was obliged to evolve an alternative and far less ambitious design which, however, is far more remarkable. He placed the main doorway off-centre in contravention of all the rules of propriety, but in order to ensure better circulation (the visitor now passes

[1] Unimaginative railings are depicted on Mackintosh's first project for the School of Art and it is not unlikely that he redesigned them after seeing Smith and Brewer's work at Tavistock Place.

[2] Published in *Academy Architecture*, 1896, also *The Studio*, 15th March 1897, p. 131.

[3] Townsend's distinctive arch motive may have been derived from American sources. A similar feature was employed by McKim, Mead and White in a New York residence *circa* 1888, and also by H. H. Richardson in his design for a lodge to a private residence in N.E. Mass.—both were illustrated in *The Builder*, 5th January 1889. In 1896 Mackintosh used a similar form—though to a much smaller scale—as a window in the east wing of the School of Art, and again as a window in the director's room.

249

through the galleries and descends to street level by a side stair and a secondary doorway), and his arrangement of window openings, his parsimonious use of mouldings, and his preference for large plain wall surfaces all point unmistakably to the twentieth century.

Yet another of Townsend's designs—a project for the porch of a country house 'Cliff Towers' (1897)—also displays a feeling for form which is distinctly modern and owes nothing to either Voysey or Shaw. But in all this work—as indeed in the Horniman Museum[2] with its curious clock tower and large mosaic panel by Anning Bell—one feels that Townsend the craftsman always takes precedence over Townsend the architect, and that he, lacking the breadth of vision and competence of a Shaw or a Mackintosh, failed to produce a work of major importance.

All the buildings reviewed here were completed before or just after the turn of the century: they are typical of much of the original work produced in England at the time. Most of the architects singled out for especial mention in this chapter, however, soon settled down to work of a more prosaic nature. The names of A. J. Slater and Sydney Greenslade, for example, are rarely met with again and, notwithstanding his achievements in the ecclesiastical field, Henry Wilson had no decisive message to convey. Messrs. Smith & Brewer built up a flourishing practice, but their work vacillated between a dignified version of Shaw—*Ditton Place*, Balcombe—and a romanticized transcription of Voysey—*Fives Court*, Pinner. The Mary Ward Settlement seems to have been an exception for soon they too were caught up in the rising wave of classicism, their *pièce de résistance* being the National Museum of Wales (1910), a monumental study in the Renaissance manner (the first premiated design of 132 submitted in open competition)—or perhaps Heal's store, Tottenham Court Road, London (1916).

Thus the initial enthusiasm aroused by Shaw and Voysey gradually waned, nor is the reason far to seek. Neither man had considered himself to be a revolutionary, and neither sought to establish a new style, much less to become the leader of a secessionist movement. For all his versatility and originality Shaw was at heart a classicist. His transition from neo-Elizabethan to Queen Anne had a most salutary effect on contemporary architectural design, but he moved

---

[1] Illustrated in *Academy Architecture*, 1897, vol. II, p. 79, and *The Studio*, vol. XIII, May 1898, pp. 239 et seq. Here the architect introduced deeply recessed windows with curved reveals, surely the first appearance of this popular twentieth-century feature.

[2] *Ibid.* Vol. XXVIII, December 1901, p. 202 et seq.

just as easily into fresh fields, and after his supreme essay, New Scotland Yard (1890), he soon reverted to a more conventional form of classicism as exemplified in the new Piccadilly Hotel and the Quadrant.

Voysey's mature style had been reached by 1900; thereafter he pursued his amiable path seemingly oblivious of the potentialities of new structural techniques and new materials. 'Architecture to me', he said in 1940, 'is a manner of growth. The traditional way of using materials has taken generations to develop. Rather than think of doing anything new, I have applied old traditions to new customs.'[1] Handicraft translated into terms of house-building by Webb, Lethaby, Shaw, Voysey and their followers established a new English domestic tradition, but in the domestic field, of course, it was possible to treat each project as a piece of craftwork, for no new planning or constructional problems were involved; the architect was concerned solely with the remodelling of the shell, the refinement and adjustment of small elements, and the decorative use of familiar materials. Once the subject was lifted out of this category, and new problems of planning arose, the artworker was at a loss. William Morris and Voysey seemed to have no message for the designer of a city hotel, a vast department store or a block of office buildings, which in any case they would not have considered necessary to the good life. On the other hand, as Norman Shaw demonstrated, the classical formula could be adapted to meet any requirement.

Shaw, then, one of the most influential personalities in the profession, drifted towards classicism and eventually joined the ranks of the academicians, and Voysey continued to design charming country houses. No one stepped into Shaw's place and no one successfully developed Voysey's thesis.

Without effective leadership, and lacking in common purpose, it is not surprising that this phase was so unfruitful. By the time Mackintosh had completed the Glasgow School of Art (1909) most practising architects had embraced the lifeless academic formalism characteristic of the closing years of the nineteenth century, and the first decade of the twentieth. Meanwhile in the domestic field, the romantic movement was sustained by such distinguished men as Sir Edwin Lutyens, E. Guy Dawber, Baillie Scott, and of course by Voysey himself.

Although this state of *laissez faire* was widespread, one or two individuals persisted on their course. Edgar Wood, for instance, continued to experiment in the north and Midlands; his Christian Science Church, Victoria Park, Manchester, is an unorthodox and attractive building in the Arts and Crafts succession and a measure of his independence. So too is *Upmeads* Stafford (1908),

[1] *The Architect's Journal*, 29th February 1940.

one of the first flat-roofed modern houses to be built in England. Leonard Stokes, too, was recognized as one of the most progressive architects of the day, and his fine sense of mass and proportion exemplified in the drawing of Convent, St. Albans (1899), (Plate 90c) finds expression in the framed structures of the National Telephone Exchange, Gerrard Street, Soho[1] and to a lesser degree in the Telephone Exchange, Parker Street, Manchester, both designed *circa* 1909. His indebtedness to Shaw is always apparent, however, and even these utilitarian buildings have their complement of classical trimmings.

Though the material evidence may be meagre when weighed against the mass of conventional and mediocre work produced at this time, it is sufficient to show that the spirit of secession was never extinguished in England. Isolated buildings such as these by Wood and Stokes, and, say, Sir John Burnet's Kodak Building, Kingsway, London (Plate 90E), one of the first buildings in which the steel frame was expressed in elevation, and the Manchester Headquarters of the Y.M.C.A., by Woodhouse, Corbett and Dean, were erected from time to time, buildings which cannot be placed in any of the convenient pigeon-holes of style, yet which presage a more rational approach to the problems of architectural design. Such work, and no doubt other examples yet to come to light, virtually constituted the English 'modern movement' of the early 1900's—the period immediately preceding the first World War. In this instance, however, 'movement' is perhaps a misnomer. The work illustrated here does not represent a movement in the generally accepted sense of the word—that is, a conscious and definite advance along well defined lines by artists motivated by a common ideal. On the continent, as we shall see, a similar spirit was afoot, but there the more progressive individuals came together in groups to discuss matters of common interest; societies were founded, journals published, exhibitions organized and manifestos issued. There the new art—the secessionist—movement was a tangible, living thing. In Britain, on the contrary, there is no indication whatever of close liaison between the Woods and the Townsends, the Stokes and the Voyseys. The English 'secessionists' did not form a group, nor had they any clearly defined aims or common objectives. Each building reviewed here is virtually an independent essay, and it is difficult, if not impossible, to discover any recognizable signs of development. It is hardly surprising therefore, that after the 1914–18 war, a new generation of architects, finding contemporary fashions in building incompatible with the demands of a rapidly changing society, should turn for inspiration to foreign sources, where indus-

[1] Illustrated in *Academy Architecture*, 1907.

trial art took exciting new forms, and the promise of an international style of architecture seemed to offer an easy solution to many, if not all, aesthetic problems. Consequently we are forced to the conclusion that there was no English modern movement in architecture as such, but a growing consciousness of the fundamental values represented by simple buildings of traditional character. Paradoxically enough, William Morris, Shaw, Voysey, and the English school are invariably acclaimed by the leaders of the continental new movement as their initial source of inspiration.[1]

What then is Mackintosh's position in relation to the developments in England?

In the architectural field as in the applied arts it is clear that he was neither the first nor the only advocate of secession in Britain. By the time the first section of the Glasgow School of Art was finished most of the buildings recorded here had been completed, and moreover had been illustrated either in *Academy Architecture* or in one of the professional journals. This is an important point. Mackintosh was able to keep abreast of events in England and to take full advantage of experiments elsewhere before he began to build. On the other hand his own architectural work remained comparatively unknown for many years. The *Glasgow Herald* Offices, Queen Margaret's Medical School, the Martyrs' School—none of which departed in any fundamental sense from contemporary Scottish practice—and Queen's Cross Church, had all appeared in *Academy Architecture* before the turn of the century (in 1894, 1895, 1896 and 1898 respectively), but, of course, above the signatures of Honeyman & Keppie. The mural decorations at Miss Cranston's Buchanan Street restaurant were published in 1898 in the same journal, when Mackintosh's name appeared for the first time. It was not until 1903, however, that the title Honeyman, Keppie and Mackintosh was appended to *architectural* projects—the Liverpool cathedral design and Pettigrew & Stephens' warehouse, Glasgow—and some years were to elapse before any important work in Mackintosh's mature style was illustrated in an English journal, namely Scotland Street School, and *Hill House*, both in 1906.

The building of the first section of the Glasgow School of Art seems to have passed unnoticed, and as far as can be ascertained, not a single illustration of the exterior had appeared in the press prior to 1909 and then only of the library

[1] 'Our whole new movement is built on the results which England has achieved from 1860 up to the mid 90's.' Muthesius in *Das Englische Haus*, p. 178.

wing.[1] Before 1903, then, Mackintosh was known to the profession mainly as a designer and decorator with a flair for the bizarre, who had once exhibited in London and subsequently obtained a good deal of publicity in *The Studio*. He had few contacts in England, and executed no work south of the border before the 1914–18 war. As far as his fellow architects were concerned he remained a remote and enigmatic figure despite the publicity afforded him by Muthesius and Koch.

Mackintosh's influence upon the course of events in the south was negligible, but of all the British pioneers he had the clearest and most direct message to convey, and he adhered to his course with commendable tenacity. Why then did the Glasgow style come to nothing, why did it not form the basis of a modern movement, and why did Mackintosh exercise so little influence in Britain when his work was greeted with such enthusiasm abroad?

It would appear that if a revolutionary movement in architecture and the minor arts is to be successfully launched, adequately sustained, and to achieve its purpose on a nation-wide scale, various conditions must be fulfilled. There must be a leader, an initiator, an advocate of new principles round whom a group of kindred spirits may gather. A club, a school, or a society may then be founded. The secessionists must have some vehicle by which their views can be propagated and by which they can convert others—they may produce a magazine, or journal, or, perhaps, find a voice in an established periodical through the agency of a sympathetic publisher—the leader himself is usually a man of some literary ability. Public interest must then be aroused by exhibitions, discussions, lectures and so forth, and finally the academies and schools of art must be won over. This broad pattern, as we shall see, was followed by architects in Austria and elsewhere—and, of course, the English Arts and Crafts movement, deriving from William Morris, achieved such notable successes in the 1890's and early 1900's because most of these conditions were met. Conversely, English architects failed to create a living, vital modern movement because only the first condition was fulfilled, and that not by a single leader, nor by a well integrated group, but by a number of individuals each working independently.

If, then, we apply the test to the Scottish artists it is possible to see why Mackintosh, undoubtedly one of the most gifted and versatile designers of the day, failed so singularly to establish himself, and to initiate a British movement.

In the first instance there was little liaison between George Walton, Oscar

[1] Pictures of the interior were reproduced in *The Studio*, vol. XIX, No. 83, Feb. 1900, pp. 53 et seq.

Paterson and other progressive artists not trained under Newbery on the one hand, and the School of Art faction on the other. All were seeking a new approach to problems of design, but none had the wisdom to see beyond the narrow limits of his own immediate circle. They had no common meeting ground, no club or society was founded independently of the School, and no attempt was made to formulate a common policy.

Then again, none of the Glasgow designers possessed either the cultural background, or the intellect of Shaw, or, with the exception of Mackintosh, the burning, prophetic zeal of the true revolutionary. Mackintosh, however, for all his creative genius, found difficulty in expressing himself lucidly by the pen. His lecture notes which survive are rambling, inconclusive and full of familiar clichés,[1] consequently his words carried little weight, and the professional journals were closed to him. Only one British magazine, *The Studio*, evinced any enthusiasm for the work of the Glasgow designer. This periodical, however, was liberal in outlook and catholic in taste; it was not the mouthpiece of a movement like the Austrian *Ver Sacrum*, nor so advanced in policy as the German *Dekorative Kunst*. Moreover Gleeson White, editor from its inception in 1893, and one of the few champions of the Glasgow style in Britain, died in 1898, just as Mackintosh came into prominence.

The innumerable continental exhibitions provided a magnificent platform for the display and propagation of the Glasgow style abroad, but as already pointed out, the work of *The Four* evoked such condemnation at the London Arts and Crafts Exhibition of 1896 that they were refused admission to subsequent exhibitions in the south. It is doubtful if Mackintosh's mature work appeared in England thereafter. His influence was thus circumscribed, and an important link with the public and the profession was denied him.

In the educational field the prospects were equally discouraging. At the turn of the century the Glasgow School of Architecture, then in its infancy, was housed in the School of Art under Newbery, with Alexander McGibbon as Director and Eugéne Bourdon, of the Atelier Pascal, Ecole des Beaux Arts, Paris, visiting Professor. The Board of Governors at this time included an imposing array of architects—William Forrest Salmon, David Barclay, William Leiper, Alexander Roche, John James Burnet and John Keppie, all men of the old school, and—with the probable exception of Salmon—solidly opposed to change in any shape or form. The possibility of establishing a progressive

---

[1] With one exception—an undated and unnamed paper read to a literary society. This is the most coherent of the few examples which survive and in all probability was written *circa* 1905–6.

teaching staff in the architectural section under these circumstances was remote indeed, though Newbery contrived to introduce a procession of distinguished instructors to join him in other departments.[1]

If, then, we accept the inevitability of Mackintosh's failure to inaugurate a new Scottish, not to mention a new British movement, it is hardly conceivable that he should have left no followers in his native city, and have had little influence on Glasgow contemporaries, yet that was virtually the case. His work aroused a certain amount of enthusiasm amongst the younger men, but enthusiasm without any real comprehension of the issues involved. Mackintosh was admired as a brilliant draughtsman, a prodigious worker, a prolific and talented designer. Nevertheless he was considered to be something of a crank, a man who indulged in dreamy fantasies remote from the real world of every-day practice. His Scottish contemporaries seem to have been completely oblivious to the deeper implications of his work, and he was never recognized as a prophet of international significance. Even James Salmon, who after Herbert MacNair's departure for Liverpool, became his intimate friend, seemed to be content merely to emulate his decorative forms. Salmon's Alexandra Park Free Church, Glasgow, designed 1898, and his Insurance Offices, 142 St. Vincent Street, Glasgow, 1899, have been mistaken frequently for works by Mackintosh; and his unpremiated competition design for the Royal Technical College, Glasgow (1901), displayed numerous borrowed details without in any way reflecting the bold functionalism of the School of Art.

Of all the sources from which a Mackintosh school might have been expected to spring, the most promising was undoubtedly the office of Honeyman and Keppie where draughtsmen and junior assistants were in close and regular contact with him. Yet even here his influence was transitory. John Honeyman retired in 1904, and Keppie and Mackintosh had discovered long before this that they had little in common: each decided to go his own way, and work in the office divided into two distinct and completely independent parts. In the late 1890's the principal assistants were George Paterson and Donald Stoddart, both of whom left Keppie soon after the turn of the century: Paterson joined John Stewart, of Glasgow, and Stoddart entered the office of A. N. Paterson, both well-known Glasgow architects. A. Graham Henderson, now (1950)

---

[1] Not least among these was Maurice Greiffenhagen, a Londoner, and a painter of out-standing merit who arrived in 1906. Two years later, C. F. A. Voysey himself was invited to take the chair of Design, but could not be persuaded however to resign his practice in the South.

256

President of the R.I.B.A. and principal of the firm, was mainly assistant to Keppie. Two younger draughtsmen, Robert Frame and William Moyes, were more directly under Mackintosh's supervision and became devoted to him. Frame emigrated to Canada (*circa* 1905) and it is believed died there some six or seven years later. William Moyes went to Australia in 1906.

In this manner, whatever influence Mackintosh was able to exert was quickly dissipated. Under such unstable conditions the formation of a nucleus of enthusiastic, progressive designers similar to, say, the Wagner School in Vienna, was out of the question. From 1906 onwards, Mackintosh himself began to lose faith and to realize that it was impossible, alone, to bring about any fundamental change in the attitude of mind of his contemporaries. He took less and less interest in the business, and long before the dissolution of the partnership, John Keppie was in complete control. Incredible as it may seem the practice remained quite unaffected by the fact that for a brief space of time, one of the most dynamic personalities in the profession had passed through its doors.

Mackintosh then, despite his many admirers in the south, had little influence on the course of events in England, and perhaps, even less on the architecture of his native country. Though he, too, gave up the struggle when the Glasgow School of Art was completed (1909), he had by that time made substantially more progress than anyone in Britain. None of his British contemporaries had produced a building comparable to the School for originality, architectural quality, and breadth of treatment. The architect's masterly handling of space, his ingenious and daring methods of fenestration displayed in the project drawings (1896), placed the building in a category by itself. Here, in fact, was a large structure, designed according to Voysey's principle, '. . . simplicity is the end and not the beginning'; in the arts and crafts succession, acknowledging tradition, and yet frankly expressing a new and adventurous spirit. In this work alone Mackintosh established his right to a place in the forefront of the modern movement at the moment when the cause began to languish in England.

THE EUROPEAN SECESSIONISTS

THE continental European has always entered upon revolution with more verve and enthusiasm than his British counterpart and whether in the political, social or intellectual field usually has carried the day with greater élan.

The artistic phenomenon known as *art nouveau* affords yet another illustration. This movement—unlike the English arts and crafts movement—was a clearly defined and conscious attempt on the part of certain designers to evolve a style entirely independent of tradition. Accepted principles of design were thrown to the winds and little cognizance taken of the natural qualities of materials—wood, for example was contorted into the most extravagant shapes and metal writhed and threshed in an unholy dance. Decorative motives were usually non-representational, flame-like or vermicular and at times positively repulsive. Cabinets, tables, chairs, doors and ornaments appear as though moulded in a soft viscous substance and structural members are no longer easily definable; the backs and legs of chairs, door stiles and rails, window bars and mullions, pillars and beams all flow sluggishly into one another. Sensuous, undulating lines dominate and in all such work we recognize the same air of melancholy,

258

the same indefinable 'maladie' that pervades the drawing of Beardsley and the designs of the Scottish group.

The researches of Giedion and Pevsner indicate that the epicentre of the new style was Brussels and it would seem that the cultural atmosphere of that city was particularly conducive to movements of this kind. Giedion points out[1] that the ground had been well prepared by painters, sculptors and musicians of an original turn of mind who, for a decade or more, had enjoyed a hearing in the Belgian capital. Renoir, Whistler, Cézanne, Van Gogh, Rodin and Debussy, for instance, had all appeared in Brussels before 1890 and as early as 1881 a weekly periodical *L'Art Moderne* had been launched and a society of progressive young artists formed—'Les XX'.

It was not until 1893, however, that *art nouveau* assumed tangible form in architecture and decoration. Its two principal exponents were Victor Horta (b. 1861) and Henry Van de Velde (b. 1863). Although by general consent Horta seems to have initiated the style in his now famous house for M. Tassel, No. 12 Rue de Turin, Brussels, Van de Velde was undoubtedly its most influential exponent, and his writings and lectures made no little impression on contemporary thought.[2]

No. 12 Rue de Turin, a narrow-fronted, four-storeyed house in a terrace, was completed in 1893. It was faced with stone but cast-iron was used freely throughout the structure—an innovation for domestic work which enabled the architect to produce a surprisingly open ground-floor plan. In the main façade the conventional forms of column, capital and base, moulded string courses and consoles are clearly discernible but none of the details is imitative. The bases of the columnar window mullions, for instance, seem to have melted and flow down over the sills; the capitals are folded upwards and grip iron lintels in which rivet-heads are accentuated, and two heavy brackets supporting a curved bay extend sluggishly down the wall in the true *art nouveau* manner. Internally, too, the house is free from historical motives; the structional members, cast-iron pillars and beams, are frankly displayed and woven into the general decorative scheme.

In the entrance hall[3] the curving iron scrolls of the column and girders are

[1] In *Space, Time and Architecture*, S. Giedion, pp. 217 et seq.
[2] The distinguished Catalan, Antonio Gaudí (Plate 91D), and some of his contemporaries, although very active in Spain, seem to have had little discernible influence upon events in Europe at this time.
[3] Illustrated in *An Introduction to Modern Architecture*, J. M. Richards, Pelican, 1940.

echoed in the mural decorations and mosaic floor, the whole forming a strange composition of structural and surface pattern. Unlike Mackintosh's linear designs, however, Horta's writing scrolls tell no story. They have no symbolic meaning; they exist merely as abstract pattern—cold, impersonal and expressionless. In this respect he differs fundamentally from the entire British school, a point which, one feels, corroborates Giedion's theory that the style as exemplified by Horta originated in iron construction, and that the whip-like vermiculations are no more than the unrolled iron volutes of a typical Belgian railway-station roof.

Van de Velde's plastic forms on the other hand were obviously derived from natural sources, though like Mackintosh he too seems to have sought inspiration in less familiar places. Formerly a painter, he turned to applied art in the early 1890's and is reputed to have followed the example of William Morris when faced with the problem of finding himself a house and furniture. He rebelled violently against contemporary standards of taste and declared that his family should not live in what he described as 'immoral surroundings', so he set to work to design a house and all its equipment.[1] This, his first architectural work, was completed in 1896 in the Avenue van der Raye, Uccle, a suburb of Brussels, and although built of traditional materials was remarkably free from stylistic caprice. In fact he produced a building of Voysey-like simplicity with shuttered windows, mansard-roofed gables and smooth plastered walls. The interiors and furniture were as plain and reticent as the house itself and show little evidence of the more exuberant forms he adopted later (Plate 91B and C).

A curious sidelight is thrown on the Belgian's attitude to design by W. C. Behrendt[2] who says that Van de Velde, once accused of torturing his materials, replied that he had been convinced for a long time of the inadequacy of wood for his designs, and that he anticipated the discovery of a more suitable material which could be cast. Unfortunately it is not said when this statement was made and two interpretations are possible. If made before 1900 it is of some significance and helps to account for the strange plastic shapes in which the designer often indulged—though it remains an extraordinary pronouncement from the man who, in 1903, pleaded for 'uncompromising logic in the use of materials'. If, on the other hand, it occurred after the turn of the century, it would appear that Van de Velde was attempting to excuse a fundamental weakness in his work

[1] Illustrated in *Van de Velde*, Karl Ernst Osthaus. Unlike No. 12 Rue de Turin, at the time of writing (1952) Van de Velde's house has been greatly altered, and none of the original interiors survives.　　　[2] *Modern Building*, W. C. Behrendt, pp. 78–9.

—a weakness common to the exponents of *art nouveau*—the search for new forms for their own sake, irrespective of tradition, logic and the nature of the materials in which they were executed.

Nevertheless Van de Velde was highly esteemed by many of his contemporaries. In 1896 the German art critic, A. J. Meier-Graefe, speaks of him as:

'One whose delicate and genuinely artistic spirit does not blind him—good workman that he is—to the necessity of giving due prominence to the practical utilitarian side of his work. To my mind,' he continues, 'Van de Velde possesses a combination of qualities of so rare a kind as to place him first among the artists of Europe today. He stands alone among the decorative workers in his genuine craftsmanship, in his absolute, certain knowledge of the necessities of his art. . . .'[1]

Meier-Graefe and S. Bing, the Parisian art dealer, were responsible for introducing Van de Velde to the French public. Both had visited the Uccle house and had been captivated by the versatility and imagination shown by the Belgian designer[2], and when Bing opened his shop in the Rue de Provence in the French capital (1896), Van de Velde was commissioned to decorate and furnish several apartments. This work attracted considerable attention and he quickly secured an influential following. In the Spring of 1897, the year in which Gleeson White introduced the Glasgow Style to Europe through the medium of *The Studio* (July) an exhibition of decorative art in the new manner was staged by five French craftsmen—Charles Plumet and Paul Dampt (furniture), Felix Aubert (fabrics), Henry Nocq (jewellery), and Alexandre Charpentier (craftwork and ceramics)—at the Gallerie des Artistes Modernes. This work too fired the imagination of the public and Paris in turn was captivated by the peculiar charms of *art nouveau*. Thereafter many designers of widely varying talents eagerly embraced the new style—Serrurier-Bovy, Bellery Desfontaines, Emile Gallé, Louis Majorelle and many others started to produce a quantity of work which for exuberance and bizarrerie has rarely been equalled.[3] In 1897 also Van de Velde exhibited in Dresden and gave added impetus to the work

---

[1] *The Studio*, vol. IX, p. 40, October 1896.

[2] In contrast, an amusing story is recorded in a book on Toulouse-Lautrec by Gotthard Jedlicka. The distinguished French painter is reputed to have remarked to his friend Joynant on the way home after calling on Van de Velde, 'Well, the only successes are the bathroom, the nursery painted with white enamel and the W.C.'

[3] Many illustrations may be found in contemporary European publications such as *Art et Décoration*, and *Der Moderne Stil* (1899). See new bibliography on p. 311.

of a group of young German artists who had begun experimenting with new decorative forms some years earlier—notably August Endell (1871–1925), architect, Otto Eckmann (1865–1902), formerly a painter, and Hermann Obrist (1863–1927). Soon a German version of the style was securely established—the *Jugendstil*—often wilder and more extravagant than its Belgian and French counterparts. The strange furniture of Bernard Pankok appeared and Richard Riemerschmid, Wilhelm Bertsch, H. E. von Berlepsch and others formulated their own interpretations in Munich, Leipzig and elsewhere.

By the turn of the century *art nouveau* was firmly entrenched in Europe. It had radiated fanwise from Brussels and the perimeter of its advance can be traced in a great arc extending from Berlin in the north-east to Paris in the south. It penetrated to Warsaw, and to Breslau on the Oder, to Dresden and Prague on the upper Elbe, to Darmstadt and Munich on the Central European plateau and eastwards to Vienna and Budapest in the Danube basin. Few countries escaped entirely from its influence. The Channel and the North Sea (and the leaders of the English Arts and Crafts movement), however, seemed to have proved an insuperable obstacle in the west, and contemporary British journals carry little evidence of the exciting events taking place abroad. Continental innovations were received in Britain with much the same hostility as greeted *The Four* when they exhibited in London in 1896. For instance George Donaldson, vice-president of the Paris Universal Exhibition of 1900, made a gift of a collection of *art nouveau* furniture to the Victoria and Albert Museum—chairs by Bing, and cabinets by Louis Majorelle, A. Darras and Emile Gallé. He observed that during the preceding decade—and these are his words—'a remarkable and distinct art development had taken place all over Europe, causing a mercantile change of quite exceptional proportions, but one of which England was practically unconscious'.

This kindly intentioned revelation evoked a tirade of abuse from certain members of the Arts and Crafts Society, who were by no means ignorant of the 'mercantile change'. Lewis F. Day (1845–1910), described by Nikolaus Pevsner as the most distinguished industrial artist of his generation, opened an outspoken attack on *art nouveau* with a letter to the *British Architect* in which he said amongst other things: 'It is the delirious art of men raving to do something new, oblivious in their rage alike of use and beauty.' And of the furniture in question: 'Whatever the munificence of the donor, it ought never to have been accepted and ought not to be sent on circulation.'[1]

[1] *The British Architect*, 28th June 1901.

John Belcher, R.A., Reginald Blomfield, Mervyn Macartney, Edward Prior then rallied to the cause and voiced their protest in *The Times* and by so doing gave the furniture a great deal of publicity. The exhibition was sent on a limited tour of Britain with a warning from the Board of Education, South Kensington, that students viewing the objects must be guided by instructors in forming an opinion.

The same point of view was expressed in the following year (1902) when Messrs. Waring & Gillow sponsored a book *Our Homes and How to Beautify Them*, in which the new style was bitterly assailed by an anonymous writer—possibly Day. In a chapter 'L'Art Nouveau on the Continent' a coloured reproduction of the dining-room of Mackintosh's *Haus eines Kunstfreundes* appeared, and the writer says:

'The aesthetic movement in its maddest moments was never half so mad as this . . . the Scotto-Continental "New Art" threatens with its delirious fantasies to make the movement for novelty a target for the shafts of scoffers and a motive for the laughter of the saner seven-eighths of mankind.'

And again:

'The authors of these dreadful designs, lacking artistic inventiveness, have been driven to seek originality in fantastic forms remote from any connection with Art.'

Thus conservative England was determined to have nothing whatever to do with the new movement, Continental or Scottish, and so successful was this campaign with its direct threat of excommunication by the men of good taste that no one ventured far from the safe haven of tradition, and never at any time was there a sign of an incipient *art nouveau* movement in this country.

It was popularly believed of course that the Glasgow Style sprang from Continental sources—or conversely that Mackintosh was the originator of the art revival abroad—no one was quite sure which theory was correct, nor did it seem to matter for *art nouveau* became a convenient epithet applicable with equal derision to either or both. And this uncertainty has persisted because little information has been forthcoming hitherto about Mackintosh's early work, and its relationship to the Continental movement of the 1890's. What then is his position in regard to *art nouveau* in Western Europe?

It is fairly certain that Horta's innovations[1] at No. 12 Rue de Turin were

---

[1] Horta is described as 'the most inspired of modern architects' in an article by Ludwig Hevesi in *Wiener Tageblatt*, 11th November 1898, but he does not seem to have been mentioned in contemporary English journals.

unknown in Britain until the late 1890's and Van de Velde is mentioned for the first time in *The Studio* in October 1896, but then only as a bookbinder. The Belgian designer did not attain to notoriety until he was 'discovered' by Bing after the completion of the Uccle house (also 1896); and illustrations of furniture by the new French school were not published in *The Studio* until 1897—by which time the style of the Glasgow Group was matured and they had exhibited in London. It is possible of course that Mackintosh visited Belgium and discovered Horta and Van de Velde for himself—if for example he went to Liège before or during the exhibition of Glasgow students' work in 1895—but this is most unlikely. Fra Newbery, the obvious source of information, could throw no light on the matter when questioned by the author, but he was convinced that Mackintosh's first continental visit, other than the Scholarship Tour of 1890, did not take place until the autumn of 1900, the time of the Exhibition at Vienna. Then again, although the Munich Secession was founded in 1891, it was concerned essentially with the fine arts, and the first *Studio* article[1] (1894) reporting the existence of a German separatist movement was devoted exclusively to painting. This could have had little effect on Mackintosh—except that it encouraged him in his struggle for independence.

If unbiased contemporary evidence is required, however, it can be found in the well-written anonymous dissertation on 'Scottish Artists' published by Koch in *Dekorative Kunst* (November 1898)—the first article on Mackintosh so far discovered by the author in a continental journal.[2] After drawing attention to the remarkable similarity between wine glasses designed by Herbert MacNair and those of Koepping, between the fabrics of Mackintosh and those of Obrist, between the 'windows' (leaded glass?) of MacNair and Van de Velde, the writer emphasizes the fact that contact between the artists was out of the question. ' . . . we are in a position to state', he says, 'that this (plagiarism) cannot be the case because we saw the Scottish work at a time when none of the other works had been published.' And then he goes on to make this observation:

'Evidently there are certain things in the air which affect our movement in spite of all nationalism and which are all the more easily explained in the knowledge that these things are concerned with purely objective logic and technical questions.'

This interesting assessment of the situation from the continental point of

[1] 'The Secessionists of Germany', by G.W., *The Studio*, vol. IV, p. 24.
[2] *L'Art Décoratif*, vol. I, 1898.

view is endorsed by Herbert MacNair himself who assured the author that *The Four* were unaffected by outside influences, for, he says: ' . . . the work of our little group was certainly not in the very least inspired by any continental movements—Indeed we knew little about these until we were well away on our own endeavours.'

There can be little doubt that the Scottish and continental movements started independently at about the same time and ran on parallel courses. Both were directly inspired by William Morris and the English School, and just as the paintings of the *Boys from Glasgow* helped to release the latent energies of the Secessionists, so strong impetus was given to the development of the Glasgow style by the work of Beardsley, Toorop, Munch, Schwabe and others.

By the time news of Van de Velde's furniture and that of the French *art nouveau* school began to filter through to Britain, however, Mackintosh's style was well developed and he was affected little by such work. It is only necessary to compare the rigid angular chairs of the Mains Street flat with the complex curvilinear forms favoured in Belgium, France and Germany at the turn of the century to realize how little either owed to the other—though all seem affected unmistakably by *maladie de la fin de siècle*.

Art nouveau was not the only movement afoot in Europe, nor was Van de Velde the sole propagator of a new gospel at the turn of the century. Many continental designers assiduously followed the activities of William Morris and Company and the Arts and Crafts societies. English domestic architecture and furniture, and the pioneer work of men like Gimson and Voysey, though by no means as stridently original as that of the Belgian and French schools, was greatly admired for its good taste and reticence. Indeed, George Walton, Baillie Scott, C. R. Ashbee and Voysey frequently exhibited abroad and executed many commissions for furniture in Europe during the late 1890's. Baillie Scott seems to have been a special favourite in Germany and Austria, where English influence was strong. It is, in fact, to Austria that we must turn in order to find the second important centre of the new movement.

The foundation of the Viennese Secession in 1897 was followed by the resignation of the Archduke Rainer as Protector of the Austrian Museum, and in 1899 of Hofrat von Storch as Director of the Kunstgewerbe-Schule (Arts and Crafts School), a position he had held for thirty years. Von Storch was succeeded by Baron Felician von Myrbach, a man who, though intended for an army career, distinguished himself as an artist, and after spending some sixteen years as an illustrator in Paris, returned to Vienna and joined the Seces-

265

sionists. Von Myrbach excelled as an organizer and teacher, and was successful in gathering together a devoted band of young and enthusiastic instructors including several of his friends and associates in the Secession—Josef Hoffmann (architecture), Koloman Moser and Alfred Roller (decorative and applied art), Arthur Strasser (sculpture).

The salutary effect of this transformation can be well imagined. Within a few years von Myrbach had succeeded in revitalizing every branch of the arts in the capital. Furthermore, his progressive policy had repercussions throughout Central Europe, for teachers trained at the Kunstgewerbe-Schule were much sought after, and carried the message of the revival far beyond the confines of Austria.

The Vienna Secessionists, however, made their debut in the applied arts at an important exhibition—the Jubilee Arts and Crafts Exhibition—held in the building of the Gartenbaugesellschaft in the Spring of 1898. For the first time work in the 'modern' manner was shown to the general public and its success was instantaneous. Here, according to a contemporary critic,[1] the old style lost the battle against the new. The interiors and furniture of two members of the Secession, J. M. Olbrich and Josef Hoffmann, attracted particular attention— Olbrich by his elaborate forms and free use of colour in the Hans Makart tradition, Hoffmann by his obvious concern with practical problems, and by the elegant simplicity of his work in the English manner.

Hoffmann designed the Secessionist Room and the Secretariat,[2] both of which were conspicuous for their relative plainness—a plainness amounting almost to austerity. The walls were undecorated, and though it is impossible now to determine the colours employed the rooms appear to have been sombre and somewhat gloomy. The chairs and tables were soundly built and severely practical, they display none of the flamboyance of French and Belgian work, nor do the rectangular cabinets and other incidental pieces. All in fact seem to fall midway between the style of Baillie Scott and that of Mackintosh— between the Englishman's work for Ernst Ludwig, Grand Duke of Hesse at Darmstadt, and the Mackintosh interior at Munich. The Darmstadt furniture did not appear in *The Studio* until July 1898, however, though it may well have been known to Hoffmann before this, and the Munich interior was not published until November of the same year.

[1] Ludwig Hevesi.
[2] Illustrated in *Deutsche Kunst und Dekoration*, vol. III, 1898, p. 197, and *Ver Sacrum*, May–June 1898, p. 7. Also at this exhibition were paintings by E. A. Walton, brother of George Walton, J. S. Sargent and Frank Brangwyn.

Naturally Hoffmann's work did not appeal to everyone and it is evident that by no means all the Viennese were eager to exchange the luxurious opulence of Makart (1840–84) the leader of fashion of the previous generation, for such studied austerity. One observer complained that the unconscious 'too much' of the past was being opposed merely by the conscious 'too little' of the present.

Olbrich on the other hand, represented a second stream within the Secessionist movement, a stream flowing more directly from *l'art nouveau*, and his arrangement of the central hall of the exhibition followed contemporary fashion more closely. Arrangement, in fact, seems a misnomer, for the exhibits—pictures, textiles and bric-a-brac of all descriptions—were assembled in groups and interspersed with palms, ferns and creeping plants. The backgrounds were colourful and richly decorated, the very antithesis of Hoffmann's careful dispositions and plain wall surfaces.

The significance of the work of the two friends was not overlooked by the critics. It was obvious that here lay the promise of a new style of furniture which, in both its manifestations, seemingly owed little to outside influences—the austerity of Hoffmann and the traditional gaiety of Olbrich, it was hoped, would serve to counteract the ferment of alien *art nouveau*.

At the Munich Secessionist Exhibition in the following year (1899)[1] this point was driven home, for work by the Viennese designers appeared very sober and refined alongside the writhing voluptuous forms affected on this occasion by Van de Velde and Pankok. Hoffmann in particular exhibited some excellent furniture, notably a well-proportioned and exquisitely made display cabinet for silver. The base consisted of a tall, narrow chest of drawers, above which was an open shelf surmounted by a cupboard glazed with square panes—two small areas of low relief carving and white metal drawer-pulls provided the only accents, otherwise the cabinet was devoid of ornament of any kind. In this piece he achieved the simplicity of Voysey and the originality of Mackintosh without emulating the stylistic mannerisms which so often date the work of both British designers. The incidence of the square as the principal decorative motive in Hoffmann's work symbolizes his rejection of *art nouveau*: its emphatic unity and uncompromising form—the antithesis of the sensuous curve—admirably suited his purpose, and soon it became one of the distinguishing features of the Viennese School.

By the turn of the century, the Viennese Secessionists and in particular Hoffmann and Olbrich had made considerable progress. And, in fact, the new

[1] Illustrated in *Deutsche Kunst und Dekoration*, vol. IV, 1899, pp. 484 et seq.

movement was firmly established in Vienna when in the autumn of 1900 the important exhibition was held to which *The Four* were invited. Generally the interiors exhibited on this occasion by the Viennese designers were elaborate and over-decorated—except for Hoffmann's room. Exhibits were frequently overcrowded or placed in isolated groups, and there was no single dominant theme either in colour or in arrangement. Hoffmann's exhibits (Plates 58c and 59b), however, were especially interesting and the striking similarity between his work and that of Mackintosh is at once apparent—his table and jewel box might well have come from the Scotsman's studio, and the tall, severely functional display cabinet may have been a Mackintosh design stripped of its beaten metal and leaded glass. Other pieces not illustrated here (*Dekorative Kunst*, vol. 4) are just as remarkable for their originality and astonishing independence —their simple ornament would have satisfied Loos, their form and proportion would have delighted Voysey, and their exquisite craftsmanship gratified the most exacting critic of the English School. In all this work plain unmoulded surfaces dominate, all metal details—lock plates, handles and the like—are of the simplest kind, and seldom does a single sensuous curve obtrude. Moreover, the exhibits were set against a background of white walls and delicately patterned, charming wallpaper.

For long it has been assumed that Hoffmann modelled his work on that of Mackintosh, but all the evidence examined by the author would indicate that this was not so. No single published illustration has been forthcoming of a complete interior in Mackintosh's mature style, nor even of one of his white rooms, before the turn of the century. The Mains Street flat was decorated and furnished in the Spring of 1900, and though it approximates most closely to Hoffmann's work at the exhibition, it was not illustrated until 1901. In any case the furniture of the two men bears individual characteristics that make nonsense of the suggestion of plagiarism at this stage, despite a strong superficial resemblance. If there had been collusion it must have taken place some years earlier before such strong personal traits developed; this raises again the problem of the interior designed by Mackintosh for an unnamed client in Munich two years earlier (Plate 58a). Did he personally supervise this work? Was it in fact an exhibition interior and not for a private patron at all? If so did he visit Munich and meet Hoffmann there? If this meeting occurred, who influenced whom?—for Mackintosh had no outstanding interiors to his credit in 1898 although work was progressing on the School of Art, but Hoffmann was one of the leading lights in the Secession and in the following year became a teacher at the Vienna Academy. These questions are impossible to answer without further information and in correspondence with the author Josef Hoffmann does not mention a meeting prior to the Eighth Secessionist Exhibition. The evidence would indicate, however, that each designer worked independently, and having a common admiration for English work—especially that of Voysey and Baillie Scott—and being motivated by similar ideals, arrived at similar conclusions. 'Professor Hoffmann's great aim', said A. S. Levetus in 1905, 'is to follow in the steps of Ruskin and William Morris, and to create a home of art in Vienna.'[1]

Illustrations of Hoffmann's work at the Vienna Exhibition demonstrate that if anything, he had made greater strides than his Scottish friend. His furniture betrays fewer idiosyncracies, and is seldom eccentric. His dining-room chairs, for example (Plate 59B), are more practical than any designed by Mackintosh and, except for the low stretcher, would be accepted without question even today. Many of his other exhibits, too, would not readily be dated earlier than the 1914–18 War, a test few of Mackintosh's designs would survive.

What then did Mackintosh contribute to the Art Revival in Central Europe?

The complete answer to this question is not to be found in the material superficialities of style, it lies rather in the psychological field—and is none the less important on that account.

In 1899 J. M. Olbrich was summoned to Darmstadt to undertake work for Ernst Ludwig, Grand Duke of Hesse, the patron of Baillie Scott and C. R. Ashbee, and in the same year Josef Hoffmann was appointed Professor at the Viennese Academy by von Myrbach. Thus at the time of the exhibition the Secession lost one of its most influential members just as the new ideas were beginning to invade the very stronghold of conservatism—the teaching academies. Von Myrbach and his staff—not unnaturally—encountered much opposition from the old school who continued to advocate a return to the safe harbour of tradition. In these circumstances the work of the Scottish Group, and especially of Mackintosh whose leadership never seems to have been in doubt for a moment, assumed new significance. It demonstrated that a virile movement, with aims and objectives closely allied to those of the Secession, was afoot in Britain, the home of propriety and good taste, and, moreover, that the centre of the movement lay in the west of Scotland, in Glasgow, a city which, as we have seen already, ranked high in the estimation of European artistic circles.

[1] *Modern Decorative Art in Austria, The Studio*, Special Number, 1906.

Mackintosh thus spoke with a voice of authority—the voice of the foreign prophet—and the whole weight of the Scottish contribution was thrown into the balance on the side of the Secessionists. His white walls and simple furniture, his delicately coloured and ingeniously contrived points of interest and the studied austerity of his arrangements gave added force to Hoffmann's thesis. His conception of the room as a work of art in which every detail must form an integral part of, and be subordinated to the whole—an aspect of interior design which had escaped the Austrians—was seized upon with enthusiasm. Almost overnight it seemed that the entire Viennese movement, with Hoffmann at its head, blazed into new life, and the next three or four years saw the outpouring of a quantity of decorative work and furnishing of a very high order, all in its whiteness and plainness bearing a striking superficial resemblance to that of Mackintosh, but revealing a wealth of original detail and a conception of design which often far transcended that of the Scottish architect himself. Interiors designed prior to 1905 by Hoffmann and his pupils—Leopold Bauer, Hans Offner, Otto Prutscher, Josef Urban and others[1]—admirably demonstrate this point and make interesting comparison with work executed in Austria before the turn of the century. And yet there was no suggestion of plagiarism. The linear patterns, the sensuous curves and the mysterious symbolism of the Scottish artists was discarded as surely and as firmly as the wilder affectations of continental *art nouveau*, and a distinctly independent Viennese style emerged.

Mackintosh and his friends thus provided an incentive, a powerful directive force, at the moment when it was most needed. The importance of their contribution cannot be over-emphasized, for thereafter Vienna in turn rapidly achieved universal recognition as one of the most progressive centres of the new movement in Europe.

THE PERIODICALS

One of the most noticeable phenomena accompanying the art revival, and in fact an indispensable adjunct to it, was the appearance or re-orientation of numerous illustrated periodicals of *The Studio* type. During the late 1890's the format of existing magazines was greatly improved, and they became excellent vehicles for the propagation of the new gospel. The indefatigable architect-

[1] Illustrated in *The Art Revival in Austria*, 1906.

270

publisher, Alexander Koch, was the most versatile propagandist of the movement. In 1888 he launched *Academy Architecture* in London with the commendable objective of bringing together 'a selection of the most prominent Architectural Drawings hung at the Royal Academy Exhibitions and interesting contemporary Architectural subjects designed in Great Britain and abroad',[1] but his continental journals were much more elegantly produced. His *Innendekoration* was first issued in 1890 and *Deutsche Kunst und Dekoration* was published at Darmstadt in 1897. Other notable journals were *Dekorative Kunst* and *Die Kunst* published at Munich in 1897 and 1899 respectively and edited by H. Bruckmann.[2] *Ver Sacrum*, mouthpiece of the Viennese Secessionists, appeared first in January 1898 and from the beginning displayed the most advanced work of the Austrian school. Joseph Hoffmann, Koloman Moser and Gustav Klimt dominated the early numbers, all of which are pervaded by the now familiar air of mournful sadness varying in intensity from the dramatic woodcuts of Moser and the sombre-eyed women of Klimt, to horribly repulsive animals and insects drawn by the painter Rudolf Bacher. Hoffmann contributed many fascinating patterns in black and white and in colour—'Buchschmuck'—often based on flower and plant forms, and closely allied to Mackintosh's linear experiments. They too formed a valuable source on which the architect subsequently drew for much of his decorative work.

These journals constituted a formidable spearhead for the advance of the new movement and with the French magazines *Art et Décoration* and *L'Art Décoratif* exerted an incalculable influence upon the trend of events abroad. They dealt not only with painting and sculpture, exhibitions, the applied arts, and interior design generally, but, like *The Studio*, frequently carried informed articles on modern building by the most progressive architects of the day, thereby admirably supplementing the more prosaic professional journals.

Despite the propaganda value of the periodicals, those seeking to break new ground in Central Europe found the transition from applied art to architecture no less difficult than did Mackintosh and his English contemporaries and again it is to Vienna that we must turn in order to discover the first signs of the new architecture. Here on 13th July 1841, was born Otto Wagner (1841–1918), one

[1] Introduction to the first volume of *Academy Architecture*.

[2] Professor Pevsner also mentions an important periodical *Pan*, first issued in 1895, which contained articles and illustrations by leading figures in the German movement. This, however, is not known to the author. (See *Pioneers of the Modern Movement*, p. 115).

271

of the most important figures in architectural history about whom far too little is known in Britain.[1]

OTTO WAGNER, 1841–1918

Wagner was educated at the Gymnasium, Kremsmünster, and the Vienna Polytechnic. He received his architectural training at the Königliche Bauschule, Berlin, and then under August Siccardsburg[2] at the Academy of Fine Arts, Vienna. The Academy, and for that matter the entire architectural field, was dominated by a well established and influential group of architects of the old school, the Gothicist Schmidt,[3] the Greek Revivalist Hansen,[4] and Ferstl, who built the Museum of Applied Art and the Technical Art School (1868–71), and the University (1885) in the renaissance manner. All of these men, with Hasenauer,[5] were responsible for the Ringstrasse and great developments in the city. Brought up and trained in this environment it is not surprising that for a time Wagner himself was immersed in classicism. He soon realized, how-ever, that the monumental formalism of his contemporaries was leading nowhere, and he could not reconcile their elaborate essays in brick and stucco with the rapid progress made in the fields of science and engineering. If architec-ture were again to become a living force, he argued, old building methods and outmoded stylistic formulae must be discarded; the practical requirements of a building must come first and new materials and modern structural techniques be exploited.

Wagner had little opportunity of developing his thesis until he was appointed successor to Frederick Schmidt as Director of the Akademie der Bildenden Kunst, Vienna, in 1894. His inaugural lecture, published in 1895 under the title

[1] No comprehensive work on Wagner has yet appeared in English, but an illustrated article on him by H. M. Priebsch was published in the *Architect's Journal*, 26th October, 1927, and a short appreciation by Hugo Haberfeld appears in *The Art Revival in Austria*, 1906.

[2] Siccardsburg, with Van der Null, designed the Vienna Opera House—built 1861–8.

[3] The Austrian architect Schmidt was responsible for the Rathaus, a German Gothic structure with Italian detail—built 1872–84.

[4] Hansen built the Imperial Academy of Fine Arts in 1874–6, and the House of Parliament —described as 'the most satisfactory example in Europe of modern work in Greek style'. *Transactions of the R.I.B.A.*, vol. IV, 1888, pp. 27 et seq.

[5] Von Hasenauer, with the architect Gottfried Semper, built the elaborate Imperial Museum for Art and Natural History (1872–84) and the Court Theatre, Vienna.

'Modern Architecture', came as a most unwelcome revelation to his colleagues. He expressed the opinion that architecture should reflect and serve the needs of modern civilization and that if the practical requirements of a problem were met and appropriate materials selected the style of the building should follow naturally; it should not be something predetermined or applied. This revolutionary philosophy cut right across the teaching of a century and made nonsense of the revivalist architecture of the Ringstrasse. It was greeted with derision by his colleagues, and hailed with delight by the younger generation as a portent of revival in a profession which appeared to them to be universally degenerate.

Wagner's outspoken opinions brought him into frequent conflict with the authorities, and comparatively few of his major schemes materialized. He was in practice in Vienna when work on the Ringstrasse commenced and during the late 1890's was busily engaged on ambitious projects of all descriptions. His well-known designs for the Metropolitan Railway were interspersed with work for commercial, public and private undertakings: for example, the Oster-reichische Länderbank; a boldly conceived scheme for an Academy of Fine Arts on the outskirts of the city (1898)—a model of which was shown at the second Secessionist Exhibition; a scheme for the Museum der Gypsab-güsse Vienna (1896); a block of flats in the Friedrichstrasse (1899), and the Kirche Steinhof (1903–7).

His firm grasp of the principles of architectural design, his mastery of the art of planning and knowledge of engineering imbued Wagner's buildings with dignity and monumentality, yet they remained within the classical tradition. All too frequently their fine proportions were marred by a veneer of ornament in what he chose to call 'Free Renaissance'—a style combining familiar classical motives with new ones of a distinctly personal nature allied to *art nouveau*. This contradiction is demonstrated clearly in the Postsparkasse Vienna (1905) considered by many to be his most successful and most original design (Plate 95). This building was constructed of brick, but the ground and first floors were faced externally with rusticated granite slabs 10 cm. thick, and the upper storeys with marble 2 cm. thick. The slabs were fixed to the wall by stone cramps 12 cm. long and 4 cm. wide which appeared on the surface as small circular studs—reminiscent of rivet heads. The attic storey was faced with panels of black tiles secured by aluminium studs—a remarkably prophetic gesture this —and embellished with the architect's favourite wreath motive. This frank expression of the use of veneer is admirable, and so, indeed, is the fine glass-roofed hall. But the wreaths and garlands are still there and the whole character

T

of the building shows that even at this time the architect could not free himself entirely from the influence of his former associates. And so, despite his theories, Wagner never completed fully the transition from the nineteenth to the twentieth centuries.

As a teacher, however, he was superb and his influence was incalculable. J. A. Lux, writing in *The Studio* (November 1903), tells us that, unlike his Viennese contemporaries, Otto Wagner selected his pupils with care and gradually eliminated the weaker men until he was left with a brilliant nucleus of ten or even less, with whom he took infinite pains. It is hardly surprising therefore to find that the two architect founder-members of the Secession, J. M. Olbrich and Josef Hoffmann, were trained by him and soon assumed leadership in the new movement.

Notwithstanding Wagner's crusade young architects of an original turn of mind had few opportunities of building in Vienna and it was not until 1898 that Olbrich entered the lists. His initial essay in the new style was the exhibition building for the Secessionists—the Secession House—a project that must have given him as much pleasure as Mackintosh enjoyed at the prospect of designing the new Glasgow School of Art.

J. M. OLBRICH, 1867–1908

Olbrich has been described by Hugo Haberfeld as 'a man highly gifted, impulsive and imaginative, a poetic interpreter of space and a decorator of rare taste', yet we have already remarked his predilection for ornamentation and the restlessness of his interior decoration. These traits are also displayed in his Wagneresque preliminary sketches for the Secession House and it is interesting to follow the design through its various stages, to see how the ultimate form gradually emerged, plain, stolid and defiant, from its fanciful neo-baroque beginnings.[1] As originally conceived, it was an ugly building with great free-standing columns each carrying a draped urn. Later, rectangular fluted pylons were substituted for the columns and the whole was enmeshed in a pattern of grotesque masks, busts and swags. Finally, after passing through several such phases, a relatively modest building emerged which expressed the aims of

[1] Well illustrated in *Deutsche Kunst und Dekoration*, vol. III, October–March 1898, pp. 199 et seq. Also *Ver Sacrum*, March 1899, and a perspective in *Osterreichische Kunst des 19. Jahrhunderts*, Ludwig Hevesi (published Leipzig, 1903), p. 283.

the Secessionists far more eloquently than all that had gone before (Fig. 27 and Plate 93A).

The principal elevation was symmetrical and consisted of three plain rectangular blocks devoid of windows. The deeply recessed copper doorway was

Figure 27. 1898. J. M. Olbrich. The Secession House, Vienna—a perspective sketch.

surrounded by a 'Frampton Tree' motive carved in a low relief, the only decoration used. The building was dominated by a hemispherical openwork cupola of gilded iron on a square base, the angles of which were carried up as stumpy towers.[1] The plan was formal and symmetrical with a large central hall surrounded by smaller apartments; the partition walls were movable, however, so that the floor area could be sub-divided as required and advantage

[1] A similar angle treatment to this was employed by Harrison Townsend in his project for the Whitechapel Art Gallery and he also used the familiar leaf motive. Townsend's design was published in *The Studio* in 1895, two years earlier than the Secession House and no doubt was known to Olbrich.

275

taken of either side or top light—an innovation that caused considerable comment at the time.

The foundation stone of the Secession House was laid on 28th April 1898, and the opening ceremony took place on 15th November of the same year. The unusual character of the building created a sensation in architectural circles and the general public, amused by Olbrich's filigree dome, christened it 'The House of the Golden Cabbage'. Thus in precisely the same way that Mackintosh achieved notoriety by the School of Art—then taking shape in Glasgow—so overnight Olbrich became one of the most discussed figures in Vienna. The Secession House, for all its ponderous formality and classical reminiscences, was just as unorthodox in the city of Schmidt and Hasenauer as Mackintosh's School of Art in the Glasgow of Burnet and Greek Thomson. In this his first building claimed an enthusiastic contemporary, Olbrich broke the ice and set free the stream of the new movement in architecture.

THE ARTISTS' COLONY, DARMSTADT

Shortly after completing the Secession House and several villas in Vienna (1899) Olbrich was summoned to Darmstadt by Ernst Ludwig, Grand Duke of Hesse, who had conceived the idea of making his city one of the foremost art centres in Europe. To this end he invited a number of distinguished artists and craftsmen to Darmstadt and commissioned Olbrich to design houses, studios, workshops and so forth for them. The scheme was quite ambitious[1]: a magnificent site on the Mathildenhohe was selected and Olbrich built houses for the artists concerned, with the exception of that for Peter Behrens which was designed by the German architect himself. The interiors and furnishings, down to the last tablecloth and teaspoon, were designed and made by the artists.

THE ERNST LUDWIG HOUSE

In addition to dwelling houses there were certain community buildings, one of the most interesting being the Ernst Ludwig House, named after the patron

[1] Illustrated in *Ver Sacrum*, vol. IX, p. 446. *Deutsche Kunst und Dekoration*, vol. VI, pp. 366 et seq.; vol. VII; vol. VIII; vol. IX. *The Studio*, vol. XXIV, pp. 91 et seq., etc.

(Fig. 28). This contained in two storeys an exhibition hall, studios, bachelors' quarters; commercial rooms, gymnasium and recreation rooms. Externally, it was long and low, with widely overhanging eaves, and rhythmically disposed windows, which, on the main elevation, were confined entirely to the ground floor —an arrangement which gave striking character to the façade. The central doorway was enclosed in a great semi-circular arch flanked by two heroic statues by Ludwig Habich, the colony's sculptor, which, unfortunately, seem much out of scale with the building itself. Ornament was confined to the door-way and the eaves, and the entire building was rendered in white rough-cast. The pleasant proportions, restful horizontal lines, and simple form of this work give it a surprising air of modernity and it is undoubtedly one of Olbrich's most successful designs (Plate 93B).

Figure 28. 1901. J. M. Olbrich. The Ernst Ludwig House, Darmstadt.

On the whole the houses were in the Austrian tradition with white rendered walls and steeply pitched tiled roofs. Several, notably those of Julius Gluckert and Ludwig Habich (Plate 93C), were remarkably adventurous despite certain neo-Renaissance details. In both of these, as in the community building, Olbrich discarded most of the surface ornament which so clearly dates his earlier work and in the Voysey-Mackintosh manner relied for effect entirely upon the arrangement of solid and void, the proportion of wall to window. Both build-ings are contemporary with *Windyhill* and *Hill House* and they indicate a similar stage of development.

Olbrich introduced many original details at Darmstadt; to take one notable instance, horizontal windows carried round the angle of a building—prospect windows—a feature which became part of the 'modern' architect's stock-in-trade after the first World War. Occasionally these were placed below light, projecting canopies; good examples of this arrangement occur in the entrance

277

pylons built for an exhibition held in the colony in 1901, and at the Hochzeitsturm (1906–7).

Olbrich continued working at Darmstadt until his premature death in 1908 shortly after the completion of the great Hochzeitsturm,[1] the 150 foot high tower of which provided the climax to the Künstlerkolonie and dominated the Mathildenhöhe.[2] During the preceding decade he had made tremendous strides and had largely divested himself of his Wagnerian legacy of neo-Renaissance ornament. The tower of the Hochzeitsturm, the Ernst Ludwig House, and the fountain court of the German pavilion at the St. Louis Exhibition (1904), place him unquestionably in the forefront of contemporary pioneers, and one can only regret that his life was cut short at this vital stage in his development.

PETER BEHRENS, 1868–1940

Before appraising the work of Josef Hoffmann, the second important figure of the Wagnerschule, it may be well to consider one of the buildings on the Mathildenhöhe which did not conform to the general pattern, the house designed by the German architect Peter Behrens (Plate 94A). Behrens, it will be remembered, some eight years later created the A.E.G. Turbine factory in the Huttlestrasse, Berlin—described by Nikolaus Pevsner as 'perhaps the most beautiful industrial building ever erected up to that time . . . a pure work of art . . .' (Plate 94c). In the Darmstadt house with its tight economical plan, quasi-Dutch gables, steeply pitched roof and green brick quoins, one can detect little evidence of the fine sense of form and proportion which characterizes the architect's later work as an industrial designer, though there may be some similarity between the rigid verticality of the façade, the hard mechanical fenestration, and his street lamps and factories of a decade later. The decoration and furnishing was heavy and overpowering with angular patterned ceilings and floors, dark woodwork and complex geometrical ornament. It is abundantly clear from this example that Behrens' metamorphosis took place well after the turn of the century and perhaps, largely as a result of his association with

---

[1] Illustrated in *Pioneers of the Modern Movement*, p. 186.

[2] It may be noted here that E. B. Kalas, in *De la Tamise à la Sprée*, claims that Olbrich derived his 'vertical arrangements' from Mackintosh. Kalas does not give his authority for this assertion nor is his view supported by the evidence of this study. Olbrich's buildings in fact are notable for their horizontality rather than for vertical arrangements.

Olbrich and the artists of the Mathildenhohe: and with Mackintosh at Turin in 1902.

JOSEF HOFFMANN, 1870–1956

On Olbrich's departure from Vienna, Josef Hoffmann became the undisputed leader of the new movement in the Austrian capital and through his eminence as a teacher, one of the most powerful influences in Central Europe. It is said that he spent much time as a student designing imaginary palaces, temples and gardens in the grand manner, and though this may be true, he too had to graduate through the applied arts. Interior design, said a contemporary critic, was the hook on which the general public was caught—and one might add, after interior design, domestic work. The formula was usually the same, whether in England, Germany or Austria. Thus Hoffmann's first architectural commission consisted of a colony of villas mainly for artists and friends, built on the Hohe Warte, a plateau on the outskirts of Vienna (1900). The houses were in the modernized traditional style favoured also by Olbrich—the Austrian equivalent of Voysey's work in England. Unlike Olbrich, however, Hoffmann did not design a building of the importance of the Secession House before the turn of the century and consequently we have no means of measuring his capabilities against his friend's achievement. In fact, some four years elapsed before he embarked upon his first large project—a Sanatorium at Pürkersdorf. During the intervening period he devoted much time and energy to the minor arts and, as we have seen, made notable progress. In 1903 he resigned from the Secession and with Koloman Moser, and the financial support of Fritz Wärndorfer, founded the Wiener Werkstätte—workshops in which, according to the precepts of William Morris, designers and craftsmen closely co-operated. Through the agency of the Werkstätte, which was largely staffed by young artists trained at the Kunstgewerbe-Schule, Hoffmann was able to propagate his ideas widely.

The Pürkersdorf Sanatorium (Plate 92), Hoffmann's first major architectural work, is the antithesis of Wagner's monumental neo-Renaissance style, and quite unlike Olbrich's Secession House. The building is the natural outcome of his initial training in the applied arts and it possesses all the characteristics of his furniture at the Vienna Exhibition of 1900—with modifications arising from his association with Mackintosh and Olbrich. The walls were rough-cast and painted white; the roof was flat with boldly projecting eaves, and the fenestration simplicity itself with meticulously placed windows of rectangular form. The whole building was almost entirely devoid of ornament and only the designer's favourite chequered border of black squares round each window, and a few small carved panels at the entrance, relieve the severity of the façades. Hoffmann made at least two notable additions to the 'modern' architect's vocabulary in this project—a tall staircase window running through three storeys and a large concrete canopy in the centre of the main elevation.

The interiors and furnishings were designed and executed under the architect's direction at the Wiener Werkstätte and they inevitably recall Mackintosh. White predominated and even here the square remained the principal decorative motive. As one might anticipate the furniture throughout was elegant and simple in form.

The Pürkersdorf Sanatorium thus represented a bold step. It was contemporary with Wagner's Postsparkasse in Vienna and Mackintosh's *Willow* Tea-Rooms and it demonstrates that Hoffmann had succeeded better than his master in throwing off the last vestiges of nineteenth-century revivalism, and, in this design at least, more effectively than Mackintosh in discarding the remnants of *art nouveau*.

Hoffmann's next important building was the Palais Stoclet,[1] a large and expensive mansion erected at Brussels in 1905. The extended plan of the house, with its large two-storeyed hall, was clearly influenced by Mackintosh's *Haus eines Kunstfreundes* project, but it is less successful. The building is faced externally with large slabs of marble framed at the angles with painted and gilded steel bands. There is an ebullient, rather ornate tower over the staircase-well— described by Goodhart-Rendel as 'just fun: quite good fun'!—a long canopy to the main entrance carried on sturdy piers, and a tall staircase window of the kind introduced at Pürkersdorf. The principal block is three storeys high, flanked by a single storey appendage with a flat roof, and attractive glazed penthouse. Despite an abundance of wrought iron, the ornate tower, and box-like contours emphasized by the curious angle treatment, the general character of the Palais Stoclet is as close to the spirit of the new movement as any of Mackintosh's domestic designs—even the *Haus eines Kunstfreundes* itself.

After this project, Hoffmann did not execute any further architectural work of significance from the point of view of this study. The Pürkersdorf Sanatorium

[1] Illustrated in *How Architecture is Made*, H. S. Goodhart-Rendel, published 1947 and based on the Sidney Jones Lectures in Art delivered at Liverpool University 1945–6, p. 57. See 'The Stoclet House', Sekler, *Essays in the History of Architecture*, 1967, pp. 228–44.

and the Palais Stoclet are two of his most venturesome projects; thereafter his work followed more conventional lines. In 1907 he built a house in Vienna[1] which, but for its canopied porch, might have been transplanted from any English suburb; and in 1913, his magnificent Wohnhaus Skywa,[2] for all its stuccoed modernity and delightful details, was of classical proportions and possessed a heavy decorated cornice with modified egg and dart ornament, a multitude of statues and a pedimented garden house. His exhibition stands at Rome in 1911,[3] at Vienna in 1912,[4] and even at the Werkbund Exhibition, Cologne,[5] in 1914, all betray the same characteristics.

Like his master Wagner, Hoffmann was a brilliant teacher and though he has comparatively few advanced architectural monuments to his credit, his influence was much stronger than might be anticipated. He maintained his position in Austria for upwards of forty years and at the time of writing (1950) continues to practise and to teach in Vienna.

Out of the Wagnerschule came other architect-designers who carried the ideals of the Secessionists still further afield, for example, Leopold Bauer, Josef Plecnik, a Slovene whose Zacherlaus office building (1903–5) in the Bauernmarkt, Vienna, is elegant and sophisticated, and Jan Kotera, one of the founders of the 'Manes' Artists' League in Czechoslovakia, who became an influential leader of the modern movement in that country. In fact the interiors and furnishings of the 'Municipal House' in Prague which are remarkably well preserved (1969) represent possibly the best and most complete examples of the Secessionist style in central Europe.

The advocates of *art nouveau* and the secessionists, important as they were, did not constitute the only groups aiming at revival in the architectural sphere, and by the end of the nineteenth century new forces were at work in Austria and Germany, forces diametrically opposed to the philosophies of *art nouveau* and of the Secession itself.

---

[1] Illustrated in *Josef Hoffmann*, Dr. Armand Weiser (published in Geneva, 1930), p. 6.
[2] *Ibid.*, pp. 10–13.   [3] *Ibid.*, pp. 4–5.
[4] *Ibid.*, pp. 8–9.   [5] *Ibid.*, pp. 17–21.

ADOLF LOOS, 1870–1933

As early as 1897, art circles in Vienna had been disturbed by an unwelcome voice other than that of *Ver Sacrum*. Adolf Loos, a young Viennese architect trained in Dresden, began to expound revolutionary views on interior decoration, furniture and clothing through the columns of the *Neue Freie Presse*. Loos had been in England and had spent three years in America *c*. 1893 where he observed the work of the new Chicago School, Adler, Sullivan and the rest—and became aware of the aesthetic possibilities of machine-made objects. On his return to Austria he enthusiastically extolled the work of the engineer, and opened an active campaign against ornament in all its forms. Not even Hoffmann escaped his attack. According to Behrendt,[1] ornament roused his passions to such an extent that on one occasion, after a heated argument in a Viennese café, he stamped out of the room exclaiming, 'Ornament is a crime!' an aphorism which was taken up by his disciples and for a time became a popular slogan.

One of Loos' first commissions was the design of a shop interior in Vienna (1898)[2] in which he attempted to translate his principles into practice. No ornament as such was employed, but the wall show-cases terminated at frieze level in a row of bow-fronted lantern-like objects, glazed in small squares forming an interesting decorative element right round the apartment.[3] The doors of the dressing cubicles—the shop was a gentlemen's outfitters ('Herrenmodegeschäft Goldmann')—were also glazed with square panes reminiscent of Mackintosh's work. Not all Loos' interiors were as pleasantly functional as this however. His *Café Museum* Vienna (1899),[4] for instance—V-shaped in plan, with billiards-tables in one wing and bentwood furniture in the other—was a grim, bleak and inelegant apartment, far removed in spirit from the Cranston tea-rooms. Some of his furniture for private clients, on the other hand—a dining-table, chairs and a dresser for Herr Stossler of Vienna (1899), and a wardrobe and buffet for Herr Gustav Turnowski [5]—is well designed and quite free from eccentricity, but the most notable room, considering its date, was a bedroom for Herr Walter Sobotka, designed in 1902.[6] In this instance

[1] *Modern Building*, W. C. Behrendt. See also 'Ornament und Verbrechen', Loos, 1908.

[2] Illustrated in *Adolf Loos*, Heinrich Kulka, Vienna, 1931, illustrations 1 and 2.

[3] The widespread popularity of the square among the 'avant garde' is interesting—and, perhaps, heralds the advent of cubist painting.

[4] Illustrated in *Adolf Loos*, Heinrich Kulka (published by Anton Schroll & Co., Vienna, 1931), illustrations 7–8.

[5] *Ibid.*, illustrations 3–6.   [6] Cf. *Adolf Loos*, Kulka, illustration 14.

282

the bedstead, panelling and wardrobe were without decoration of any kind. The figure of the wood and the form of the pieces themselves being considered of sufficient interest, accents were provided by flowers, the carpet and the soft furnishings only. This room should be compared·with Mackintosh's bedroom at Mains Street (1900) and with the interior work of Van de Velde and others if the extraordinary purity of the design is to be fully appreciated.

Few of Loos' projects reached such a high standard, however, and he seems to have made little headway as an architect for a considerable time. In 1907, for example, he was still designing in a form of Wagneresque neo-Renaissance as exemplified by his project for the Kriegsminesterium, Vienna,[1] and his first unmistakable deviation from contemporary practice did not occur until 1910 when he built the Haus Steiner, Vienna (Plate 94D). Thus, despite his proselytism Loos did not become an important force in the new movement for some years, while Mackintosh, Olbrich and Hoffmann went from strength to strength and rapidly acquired international fame.

In Western Europe at the turn of the century events began to move swiftly. In 1903, the year in which Hoffmann relinquished his chair at the Vienna Academy to found the Wiener Werkstätte, Hermann Muthesius returned to Germany from London full of enthusiasm for the work of British designers, and eager to propagate his personal views in the soil prepared by the advocates of *art nouveau*. Professor Pevsner tells us that he was appointed superintendent of the Arts and Crafts Schools of the Prussian Board of Trade, and at once began to use his influence to bring about radical changes in the field of art education, to which end he invited Peter Behrens to Düsseldorf and Hans Poelzig to Breslau, each as head of the Arts and Crafts Academy in these cities. At this time, too, Henry Van de Velde became principal of the Weimar Art School (where he was succeeded by Walter Gropius in 1914) and Bruno Paul head of the Berlin School of Arts and Crafts. In this manner the spirit of the new movement was widely disseminated and the gains already made rapidly consolidated.

The view implicit in Loos' philosophy, that industrial design and the product of the machine might be as a legitimate a form of artistic expression as handicraft, had been voiced in England by Cobden Sanderson, Lewis Day and others before him; it was foreshadowed in the quasi-engineering designs of Wagner and Horta and in the neo-Romanesque buildings of Berlage in Holland. This theme —a symptom of awakening consciousness to the potentialities of the twentieth

---

[1] *Adolf Loos*, Kulka, illustrations 33–4.

283

century—was taken up with avidity by Hermann Muthesius, and it found an echo across the Atlantic in the explosive writings of Frank Lloyd Wright.[1]

Muthesius seems to have been responsible for bringing matters to a climax in Western Europe in 1907 when largely at his invitation a number of enterprising manufacturers and designers came together and launched the Deutsche Werkbund, an association formed with the object of improving the standard of machine-made products by encouraging closer co-operation between architect, designer, workman and manufacturer. One of the most important figures associated with the Werkbund was Peter Behrens now emancipated from the subtle charms of the Darmstadt Künstlerkolonie and appointed architect to the important A.E.G. (General Electric Company, of Berlin). It was from such beginnings that yet another stream of the new movement, the rationalist or functionalist stream sprang.

In a lucid exposition of the situation Professor Pevsner[2] states that the Deutsche Werkbund did not easily find a solution to the controversial problems of art and industry, nor to the closely related question of architectural design. One faction, headed by Muthesius, favoured standardization, and a second, with Van de Velde as spokesman, insisted that individuality be preserved—a view not unexpected from the protagonist of *art nouveau*. This fundamental divergence of opinion persisted for some years but resolved itself at the Werkbund Exhibition at Cologne in 1914 when there appeared side by side buildings by Adolf Meyer and Walter Gropius, two of Behrens' former pupils; Bruno Taut; Van de Velde and Josef Hoffmann.

Hoffmann's Austrian pavilion[3] was built on sound traditional lines with solid load-bearing walls and steeply pitched gables. It had fluted piers—without either base or cap—and an arcaded courtyard; it was an inoffensive charming building that admirably represented the Secession and the craftsmen of the Wiener Werkstätte. Van de Velde designed the Exhibition Theatre[4] (Plate 91E), a strange rather repulsive structure, hugging the earth, and made up of many elements which flowed together and were covered by a variety of pitched roofs, a building well within the *art nouveau* succession. The German, Bruno Taut, on the other

---

[1] See paper read in Chicago by F. L. Wright in 1903—'The Art and Craft of the Machine' —reprinted *Modern Architecture* Princeton, 1931.

[2] *Pioneers of the Modern Movement.*

[3] Illustrated in *Josef Hoffmann*, Armand Weiser, pp. 17 et seq.

[4] Well illustrated in *H. Van de Velde*, Karl Ernst Osthaus, p. 126 et seq., and also in *Modern Architecture*, Bruno Taut, 1929, p. 53, and *Groszstadt Architektur*, Ludwig Hilberseimer.

hand, designed an extraordinary glass house[1] of circular plan, lightly framed in reinforced concrete and covered by a many faceted glass 'dome' of network construction. This daring experiment attracted a good deal of attention, for it was devised to reveal the possibilities of glass as a building material and in addition to its ingenious dome had walls made of glass bricks, and many other innovations.

The building of greatest significance, however, was a model factory and office designed by Walter Gropius and Adolf Meyer of Berlin (Plate 75c). This was steel framed with boldly projecting concrete roofs, spiral staircases contained in transparent semicircular bays, and diaphanous curtain walls of glass suspended in front of the main structure—a development of the system introduced by the architects at their 'Fagus' factory at Ahlfeld in 1911. In this building were revealed as never before the architectural potentialities of the new materials—steel, concrete and plate glass. It was demonstrated that walls could be dissolved into thin transparent membranes, roofs and floors could be thrust forward without visible means of support, and the plan of a building could be freed of solid load bearing partitions. Lightness and flexibility were the most striking characteristics of the German work at Cologne, characteristics that were thrown into greater relief by the presence of buildings in a more traditional vein by Hoffmann, Van de Velde and others. Here in fact can be recognized quite clearly two diametrically opposite views on the nature of modern architecture; that of Van de Velde and Hoffmann representing *art nouveau* and the Secession—renaissance through the handicrafts and by means of traditional building methods; and that of the Gropius faction postulating an entirely new conception of architectural design based on scientific rationalism and the exploitation of new materials.

Professor Pevsner claims, and rightly so, that the presence of Gropius' model factory at Cologne demonstrated indisputably the trend of future developments, it gave form and substance to the dream of an international style, a twentieth-century architecture.

And so again the familiar cycle is complete, and the emergence of the new architectural style exemplified by Gropius' factory can be traced from its source in the minor arts, this time, however, from the industrial design and machine art of the Deutsche Werkbund. Moreover, an identical pattern is followed and in maturity the style takes upon itself many of the characteristics displayed by the art form from which it springs. We recognize in Gropius' building at

[1] Cf. *Modern Architecture*, Bruno Taut, p. 56.

285

Cologne or in Taut's glass-house, the same sleek metallic precision that distinguishes the silver boxes of Ehmcke, or the functional street lamps of Behrens. The art worker, the individual craftsman, is superseded by the engineer and the machine, and for the sympathetic traditional materials wood, brick and stone, are substituted the man-made synthetics, steel, concrete and glass.

From the ground covered in this chapter it has become increasingly apparent that secessionist trends in Europe—using the term secessionist in its broadest sense—were widespread, and did not by any means constitute a single organized movement, much less a movement centred on Glasgow. At least four separate and largely independent sources can be recognized, each with its influential group of adherents and its peculiar characteristics: *Art Nouveau*, the Central European Secessionists and the Glasgow Group, all of whom virtually form one main stream, directly, or indirectly deriving from Morris and the English School. The fourth source, represented by Loos, Behrens and Gropius (and the Frenchmen Auguste Perret and Mallet Stephens), is a little apart and forms a second stream which, as the twentieth century advanced, assumed greater and greater importance. By the outbreak of the first world war the streams had diverged and two conflicting views on the meaning and purpose of architecture had crystallized—that of the architect romanticist and that of the industrial designer, the engineer, the architect-rationalist.

It now remains to determine to which stream, if either, Mackintosh belonged and to assess the importance of his work in relation to the work of his contemporaries.

His precise position is not easy to define. The second section of the School of Art (1907–9) is contemporary with Behrens' Turbine Factory, and, with its thrilling cascades of metal and glass and boldly cantilevered conservatory, seems at first glance to belong unmistakably to the Gropius faction. Yet it contains much decorative detail, both internally and externally, and, it will be remembered, the west elevation was intended to embody sculptured figures of St. Francis and Cellini! Moreover, its designer did not refrain from combining traditional and modern architectural forms, nor did he hesitate to employ at one and the same time, old building methods and new structural techniques. None of these apparent contradictions would have been condoned by the purists—by Loos and the German group—however greatly they might have admired his imaginative experiments.

The Secessionists, on the other hand, did not find Mackintosh's continual

286

preoccupation with decoration and his reluctance to depart far from tradition unduly disturbing, yet none of them adventured so fearlessly into the realms of spatial composition and structural experiment. Hoffmann, for example, was clearly dominated by a similar urge to decorate—in his case a legacy from the epoch of Makart. The 'artistic sentiment' which caused him to place chequered borders round the windows of the Pürkersdorf Sanatorium, and a fanciful tower on the Palais Stoclet, persisted in 1914 and impelled him to use fluted piers, pedimented gables and arcades at the Cologne Exhibition, where Gropius employed steel and glass.

Mackintosh thus had a foot in both camps—but he walked alone, treading a solitary path somewhere between the uncompromising materialism of the German school, and the pleasant romanticism of the Secessionists, subscribing to both, indebted to neither. His importance on the international stage is best expressed by Muthesius who, in commenting on the *Haus eines Kunstfreundes* project, had no hesitation in claiming that the Scottish architect was far in advance of his contemporaries. The elevations, he said, were absolutely original —'unlike anything else known'—and admirably expressed the adventurous spirit of the age. He concluded his critical review with these words: ' . . . if one were to go through the list of truly original artists, the creative minds of the modern movement, the name of Charles Mackintosh would certainly be included even amongst the few that one can count on the fingers of a single hand.' The significance of this pronouncement from a man who himself was shortly to play such a vital part in the new movement can hardly be overestimated, and its accuracy is borne out by the evidence contained in this study.

It is the first project for the Glasgow School of Art, however, that must always be the yardstick by which Mackintosh's independence and creative genius is measured. By 1896, when the School was designed, no one in Europe, not even Horta, had produced a scheme of the originality, and what is more, the architectural quality, of this work. Mackintosh's unconventional façades, his free planning, and his disdain of fashionable ornament make Olbrich's Secession House and Wagner's railway stations seem dated and almost banal. When he submitted this project in competition, Van de Velde and Hoffmann had scarcely begun to build, Loos and Muthesius had not committed themselves in print. Behrens was still within the *art nouveau* fold, Berlage had not embarked upon his quasi-Romanesque project for the Amsterdam Stock Exchange—since hailed with much delight by the historians—and Frank Lloyd Wright, with few buildings to his credit, was quite unknown in Europe.

Thus it can be claimed with some justification that Mackintosh erected the first important architectural monument to the new movement in Europe. The School of Art, however, is not a cold, impersonal essay in an international style; it does not stand stark and naked—the 'bald erection' visualized by the governors—nor does it shock our inherent sense of order and harmony. It is, in fact, a building of extraordinary quality and is still recognized by those who use it as one of the best of its kind. Its spatial organization reflects and is expressive of its function and, together with the subtle excellence of its natural lighting, provides an endless source of pleasure for those working in it, and for those who now come from many parts of the world to see it. The building is small enough, and its planning lucid enough, to make total comprehension easy for the layman as well as the professional, and the richness and variety of its detail add surprise and delight. In this his first and last building of consequence, spanning the few years from 1896–1909 in which his creative genius found full expression, he produced a living, vital work of art, anticipating future trends yet resting firmly within the Scottish tradition. That indeed was his objective, and it will remain his distinctive contribution to modern architectural history.

EPILOGUE

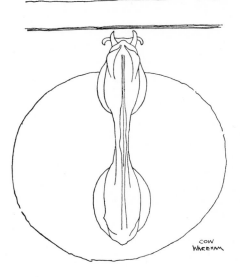

COW
WAREHAM

U

EPILOGUE

THE Mackintoshes had retained the lease of the Glebe Place studios during and after their brief stay in France, and on Margaret's death, the contents were valued. There were twenty-six water-colours and five flower paintings, a large collection of miscellaneous architectural drawings, sketches and photographs, some furniture and personal effects. According to the official assessment the entire contents of the two studios were 'practically of no value'—they were estimated to be worth £88 16s. 2d.!

Eventually everything was disposed of by the executors, except the drawings and paintings which were sent to Glasgow and held in trust by William Davidson for Mr Sylvan MacNair, only son of Herbert and Frances MacNair, then living in South Africa. An attempt was made to realize on the collection in May 1933 when a Memorial Exhibition was arranged at the McLellan Galleries, Glasgow,[1] by Mr. Davidson and Mr. Geoffrey Waddell—a great admirer of the architect's work. A few of the paintings and drawings were sold, some were given away, and the rest were stored in the basement of Mr. Davidson's city

[1] It was suggested that the Exhibition be transferred to London to the Royal Institute of British Architects, but after lengthy correspondence nothing came of the project.

291

warehouse where they remained undisturbed, and to all intents and purposes forgotten, until the author commenced this investigation in 1940.

The discovery of the collection was an exciting experience. The offices were hung with framed pictures and drawings, and the basement room, with its piles of dust-ladened folios and parcels, seemed a veritable treasure house. Many hours were spent sorting, classifying and recording the hundreds of sketches and drawings that came to light—a task in which William Davidson took a kindly interest, often lending a hand himself, and encouraging his staff to do the same. In retrospect one cannot but be astonished at the patient forbearance of these good people, for few such business concerns can have been blessed—or cursed—with a research student in the cellar at lunch-times, in the evening and at the weekends. Mr. Davidson's sole concern, however, was that justice should be done to his old friend and idol, Mackintosh. He resented bitterly the indifference of his fellow citizens to the claims of one whom he considered to be the greatest architect Scotland had produced, and he was determined not to let the drawings out of his care until they could be properly housed.

As time passed it became obvious that some attempt should be made to safeguard the collection, and if possible, to arrange a permanent exhibition of the Mackintoshes' work in Glasgow. This rather delicate question the author raised frequently, but the insuperable obstacle was always that of finding suitable accommodation. Mr. Davidson would not agree to send even a selection of the drawings to the Royal Institute of British Architects—the most appropriate home for them—nor even to the Victoria and Albert Museum, and he refused adamantly to send them to the Glasgow Corporation Art Galleries unless an assurance were given that they would be adequately and permanently displayed: nor would he contemplate giving them to the School of Art except on similar terms. In neither case was the assurance forthcoming; space at both institutions being at a premium. Moreover, local interest in Mackintosh at this time had not been sufficiently awakened.

Failing the two most obvious centres in Glasgow the only alternative that came to mind was the Mackintoshes' former home, No. 78 Southpark Avenue, a doubly attractive proposition in that the architect's original decorations and furniture had been carefully preserved. In view of its situation within an area intended for development by Glasgow University, the author suggested that the possibility of acquiring the property, if at any time it should come on the market, might be investigated. Through the good offices of Professor C. J.

Fordyce and Professor John Walton this proposition was favourably received, and the necessary steps taken.

Unfortunately Mr. Davidson's dream of a permanent Mackintosh Exhibition did not materialize during his lifetime, nor did he live to see the completion of this study in which he had taken such a benevolent interest. He had been in failing health for some years and, after a protracted illness this kindly old man, one of the most stalwart of Mackintosh's champions, died in the summer of 1945.

The Davidson family decided to sell the Southpark Avenue house, and on 15th November 1945, it was bought by the University. At the same time most of the original furniture designed by Mackintosh was presented by Dr. Cameron and Mr. Hamish Davidson to the University in memory of their father—a generous and valuable gift.[1] Shortly afterwards Mr. Sylvan MacNair relinquished his claim to the drawings and now they, too, are safely housed in the Hunterian Museum, Glasgow University.[2]

In this manner a representative collection of the artists' work has been secured and, moreover, some of the furniture can be seen in its original setting. But the Southpark Avenue house could not be made into a museum as the author had hoped, and at present it is occupied by a senior member of the University staff. It is anticipated that a permanent home for the Mackintosh collection will be provided in future extensions to the University, and the possibility of reconstructing the best Southpark Avenue interiors as a background to the exhibits should not be overlooked.

The story is not quite ended, however. Southpark Avenue is rather remote from the centre of the city and it seemed that the Mackintoshes should be represented adequately in the School of Art, the centre to which all interested visitors inevitably gravitate. The publicity accorded to the acquisition of No. 78 Southpark Avenue by the Scottish press and the architectural journals aroused a good deal of interest, and shortly afterwards the author prevailed upon Mr. Henry Y. Allison, acting Director of the School of Art, to start a Mackintosh collection, using as a nucleus, the furniture and drawings already in the

---

[1] See 'A. Mackintosh House in Glasgow', T. Howarth, *Journal of the R.I.B.A.*, vol. LIII, 1946. 'Some Mackintosh Furniture Preserved', T. Howarth, *The Architectural Review*, vol. C, 1946.

[2] The drawings, photographs, sketch-books and the like, were catalogued in September 1946 by the author. Drawings by Margaret Macdonald and by the MacNairs are included in the collection.

building.[1] Research in connection with this study had revealed the presence of many potential exhibits in the hands of kindly disposed individuals, and the success of an exhibition room seemed assured once the project was given official status. While the plan was taking shape, Mr. Douglas Percy Bliss was appointed Director and he, too, gave the scheme his wholehearted support. And then came a magnanimous gesture from the governors who, in approving the project, decided that the work should be housed in the old board-room—one of the finest apartments in the School. The decoration of this room and the collection and arrangement of exhibits was left in the hands of the author and the deputy director, Mr. H. Jefferson Barnes, and an appeal for further work by the artists was circulated. The response was most gratifying and many pieces came to hand. The sceptics were confounded, and the room was formally opened on 17th April 1947, by Miss Nancy Mackintosh after an address by Sir Frank Mears of Edinburgh. Now the School of Art possesses an excellent collection of furniture, water-colours and drawings by the architect and his wife, worthily housed, and conveniently situated in the centre of the city.

Since then there has been a remarkable change in public opinion. This may be measured by the fact that in 1950 when the lease of the Ingram Street tea-rooms expired and the premises were advertised for sale, Glasgow Corporation, in response to many appeals in the press and elsewhere, stepped in and bought them—complete with furniture—at a cost of £23,000. The interior is to be restored and the rooms used for cultural purposes, meetings of societies and so forth, and one part will be kept as a memorial to the Mackintoshes.

Thus it can be claimed with some justification that the prophet at last has found honour in his own country. It is hoped now that the collections of furniture and drawings described here will be maintained and augmented, and that Mackintosh's architectural work in Glasgow and its environs will be saved from further mutilation.

---

[1] The School possessed several large pieces of furniture given by Mr. Davidson when he left *Windyhill*. The most notable piece is the white-painted bed (Plate 34c).

CHRONOLOGICAL TABLE (1860–1933)

In this table the left-hand column is devoted to Mackintosh and the *Four*. The right-hand column contains the names of well-known contemporary buildings and the date of birth of many architects and designers. Thus by comparison Mackintosh's work may be seen in correct perspective, and the swiftly changing pattern of events during the period under review be appreciated more readily.

Buildings in one or other of the revivalist styles are distinguished by an asterisk. All names refer to architects unless stated otherwise; the date of death is signified thus—(d. 1850).

GENERAL

1860   *Westminster Palace, London, completed. Barry & Pugin.
      Edgar Wood born (d. 1935).
      Karl Moser, painter (d. 1936).

1861   William Morris, Marshall, Faulkner & Company founded.
      Victor Horta (d. 1947)
      Hermann Muthesius (d. 1927).
      Charles Plumet (d. 1928); designer.
      Bernard Maybeck (d. 1957).

1863   C. R. Ashbee (d. 1942).
      Raymond Unwin (d. 1940).

CHARLES RENNIE MACKINTOSH AND THE 'FOUR'		GENERAL
		Edvard Munch (d. 1944); painter.
		Gustav Klimt (d. 1918); painter.
		Henry van de Velde (d. 1957).
		Herman Obrist (d. 1927); designer.
	1864	Robert Lorimer (d. 1929).
		Ernest Gimson (d. 1920).
		Otto Eckmann (d. 1902).
Margaret Macdonald born (d. 1933).	1865	Baillie Scott (d. 1940).
		Talwin Morris (d. 1912); designer.
		Joseph Paxton died (b. 1803).
	1866	*Work began on Glasgow University and on St. Pancras Station, London; architect, Sir Gilbert Scott, R.A. (1810–77)
		W. Kandinski (d. 1944); painter.
	1867	George Walton (d. 1933).
		Frank Brangwyn (d. 1956); painter.
		J. M. Olbrich (d. 1908).
		Hector Guimard (d. 1942).
		Queen's Park Church and Gt. Western Terrace, Glasgow, by 'Greek' Thomson.
C. R. Mackintosh born (d. 1928).	1868	*Manchester Town Hall (completed 1877) by Alfred Waterhouse.
Herbert MacNair born (d. 1953).		Richard Riemerschmid (d. 1957).
		Peter Behrens (d. 1940).
		Charles Greene USA (d. 1957).
	1869	Frank Lloyd Wright (d. 1959).
		Edwin Lutyens (d. 1944).
		Tony Garnier (d. 1948).
		Hans Poelzig (d. 1936).
	1870	*Keble College Oxford, by William Butterfield.
		Adolf Loos (d. 1933).
		Josef Hoffmann (d. 1955).
	1871	Charles Brewer (d. 1925).
		August Endell (d. 1925).
	1872	*Albert Memorial, London, by Sir Gilbert Scott.
		Ambrose Heal (d. 1959); furniture designer.
		Aubrey Beardsley (d. 1898); illustrator.
		Robert Maillart (d. 1940); engineer.

296

CHARLES RENNIE MACKINTOSH AND THE 'FOUR'	GENERAL
	1873 Eliel Saarinen (d. 1950).
Frances Macdonald born (d. 1921).	1874 *London Law Courts (1874–82) built by G. E. Street (1824–81). *Opera House, Paris, by Charles Garnier. Auguste Perret (d. 1954). Bruno Paul (d. 1954).
C. R. Mackintosh at Reid's Public School, Glasgow.	1875 'Swan House', Chelsea; by R. N. Shaw (Plate 87D). 'Greek' Thomson died (born Glasgow 1817).
	1876 Rounton School, Yorkshire, by Philip Webb (Plate 88A). Bon Marché Store, Paris, Eiffel and Boileau. Furniture Warehouse, Glasgow, by J. Honeyman (Plate 18A).
C. R. Mackintosh at Alan Glen's High School.	1877 Society for the Protection of Ancient Buildings founded by Wm. Morris.
	1878 Flat-roofed house by Mackmurdo at Enfield. Gottfried Semper died (born Hamburg 1803).
	1879 Glasgow Art Institute founded. Eugène Freyssinet (d. 1926); engineer.
	1880 Bruno Taut (d. 1938).
	1881 'Clouds' (Plate 87A and B), by Philip Webb. The periodical *L'Art Moderne* launched in Brussels. Pablo R. Picasso (d. 1973); painter. Adolf Meyer (d. 1929).
	1882 *Japan, its Architecture, Art and Art Manufactures.* C. Dresser. Mackmurdo founded the Century Guild. C. F. A. Voysey in practice. D. G. Rossetti died; poet.
	1883 *Glasgow Municipal Buildings, foundations laid. *Palais de Justice, Brussels, completed by Poelaert. La Sagrada Familia, Barcelona, begun (to 1926) by Gaudí.

297

CHARLES RENNIE MACKINTOSH AND THE 'FOUR'		GENERAL
		Walter Gropius (d. 1969).
		Theo Van Doesburg (d. 1931); painter.
		Otto Bartning (d. 1959).
Professional Training Begins. Apprenticed to John Hutchison, architect. Commenced evening classes at Glasgow School of Art.	1884	The Art Workers' Guild founded. Willem Dudok born.
Awarded a school prize for painting in monochrome.	1885	Francis H. Newbery appointed headmaster of the Glasgow School of Art. Guell Palace, Barcelona, by Gaudí. Erik Gunnar Asplund (d. 1940).
Awarded a school prize: work generally highly commended. Sketched Glasgow Cathedral. Drawing from the cast (Plate 2A).	1886	McGibbon and Ross's *Castellated and Domestic Antiquities of Scotland* published. H. H. Richardson died Boston (b. 1838). Miës van der Rohe (d. 1969). Mallet-Stevens born Paris (d. 1945). Auditorium Building, Chicago, Louis H. Sullivan.
Awarded two prizes by the Glasgow Institute of Architects.	1887	*Imperial Institute, South Kensington (completed 1893) by T. E. Collcutt. Le Corbusier (d. 1966). Erich Mendelsohn (d. 1953).
Awarded Bronze Medal at South Kensington and two of the Glasgow Institute's prizes.	1888	First International Exhibition at Glasgow (Plate 66A). The Arts and Crafts Exhibition Society founded and first exhibition held. *Academy Architecture* launched by Alexander Koch. Guild and School of Handicraft founded by C. R. Ashbee. G. T. Rietveld born Utrecht. Sant' Elia born Como (d. 1916).
Mackintosh in Practice. Joined John Honeyman & Keppie. Awarded one of the Queen's Prizes at South Kensington, also several School prizes, a free studentship and the Glasgow Institute's Design Prize. Sketches at Elgin.	1889	George Walton practising as a decorator in Glasgow. Holy Trinity Church, Sloane St., London, by J. D. Sedding. Forth Bridge completed. Eiffel Tower and Halle des Machines (span 373 feet), built for Paris Exhibition. Leiter Building, Chicago, by W. Le B. Jenney, one of the first framed buildings of the 'Chicago School'.

298

CHARLES RENNIE MACKINTOSH AND THE 'FOUR'

GENERAL

First Experimental Designs.

Cabinet and frieze of cats, Dennistoun (Plate 5A).

'A Public Hall'. Awarded Alexander Thomson Scholarship (Fig.1).

'Redclyffe', Mackintosh's first commission (Plate 4).

'A Science and Art Museum' (Plate 2B).

Awarded National Silver Medal, South Kensington.

Glasgow Art Galleries Competition (Plate 19A).

Sketches at Largs, Ayrshire.

1890 New Scotland Yard by Norman Shaw.
Innendekoration first published.
Rousseau, Gauguin painting. Van Gogh died.
Getty Tomb, Chicago, by L. H. Sullivan.
*The Reichstag, Berlin, by Paul Wallot.
Wainwright Building, St. Louis, by L. H. Sullivan.
Reliance Building, Chicago, by Burnham & Root.
J. J. P. Oud born Holland (d. 1936).

Scholarship tour in Italy.

Scottish Baronial Architecture—a paper read to the Glasgow Architectural Association.

The Macdonald sisters first mentioned in the School of Art records.

1891 Glasgow Corporation purchased Whistler's 'Carlyle'.
'A Town Mansion' (Fig. 25) by J. A. Slater.
Project, 'A Studio' (Fig. 26), and Nos. 14 & 16, Hans Road, Chelsea, built by C. F. A. Voysey.
'Avon Tyrrell', Hampshire, by W. R. Lethaby (Plate 87C).
J. D. Sedding died.
Kelmscott Press founded by Wm. Morris.
Beardsley illustrated 'Morte d'Arthur'.
Munich Secession founded.
Gio Ponti born Italy.
Pier Luigi Nervi born Italy.

Soane Medallion Competition, 'A Chapter House' (Fig. 2).

Awarded National Gold Medal, South Kensington.

Italy—a paper read to the Glasgow Architectural Association.

1892 Lorimer practising in Scotland.
*Extension to the Athenaeum, Glasgow, by John Burnet (Plate 18B).
Richard Neutra born Vienna (d. 1970).

L'Art Nouveau in Belgium.

Project for 'A Railway Terminus' (Plate 3).

Architecture—a paper read to the Glasgow Architectural Association.

Tower of *Glasgow Herald* Building designed (?) (Fig. 10).

'Girl in the East Wind' (Plate 6A), by Frances Macdonald.

'The Harvest Moon' by Mackintosh (1892?).

1893 *William Leiper built the Kelly Mansion (Plate 32B).
C. F. A. Voysey built 'Perrycroft', Malvern.
Oscar Wilde's *Salome* published.
The Studio monthly journal launched; work by Beardsley, C. F. A. Voysey and Toorop illustrated.
'The Cry' by Edvard Munch.

299

CHARLES RENNIE MACKINTOSH AND THE 'FOUR'		GENERAL
Canal Boatmen's Institute, Port Dundas (Plate 19B), designed at the office (?). Sketches at Lamlash, Arran.		No. 12, Rue de Turin, Brussels, built by Victor Horta (Plate 91A). Chicago World Fair. Winslow House, Illinois, built by Frank Lloyd Wright. Hans Scharoun born Bremen.
'Conversazione' Programme (Fig. 3). 'Spring' (Plate 7A) and 'Autumn' in the Scrap Books. 'November 5th', by Margaret Macdonald (Plate 60), and 'A Pond', by Frances Macdonald (Plate 7B). Drawing 'The Tree of Influence' (Plate 6B). Queen Margaret's Medical College (Fig. 11). Project for Royal Insurance Building, prepared in the office (Plate 19C). Sketches at Stirling, Wareham and Chipping Campden; flower studies at Langside.	1894	*The Yellow Book* published. *Pathological Building, Glasgow Infirmary, John Burnet (Plate 18C). *Tower Bridge, London, by Barry and Jones. James Pryde and William Nicholson (the Beggarstaff Brothers) exhibited posters in London. Otto Wagner appointed Professor of Architecture, Vienna. Work of British artists exhibited in Vienna. Guarantee Building, Buffalo, by L. H. Sullivan. St. Jean de Montmartre, Paris, by Baudot.
Martyrs' Public School (Plate 20). Interior details at 'Gladsmuir', Kilmacolm, for the Davidsons. Posters and Craftwork (Plates 8 and 9). Sketches at Christchurch, Hampshire, and Oxford. (Herbert MacNair in practice alone.)	1895	C. R. Ashbee's 'Magpie and Stump', Chelsea, built. Charles Hiatt's book *Picture Posters* published. Patrick Geddes' quarterly *Evergreen* appeared. Mary Ward Settlement, designed by Smith and Brewer (Plate 90B). *Westminster Cathedral in the Byzantine style, commenced. J. F. Bentley. Otto Wagner published *Modern Architecture*. Van de Velde built his house at Uccle, Brussels (Plate 91B and C). Richard Buckminster Fuller born. Hotel Solvay, Brussels, by Horta.
The Glasgow Style Emerges. Glasgow School of Art Competition (Fig. 15). Decorations, Buchanan St. Tea-Rooms (Plate 48). Posters, furniture and paintings, etc., exhibited in London.	1896	Death of William Morris. Maison du Peuple, Brussels, by Horta. E. A. Hornel and George Henry, painters, returned to Glasgow from Japan.

CHARLES RENNIE MACKINTOSH AND THE 'FOUR'

Sketches at Worsted.

(Margaret and Frances Macdonald at 128, Hope Street, Glasgow, illustrating William Morris's *Guinevere*, and *The Christmas Story*.)

Glasgow School of Art—building commenced (1897–9).

Queen's Cross Church designed (Plate 70).

Furniture designed for the Argyle St. Tea-Rooms (Plate 49B).

Important articles on the Glasgow Designers published in *The Studio*.

Sketches in East Anglia.

'Spring' and 'Summer': gesso panels by the Macdonald sisters, in the Glasgow Art Galleries Collection ('Autumn' and 'Winter', 1898).

C. R. M., salary £12 per month.

Project for the Glasgow Exhibition, 1901 (Plates 67–8).

First illustrations of furniture in *Dekorative Kunst*.

Ruchill Street Church Halls, Glasgow

Several cabinets for Alexander Seggie of Edinburgh.

Gravestone, Kilmacolm (Plate 71C).

Sketches: Tavistock and Exeter.

(Herbert MacNair appointed Instructor of Design at Liverpool University.)

GENERAL

Paul Gauguin exhibited in Paris.

S. Bing opened his shop 'L'Art Nouveau' in Paris—interiors designed by Van de Velde.

Hermann Muthesius arrived in London.

1897 George Walton moved from Glasgow to London.

Whitechapel Art Gallery built. C. H. Townsend (Plate 90D).

Adolf Loos advocating new principles of design in Vienna.

August Endell designed the Atelier Elvira at Munich.

Exhibition of *art nouveau* furniture in Paris.

Henry van de Velde exhibited furniture at Exhibition of Applied Arts at Dresden.

Vienna Secession founded.

Deutsche Kunst und Dekoration and *Dekorative Kunst* launched in Germany. *Art et Décoration* and *L'Art Décoratif* in France.

1898 Aubrey Beardsley and Sir E. Burne-Jones died.

Baillie Scott designed interiors and furniture for the new Palace at Darmstadt.

Project for a town church. S. A. Greenslade (Plate 90A).

George Walton decorated and furnished 'Lead Cameron', Glasgow (Plate 11B) and began work on the Kodak Showrooms.

August Endell published a treatise on basic building proportions.

Stock Exchange, Amsterdam (1898–1903). H. P. Berlage.

First Exhibition of Applied Art held in Vienna.

The Secession House, Vienna, built by J. M. Olbrich (Plate 93A).

The Secessionists' Journal *Ver Sacrum* first appeared.

Guell Chapel Sta. Coloma (to 1915), by Gaudí.

Tomorrow by Ebenezer Howard, advocating garden cities.

301

CHARLES RENNIE MACKINTOSH AND THE 'FOUR'		GENERAL
Glasgow School of Art—East wing completed.	1899	No. 25, Cadogan Gardens (Plate 87E), by A. H. Mackmurdo.
'Windyhill' designed for William Davidson, Jnr. (Plates 33–5).		Eduardo Torroja born Madrid (d. 1961).
Dining-room cabinets illustrated in *Dekorative Kunst* (Plate 58A).		Talwin Morris died.
Queen's Cross Church completed.		Secessionist Exhibition at Munich: furniture and decorations by Hoffmann and Olbrich.
The Macdonalds move to Dunglass Castle—Mackintosh interior (Plate 11A).		J. M. Olbrich summoned to Darmstadt.
Frances Macdonald and Herbert MacNair married.		*Die Kunst* first published.
C. R. M., salary £16 per month.		Waller House, Chicago, by Frank Lloyd Wright (Plate 15B).
		Carson, Pirie, Scott Store, Chicago, by Louis H. Sullivan.
		E. Maxwell Fry born.
		Garden City Movement founded by Ebenezer Howard.
		Clock Tower, Lindley (Plate 89C), by Edgar Wood.
Mackintosh Exhibits Abroad.		*Emergence of the Viennese School.*
Margaret Macdonald and Charles Mackintosh married.	1900	John Ruskin died.
Decoration and furnishing of 120, Mains St., Glasgow (Plates 12–16).		The Deanery, Sonning, by Sir Edwin Lutyens.
Ingram Street Tea-Rooms decorated.		The Orchard, Chorley Wood (Plate 88C), by C. F. A. Voysey.
Exhibition at the Secession House, Vienna (Plate 59).		J. Cobden Sanderson and Emery Walker founded the Doves Press.
Interiors, Kingsborough Gardens, Glasgow (Plate 17A).		Fricke House, Chicago, by Frank Lloyd Wright (Plate 94B).
Fritz Wärndorfer visits the Mackintoshes at Glasgow (?).		J. M. Olbrich at work on the Künstlerkolonie, Darmstadt.
Decorations, St. Serf's Church, Dysart, Fife (?).		8th Secessionist Exhibition, Vienna.
Interiors at Queen's Place, Glasgow (1901?).		Paris Universal Exhibition.
		Henry van de Velde, appointed Principal, Weimar Academy of Art.
		★Petit Palais, Paris, by Charles Girault.
		Parc Guell, Barcelona (to 1914), by Gaudí.
'Windyhill' completed.	1901	Second International Exhibition at Glasgow (Plate 66B).
Ingram Street Tea-Rooms decorated (Plates 50–2).		'The Leys', Elstree, by George Walton (Plate 88B).
Projects: 'A Town House for an Artist' and 'A Country Cottage for an Artist' (Plates 44–5).		House at Darmstadt, by Peter Behrens (Plate 94A).

CHARLES RENNIE MACKINTOSH AND THE 'FOUR'

GENERAL

Gate Lodge, Auchenbothie, Kilmacolm built.
Menus designed for the Annual Dinner of the R.I.B.A.
Stands at International Exhibition, Glasgow, illustrated in *The Studio*.
Daily Record Office, Glasgow (Plate 69).
Project: Haus Eines Kunstfreundes (Plates 61–3).
Illustrated article in *Die Kunst* furniture exhibited at Dresden and Berlin (?).
Sketches and Flower studies, Holy Island, Northumberland.
Salary £20 per month.

1901 'Cité Industrielle'—first modern town plan with reinforced concrete houses, schools, stations, etc. Tony Garnier.
Pavilion of the Plastic Arts, and Ernst Ludwig House, Darmstadt, by J. M. Olbrich (Plate 93).
Paul Hankar died (b. 1859).
Louis Kahn born Estonia (d. 1974).

Exhibited at Turin (Plate 64B).
Wärndorfer Music Salon, Vienna, (Plate 60).
Liverpool Cathedral project in preparation (Plates 72–3).
'Haus Eines Kunstfreundes' design published.
'Hill House', Helensburgh, designed for W. W. Blackie (Plates 36–42).
A paper entitled *Seemliness*.
Drawings for house at Kilmacolm (unknown) in Glasgow University collection.
Illustrated articles in *Dekorative Kunst* and *Deutsche Kunst und Dekoration*.

1902 Alexandra Park Free Church, by James Salmon.
International Exhibition of Decorative Art, Turin (Plates 64–5).
August Endell designed the Buntes Theatre, Berlin.
Bedroom for Walter Sobotka, Vienna, by Adolf Loos.
Arne Jacobson born Copenhagen.

Liverpool Cathedral project published.
'Hous'hill' alterations and furnishing commenced (Plates 46–7).
The Willow Tea-Rooms designed (Plates 53–7).
Exhibition of furniture, Moscow.

1903 *Liverpool Cathedral Competition won by Giles Gilbert Scott.
J. McNeill Whistler died.
Concrete apartment house, No. 25, Rue Franklin, Paris, by August Perret.
Letchworth Garden City founded. Parker and Unwin.
Wiener Werkstätte founded.
Hermann Muthesius returned to Germany from London.
Frank Lloyd Wright's manifesto *The Art and Craft of the Machine*, Chicago.
Winslow House, River Forest, Frank Lloyd Wright.

John Honeyman retired; Mackintosh became a partner in the firm.

1904 Pürkersdorf Sanatorium, Vienna, by Josef Hoffmann (Plate 92).

CHARLES RENNIE MACKINTOSH AND THE 'FOUR'		GENERAL
Furniture, Holy Trinity Church, Bridge of Allan (Plate 74). Scotland Street School, Glasgow, designed (Plates 75A–6A). The Willow Tea-Rooms opened (October). Sketches and Flower studies at St. Mary's, Scilly Islands.		*Das Englische Haus*, by Hermann Muthesius, published in Germany. Larkin Building, Buffalo, by Frank Lloyd Wright. Émile Gallé died (b. 1846); designer.
Illustrated articles on 'Hill House' and the Willow Tea-Rooms in *Deutsche Kunst und Dekoration* and *Dekorative Kunst*. Fireplace for Miss Rowat, Paisley. Hall furniture (chairs), Windyhill. 'Faded Rose', a flower study—Glasgow Corporation Collection. Painted wall panels for the Wärndorfer Music Salon (1906?). Eulogy on the Mackintoshes by Kalas in *De la Tamise à la Sprée*. Gravestone, East Wemyss, Fife. Sketches at Stopham and Saxlingham, Sussex.	1905	Palais Stoclet, Brussels, by Josef Hoffmann. Postsparkasse, Vienna, by Otto Wagner (Plate 95). Reinforced concreted bridges in Switzerland by Maillart. Miës van der Rohe joined Bruno Paul at Berlin (1905–7). Klimt, von Myrbach, Hoffmann and others left the Secession. Casa Milá, Barcelona, by Gaudí. Casa Battló, Barcelona, by Gaudí (Plate 91D).
Elected Fellow of the R.I.B.A. (3rd December). Charles and Margaret Mackintosh move to No. 78, Southpark Avenue. Glasgow School of Art: West wing redesigned. 'Mosside', Kilmacolm, for H. B. Collins, Esq. (Plate 43C). 'Auchinibert', Killearn, for F. J. Shand, Esq. (Plate 43A). 'The Dutch Kitchen', Argyle Street Tea-Rooms (Plate 49A). 'The Oak Room', Ingram Street Tea-Rooms (Plate 51A). Organ case and pulpit, Abbey Close Church, Paisley. 'Hill House' illustrated in *Academy Architecture*. Sketches on Holy Island, Northumberland.	1906	Lion Chambers, Glasgow, by Salmon and Son: first reinforced concrete building in that city. ★Ardkinglass, Argyle, by Sir Robert Lorimer (Plate 32A). ★War Office, Whitehall, by William Young. ★Central Hall, Westminster, by Lanchester and Rickards. Philip Johnson born U.S.A. Garage Ponthieu, Paris, by Perret. Weimar School of Applied Arts founded and built (1906–14) by Van de Velde. F. R. S. Yorke (d. 1962).
Glasgow School of Art, West Wing, building commenced.	1907	Deutsche Werkbund founded. J. M. Olbrich built the Hochzeitsturm,

CHARLES RENNIE MACKINTOSH AND THE 'FOUR'

GENERAL

'Hill House' illustrated in *Year Book of Decorative Art*.

at Darmstadt.
Walter Gropius joined Peter Behrens.
Oscar Niemeyer born Rio de Janeiro.
Hampstead Garden Suburb, Sir Edwin Lutyens.

1908

Elected Fellow of Royal Incorporation of Architects in Scotland.
Doorway to the Lady Artists' Club, Blythswood Square, Glasgow.
Auchinibert illustrated in *Academy Architecture*.
Sketches at Cintra, Portugal.

The White House, Shiplake, by George Walton (Plate 88D).
J. M. Olbrich died.
Miës van der Rohe joined Peter Behrens.
Frederick Gibberd born.
Gamble House, Pasadena, by C. & H. Greene.
'Upmeads', Stafford, by Edgar Wood (Plate 89A).

1909

C. R. Mackintosh in Decline.
The West wing of the Glasgow School of Art completed.
Exhibited at Kunstschau, Vienna.
'The Four Queens', gesso panels by Margaret Mackintosh for the 'Hous'hill'.
Flower studies at Withyham, Kent.
Sketches of cottages in Sussex.

*Selfridge's Emporium, Oxford Street, London, by Burnham.
Peter Behrens built the A.E.G. Turbine Factory, Berlin (Plate 94C).
Futurist Movement began, Italy.
School, Sagrada Familia, Barcelona, by Gaudí.
Robie House, Chicago, by Frank Lloyd Wright.

1910

Sketches of gravestones, Penshurst, Kent.
Flower studies at Chiddingstone, Kent.

Kodak House, Kingsway, London, by Sir John Burnet (Plate 90E).
*Smith and Brewer designed National Museum of Wales.
Bruno Paul designed first 'unit' furniture.
Adolf Loos built the Steiner House, Vienna (Plate 94D).
The Jahrhunderthalle, Breslau (1910–12), by Max Berg. Reinforced concrete dome, 213 feet diameter.
Christian Science Church, Berkeley, by Bernard Maybeck.
Post-Impressionist exhibition held in London.
Monograph on Frank Lloyd Wright published in Berlin.

1911

'The Cloister Room' and 'The Chinese Room' at Ingram Street (Plate 51 C and B).

Fagus Factory, Berlin, by Walter Gropius (1911–14).

CHARLES RENNIE MACKINTOSH AND THE 'FOUR'

GENERAL

'The White Cockade' Restaurant for Miss Cranston at Glasgow Exhibition.

Lettering of Talwin Morris' Memorial Stone.

Flower studies at Bowling, Dumbartonshire.

Stockholm Town Hall commenced. Ragnar Östberg.

Taliesin I, Wisconsin, by Frank Lloyd Wright.

1912 *London County Hall commenced; Ralph Knott.

Richard Norman Shaw died (b. 1831).

Frank Furness died (b. 1839), Philadelphia.

Centenary Hall, Breslau, by Max Berg.

Exhibited furniture in Moscow (?).

Further alterations at 'Moss-side', Kilmacolm.

Mackintosh left Honeyman & Keppie.

1913 Miës van der Rohe in practice at Berlin.

Kenzo Tange born Japan.

*New Delhi (to 1930) by Sir Edwin Lutyens and Sir Herbert Baker.

The Mackintoshes moved to Walberswick, Suffolk, and took seriously to painting.

(John Honeyman died.)

1914 The Design and Industry Association founded.

Futurists' exhibition 'Città Nuova'.

Exhibition at Cologne. Important contributions by Walter Gropius (Plate 75c), Van de Velde (Plate 91e), Bruno Taut and others.

Taliesin II, Wisconsin, by Frank Lloyd Wright.

*Lincoln Memorial Washington (1914–22) by Henry Bacon.

1914–18, FIRST WORLD WAR

The London Phase.

The Mackintoshes settled in Chelsea.

1915 Philip Webb died (b. 1831).

Anatole Baudot died in Paris (b. 1834).

*Fine Arts Building, San Francisco Exposition, by Maybeck.

No. 78, Derngate for W. J. Bassett-Lowke (Plates 76b and 77).

The 'Dugout', an addition to the 'Willow' Tea-Rooms (1917?).

Fabric designs for Messrs. Foxton and Messrs. Sefton of London.

1916 Smith and Brewer built Heal's Store, London.

Reinforced concrete airship hangars, Orly, France, by Freyssinet.

Imperial Hotel, Tokio, by Frank Lloyd Wright.

Clocks for Mr. Bassett-Lowke (Plate 77).

Decorations and furniture for F. Jones, Esq., Northampton.

1917 Ozenfant and Jeanneret (Le Corbusier) join forces as painters—*Purisme*.

306

CHARLES RENNIE MACKINTOSH AND THE 'FOUR'		GENERAL
Adhesive labels for W. J. Bassett-Lowke, Ltd. (Plate 81c).		'de Stijl' movement launched in Holland (incl. Mondrian, Van Doesburg, Oud). Rodin died (b. 1840).
The 'Peace Panels' (or the 'Little Hills') for Miss Cranston (Plate 81A).	1918	J. J. P. Oud, De Klerk, P. Kramer, W. M. Dudok and others at work in Holland. Many advanced designs in reinforced concrete executed at this time in Western Europe. Otto Wagner died (b. 1841). Gustav Klimt died (b. 1862).
Memorial fireplace for the 'Dugout'. Cottage at East Grinstead for E. O. Hoppé. (William Davidson bought No. 78, Southpark Avenue.)	1919	Walter Gropius succeeded Van de Velde at Weimar, and founded the Bauhaus. Sketches of steel and concrete buildings by Eric Mendelsohn exhibited at Berlin. Citrohan house by Le Corbusier.
Proposed studios in Chelsea (Plate 78). Proposed studio flats for the Arts League of Service (79A). Proposed Theatre for Margaret Morris (79B).	1920	Einstein Tower, Potsdam Observatory, Eric Mendelsohn. Constructivism; First Manifesto.
Book covers designed for W. W. Blackie & Sons.	1921	Paul Klee and Theo van Doesburg joined the Bauhaus. La Cité Moderne, Brussels, built by Victor Bourgeois. Glass Skyscraper project, Berlin, by Miës van der Rohe.
W. J. Bassett-Lowke engaged Peter Behrens to design his house 'New Ways', completed 1925 (Plate 76c).	1922	*Form and Civilization*, by W. R. Lethaby, published in London. Wassily Kandinsky joined the Bauhaus. Le Corbusier began to build. Chicago Tribune Tower Competition, won by Raymond Hood.
The Mackintoshes settled at Port Vendres. Charles Mackintosh devoted himself entirely to painting.	1923	L. Moholy-Nagy joined the Bauhaus. Stockholm City Hall completed, by Ragnar Östberg. Reinforced concrete church at Le Raincy, Paris, by the Perret Brothers. Millard House, Pasadena, Frank Lloyd Wright. Gustav Eiffel died in Paris (b. 1832). *Vers un Architecture* by Le Corbusier published in France.

307

CHARLES RENNIE MACKINTOSH AND THE 'FOUR'		GENERAL
Margaret Mackintosh executed designs for the Queen's Doll's House.	1924	Marcel Breuer joined the Bauhaus. Workers Houses, Hook of Holland, by J. J. P. Oud. Louis Sullivan died (b. 1856, Boston). Quartier Moderne Fruges, Pessac (1924–6), by Le Corbusier.
Paintings exhibited at the 5th International Exhibition, Chicago.	1925	Leonard Stokes died. English edition of Mendelsohn's *Structures and Sketches* published. The Bauhaus moved to Dessau. First tubular steel chairs by Breuer. Goetheanum at Dornach by Rudolf Steiner. 'Der Ring' founded, Berlin. 'New Ways', Northampton, by Behrens (Plate 76c).
	1926	The New Bauhaus built by Gropius, at Dessau. Adelaide House, London, by Burnet, Tait & Lorne. St. Antonius' Church, Basel, by Karl Moser. Antonio Gaudí (b. 1859) died Barcelona.
The Mackintoshes returned to London.	1927	League of Nations Palace Competition. Le Corbusier's *Vers un Architecture* translated into English. Le Corbusier's famous house at Garches built. Weissenhof Siedlung, Stuttgart. Muthesius died (b. 1861). Lovell House, Los Angeles, by Richard Neutra.
Charles Mackintosh died.	1928	C. H. Townsend died. English translation of Le Corbusier's *Urbanisme*. Shakespeare Memorial Theatre, Stratford, by Scott, Chesterton & Shepherd. Foundation of CIAM. Van Nelle Factory, Rotterdam, by Brinkman and Van de Vlucht. Hilversum Town Hall by Dudok. Steel Church, Cologne, Otto Bartning. Jan Toorop died (b. 1858); painter.

CHARLES RENNIE MACKINTOSH AND THE 'FOUR'		GENERAL
Margaret Mackintosh returned to Chelsea.	1929	Salvation Army Hostel, Paris, by Le Corbusier.
		Great Siemensstadt Housing project, Berlin, by Gropius.
		Modern Architecture, by Bruno Taut, published.
		Barcelona Exposition, remarkable German pavilion, by Miës van der Rohe.
	1930	Tugendhat House, Brno, by Miës van der Rohe (Plate 47A).
		Sports Stadium, Florence, by Nervi.
	1931	*Daily Express* Building, Fleet Street, London, by Sir E. Owen Williams.
		Swiss Pavilion, University City, Paris, by Le Corbusier.
	1932	Messrs. Boots Factory, Beeston, by Sir E. Owen Williams.
		Paimio Sanatorium, Finland, by Alvar Aalto.
Margaret Macdonald died.	1933	Adolf Loos died.
Memorial Exhibition to the Mackintoshes held in Glasgow.		George Walton died.
		House at Platt, Kent, by Colin Lucas (Plate 44D).
		Highpoint Flats, and Penguin Pool, London Zoo, by Tecton.
		The advent of Nazism in Germany.
		Louis Comfort Tiffany died (b. 1848); designer.

In 1933–4 the modern movement was firmly established in Britain. It gained considerable impetus thereafter from the work of several distinguished European refugees who practised in England for a few years before settling in America—notably Walter Gropius, Marcel Breuer and Eric Mendelsohn. Among the most influential English architects of the day were Serge Chermayeff; Messrs. Connell, Ward and Lucas; E. Maxwell Fry; Frederick Gibberd; Raymond McGrath; Christopher Nicholson; 'Tecton'; F. R. S. Yorke; and Wells Coates, a Canadian domiciled in England; there were no comparable figures in Scotland at this time.

BIBLIOGRAPHY

PART ONE **The most important references to Mackintosh's mature work, arranged in chronological order. The interesting grouping of publications should be noted.**

1896. *The Studio*, vol. X, pp. 203–5. Arts and Crafts Exhibition, London. Two pictures and favourable comment in the text. (Paintings by the Macdonald Sisters and Herbert MacNair were illustrated in *The Yellow Book*, vol. X, July, 1896.)

1897. *The Studio*, vol. XI, pp. 86 et seq., 226 et seq. Well-illustrated articles, 'Some Glasgow Designers and their Work'. Gleeson White.

1898. *Dekorative Kunst*. November. Bruckmann, Munich. An article 'Scottish Artists', author anonymous.

1899. *Dekorative Kunst*. May. Several pictures of furniture.

1900. *The Studio*, vol. XIX, pp. 48 et seq. The Glasgow School of Art. Four indifferent pictures of the interior. No reference to Mackintosh in the text.

1900 *Ver Sacrum*, vols. III and IV, Vienna. A review of work at the Eighth Secessionist
& Exhibition, including the Scottish Section.
1901.

1901. *Die Kunst*. February. Bruckmann, Munich. 'Die VIII Ausstellung der Wiener Secession.' Excellent illustrations of the Scottish Section.

1901. *Modern British Domestic Architecture*. Special Summer Number of *The Studio*, pp. 110 et seq. Five good pictures of the Mains Street flat. No reference in the text.

1902. *Arte Italiana Decorativa ed Industriale*, vol. XI, pp. 61–8 and plates 45–6. The Scottish Section at Turin.

1902. *Meister der Innenkunst*. Koch, Darmstadt. Folio of drawings. Haus eines Kunst-freundes Competition. Long preface by Hermann Muthesius.

1902. *The Studio*, vol. XXVI, pp. 91 et seq. Turin Exhibition. Well illustrated article on the Scottish Section.

1902. *Deutsche Kunst und Dekoration*. September. Koch, Darmstadt. 'Mackintosh und die Schule von Glasgow in Turin.' George Fuchs. Excellent pictures of the Scottish Section. (A well-illustrated article on Margaret Macdonald's work was published in this journal in May, 1902.)

1902. *Dekorative Kunst*. March. 'Die Glasgower Kunstbewegung.' Hermann Muthesius. Many excellent pictures of *Windyhill* and of projects not published elsewhere.

1903. *Das Englische Haus*. Hermann Muthesius. Vols. I and III. A monumental work widely used by architects. Many references to Mackintosh. Appreciation, good illustrations.

1903. *Mir Iskusstva*, No. 3, p. 117. Illustration of exhibition stand at Moscow.

1903. *The British Architect*. 13th March. Liverpool Cathedral project drawings.

1905. *Deutsche Kunst und Dekoration*. March. 'The Hill House', Helensburgh. Fernando Agnoletti. Article and thirty-five superb illustrations.

1905. *Dekorative Kunst*. April. 'A Mackintosh Tea-Room in Glasgow' (the *Willow*). Another beautifully illustrated article. Author anonymous.

1905. *De la Tamise à la Sprée*, Michaud, Rheims. 'The Art of Glasgow.' E. B. Kalas. A short paper on the Mackintoshes. (A translation was published in the Mackintosh Memorial Exhibition Catalogue, 1933.)

1906. *The Studio*, vol. XXXIX, pp. 32 et seq. 'Modern Decorative Art in Glasgow.' J. Taylor. An article and seven pictures of the Argyle Street Tea-Rooms.

1906. *Academy Architecture*. Scotland Street School, perspective drawing and plans; pictures and plans of Hill House.

1906. *The Builder's Journal and Architectural Engineer*. 28th November, pp. 267–9. Façade of the *Willow*. Photographs and plans of Scotland Street School.

1907. *Studio Year Book of Decorative Art*, pp. 32–3. Hill House, three pictures. Interiors of Hous'hill, five pictures.

1910. *A Creel of Peat—Stray Papers*. Adelphi Press. Desmond Chapman-Huston. Contains a short essay on the Mackintoshes. Not illustrated.

1917. *The Year Book of Decorative Art*, p. 79 and pp. 122–3. Gesso panels and fabric designs. (1920. *The Ideal Home* September. Long article on No. 78 Derngate, Northampton. Well illustrated. No reference to Mackintosh.)

1928. (Mackintosh died: obituary notices appeared in *The Times* and in the Scottish press.)

1929. *Modern Architecture*. Bruno Taut. Pub. *The Studio*. Four good illustrations, short reference in the text.

1930. *Artwork*, vol. VI, No. 21. Spring. 'Charles Rennie Mackintosh, his Life and Work.' Desmond Chapman-Huston. The first attempt at a biographical appreciation, and the source used by most subsequent writers—but contains many factual errors.

1933. Alan Glen's School Magazine, Midsummer Number, pp. 18–19. An appreciation.

1933. *The Studio*, vol. CV, pp. 344–52. 'Charles Rennie Mackintosh—a Neglected Genius.' E. A. Taylor. (Well illustrated.)

1933. *The Quarterly Illustrated*. Journal of the Royal Incorporation of Architects in Scotland. Spring. No. 42, pp. 11–14. 'Charles Rennie Mackintosh.' J. J. Waddell.

1933. *The Listener*, vol. X, pp. 98–100. 'Charles Rennie Mackintosh.' Alan D. Mainds, Professor of Fine Art, Durham University.

1933. *The Builder*. July 7th. 'Charles Rennie Mackintosh'—by Campbell Mackie.
The five preceding articles, with innumerable shorter appreciations in the press, were inspired by W. R. Davidson and J. J. Waddell, sponsors of the Mackintosh Memorial Exhibition held at Glasgow in 1933. A catalogue of the Exhibition was published.

1934. *Twentieth Century Houses*, pp. 77–9, etc. Raymond McGrath. A short biography and two illustrations.

1935. *Architectural Review*, vol. LXXVII. 'The Glasgow Interlude.' P. Morton Shand. A protest against the extravagant claims made by some of Mackintosh's admirers.

1936. *Pioneers of the Modern Movement*. Nikolaus Pevsner—an excellent appraisal of Mackintosh's contribution.

1939. *Country Life*. 'Charles Rennie Mackintosh (1867–1933)' (*sic*). Nikolaus Pevsner. A short illustrated article.

1945. *Transactions of the Scottish Ecclesiological Society*, 1945. 'Queens Cross Church.' T. Howarth. Illustrated.

1945. *The Glasgow Herald:* An article on the Mackintoshes. T. Howarth.

1946. *Journal of the R.I.B.A.*, vol. LIII. 'A Mackintosh House in Glasgow.' T. Howarth. Illustrated.

1946. *Architectural Review*, vol. C. 'Some Mackintosh Furniture Preserved.' T. Howarth. Illustrated.

1948. *The Magazine of Art*, vol. XLI. Pub. Museum of Modern Art, U.S.A. 'Mackintosh and the Scottish Tradition.' T. Howarth. Illustrated.

1950. *Journal of the R.I.B.A.*, vol. LVIII, No. 1. 'C. R. Mackintosh, Architect and Designer.' T. Howarth. The edited manuscript of a talk broadcast in the Third Programme of the B.B.C. Illustrated.

1950. Monograph in Italian in the series 'Architetti del Movimento Moderno'. Il Balcone, Milan. 'C. R. Mackintosh', by Professor Nikolaus Pevsner.

PART TWO Books of general reference, journals and periodicals.

Behrendt, W. C.	*Modern Building*, 1937.
Billings, R. W.	*Baronial and Ecclesiastical Antiquities of Scotland*, 1845–52.
Blomfield, Sir Reginald.	*Modernismus.*
	The Work of Ernest Newton, 1925.
	Richard Norman Shaw, 1940.
Boardman, Philip.	*Patrick Geddes*, 1944.
Briggs R. A.	*Homes for the Country*, 1904.
Burdett, Osbert.	*The Beardsley Period*, 1925.
Casson, Hugh.	*An Introduction to Victorian Architecture*, 1948.
Casteels, Maurice.	*The New Style* (translated from the French by Maurice Casteels), 1931.
Chapman-Huston, D.	*The Lamp of Memory*, 1949.
Clark, Sir Kenneth.	*The Gothic Revival*, 1928.
Cobden-Sanderson, T. J.	*The Arts and Crafts*, 1905.
Elder, Eleanor.	*The Travelling Players*, 1939.

Fergusson, J. D.   *Modern Scottish Painting*, 1943.
Fletcher, B. & H. P.   *The English House*, 1910.
Gaunt, William.   *The Pre-Raphaelite Tragedy*, 1942.
                                       The Aesthetic Adventure, 1945.
Giedion, Sigfried.   *Space, Time and Architecture*, 1941.
Gimson, E.   *Ernest Gimson, His Life and Work*, 1924.
Goodhart-Rendel, H. S.   *How Architecture is Made*, 1947.
Gropius, Walter.   *The New Architecture and The Bauhaus*, 1935.
Hannah, Ian C.   *The Story of Scotland in Stone*, 1934.
Harbron, Dudley.   *Amphion*, 1930.
Hevesi, Ludwig von.   *Österreichische Kunst Des 19. Jahrhunderts*, 1903.
Hiatt, Charles.   *Picture Posters*, 1895.
Hudson, Derek.   *James Pryde (1866–1941)*, 1949.
Hurd, Robert & Alan Reiach.   *Building Scotland*, 1944.
Jackson, Holbrook.   *The Eighteen Nineties*, 1927 (2nd edit.).
                                       William Morris, 1926.
                                       William Morris and the Arts and Crafts, 1934.
Kalas, E. B.   *De la Tamise à la Sprée*, 1905.
Koch, Alexander.   *Handbuch Neuzeitlicher Wohnlungskultur*, 1914.
Kotéra, Jan.   *Práce mé a mych žánku, 1898–1901*, 1901.
Kulka, Heinrich.   *Adolf Loos*, 1931.
Lethaby, W. R.   *Philip Webb and His Work*, 1935.
Lux, A. J.   *Otto Wagner*, 1914.
MacKail, J. W.   *The Life of William Morris*, 1899.
Martin, David.   *The Glasgow School of Painters*, 1897.
Maxwell, Sir John Stirling.   *Shrines and Homes of Scotland*, 1938.
McGrath, Raymond.   *Twentieth Century Houses*, 1934.
McGibbon & Ross.   *Castellated and Domestic Architecture of Scotland*, 5 Vols. 1887–92.
                                       The Ecclesiastical Architecture of Scotland, 3 Vols. 1896–7.
Morris, May.   *Collected Works of William Morris*, 24 Vols. 1910–15.
Muir, James Hamilton.   *Glasgow in 1901*.
Munro, Neil.   *Erchie, circa* 1910.
Muthesius, Anna.   *Das Eigenkleid der Frau, circa* 1906.
Muthesius, Hermann.   *Das Englische Haus*, 1904–05.
                                       Die Englische Baukunst der Gegenwart, 1900.
                                       Das Moderne Landhaus, 1905.
                                       Die Neuere Kirchliche Baukunst, 1901.
                                       Haus Eines Kunstfreundes, 1902.
Nichol, James (editor).   *Domestic Architecture in Scotland*, 1908.
Osthaus, Karl Ernst.   *Van de Velde*, 1920.
                                       Die Neue Bankunst, 1920.
Pennell, E. P. & J.   *The Life of James (Abbott) McNeill Whistler*, 1911.
Pevsner, Nikolaus.   *Pioneers of the Modern Movement*, 1936.
Platz, G. A.   *Die Baukunst der Neuester Zeit*.
Richardson, A. E.   *Monumental Classic Architecture in Great Britain and Ireland during the 18th and 19th Centuries*, 1914.
Ross, Robert.   *Aubrey Beardsley*, 1909.

Rossetti, D. G.   *The House of Life* and other works.
Roth, Alfred.   *The Reality of the New Architecture*, 1940.
Ruskin, John.   *Lectures in Architecture and Painting*, 1853.
    Seven Lamps of Architecture, etc. 1849.
    The Two Paths, 1859.
Scott, Sir George Gilbert.   *Personal and Professional Recollections*, 1879.
Scott, H. Baillie.   *Houses and Gardens*, 1906.
Scott-Moncrieff, George (editor).   *The Stones of Scotland*, 1938.
Sharp, William & E. A.   *Progress of Art in the Century*, 1906.
Sparrow, W. Shaw.   *The Modern Home*, 1906.
    Our Homes and How to Make the Best of Them, 1909.
Symons, Arthur.   *Aubrey Beardsley*, 1905.
Tallmadge, T. E.   *The Story of Architecture in America*, 1928.
Taut, Bruno.   *Modern Architecture*, 1929.
Taylor, Charles.   *The Levern Delineated*, 1831.
Tranter, N. G.   *The Fortalices and Early Mansions of Southern Scotland*, 1934.
Van de Velde, Henry.   *Die Renaissance im Modernen Kunstgewerbe*, 1910.
Voysey, C. F. A.   *Individuality*, 1915.
Veronesi, Giulia.   *J. M. Olbrich*, 1948.
Weaver, Sir Lawrence.   *Houses and Gardens by Sir Edwin Lutyens*, 1921.
Weiser, Dr. Armand.   *Josef Hoffmann*, 1930.
Wilenski, R. H.   *The Modern Movement in Art*, 1935.
Willmott, Ernest.   *English House Design*, 1911.
Wirth, Dr. Zdenek.   *Josef Gočár*, 1930.

PERIODICALS

Academy Architecture.
The Architect.
The Architects' Journal.
The Architectural Record.
The Architectural Review.
Artwork.
The Art Journal.
Art et Décoration.
L'Art Décoratif.

The British Architect.
The Builder.
The Builders' Journal and Architectural Engineer.
The Building News.

Country Life.
The Craftsman.

Dekorative Kunst.
Der Architekt.

Deutsche Kunst und Dekoration.
Die Kunst.

Innendekoration.

The Journal of the R.I.B.A.
The Journal of Decorative Art and The British Decorator.

Kunst und Handwerke.

The Listener.

Magyar Iparmuveszet.
The Magazine of Art.

The Quarterly. The Journal of the Royal Incorporation of Architects in Scotland.

Revue du Vrai et du Beau.

BIBLIOGRAPHY

The Scottish Field.	*The Transactions of the Scottish Ecclesio-*
The Studio.	*logical Society.*
The Studio Year Books.	*Ver Sacrum.*

COLLECTED PAPERS, ETC.

'Arts and Crafts Essays.' — By members of the Arts and Crafts Exhibition Society, 1893.

'Art and Life and the Building and Decoration of Cities.' — Lectures by members of the Arts and Crafts Exhibition Society—W. R. Lethaby and others.

'The Art Revival in Austria.' — *The Studio*, 1906.

'The British Home of Today.' — Edited by W. Shaw Sparrow, 1904.

'A Creel of Peat', Essays. — Desmond Chapman-Huston, 1910.

'Ein Skizzen, Projekte und Ausgefuhrte Bauwerke von Otto Wagner.' — Vienna, 1906.

'Evergreen.' — An illustrated quarterly. Edited by Patrick Geddes, 1896.

'Glasgow Contemporaries.' — Biographical Notes about local celebrities, *circa* 1902.

'Glasgow Who's Who.' — Pub. *circa* 1910.

'Modern British Architecture and Decoration.' — *The Studio*, 1901.

'Der Moderne Stil.' — Folio, published Stuttgart.

'Our Homes and How to Beautify Them.' — Sponsored by Messrs. Waring & Gillow, 1902.

'Recent English Domestic Architecture.' — Pub. *Architectural Review*, 1908.

'Scotland.' — Robert Hurd, Sir Stanley Cursitor and others, 1947.

'Wagnerschule—Projekte, Studien und Skizzen aus der spezialschule für architecktur des oberbaurat Otto Wagner.' — Leipzig, 1910.

'The Yellow Book.' — An illustrated quarterly, 1894, et seq.

'Bauten der Arbett und des Verkehrs aus Deutscher Gegenwart.' — Pub. Leipzig, *circa* 1929 et seq.

PART THREE Selected books, brochures and articles specifically on Mackintosh, or some aspect of his work.

Alison, Filippo, *Charles Rennie Mackintosh as a Designer of Chairs.* A Catalogue-Brochure, 'documenti di Casabella', Milan and Warehouse Publications, London, 1974. 106 pp. Excellent illustrations. Introduction, McLaren Young, 'Mackintosh and Italy'; a well-documented essay on Mackintosh's scholarship tour of 1891. Text in English by Filippo Alison. This publication served as a catalogue for the exhibition of reproductions of Mackintosh furniture that has had wide circulation in Italy and the U.S.A. in 1974–6.

Barnes, H. Jefferson, *Charles Rennie Mackintosh:* Furniture, 35 pp.; Ironwork and Mackintosh, 38 pp. Brochures describing selected examples in the Glasgow School of Art Collection; splendidly illustrated with photographs and measured drawings. Glasgow School of Art, 1964. In the same series *Charles Rennie Mackintosh and the Glasgow School of Art.*

316

Doak, Archibald M. (Ed.), *Architectural Jottings by Charles Rennie Mackintosh*. Selected by Andrew McLaren Young. Published by the Glasgow Institute of Architects in 1968 marking not only the centenary of Mackintosh's birth, but the centenary of the founding of the Institute. 32 pp.

MacLeod, Robert, *Charles Rennie Mackintosh*, Hamlyn, 1968. 160 pp. This very useful book was published just before the Mackintosh Centennial Exhibition of 1968. It contains many excellent photographs that admirably complement those in our present volume. The author's main contribution lies in the field of contemporary architectural theory; he extends our knowledge of Mackintosh's British sources and, through a careful examination of the architect's lecture notes, compares his philosophy to that of Pugin, Ruskin, Lethaby and others.

The Architectural Review, vol. 144 (November 1968), pp. 355 et seq. 'Charles Rennie Mackintosh', a well-illustrated paper on Mackintosh's British sources by David Walker. Reprinted in *The Anti-Rationalists* (Richards and Pevsner, Eds).

The Connoisseur, vol. 183, No. 738 (August 1973), pp. 280–8. 'Remembering Charles Rennie Mackintosh', a recorded interview with Mary Newbery Sturrock: by June Bedford and Ivor Davies.

Newsletter of the Charles Rennie Mackintosh Society. 1307 Argyle Street, Glasgow G.3. Published quarterly and devoted to many aspects of the architect's work, and current events relating to the Glasgow designers and their contemporaries.

The Scottish Art Review, Special Number, vol. XI, No. 4 (1968) to mark the centennial of Mackintosh's birth, Glasgow Art Gallery and Museum's Association. 21 pp. This issue contains the text by Mackintosh explaining his curious water-colour drawing of 1894, 'Cabbages in an Orchard'. 'Memories' of the architect are provided by Hamish R. Davidson, whose father commissioned 'Windyhill', and by Walter W. Blackie for whom Mackintosh designed 'Hill House'. There is a translation of Hermann Muthesius' observations of 1904 on the Glasgow Style introduced by Eithne O'Neill and a short essay 'Odd Man Out' by Henry Hellier. Mr. Hellier says that in 1909, the date of the completion of the Glasgow School of Art, Francis H. Newbery exhibited at the Glasgow Fine Art Institute his well-known portrait group of the Building Committee of the Board of Governors of the School. It did not include Mackintosh. However, he painted later a large portrait of the architect that was exhibited in February 1914. Newbery offered his portrait group to the Board and it was accepted. When the unveiling ceremony took place on 18 May 1914 it was seen that Mackintosh's figure had been added to the left of the group—a smaller version of the large portrait—and the whole canvas redated 1914. Newbery thus ensured that his protégé should be given his rightful place alongside those who bore the responsibility for implementing his design. The addition was not discovered until the picture was cleaned and re-lined by Mr. Harry MacLean in 1963.

L'architettura, vol. 13, May and July 1967. pp. 60–4; 130–4; 200–4; 270–4. 'La Mano di Mackintosh', a four-part appraisal by Luciano Rubino with excellent illustrations.

Casabella, No. 376 (1973), pp. 17–26. 'C. R. Mackintosh'. Filippo Alison with notes by Giovanni K. Konig. Text in Italian and English. A rather esoteric paper on Mackintosh's work with especial reference to his furniture of which Alison has obtained meticulous measured drawings. Also Nos 380–381, 1973. pp. 33–42. 'A Critical Survey of Mackintosh's Works'. Filippo Alison. Text in Italian and English. Important for its excellent drawings of the Glasgow School of Art library. Alison gives credit for the 'Geometrical surveys' (measured drawings?) in Glasgow to Vicenzo Forino and for the graphic presentation to Luigi Falanga.

317

BIBLIOGRAPHY

PART FOUR   Major exhibitions of Mackintosh's work and catalogues.

Charles Rennie Mackintosh 1868–1928. Saltire Society, The Royal Mile, Edinburgh, 1953. An exhibition sponsored by the Saltire Society and the Arts Council of Great Britain for the Edinburgh Festival. This was the first comprehensive exhibition of Mackintosh's work since the 'Memorial Exhibition' staged in Glasgow after the death of Margaret Macdonald Mackintosh in 1933. This exhibition was shown subsequently in Newcastle upon Tyne, Manchester; Liverpool, Bristol, London, and finally in Glasgow. Catalogue and text by Thomas Howarth.

Charles Rennie Mackintosh 1868–1928: Architecture, Design and Painting. Royal Scottish Museum, Chambers Street, Edinburgh, 17 August to 8 September 1968. An exhibition sponsored by the Edinburgh Festival Society and arranged by the Scottish Arts Council. This superb exhibition was shown also at the Victoria and Albert Museum, London. Selected exhibits were sent to Darmstadt and to Vienna in 1969. Catalogue and text by Andrew McLaren Young: excellent illustrations.

Charles Rennie Mackintosh 1868–1928. Hessischen Landesmuseum in Darmstadt. 27 February to 4 May 1969. Sponsored by the British Council. Exhibits selected from Edinburgh Festival Exhibition of 1968. Catalogue 134 pp.: well illustrated. Introductory articles in English (McLaren Young) and German. Text in German.

Charles Rennie Mackintosh. Museum des 20. Jahrhunderts, Schweizergarten, Wien III. 7 June to 20 July 1969. This exhibition was transferred to Vienna from Darmstadt—see above. Catalogue 52 pp.: well illustrated. Text in German. Foreword by Werner Hofmann. Introduction by McLaren Young; important contribution by Eduard Sekler. 'Mackintosh und Wien'.

Furniture, *objets d'art*, paintings and drawings by the Mackintoshes have been shown individually, or in small groups, at innumerable exhibitions in Europe and the U.S.A. Items from my personal collection for example have been to cities as widely separated as Zürich, London and Toronto, and, of course, to many places in the U.S.A. including Frank Lloyd Wright's Taliesin East, Wisconsin. The advent of commercially reproduced pieces, however beautifully made, does not seem to detract from the public's desire to see the original work which, in any case, is of particular interest to the specialist.

PART FIVE   Miscellaneous, including films.

There are two films on Mackintosh. The first of these, which I prefer in spite of a rather rough soundtrack, was produced in 1965. The second was made at the time of the Centennial Exhibition, Edinburgh in 1968:

Charles Rennie Mackintosh, 18 minutes: colour. Educational Films of Scotland, 1965.

Mackintosh, 30 minutes: colour. International Film Association, Scotland, 1968.

Among the more curious by-products of the new enthusiasm for Mackintosh are the following:

1. *Paisley Rocketeers' Society*. To mark the exact centenary of Mackintosh's birth 28 December 1968 the Paisley Rocketeers' Society launched a rocket from the garden of Hill House.

   One hundred special first issue covers were printed with simulated postage stamps depicting a future rocket mail service. The envelopes were overprinted 'Charles Rennie Mackintosh Centenary 1868–1928' and carried the legend 'Aquajet 17, Shot A, 28 Dec. 1968': also a normal 4 pence stamp! I am indebted to Mr. John D. Stewart of the Paisley Society for information about this fascinating event, and for a first issue envelope.

318

2. *Charles Rennie Mackintosh Society*. The Autumn 1975 Newsletter of the Society advertises, of all things, Mackintosh T-shirts 'proudly bearing our symbol on the front in black with CRM lettered across the top—ridiculous but gorgeous!!' This Society, however, the most successful of several attempts over the past thirty years to launch such a group, is very active indeed, produces a lively newsletter, and deserves encouragement.

3. Mackintosh Christmas cards and Mackintosh posters have been commercially produced for some years. And now we have Italian-made reproductions of Mackintosh furniture! It is rather sad that these were not made of British material by British craftsmen working in Scotland.

PART SIX   A selection of publications relevant to the subject in most of which reference is made to Mackintosh's contribution.

Abbate, Francesco (Ed.), *Art Nouveau: The Style of the 1890's*, London, New York, Octopus Books, 1972. 158 pp.

Amaya, Mario, *Art Nouveau*, London, Studio Vista, 1968. 168 pp.

Archer, J. H. G., *Edgar Wood (1860–1935) A Manchester 'Art Nouveau' Architect*, reprinted from the *Transactions of the Lancashire and Cheshire Antiquarian Society*, vols. 73–74, 1963–4, Manchester, 1966. pp. 153–87.

Aslin, Elizabeth, *The Aesthetic Movement: Prelude to Art Nouveau*, London, Elek, 1969. 192 pp.

Banham, Reyner, *Age of the Masters*, London, Architectural Press, 1975. 170 pp.

Barilli, Renato, *Art Nouveau*, London, New York, Hamlyn, 1969. 157 pp.

Bing, Samuel, *Artistic America, Tiffany Glass and Art Nouveau*, Cambridge, Mass., M.I.T. Press, 1970. 260 pp.

Borsi, Franco and Portoghesi, Paolo, *Victor Horta*, Brussels, M. Vokaer, 1970. 413 pp.

Brooks, H. A., *The Prairie School*, Toronto, 1973.

Citroen, K. A., *Jugendstil*, Darmstadt, Hessisches Landesmuseum, 1962. 181 pp.

Clark, Robert Judson (Ed.), *The Arts and Crafts Movement in America 1876–1916*, Princeton, 1972. 190 pp.

Cremona, Italo, *Il Tempo dell'Art Nouveau: Modern Style, Sezession, Jugendstil, Arts and Crafts, Floreale, Liberty*, Florence, Valecchi, 1964. 230 pp.

Descharnes, R. and Prévost, C., *Gaudi the Visionary*, London, 1971. 247 pp.

Funk, Anna-Christa, *Art Nouveau in England und Schottland*, Hagen, Druck, Westruck, 1968. 52 pp.

Gebhard, David, *Charles F. A. Voysey*, Santa Barbara, 1970. 75 pp.

Geretsegger, Heinz, *Otto Wagner, 1841–1918: the Expanding City*, New York, Praeger, 1970. 276 pp.

Gillon, Edmund Vincent, *Art Nouveau: An Anthology of Design and Illustration from the Studio*, New York, Dover, 1969. 89 pp.

Gomme, Andor and Walker, David, *Architecture of Glasgow*, London, 1968. 320 pp.

Hammacher, A. M., *Le Monde de Henry van de Velde*, Paris, Hachette, 1967. 352 pp.

Hitchcock, Henry-Russell, *Architecture: Nineteenth and Twentieth Centuries*, Baltimore, 1958. 498 pp.

Hüter, Karl-Heinz, *Henry van de Velde: Sein Werke bis zum Ende seiner Tätigkeit in Deutschland*, Berlin, Akademic-Verlage, 1967. 286 pp.

Jullian, Philippe, *The Triumph of Art Nouveau: Paris Exhibition, 1900*, London, Phaidon, 1974. 216 pp.

BIBLIOGRAPHY

Kornwolf, James D., *M. H. Baillie-Scott and the Arts and Crafts Movement*, Baltimore and London, Johns Hopkins Press, 1972. 588 pp.

Madsen, Stephen Tschudi, *Art Nouveau*, London, Weidenfeld and Nicolson, 1967. 256 pp.

Pevsner, Nikolaus, *Sources of Modern Architecture and Design*, New York, Praeger, 1968. 216 pp.

Rheims, Maurice, *Flowering of Art Nouveau*, New York, Abrams, 1966. 450 pp.

Richards, J. M. and Pevsner, Nikolaus (Eds), *The Anti-Rationalists*, London, Architectural Press, 1973. 141 pp.

Schmutzler, Robert, *Art Nouveau*, New York, Abrams, 1962. (English edition of *Art Nouveau-Jugendstil*, Stuttgart, 1962. 322 pp.)

Schneck, Adolf Gustav, *Neue Möbel von Jugendstil bis Heute*, München, Bruckmann, 1962. 159 pp.

Scully, Vincent J., *The Shingle Style*, New Haven and London, 1955. 181 pp.

Seling, Helmut (Ed.), *Jugendstil*, Heidelberg, Keyser, 1959. 459 pp.

Selz, Peter and Constantine, Mildred (Eds), *Art Nouveau: Art and Design at the Turn of the Century*, New York, Museum of Modern Art, 1960. 192 pp.

Service, Alastair (Ed.), *Edwardian Architecture and its Origins*, London, Architectural Press, 1975. 504 pp.

Taylor, John Russell, *The Art Nouveau Book in Britain*, London, Methuen, 1966. 176 pp.

Waissenberger, Robert, *Die Wiener Sezession. Eine Dokumentation*, Vienna, Jugend and Volk, 1971. 295 pp.

Wittkower, R. (Ed.), *Studies in Western Art: Problems of the Nineteenth and Twentieth Centuries*, Princeton, 1963. 80 pp.

ACKNOWLEDGMENTS

Many people have shown an interest in this work and the author acknowledges his indebtedness to each of the following who in some specific way helped in its preparation:

Mr. Alexander Adam.
Mr. Henry Y. Allison.
Rev. John Anderson.
Mr. J. Craig Annan.
Mr. Thomas C. Annan.
Mr. & Mrs. H. Jefferson Barnes.
Mr. W. J. Bassett-Lowke.
Mr. & Mrs. W. W. Blackie.
Mr. Douglas Percy Bliss.
Major Desmond Chapman-Huston.
Mr. Hamish R. Davidson.
Mr. P. Wylie Davidson.
Dr. W. Cameron Davidson.
Mr. J. D. Fergusson.
Mr. J. A. Harris.
Rev. George S. Hendry.
Mr. Herbert L. Honeyman.
Dr. T. J. Honeyman.
Mr. E. O. Hoppé.
Mr. Robert Hurd.

Dr. & Mrs. Jubb.
Sir Frank & Lady Mears.
Mr. James Meldrum.
Mr. William Moyes.
Mr. & Mrs. Francis H. Newbery.
Mr. Alexander Orr.
Sir John Richmond.
Sir William Robieson.
Professor & Mrs. Randolph Schwabe.
Dr. Eduard F. Sekler.
Mr. Alexander Smellie.
Mr. Herbert Smith.
Mr. W. Morrison Smith.
Mr. Harold Squire.
Mr. Macaulay Stevenson.
Mr. E. A. Taylor.
Mr. Allan Ure.
Mr. Cowles Voysey.
Mr. Alan Walton.
Professor & Mrs. John Walton.

321

ACKNOWLEDGMENTS

Mr. William Ward.
Miss Helen L. Bell.
Miss Elizabeth Brown.
Miss De C. L. Dewar.
Mrs. Dunderdale.
Miss Lucy Johnstone.
Mrs. Catherine Cameron Kay.
Miss Jessie Keppie.
Miss Knox-Arthur.
Mrs. Elsie Lang.
Miss Ann Macbeth.
Mrs. Charles Macdonald.
Miss Mary McKechnie.
Mrs. K. McNeil.
Miss J. B. Mavor.
Mrs. Gordon Miller.
Miss Margaret Morris.
Mrs. Talwin Morris.

Miss Agnes Raeburn.
Mrs. Lucy S. Ritchie.
Mrs. Jessie M. King-Taylor.
Miss J. J. Waddell.
Mrs. Fritz Wärndorfer.

M. le Corbusier.
Mr. W. M. Dudok.
Mr. Charles Greene.
Professor Walter Gropius.
Professor Josef Hoffmann.
Mr. Bernard Maybeck.
Mr. Eric Mendelsohn.
Mr. Ludwig Miës van der Rohe.
Mr. Auguste Perret.
Mr. Henry van de Velde.
Mr. Frank Lloyd Wright.

ILLUSTRATIONS

Many of the pictures are taken from the author's collection. For permission to reproduce photographs or to copy published illustrations thanks are due to:

Academy Architecture, 10A, 11B, 18B and C, 19C, 20A, 32B, 70A, 75A and B, 90A and C. Figs. 11, 12 and 18.

T. & R. Annan & Sons, Ltd., 14A, 15A, 21, 25, 33, 34A, 35, 42A, 46, 47B, 48, 49, 50C, 53, 56C, 66, 67A, 71C, 86.

Mr. H. Jefferson Barnes, 78, 79A.

Mr. W. J. Bassett-Lowke, 76B and C, 77.

Messrs. B. T. Batsford, Ltd., 87A and D.

Messrs. Bedford-Lemere & Co., Ltd., 30, 31.

Mr. John Brandon-Jones, 87B and C, 88A.

Messrs. F. Bruckmann, Verlag, Munich, 17A, 34B and C, 58, 59, 64.

The Builder, 3, 19A and B, 70B. Figs. 1, 2, 25, 26.

Country Life, 32A, 89A.

Glasgow Art Gallery, 86E.

Glasgow University, 2, 49B, 54, 55, 56A, 57, 67B, 68, 69, 70B, 72, 73, 79B, 80A, B and D, 84, 85. Fig. 10.

Glasgow School of Art, 82, 83.

Mr. Hugh Gray, 71A.

Professor Walter Gropius, 75C.

Mr. Arthur Hickman, 9B.

Mr. E. O. Hoppé, 1.

Mr. Herbert L. Honeyman, 18A.

Messrs. Alexander Koch, Verlag, Stuttgart, 40, 42B, 61, 62, 63, 65, 94A.

Messrs. Kodak, Ltd., 90E.

Messrs. K. R. Langewiesche, Verlag (from *Blauen Buchern*), 94C.

Archivo Mas, Barcelona, 91D.

Museum of Modern Art, New York, 60B.

New York Public Library, 8A.

Mr. Ludwig Miës van der Rohe, 47A.

Royal Institute of British Architects, 88B.

Mr. J. Henry Sellers, 89B and C.

Dr. E. Sekler and Dr. Rudolf Boeck (and Lichtbildwerk-Stätte, Alpenland), 92A, 93A, 94D, 95.

The Studio, 8E, 9F, 10B, 47C, 49B and C, 60A; (from *The Art Revival in Austria* (Haberfeld), 92B, C and D.

Trinity College Library, Dublin, and Urs Graf, Verlag, 9A.

Mr. Henry van de Velde, 91B, C and E.

Guilia Veronese and the Editor, *Il Balcone*, Milan, 93B and D. Figs 27, 28.

Professor Basil Ward, 44D.

Mr. Frank Lloyd Wright and the Chicago Photographing Company, 15B, 94B.

INDEX

Y*

PLATE I

CHARLES RENNIE MACKINTOSH, 1868–1928. CAMERA STUDY BY E. O. HOPPÉ *circa* 1920

PLATE 2

A. 1886. A DRAWING IN SEPIA FROM THE CAST. ONE OF THE EARLIEST SURVIVING DRAWINGS BY MACKINTOSH

B. 1890. A SCIENCE AND ART MUSEUM. A DESIGN AWARDED THE NATIONAL AND QUEEN'S PRIZE AT SOUTH KENSINGTON

PLATE 3

ELEVATION

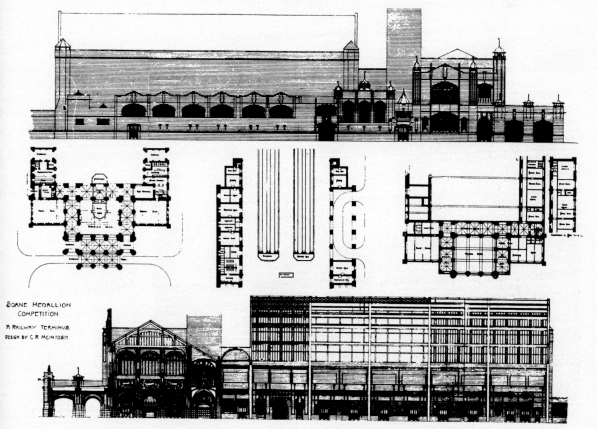

SOANE MEDALLION
COMPETITION

A RAILWAY TERMINUS.

DESIGN BY C R MCINTOSH

1892. A RAILWAY TERMINUS. UNPREMIATED DESIGN FOR THE SOANE MEDALLION COMPETITION

A. 1890. 'REDCLYFFE', SPRINGBURN, GLASGOW. MACKINTOSH'S FIRST COMMISSION. VIEW FROM THE SOUTH-WEST

B. 'REDCLYFFE' FROM THE NORTH-WEST

PLATE 5

A. *circa* 1890. MACKINTOSH'S STUDIO BEDROOM AT DENNISTOUN. NOTE THE FRIEZE OF CATS

B. 1890. 'REDCLYFFE.' DRAWING-ROOM FIREPLACE

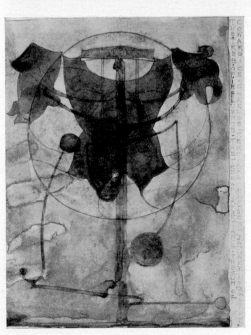

PLATE 6

EARLY WATER-COLOUR
DRAWINGS AND BOOK
COVERS

A. 1893.
FRANCES MACDONALD.
'ILL OMEN' OR
'GIRL IN THE EAST WIND'

B. 1895.
C. R. MACKINTOSH.
'THE TREE OF INFLUENCE'

C. 1894.
MARGARET MACDONALD.
'NOVEMBER 5TH'

D. 1894. MACDONALD.
'THE STORY OF A RIVER'

B   C   D

PLATE 7

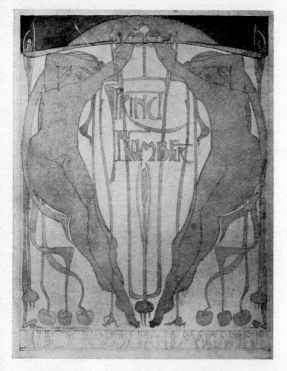

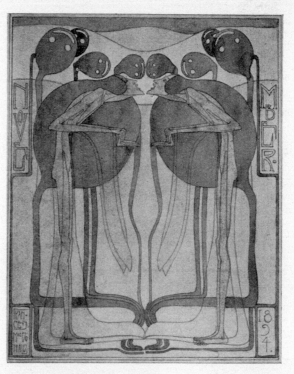

A. 1894. C. R. MACKINTOSH. 'SPRING'

B. 1894. FRANCES MACDONALD. 'A POND'

C. 1893. C. R. MACKINTOSH. A DESIGN FOR THE DIPLOMA AWARDED BY THE GLASGOW
SCHOOL OF ART CLUB

PLATE 8

A. EIGHTEENTH-CENTURY JAPANESE TRIPTYCH BY UTAMARO. 'A GEISHA PERFORMANCE'

B. *circa* 1890. JAN TOOROP. 'THE THREE BRIDES'

C

C. and D. *circa* 1895. F. & M. MACDONALD. ILLUMINATED MS. 'ANNUNCIATION' AND 'NATIVITY' $11\frac{1}{4}'' \times 2\frac{1}{2}''$

D

E. (*left*) 1896. F. & M. MACDONALD CLOCK FACE IN BEATEN BRASS $11\frac{1}{4}'' \times 2\frac{1}{2}''$

E

PLATE 9

A. SIXTH CENTURY A.D. INITIAL,
THE BOOK OF KELLS

B. 1897. JAMES PRYDE.
'PIERROT'

C. 1894. AUBREY BEARDSLEY.
'THE PEACOCK SKIRT'

D. and E. REPOUSSÉ WHITE
METAL PLAQUES. 'THE ILIAD'
20″×6″. BY F. & M. MACDONALD

F. (left) 1896. C. R. MACKINTOSH.
A POSTER 7′8″×3′2″

F

PLATE 10

A. *circa* 1895. A TYPICAL CONTEMPORARY INTERIOR BY A FIRM OF SCOTTISH ARCHITECTS

B. *circa* 1899.
THE MacNAIRS'
STUDIO FLAT.
THE DINING-
ROOM

PLATE 11

A. 1899. C. R. MACKINTOSH. THE DRAWING-ROOM FIREPLACE, DUNGLASS CASTLE

B. 1898. GEORGE WALTON. 'LEAD CAMERON', Nr. GLASGOW. THE DRAWING-ROOM

PLATE 12

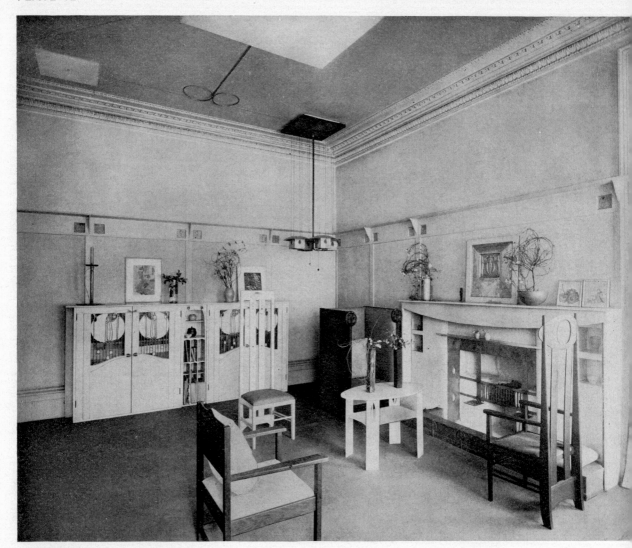

A. 1900. THE MACKINTOSHES' STUDIO
FLAT, 120 MAINS STREET, GLASGOW.
THE DRAWING-ROOM

B. 1900. A CHAIR PAINTED WHITE AND
UPHOLSTERED IN LINEN

PLATE 13

A. 1900. THE MACKINTOSHES' STUDIO FLAT, 120 MAINS STREET, GLASGOW. THE DRAWING-ROOM

and C. *circa* 1903. WHITE CABINET. INLAID FIGURES OF ENAMEL
ND LEADED GLASS

C

PLATE 14

A. 1900. 120 MAINS STREET, GLASGOW. THE STUDIO FIREPLACE

B. 1900. C. F. A. VOYSEY
'THE ORCHARD',
CHORLEY WOOD.
DINING-ROOM

PLATE 15

A. 1900. C. R. MACKINTOSH. 120 MAINS STREET, GLASGOW. THE DINING-ROOM

899. FRANK LLOYD
IGHT. WALLER HOUSE,
CAGO. DINING-ROOM.
TE LARGE WINDOW
D MARKED HORIZON-
ITY

PLATE 16

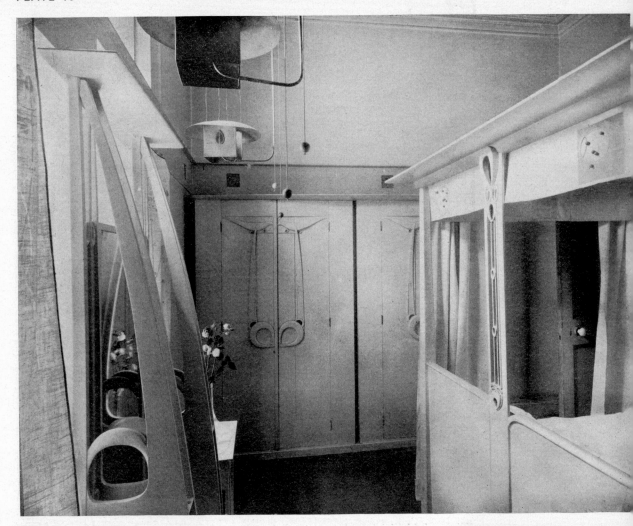

A. 1900. C. R. MACKINTOSH. 120 MAINS STREET, GLASGOW. THE BEDROOM

B. BEDROOM CHAIR WITH LINEN BACK AND SEAT

C

C. BEDROOM TABLE, PAINTED WHITE WITH PURPLE ENAMEL INLA

PLATE 17

A. *circa* 1900. NO. 34 KINGSBOROUGH GARDENS, GLASGOW. THE DRAWING-ROOM FIREPLACE

1900. C. F. A. VOYSEY.
E ORCHARD', CHORLEY
OOD. LOUNGE HALL

PLATE 18

B

A. 1872. JOHN HONEYMAN. FURNITURE WAREHOUSE, GLASGOW. CAST IRON CONSTRUCTION

B. 1892. JOHN BURNET, SON AND CAMPBELL. THE ATHENÆUM, GLASGOW

C. 1894. JOHN BURNET, SON AND CAMPBELL. PATHOLOGICAL BUILDING, GLASGOW UNIVERSITY

C

PLATE 19

A. 1890. GLASGOW ART GALLERIES COMPETITION: UNPREMIATED DESIGN

DESIGNS PREPARED IN THE OFFICE OF JOHN HONEYMAN & KEPPIE

893. CANAL BOATMEN'S INSTITUTE, PORT DUNDAS
EXECUTED

C. 1894. ROYAL INSURANCE BUILDING, GLASGOW
UNPREMIATED DESIGN

PLATE 20

A

1895. MARTYRS' PUBLIC SCHOOL, GLASGOW

A. PERSPECTIVE DRAWING BY MACKINTOSH

B. ROOF TRUSS IN MAIN HALL

C. DOORWAY

B

C

PLATE 21

1897–9. GLASGOW SCHOOL OF ART, NORTH FAÇADE

PLATE 22

THE GLASGOW SCHOOL OF ART.

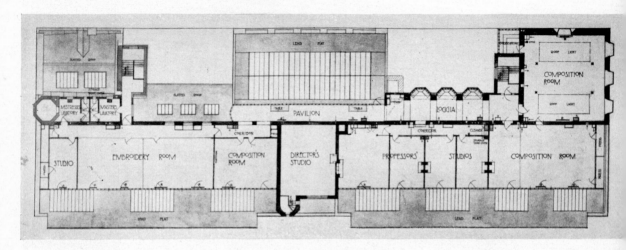

A. SECOND FLOOR PLAN

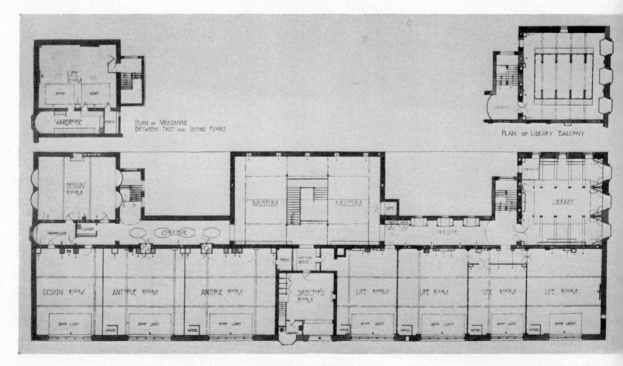

B. FIRST FLOOR PLAN

GLASGOW SCHOOL OF ART. PLANS DRAWN IN 1910 SHOWING FINAL LAYOUT OF INTERIOR (FOR GROUND FLOOR PLAN (1896), SEE FIG. 15)

PLATE 23

THE GLASGOW SCHOOL OF ART.

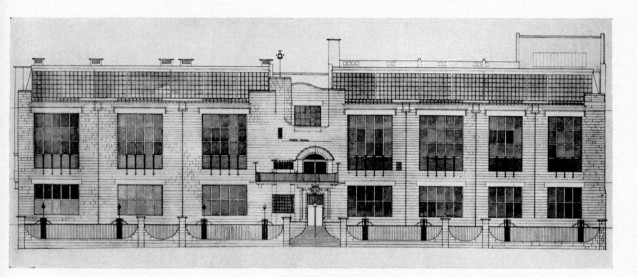

A. GLASGOW SCHOOL OF ART. NORTH ELEVATION DRAWN IN 1910 SHOWING ATTIC STOREY

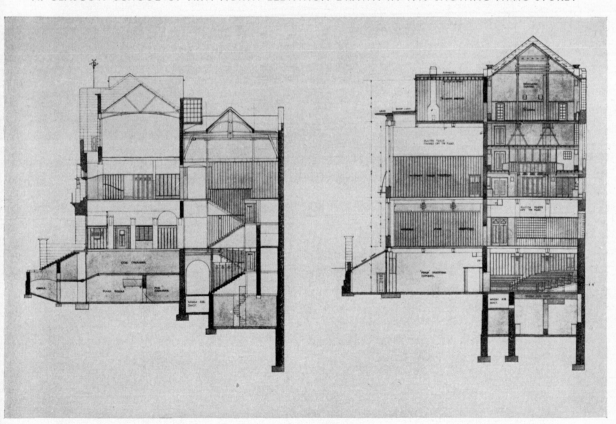

B. SECTION THROUGH ENTRANCE HALL AND
THE MUSEUM HALL

C. SECTION THROUGH LIBRARY AND
LECTURE ROOM

PLATE 24

1897–9. GLASGOW SCHOOL OF ART. EAST FAÇADE—THE TWO WINDOWS ON THE
RIGHT ARE LATER ADDITIONS

PLATE 25

1907–9. GLASGOW SCHOOL OF ART. VIEW OF LIBRARY WING FROM THE SOUTH-WEST

PLATE 26

A

B

A. 1907–9. CONSERVATORY

B. 1907–9. 'THE HEN RUN'

GLASGOW SCHOOL OF ART.
DETAILS

C. 1907–9. THE WEST DOORWAY

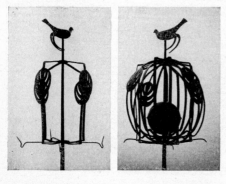

D. 1897–9. WROUGHT IRON EMBLEMS

C

PLATE 27

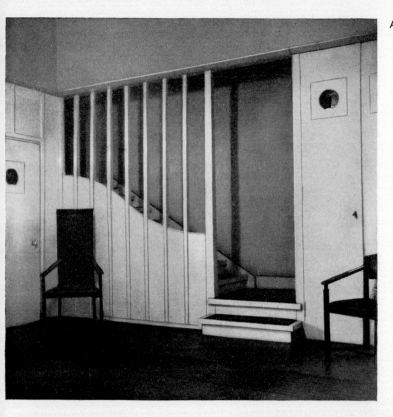

A

B

A. 1897–9. HEADMASTER'S ROOM.
STAIRCASE TO PRIVATE STUDIO

B. 1907–9. PILASTER CAPITAL IN
THE BOARD ROOM

GLASGOW SCHOOL OF ART.
DETAILS

C. 1907–9. ON THE TOP FLOOR OF THE WEST WING. 'THE LOGGIA'

PLATE 28

B. STAIRCASE IN THE EAST WING, ADDED *circa* 1907

A. WROUGHT IRON BRACKETS, NORTH FAÇADE

GLASGOW SCHOOL OF ART. DETAILS

PLATE 29

1897–9. GLASGOW SCHOOL OF ART. THE PRINCIPAL STAIRCASE

PLATE 30

1907–9. GLASGOW SCHOOL OF ART. THE LIBRARY

PLATE 31

1907–9. GLASGOW SCHOOL OF ART. THE LIBRARY

PLATE 32

Country Life

A. 1906–8. SIR ROBERT LORIMER, 'ARDKINGLASS', ARGYLLSHIRE

B. *circa* 1893. WILLIAM LEIPER. KELLY MANSION ON THE CLYDE ESTUARY. DESTROYED BY FIRE

THE SCOTTISH BARONIAL STYLE. TWO CONTRASTING EXAMPLES

PLATE 33

1899–1901. C. R. MACKINTOSH. 'WINDYHILL', KILMACOLM, FOR W. DAVIDSON.
VIEW FROM THE SOUTH

PLATE 34

A. 1899–1901. 'WINDYHILL', KILMACOLM. VIEW FROM THE NORTH

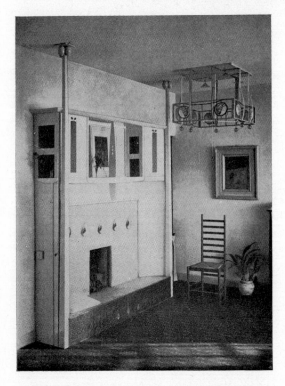

B. 1899–1901. DRAWING-ROOM FIREPLACE

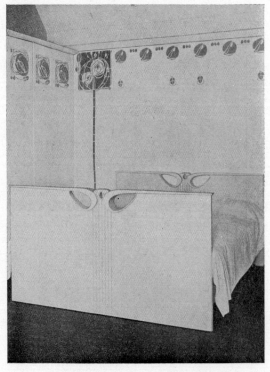

C. 1899–1901. PRINCIPAL BEDROOM

PLATE 35

A. 1899–1901. 'WINDYHILL.' DETAIL OF MAIN ENTRANCE

B. 1899–1901. 'WINDYHILL.' ENTRANCE HALL

PLATE 36

1902-3. 'HILL HOUSE', HELENSBURGH, FOR W. W. BLACKIE. VIEW FROM THE SOUTH-WEST.

PLATE 37

A. 1902–3. 'HILL HOUSE', HELENSBURGH, FROM THE SOUTH-WEST. (FOR PLANS, SEE PAGE 100)

B. 'STENHOUSE', EDINBURGH. A TYPICAL SEVENTEENTH-CENTURY SCOTTISH TOWN HOUSE.
(COMPARE WITH 'A' ABOVE)

PLATE 38

A. 1902–3. 'HILL HOUSE' FROM THE SOUTH. NOTE THE ANGLE TURRET

B. 1902–3. 'HILL HOUSE' FROM THE NORTH. NOTE THE STAIRCASE BAY

PLATE 39

1902–3. 'HILL HOUSE.' THE LIBRARY

PLATE 40

B

A

1902–3. 'HILL HOUSE.' THE ENTRANCE HALL. IN 'A' THE MAIN DOOR AND STAIRCASE CAN BE SEEN

PLATE 41

1902-3. 'HILL HOUSE.' THE BAY WINDOW. PAINTED WHITE; SEAT ORIGINALLY UPHOLSTERED IN LINEN WITH STENCILLED FLORAL MOTIVES

PLATE 42

1902–3.
'HILL HOUSE',
HELENSBURGH.

THE PRINCIPAL
BEDROOM WITH
BUILT-IN WARD-
ROBES AND
FURNITURE

PLATE 43

A. 1906. 'AUCHINIBERT', KILLEARN. THE ENTRANCE.
(SEE ALSO FIG. 18, PAGE 110)

A

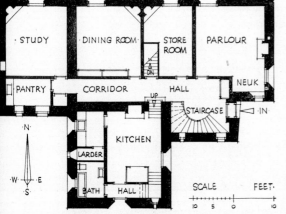

B. 1906. 'MOSSIDE', KILMACOLM: THE PLAN

STUDY — DINING ROOM — STORE ROOM — PARLOUR — PANTRY — CORRIDOR — HALL — NEUK — UP — DN — STAIRCASE — IN — KITCHEN — LARDER — BATH — HALL

N W E S

SCALE FEET
10 5 0 10

C. (left)
1906. 'CLOAK', KILMACOLM,
FROM THE DRIVE. THE SOUTH-WEST

PLATE 44

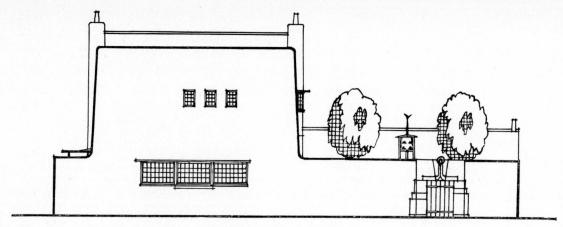

A. SOUTH ELEVATION

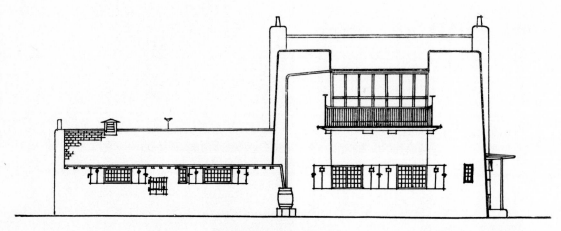

B. NORTH ELEVATION

D. 1933. COLIN LUCAS. HOUSE BUILT IN
CONCRETE AT PLATT, KENT

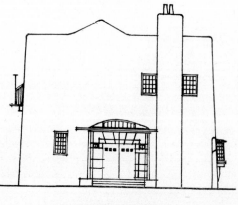

C. WEST ELEVATION

1901. PROPOSED COUNTRY
COTTAGE FOR AN ARTIST

PLATE 45

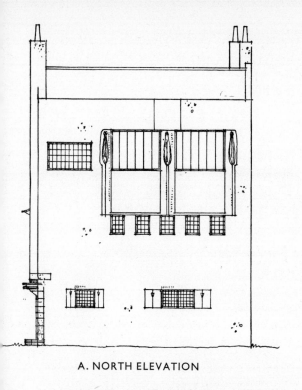

A. NORTH ELEVATION

B. SOUTH ELEVATION

GROUND FLOOR

FIRST FLOOR

SECOND FLOOR

PLANS OF TOWN HOUSE

· FIRST FLOOR PLAN

GROUND FLOOR PLAN

N

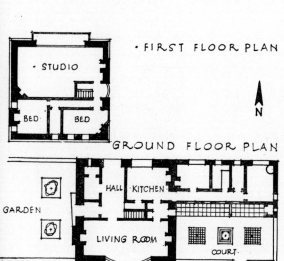

GARDEN

PLANS OF COUNTRY COTTAGE
(SEE PLATE 44)

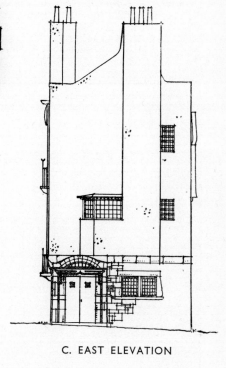

C. EAST ELEVATION

1901. A TOWN HOUSE FOR AN ARTIST

PLATE 46

circa 1906. 'HOUS'HILL', NITSHILL, GLASGOW, FOR MISS CRANSTON. THE MUSIC-ROOM

PLATE 47

B. 1906. 'HOUS'HILL.' BEHIND THE SCREEN IN THE MUSIC-ROOM

C. (left) 1906. 'HOUS'HILL.' MUSIC-ROOM FIREPLACE

A. 1930. TUGENDHAT HOUSE, BRNO. MIËS VAN DER ROHE. DINING AREA

PLATE 48

1897. BUCHANAN STREET TEA-ROOMS, GLASGOW. MURAL DECORATION BY MACKINTOSH;
FURNITURE BY GEORGE WALTON

PLATE 49

A. 1905. ARGYLE STREET TEA-ROOMS. THE DUTCH KITCHEN

B. 1897. ARGYLE STREET TEA-ROOMS.
SMOKING ROOM. DECORATIONS AND
FURNISHINGS BY GEORGE WALTON.
MOVABLE FURNITURE BY MACKINTOSH

C. 1896. BUCHANAN STREET TEA-ROOMS.
MURAL BY GEORGE WALTON. COMPARE
WITH PLATE 48

C B

PLATE 50

1901. INGRAM STREET TEA-ROOMS

A. DINING-ROOM, PAINTED WHITE; FURNITURE IN OAK

B. (*left*) DETAIL OF CASH DESK

C. (*below*) CUTLERY DESIGNED BY MACKINTOSH (SEE ALSO PLATE 51)

PLATE 51

A. *circa* 1906. THE OAK ROOM

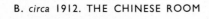

B. *circa* 1912. THE CHINESE ROOM

C. *circa* 1911. THE CLOISTER ROOM

PLATE 52

1912. INGRAM STREET TEA-ROOMS. DETAIL OF SCREENS IN THE CHINESE ROOM

PLATE 53

1904. 'THE WILLOW' TEA-ROOMS, SAUCHIEHALL STREET. THE FAÇADE

PLATE 54

1904. 'THE WILLOW' DINING-ROOM, SHOWING CASH DESK, STAIRCASE AND CENTRAL FEATURE

PLATE 55

A. 1904. 'THE WILLOW' GALLERY TEA-ROOM, PAINTED WHITE

B. 1904. 'THE WILLOW' DINING-ROOM BELOW GALLERY, FURNISHED IN OAK

PLATE 56

A. VIEW FROM STAIRCASE SHOWING WROUGHT METAL
BALUSTRADE AND PLASTER FRIEZE

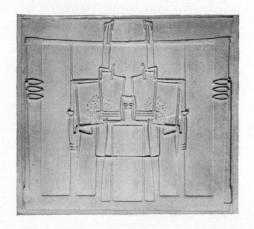

B. ONE UNIT OF THE PLASTER FRIEZE
C. (right) 'ROOM DE LUXE'
GESSO PANEL BY MARGARET MACDONALD

1904. 'THE WILLOW' TEA-ROOMS

C

PLATE 57

A. 'THE WILLOW' TEA-ROOMS. ROOM DE LUXE. GENERAL VIEW

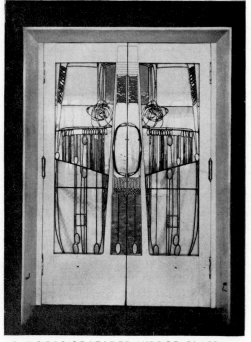

B. CRYSTAL CHANDELIER

C. DOORS OF LEADED MIRROR GLASS

PLATE 58

A. 1898. INTERIOR AT MUNICH. CUPBOARDS BY MACKINTOSH; FURNITURE BY K. BERTSCH

B. SECRETAIRE BY C. R. ASHBEE   C. CABINET BY JOSEF HOFFMANN

1900. SECESSIONIST EXHIBITION, VIENNA

PLATE 59

A. 1900. SECESSIONIST EXHIBITION, VIENNA: SCOTTISH SECTION BY MACKINTOSH

B. FURNITURE EXHIBITED BY JOSEF HOFFMANN

C. FURNITURE EXHIBITED BY MACKINTOSH

PLATE 60

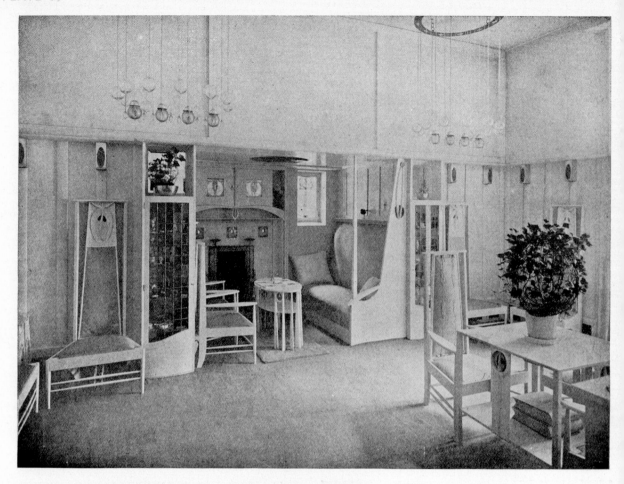

A. (*above*)
GENERAL VIEW, SHOWING
FIREPLACE

B. (*left*) THE GRAND PIANO
WITH WINDOW SEAT IN
BACKGROUND

circa 1902. WÄRNDORFER MUSIC
SALON, VIENNA

PLATE 61

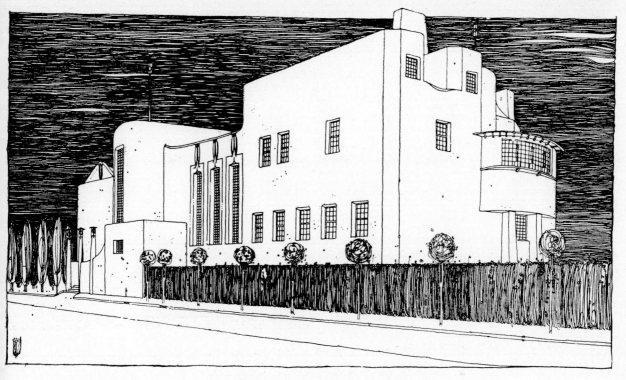

A. VIEW FROM THE NORTH-WEST

B. VIEW FROM THE SOUTH-EAST

1901. HAUS EINES KUNSTFREUNDES COMPETITION

PLATE 62

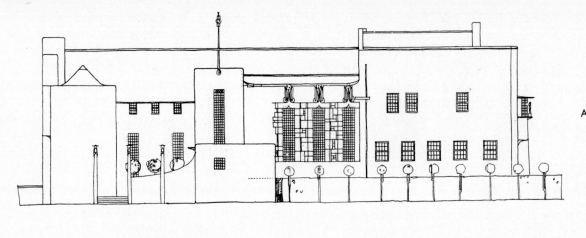

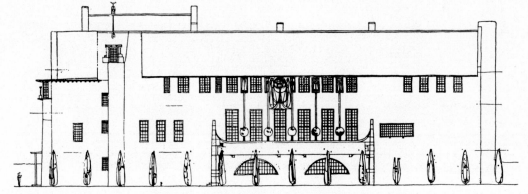

A. and B. NORTH AND SOUTH ELEVATIONS BY MACKINTOSH
(FOR PLANS, SEE PAGE 159, FIGURE 21)

C and D. NORTH AND SOUTH ELEVATIONS BY BAILLIE SCOTT—THE WINNING DESIGN

1901. HAUS EINES KUNSTFREUNDES COMPETITION

PLATE 63

B. DINING-ROOM BY MACKINTOSH

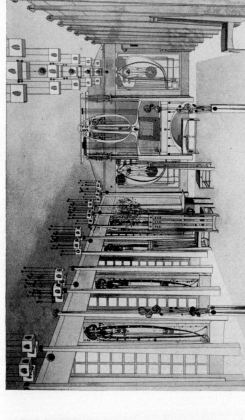

D. MUSIC-ROOM BY MACKINTOSH

A. DINING-ROOM BY BAILLIE SCOTT

C. MUSIC-ROOM BY BAILLIE SCOTT

1901. HAUS EINES KUNSTFREUNDES COMPETITION

PLATE 64

A. PAVILION BY SIGNOR D'ARONCO OF CONSTANTINOPLE, ARCHITECT TO THE EXHIBITION

1902. INTERNATIONAL EXHIBITION OF DECORATIVE ART AT TURIN

B. THE ROSE BOUDOIR BY MACKINTOSH

C. DISPLAY CABINET BY MACKINTOSH

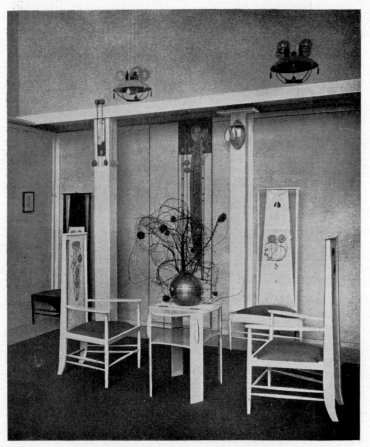

B

C

PLATE 65

1902. INTERNATIONAL EXHIBITION
OF DECORATIVE ART AT TURIN.
TYPICAL STANDS

A. SALON BY BUGATTI, ITALY

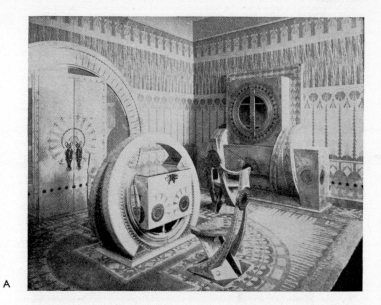

A

B. INTERIOR WITH BALCONY BY
SNEYERS & CRESPIN, BELGIUM

C. THE SCOTTISH SECTION,
H. & F. MACNAIR

D. DISPLAY CABINET BY HENRY
VAN DE VELDE, BELGIUM

B

D   C

PLATE 66

A. 1888. JAMES SELLARS. INDUSTRIAL HALL, AT THE FIRST INTERNATIONAL EXHIBITION HELD IN GLASGOW

B. 1901. JAMES MILLER. INDUSTRIAL HALL, INTERNATIONAL EXHIBITION, GLASGOW

PLATE 67

A. 1898. MACKINTOSH. PERSPECTIVE DRAWING OF PROJECT FOR THE INTERNATIONAL EXHIBITION, GLASGOW, 1901. WITH KELVINGROVE ART GALLERY IN RIGHT BACKGROUND

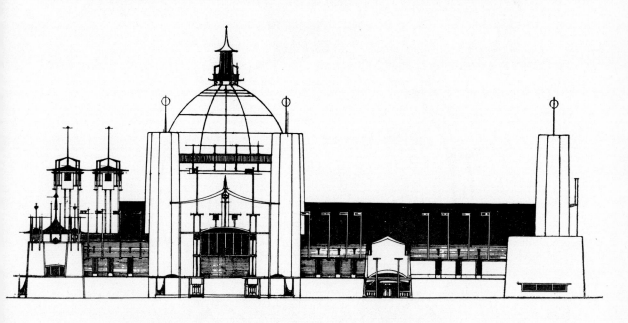

B. 1898. MACKINTOSH. SIDE ELEVATION OF INDUSTRIAL HALL (NOT EXECUTED)

PLATE 68

INTERNATIONAL EXHIBITION GLASGOW 1901
COMPETITION DESIGN FOR BUILDINGS

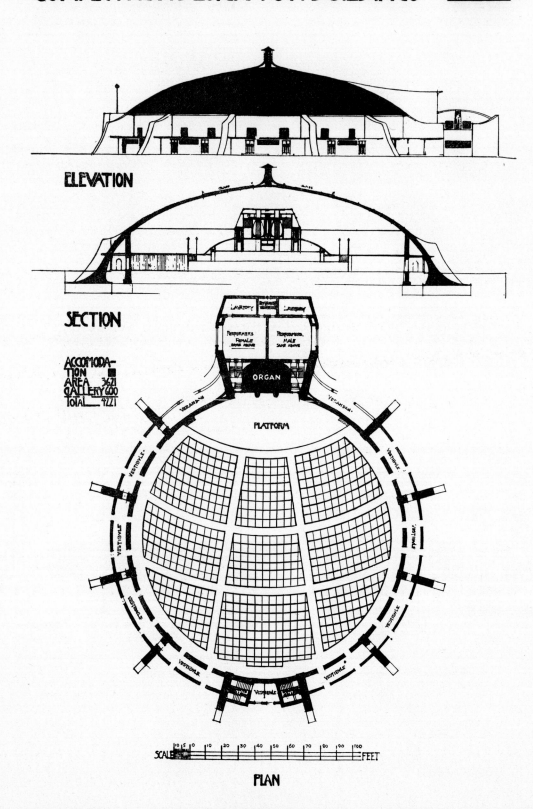

ELEVATION

SECTION

ACCOMODA-
TION
AREA 3621
GALLERY 600
TOTAL 4221

PLAN

PLATE 69

1901. 'DAILY RECORD' OFFICE, GLASGOW.
PERSPECTIVE DRAWING OF THE BUILDING AS
EXECUTED

PLATE 68 (opposite)
1898. MACKINTOSH. PROJECT FOR CONCERT HALL,
INTERNATIONAL EXHIBITION, GLASGOW, 1901
(NOT EXECUTED)

PLATE 70

MERRIOT CHURCH
SOMERSETSHIRE.

1897. QUEEN'S CROSS CHURCH OF SCOTLAND, GLASGOW
PERSPECTIVE DRAWING BY MACKINTOSH OF BUILDING AS EXECUTED, AND
A SKETCH (1895) OF MERRIOTT CHURCH, SOMERSET, WHICH DISCLOSES
THE ORIGIN OF THE UNUSUAL TOWER AT QUEEN'S CROSS CHURCH

PLATE 71

1897. QUEEN'S CROSS CHURCH, GLASGOW. A. THE CHANCEL

B. THE AISLE, WITH GALLERY ABOVE

C. 1898. GRAVESTONE, KILMACOLM

C   B

PLATE 72

THE DESIGN SUBMITTED BY MACKINTOSH. PERSPECTIVE VIEW FROM THE SOUTH-WEST, EMPHASIZING THE BOLD MASSING AND SHOWING THE UNUSUAL BUTTRESSES TO THE NAVE

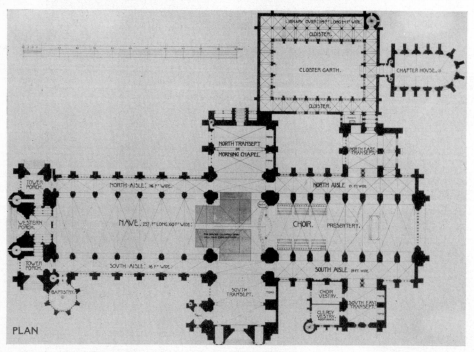

PLAN OF THE CATHEDRAL, CLOISTER AND CHAPTER HOUSE

1903. LIVERPOOL CATHEDRAL COMPETITION

PLATE 73

A. SOUTH ELEVATION

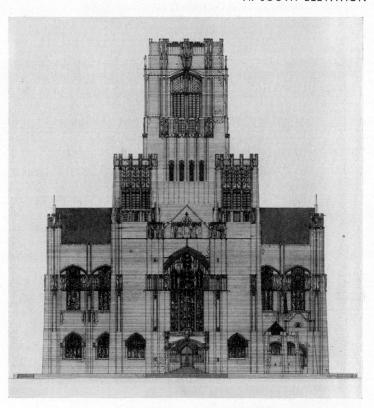

B. WEST FRONT

1903. LIVERPOOL CATHEDRAL COMPETITION

PLATE 74

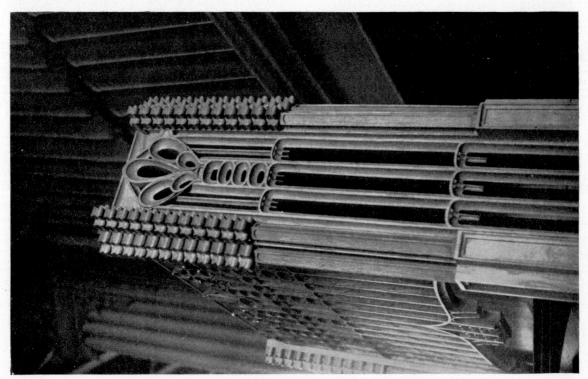

1906. HOLY TRINITY CHURCH, BRIDGE OF ALLAN. DETAILS OF THE ORGAN SCREEN AND THE COMMUNION TABLE EXECUTED IN LIGHT OAK

PLATE 75

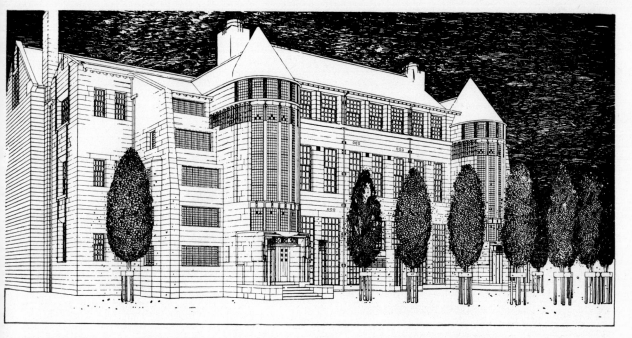

A. 1904. SCOTLAND STREET SCHOOL, GLASGOW. PERSPECTIVE DRAWING, VIEW FROM THE NORTH-EAST. PLANS BELOW

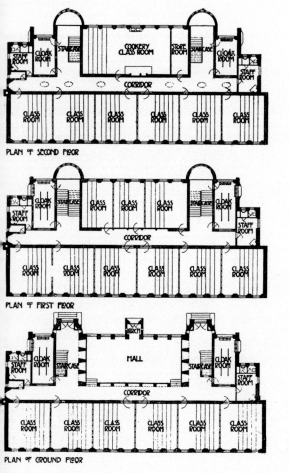

PLAN OF SECOND FLOOR

PLAN OF FIRST FLOOR

PLAN OF GROUND FLOOR

B

C. 1914. WALTER GROPIUS. EXHIBITION BUILDING AT COLOGNE. MODEL FACTORY AND OFFICE

PLATE 76

A. 1904. SCOTLAND STREET SCHOOL. VIEW FROM NORTH-EAST, WITH CARETAKER'S HOUSE IN THE BACKGROUND

B. 1916. NO. 78 DERNGATE, NORTHAMPTON, FOR MR. BASSETT-LOWKE. EXTENSION TO GARDEN FRONT

B

C. 1925. 'NEW WAYS', NORTHAMPTON, DESIGNED BY PETER BEHRENS

C

PLATE 77

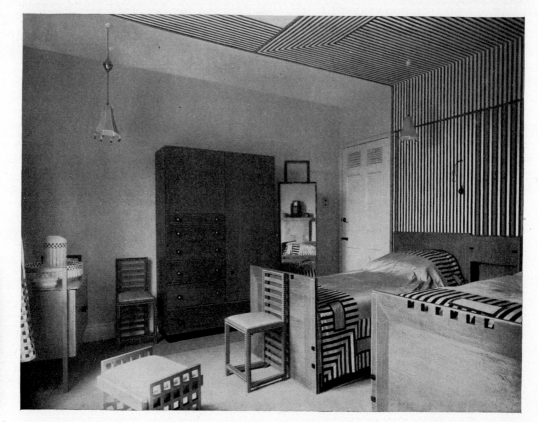

1916. NO. 78 DERNGATE, NORTHAMPTON. REMODELLED INTERIOR. LOUNGE HALL AND
GUESTS' BEDROOM

PLATE 78

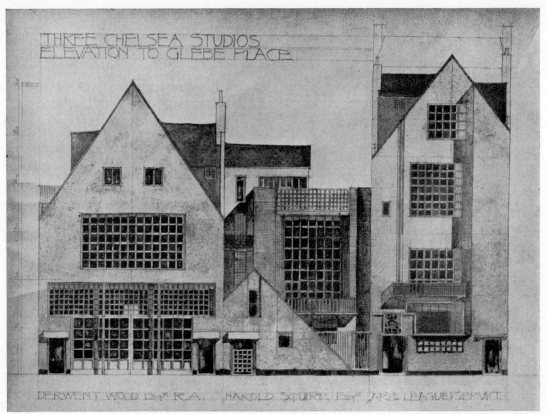

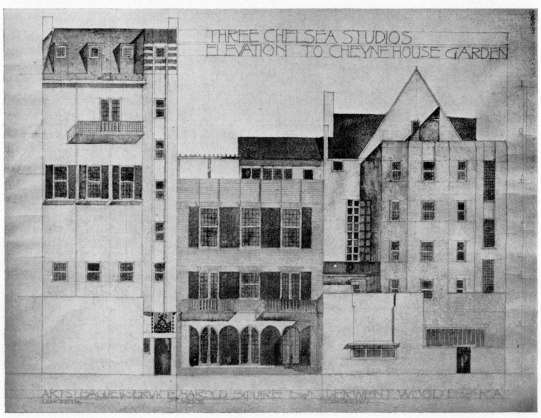

1920. PROPOSED ARTISTS' STUDIOS, CHELSEA. ELEVATIONS TO GLEBE PLACE AND TO
CHEYNE HOUSE GARDEN

PLATE 79

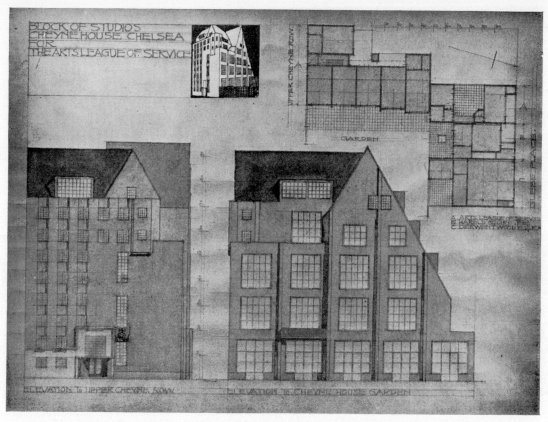

A. 1920. PROPOSED STUDIOS FOR THE ARTS LEAGUE OF SERVICE, CHELSEA

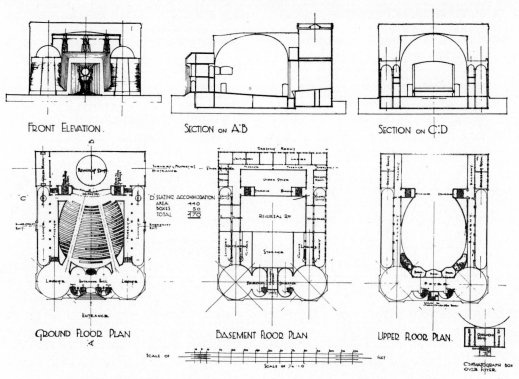

B. 1920. PROPOSED THEATRE IN CHELSEA FOR MARGARET MORRIS

PLATE 80

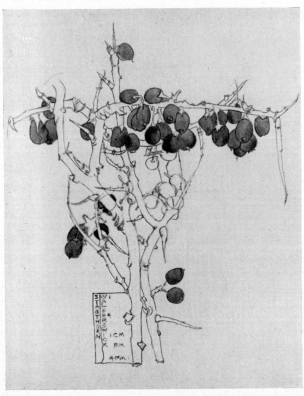

A. JAPONICA, CHIDDINGSTONE, DORSET, 1910

B. LARKSPUR, WALBERSWICK, 1914

C. STAGTHORN, WALBERSWICK, 1914

D. MIMOSA AMELIE, LES BAINS, 1924

FLOWER STUDIES BY CHARLES AND MARGARET MACKINTOSH. $10\frac{1}{2}'' \times 8\frac{1}{2}''$

PLATE 81

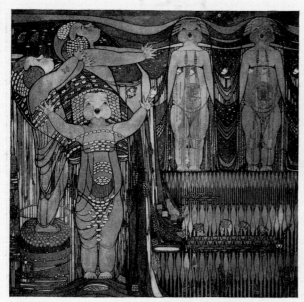

A. *circa* 1919. 'THE LITTLE HILLS.' PAINTED ON CANVAS: TWO PANELS 40" × 40"

B. *circa* 1920. FLOWER STUDY. 9"×9". FABRIC DESIGN

C. *circa* 1918. ADHESIVE LABELS. 2¼" × 1⅜". IN BRILLIANT PRIMARY COLOURS

PLATE 82

1927. C. R. MACKINTOSH. 'THE ROCKS.' WATER-COLOUR. 12″ × 10″ (approx.)

PLATE 83

1927. C. R. MACKINTOSH. LE FORT MAILLERT. WATER-COLOUR. $13\frac{1}{2}'' \times 10\frac{1}{2}''$

PLATE 84

1927. C. R. MACKINTOSH. 'LA RUE DU SOLEIL.' WATER-COLOUR. 15½″ × 15″

PLATE 85

1927. C. R. MACKINTOSH. 'THE LITTLE BAY.' WATER-COLOUR. $15\frac{1}{2}'' \times 15''$

PLATE 86

MARGARET MACDONALD
MACKINTOSH, *circa* 1903

MISS CATHERINE
CRANSTON

FRANCIS H. NEWBERY
PORTRAIT BY MAURICE
GREIFFENHAGEN

HONEYMAN & KEPPIE'S STAFF
circa 1890

J. H. MACNAIR (*centre*)
C. R. MACKINTOSH (*right*)
ALEXANDER McGIBBON (*seated*)
CHARLES WHITELAW (*seated right*)

C. R. MACKINTOSH, *circa* 1903

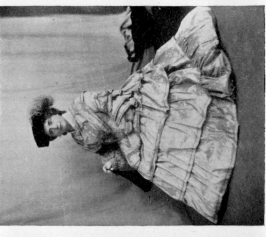

PLATE 87

A. 1881–6. PHILIP WEBB. 'CLOUDS'

B. 1881–6. THE HALL AT 'CLOUDS'

THE ENGLISH REVIVAL

C. (left)
1891. W. R. LETHABY. 'AVON TYRRELL',
HAMPSHIRE

D. (left)
1876. R. N. SHAW.
'SWAN HOUSE', CHELSEA

E. (right)
1899. A. H. MACKMURDO.
25 CADOGAN GARDENS

PLATE 88

A. 1876. PHILIP WEBB. ROUNTON SCHOOL, YORKS

B. 1901. GEORGE WALTON. 'THE LEYS', ELSTREE

C. 1900. C. F. A. VOYSEY. 'THE ORCHARD', CHORLEY WOOD

D. 1906. GEORGE WALTON. 'THE WHITE HOUSE', SHIPLAKE

PLATE 89

Country Life

A

A. 1908. 'UPMEADS', STAFFORD

EDGAR WOOD

B. 1891. DRAWING-ROOM IN
THE ARCHITECT'S OWN HOUSE
MIDDLETON, LANCASHIRE

B

C. 1899–1902. CLOCK TOWER, LINDLEY, YORKS

PLATE 90

A. 1898. ENGLISH ART NOUVEAU.
SYDNEY GREENSLADE, A TOWN
CHURCH

B. 1898. SMITH AND BREWER.
MARY WARD SETTLEMENT,
LONDON

C. (left)
1899. LEONARD STOKES.
CONVENT, ST. ALBANS

D. (right)
1897–9. C. H. TOWNSEND.
WHITECHAPEL ART
GALLERY

E. (left)
1910. SIR JOHN BURNET AND
PARTNERS. KODAK HOUSE,
KINGSWAY, LONDON.
STEEL FRAMED STRUCTURE
FRANKLY EXPRESSED

PLATE 91

B

A. 1893. VICTOR HORTA. NO. 12 RUE DE TURIN, BRUSSELS. CAST IRON AND STONE FACADE

C

B and C. 1895. HENRY VAN DE VELDE. HOUSE AT UCCLE, BRUSSELS. EXTERIOR AND DINING-ROOM

D. (left). 1906. ANTONIO GAUDÍ. CASA BATLLO, BARCELONA

E. 1914. HENRY VAN DE VELDE. EXHIBITION THEATRE, COLOGNE

PLATE 92

B

C

A. 1904. PÜRKERSDORF SANATORIUM, VIENNA.
PERSPECTIVE DRAWING OF THE MAIN FAÇADE
BY THE ARCHITECT

B. SUBSIDIARY DOORWAY; NOTE METAL CANOPY
AND CHEQUERED DECORATION

C. THE DINING-ROOM PAINTED WHITE

D. *circa* 1904. A VILLA AT VIENNA

JOSEF HOFFMANN, VIENNA

D

PLATE 93

A. 1898. THE SECESSION HOUSE, VIENNA

B. 1901. ERNST LUDWIG HOUSE, KUNSTLERKOLONIE, DARMSTADT *(top right)*

C. 1901. SKETCH OF HOUSE FOR LUDWIG HABICH AT DARMSTADT *(right)*

D. 1901. PAVILION OF THE PLASTIC ARTS, THE KUNSTLERKOLONIE, DARMSTADT

J. M. OLBRICH, VIENNA

PLATE 94

B

C

D

A. 1901. PETER BEHRENS. HOUSE AT THE KUNSTLERKOLONIE, DARMSTADT

B. *circa* 1900. LLOYD WRIGHT. FRICKE HOUSE, CHICAGO. WRIGHT'S STYLE ALREADY WELL DEVELOPED

C. 1909. PETER BEHRENS. A.E.G. FACTORY, BERLIN. A MATURE WORK IN STEEL AND GLASS

D. 1910. ADOLF LOOS. HOUSE, VIENNA. COMPARED WITH 'UP-MEADS', PLATE 89A

PLATE 95

1905.
POSTSPARKASSE,
VIENNA

A. ELEVATION
FACED IN GRAN-
ITE SLABS

B. MAIN HALL IN
STEEL AND GLASS

OTTO
WAGNER,
VIENNA

PLATE 96

1907–9. MACKINTOSH. GLASGOW SCHOOL OF ART: DETAIL OF THE LIBRARY WING

DATE DUE